P9-EDF-433

# Web Security

## *A Matter of Trust*

O'REILLY™

# WORLD WIDE WEB JOURNAL

## WEB SECURITY: A MATTER OF TRUST    Volume 2, Issue 3, Summer 1997

*Publisher:* Dale Dougherty

*Series Editor:* Rohit Khare

*Managing Editor:* Donna Woonteiler

*News Editor:* Dave Sims

*Production Editor:* Nancy Crumpton

*Technical Illustrator:* Chris Reilley

*Software Tools Specialist:* Mike Sierra

*Quality Assurance:* Ellie Fountain Maden

*Cover Design:* Hanna Dyer

*Text Design:* Nancy Priest, Marcia Ciro

*Subscription Administrator:* Marianne Cooke

 This book is printed on acid-free paper with 85% recycled content, 15% post-consumer waste. O'Reilly & Associates is committed to using paper with the highest recycled content available consistent with high quality.

ISSN: 1085-2301

ISBN: 1-56592-329-4                                                                          7/1/97

## W3C Administration

Jean-François Abramatic
  W3C Chairman and Associate
  Director, MIT Laboratory for
  Computer Science
  jfa@w3.org

Tim Berners-Lee
  Director of the W3C
  timbl@w3.org

Vincent Quint
  Deputy Director for Europe
  Vincent.Quint@w3.org

Nobuo Saito
  W3C Associate Chairman
  and Dean, Keio University
  nobuo.saito@w3.org

Alan Kotok
  W3C Associate Chairman
  kotok@w3.org

Tatsuya Hagino
  hagino@w3.org
  Deputy Director, Asia

## User Interface

Vincent Quint
  Domain Leader
  Vincent.Quint@w3.org

Bert Bos
  bert@w3.org

Ramzi Guetari
  guetari@w3.org

Arnaud Le Hors
  lehors@w3.org

Håkon Lie
  howcome@w3.org

Chris Lilley
  chris@w3.org

Dave Raggett
  dsr@w3.org

Irène Vatton
  Irene.Vatton@w3.org

Daniel Veillard
  Daniel.Veillard@w3.org

## Technology and Society

Jim Miller
  Domain Leader
  jmiller@w3.org

Eui-Suk Chung
  euisuk@w3.org

Daniel Dardailler
  danield@w3.org

Philip DesAutels
  philipd@w3.org

Joseph Reagle
  reagle@w3.org

Ralph Swick
  swick@w3.org

## Architecture

Dan Connolly
  Domain Leader
  connolly@w3.org

Anselm Baird-Smith
  abaird@w3.org

Jim Gettys
  jg@w3.org

Philipp Hoschka
  Philipp.Hoschka@w3.org

Yves Lafon
  lafon@w3.org

Ora Lassila
  lassila@w3.org

Henrik Frystyk Nielsen
  frystyk@w3.org

## Cross Areas and Technical Support

Janet Bertot
  bertot@w3.org

Stephane Boyera
  Stephane.Boyera@w3.org

Daicho Funato
  daichi@w3.org

Tom Greene
  tjg@w3.org

José Kahan
  Jose.Kahan@w3.org

Sally Khudairi
  khudairi@w3.org

Stéphan Montigaud
  montigaud@w3.org

Luc Ottavj
  ottavj@w3.org

Pierre Fillault
  fillault@w3.org

Takeshi "Yamachan" Yamane
  yamachan@w3.org

## Administrative Support

Pamela Ahern
  pam@w3.org

Beth Curran
  beth@w3.org

Susan Hardy
  susan@w3.org

Marie-Line Ramfos
  ramfos@w3.org

Josiane Roberts
  Josiane.Roberts@inria.fr

Yukari Mitsuhashi
  yukari@w3.org

Access Company Limited

Adobe Systems Inc.

Aérospatiale

AGF.SI

Agfa Division, Bayer Corp.

Agranat Systems, Inc.

Alcatel Alsthom Recherche

Alfa-Omega Foundation

Alis Technologies, Inc.

America Online, Inc.

American International Group Data Center, Inc. (AIG)

American Internet Corporation

Apple Computer, Inc.

ArborText, Inc.

Architecture Projects Management Ltd.

AT&T

Attachmate Corporation

BELGACOM

Bellcore

Bitstream, Inc.

British Telecommunications Laboratories

Bull S.A.

Canal +

Canon, Inc.

Cap Gemini Innovation

Center for Mathematics and Computer Science (CWI)

CERN

CIRAD

CNR—Instituto Elaborazione dell'Informazione

CNRS

Commissariat a L'Énergie Atomique (CEA)

CompuServe, Inc.

Computer Answer Line

CosmosBay

Council for the Central Laboratory of the Research Councils (CCL)

CyberCash, Inc.

Cygnus Support

Daewoo Electronics Company

Dassault Aviation

Data Research Associates, Inc.

Defense Information Systems Agency (DISA)

Deutsche Telekom—T-Online

Digital Equipment Corporation

Digital Vision Laboratories Corporation

DigitalStyle Corporation

Direct Marketing Association, Inc.

Eastman Kodak Company

École Nationale Supérieure d'Informatique et de Mathématiques Appliquées (ENSIMAG)

EDF

EEIG/ERCIM

Electronic Book Technologies, Inc.

ENEL

ENN Corporation

Enterprise Integration Technology

ERICSSON

ETNOTEAM S.p.A.

Firefly Network, Inc.

First Virtual Holdings, Inc.

FirstFloor Software, Inc.

Folio Corporation

Foundation for Research and Technology (FORTH)

France Telecom

FTP Software

Fujitsu Limited

Fulcrum Technologies, Inc.

GCTECH, Inc.

GEMPLUS

General Magic, Inc.

Geoworks

GMD Institute FIT

Graphic Communications Association

Grenoble Network Initiative

GRIF S.A.

Groupe ESC Grenoble

Harlequin Inc.

HAVAS

Hewlett Packard Laboratories, Bristol

Hitachi, Ltd.

Hummingbird Communications Ltd.

IBERDROLA S.A.

IBM Corporation

ILOG, S.A.

InContext Systems

Industrial Technology Research Institute

Infopartners

INRETS

Institut Franco-Russe A.M. Liapunov

Intel Corporation

Intermind

Internet Profiles Corporation

Intraspect Software, Inc.

Joint Info. Systems Comm. of the UK Higher Ed. Funding Council

Justsystem Corporation

K2Net, Inc.

Kumamoto Institute of Computer Software, Inc.

Lexmark International, Inc.

Los Alamos National Laboratory

Lotus Development Corporation

Lucent Technologies

Mainspring Communications, Inc.

Marimba, Inc.

Matra Hachette

MBED Software

MCI Telecommunications

Metrowerks Corporation

Michelin

Microsoft Corp.

MITRE Corporation

Mitsubishi Electric Corporation

MTA SZTAKI

National Center for Supercomputing Applications (NCSA)

National Security Agency (NSA)

National University of Singapore

NCR

NEC Corporation

Netscape Communications

NeXT Software, Inc.

NHS (National Health Service, UK)

Nippon Telegraph & Telephone Corp. (NTT)

NOKIA Corporation

Novell, Inc.

NTT Data Communications Systems Corp.

Nynex Science & Technology, Inc.

O'Reilly & Associates, Inc.

Object Management Group, Inc. (OMG)

OCLC (Online Computer Library Center, Inc.)

Omron Corporation

Open Market, Inc.

Open Software Foundation

Oracle Corp.

ORSTOM

Pacifitech Corporation

Philips Sound and Vision

PointCast Incorporated

Pretty Good Privacy, Inc.

Prodigy Services Corporation

Progressive Networks

Public IP Exchange, Ltd. (PIPEX)

Raptor Systems, Inc.

Reed-Elsevier

Reuters Limited

Rice University for Nat'l HCPP Software

Riverland Holding NV/SA

Royal Melbourne Institute of Technology

Security Dynamics
    Technologies, Inc.
Sema Group
SICS
Siemens-Nixdorf
Silicon Graphics, Inc.
SLIGOS
SoftQuad. Inc.
Software 2000
Sony Corporation

Spyglass, Inc.
STET
Sun Microsystems Corporation
SURFnet bv
Swedish Institute for Systems
    Development (SISU)
Syracuse University
Tandem Computers Inc.
Technische Universitat Graz
Teknema Corporation

Telequip Corporation
Terisa Systems, Inc.
The Hong Kong Jockey Club
Thomson-CSF
TIAA-CREF
Toshiba Corporation
TriTeal Corporation
U.S. Web Corporation
UKERNA
Unwired Planet

Verity, Inc.
VTT Information Technology
webMethods, Inc.
Wolfram Research, Inc.
WWW. Consult Pty Ltd.
WWW–KR
Xerox Corporation
Xionics Document
    Technologies, Inc.

# C O N T E N T S

*This issue's cover was illustrated by Marina Thompson.*

# C O N T E N T S

# C O N T E N T S

EVER SINCE I TOOK THE HELM of the *World Wide Web Journal* a year ago, I have been both dreading—and eagerly anticipating—putting together a Web security issue. Dreading it because, as W3C's original "security maven," I know how numbingly dry cryptographic technology debates can be. I was also aware that any attempt to capture the details of today's algorithms, formats, and protocols could result in chasing a mirage of futures, since these details are so dramatically in flux. Most of all, I had a nagging sense our readers— even hardcore research and development types—would not be well served by "Yet Another Web Security How-To Book," dissecting the innards of Secure Sockets Layer (SSL) or Secure-HTTP.

On the other hand, I was excited about the prospect of developing a very different kind of resource. While we do describe the fundamentals of cryptography, tips and tricks for secure Web programming, and even offer an SSL how-to, I am especially proud of how *Web Security: A Matter of Trust* indeed refocuses the debate on the nature of trust in an open, distributed system like the Web.

The Web of Trust radiates outward from the basic challenge of securing Web transactions. Below HTTP, we need private network connections and reliable naming services for locating Internet devices. We need standard trust management tools on top of Web clients and servers to help automate everyday trust decisions using signed assertions: Is this applet safe? Should Junior be able to access *playboy.com*? Did she really say that?!

To address these questions, W3C is working on digitally signed assertions: the architecture and specifications are in this issue. Using these tools we can begin to develop trusted Web applications like electronic payments, electronic commerce, and electronic health care. But most of all, we need to reach within ourselves, to promulgate a new philosophy for weaving a Web of Trust amongst the people, computers, and organizations on the Net.

One beauty of the *Web Journal* is that we have the freedom to step outside narrow technological concerns to consider the impact of the Web on the world. In this issue, we also consider what society and policymakers have to say about our headlong rush to mirror human communities on the Web. This ranges from the practical—such as concerns about digital signature legality—to the philosophical—such as our fundamental right to privacy enabled by strong cryptography. We report on what several state and national governments are doing in response to these issues, including an interview with U.S. FTC Commissioner Christine Varney.

These implications become acute as we recapitulate more of our real world within the Web. The challenge is not *how* we should explicitly move "secure" institutional applications like banking and top-secret documents on to the Web but, rather, to provide the infrastructure for automatable Trust Management for everyday life. We need to protect our own identities and be sure of our correspondents'. We need to share our opinions with each other about what's good and bad out there on the Web. We need to bring back accountability, as exemplified in Tim Berners-Lee's infamous "Oh, Yeah?" button, which demands feedback not just from the publisher, but from the community of *readers*. The future is in *our* hands: as users, as developers, as webmasters, as citizens.

Welcome to the seventh issue of the *World Wide Web Journal.* I think it's a lucky issue, and I'm not just saying that because I'm featured in all three sections! I think the readers are the lucky ones: *Web Security: A Matter of Trust* contains an outstanding team of contributors, a timely set of specifications, and a gamut of security-related technical papers—all in all, a fine example of O'Reilly's and the W3C's joint mission for W3J.

**One Down, . . .**

This issue marks my first full year editing the *World Wide Web Journal.* It seems longer—I changed jobs twice within the Consortium and left recently to join the Ph.D. program at the University of California at Irvine—pausing at MCI's Internet Architecture division in between. W3J has been an adventure on several fronts: dealing with a print publication while working in "Web time"; refining our editorial mission using the "ready, fire, aim" technique; and continuously expanding our vision. It seems to be working: both *Advancing HTML: Style and Substance* and *Scripting Languages: Automating the Web* sold very well in retail, new subscriptions are adding up, and we are pleased to welcome Dale Dougherty, President of Songline Studios and Publisher of Web Review, to the W3J team.

A great deal of credit is due to Managing Editor Donna Woonteiler, who takes care of W3J day in and day out. For this issue, thanks also to O'Reilly Editor Debby Russell for reviewing several articles, Simson Garfinkel for helping identify topics, and Sally Khudairi, W3C's Promotion and Dissemination Domain Leader, for acting as W3C's liason. Last, but not least, a hearty congratulations to our authors, who are ultimately responsible for our success.

Our next topic will be eXtensible Markup Language (XML). The Fall 1997 issue will herald the return of Guest Editor Dan Connolly, W3C's Architecture Domain Leader (who also edited W3J Volume 1, Number 2, *Key Specifications of the World Wide Web*). Dan was one of the original champions of structured markup for the World Wide Web and leaders of the XML effort, so I'm confident we're in good hands. The XML issue will be an authoritative, timely guide to the entire range of issues surrounding this new specification for authors, software developers, and researchers.

Until next "Web-year," then . . . ∎

Rohit Khare
*editor@w3j.com*
June 1997, Boston, Massachusetts

# INTERVIEW
## CHRISTINE VARNEY
### Talks About
### Advancing Commerce and
### Protecting Consumers

**F**rom the trust that forms the basis of Web commerce to the anti-trust concerns of smaller Web-based businesses, many of the current up-in-the-air issues on the Web will find their way to the Federal Trade Commission in Washington, D.C. And Commissioner Christine Varney is already preparing to deal with them.* Appointed to the FTC in late 1994, Varney, 41, has always taken a special interest in Internet-related commerce issues. Recently, for example, she helped organize a public workshop on Consumer Information Privacy.† In fact, conference preparations were in full swing when she stopped long enough to chat with D.C. Denison about some of the pressing issues facing the FTC and the World Wide Web.

**Q:** *From reading your speeches, I get the feeling your approach to Internet fraud is: "A swindle is a swindle is a swindle, no matter where it happens."*

**A:** And if it sounds too good to be true, it probably is. Yes, that's my view: when you're talking about your garden-variety fraud, it's a scam whether it's through the mail, on the phone, or on the Internet. Although sometimes on the Internet, it can be a little more difficult to figure out that you're getting scammed.

**Q:** *Can you think of an example?*

**A:** Let's say that someone in your family comes

---

* The images of Christine Varney you see on this page were taken from a QuickTime movie, courtesy of CNET's *NEWS.COM.*
† See the sidebar for a sample of the developments and proposals that came out of the FTC hearings, which took place June 10–13, 1997. For more information about the workshop see *http://www.ftc.gov/bcp/privacy2/index.html.*

down with cancer. You go all around the Web, and you're looking for everything you can find on that form of cancer. Then you happen into what looks like a pretty good discussion group on the topic. And someone in the group is saying, "You know there's this tree bark in Mexico, and it's administered by this clinic. And it saved my husband's life." Then someone else says, "Yeah, we went too, and it saved our life as well." So you say, "Tell me more about it. And you get into some long discussion over the next few days or weeks, and you never find out, because it's never disclosed to you, that the person putting up this posting owns the trees, and the bark, and the charter company which is the only way to get there, and the institute that you have to stay in while you're there. So it's never disclosed to you that the people you're chatting with have a pecuniary interest in any decision you may make. If you have that knowledge, it may influence your decision making.

**Q:** *So there are special cases on the Internet.*

**A:** Right. The wonderful thing about the Web and the Internet is that you're able to go and get information from any variety of sources, unfiltered, uncensored. But at the same time, you don't always have the ability to judge if there are any other motivations from the people who are offering the opinions.

**Q:** *You appear to support the view that the government should resist the impulse to create laws regarding Internet commerce.*

**A:** Well, that kind of behavior that I just mentioned could be prosecuted under our existing laws under either our deception authority or our fraud authority. So we don't need new law to prosecute that.

**Q:** *And some of these issues aren't new to the FTC. They've already come up in connection with credit cards, 900 numbers, and credit reporting bureaus.*

**A:** Absolutely. In my view, there may not be a lot of new law that's needed in order to prosecute abuses that occur on the Internet. But there are exceptions—for example, junk mail spamming. There is a cost to receiving unsolicited junk mail—it's the cost of the time it takes to get online, open your mail, and trash it. It may be a minimal cost, but it's a cost.

The same thing happened with unsolicited faxes. And Congress passed a law prohibiting that. We may have to do the same with regard to the Internet. You always have to balance First Amendment rights, free speech, and commercial speech. But unsolicited junk mail has some costs associated with it, so we'll see where that one goes.

**Q:** *Do you support the creation of an industry-based, market-based privacy solution?*

**A:** I think that privacy has many facets; there may be a marketplace for privacy in some instances. When individuals go on the Internet and they are dealing one-on-one with interactions or transactions, there's a true marketplace for privacy. If the individuals demand to know the privacy practices of the sites they are visiting, and refuse to go to sites that don't disclose their privacy practices, then there's a marketplace for privacy. Perhaps there will be tech-

# Internet Privacy Developments at FTC Hearings

A recent FTC Public Workshop on Consumer Online Privacy, held in Washington from June 10–13 1997, and hosted by Commissioner Christine Varney, generated a surprising number of developments. Among them:

- The announcement of a W3C Platform for Privacy Preferences (P3) Project, which allows Web sites to easily describe their privacy practices, as well as set policies about the collection and use of their personal data. Between the Web site's practices and the user's preferences, a flexible "negotiation" allows services to offer the preferred level of service and data protection to the user. If there is a match, access to the site is seamless; otherwise the user is notified of the difference and is offered other access options to proceed.

- Microsoft announced that it will collaborate with Netscape, Firefly, and VeriSign on the creation of an Open Profiling Standard (OPS). OPS is designed to control how information collected by Web-based companies is used. The standard will be developed under the auspices of the W3C's Privacy Working Group.

- A group of eight database companies announced practices and guidelines for collecting personal information online. The participating companies include Lexis-Nexis, ChoicePoint, Database Technologies, Experian, First Data InfoSource/Donnelly Marketing, IRSC, Metromail, and Information America.

- TRUSTe, backed by companies such as Oracle, Netscape, CyberCash, and IBM, unveiled a set of logos that will inform visitors to Web sites how the information collected on the site will be used.

- Lucent Technologies demonstrated a "personal Web assistant" that is designed to protect the privacy of Web users. The Web assistant allows users to register at sites under a new identity, and continue to use that identity on future visits.

- McGraw-Hill announced a new online privacy policy that will inform Web site visitors how personal data will be collected, and give users the option to prohibit the distribution of this data.

- The Direct Marketing Association announced that it has drafted disclosure standards for its members. Although its policy is not mandatory, DMA president Robert Wientzen promised that eighty percent of DMA member Web sites would employ the standards within a year.

These proposals, and others offered at the FTC workshop, appear to confirm Commissioner Varney's strategy of encouraging "market-based" privacy solutions over government regulation. But the FTC, and Congress, will no doubt be watching the follow-though over the next year, as they decide where and when government regulators will get involved with the Internet.

nological solutions, and people will be able to make money by providing higher and lower levels of privacy, and figuring out disclosure codes and all kinds of stuff. There are arenas where I don't think there is a marketplace for privacy. One is children. The other is for the collection of data about you when you're not involved in the interaction or the transaction with the entity that's doing the data collection.

It's almost analogous to credit bureaus. There has arisen an industry whose sole purpose and product is to collect information about you, without your knowledge or consent, and then sell it. Sometimes that's a valuable function in society. One of the companies that does this stuff was engaged in the search for the alleged Oklahoma bomber. And they found him within five minutes. It also turns out that the guy who originally got the license to distribute RU-486 in the United States was a convicted felon. The way they eventually found this out was by using one of these services.

So there can be legitimate societal uses for this information. But there can also be wild and rampant abuses. Individuals have no knowledge about what's being collected on them, and what's being used, what's being done with it. And that's an area where the government could get involved.

**Q:** *In the past you've suggested that the W3C's PICS (Platform for Internet Content) protocol could be useful in this area.*

**A:** Absolutely. For the one-on-one interactions and transactions—I think it's great. Last June, at our privacy hearings, I said "Why can't you take a PICS approach to privacy? Can't we go to the W3C, and see if they can take the technology they are developing and do a protocol for privacy—so that your privacy preference can precede you everywhere you go?" PICS is invisible—you just download software into your hard drive; and it's easy to use. If you go somewhere that doesn't support your privacy preference, a flag comes up. It indicates that this place either doesn't have a privacy policy

---

*"I don't think that there's any such thing as valid consent from a 10-year old. . . . What do you do about those sites that spring up before they can be blocked and collect enormous amounts of information from children?"*

---

or won't accept this one. Then you can make a decision as to whether or not you want to continue. I'm not sure, however, whether PICS will work for the non one-on-one interactions and transactions—the so-called "Look Up" industry, the information collection industry.

**Q:** *The information collection industry is a lot older and bigger than just the Internet.*

**A:** Right. But what these new companies are doing is they're going to places like Double-Click—they're getting a lot of data about you and they are marrying it with public record data that they already have. And then they come up with extensive profiles. It is an old industry, but it's changing. The ease with which information can be collected and aggregated in the digital age was unimaginable two or three years ago.

**Q:** *So that's an area that the FTC might be looking at?*

**A:** We are. We've been asked by the Senate to make a recommendation in regard to what they call "Look Up" services. We view it as a little bit broader than that: we view it as electronic databases that have gathered information about individuals without their knowledge or consent.

**Q:** *Do you give your credit card number over the Internet?*

**A:** Absolutely. I shop at *Amazon.com* and *CDNet.*

**Q:** *No precautions?*

**A:** I'm not particularly worried about my credit card getting ripped off in the transmission. As everyone says, it's more likely to get ripped off at a restaurant or in a phone transaction. I think the bigger problem with credit cards is very sophisticated hackers who can break into databases, and take out a thousand credit card numbers, and use them simultaneously. I don't think the danger is so much with individual credit cards; it's really the databases.

**Q:** *Last year you organized an "Internet Pyramid Surf Day."*

**A:** Oh yeah, that was my baby. We got all our state attorney generals, and our staff here in Washington. We identified a day and time and said, "Okay, everybody online now! Go!" There were probably a hundred of us, and we all spent four or five hours surfing the net, looking for scams.

**Q:** *What did you do when you found them?*

**A:** When we found something that looked suspicious, we sent an electronic message that said, "You may not be aware of it, but there are a whole series of rules that govern enterprises that are involved with multilevel distribution. And the Web site you have does not appear to comport with these rules." So we gave them notice. We didn't say, "You're busted. Stop." And we didn't undertake huge investigations. We just surfed and visited places that on their face did not appear to comport with the multilevel distribution rules that apply on the state or federal level.

**Q:** *How many did you identify?*

**A:** About five hundred sites. Then we went back a couple of weeks later, and about half of them were down.

**Q:** *And the rest?*

**A:** Of the half that were still up, we started doing a little investigation, and probably some cases will come out of that.

**Q:** *What did you learn from that exercise?*

**A:** That there are a lot of fools on the Internet who don't think they're going to get caught.

**Q:** *What are the biggest categories of Internet fraud?*

**A:** Let's see: there are travel scams, investment opportunity scams, business opportunity scams, and old fashioned pyramid schemes: send us $5 and we'll send you $20.

**Q:** *I think I got one of those in my email box this morning.*

**A:** Send it to us. We'll take a look at it.

**Q:** *Trust is a big issue on the Web: am I the person I say I am. Is that one of the FTC's concerns?*

**A:** The Clinton administration is very interested in promoting commerce on the Internet, electronic commerce. And I have said, many times, that there are four elements that are necessary for Internet commerce to really take off:

1. *Authenticity*—that you are who you say you are.

2. *Security*—nothing's going to happen to your credit card.

3. *Privacy*—you know what information is being collected about you, and what's being done with it.

4. *Recourse*—if you're unhappy with the transaction, you know you can get your money back.

All of these include some level of trust. And until the Internet evolves to the point where those four can be assured, I don't think electronic commerce is going to take off.

**Q:** *Is it the government's role to make those things happen?*

**A:** That's the big question: what is the appropriate level of government in any of those. Right now everybody says, "Government stay

out. Because if you get involved, you'll only muck it up." But at some point, I think that dialogue is going to change. For example, banks will be coming to the government and saying, "You're going to have to set some floors for doing business on the Internet, because we're getting killed by shady operators." We may see the National Retail Federation coming to the FTC or to Congress and saying, "You need to set some floors for recourse and redress on the Internet. Because some people are going out of business the second they sell everything, and people are left holding the bag. And it's really discouraging commerce on the Internet."

So right now the view is: Do nothing. Stay out of the way. I suspect that that view will evolve over time to a point where the various sectors of the economy that want to be active on the Internet, will identify the need for the government to come in and set some floors.

**Q:** *But you want to give those sectors the opportunity to come up with an industry-based solution first?*

**A:** Absolutely. Because technological solutions, which we can't even imagine yet, will be viable on the Internet. And government solutions may retard technical innovation.

**Q:** *Does everything change when you're talking about kids?*

**A:** For me it does. Because I don't think there's any such thing as valid consent from a 10-year-old. To the extent that blocking software really works, I think that can be a great help to parents. But what do you do about those sites that spring up before they can get blocked, that collect enormous amounts of information from children about their families and then sell it? That's where the FTC might get involved.

**Q:** *What are your favorite search phrases?*

**A:** "Get Rich Quick," "Free Travel," "Fast Money." I just put in any words like that that come into my head. In fact I think there's an area in Yahoo! Business and Economy called "Get Rich Quick." It's really very funny.

**Q:** *Going from trust to anti-trust, what are the biggest issues in that arena, in your opinion?*

**A:** Well I don't think they're specifically Internet-related, but they are high tech related—bio high tech and electronic high tech. When you're in a high tech field, you're usually dealing with high degrees of R&D. And when you see companies either merging, joint-venturing, or entering into other kinds of strategic alliances—it's sometimes, in high tech, very hard to figure out where there might be anti-competitive consequences. Because you can't figure out whether vertical integration is simply more efficient, or whether it's choking competition.

For example, you'll see that Microsoft integrates its Internet Explorer browser into its operating system, and Netscape creates an operating system. Now what you're seeing is what we had previously thought of as two product markets collapsing into one market—the browser market and the operating system market are now one market.

Say, for example, that we never thought of Microsoft as being in the browser market at all. Under traditional anti-trust theory, there would be no problem with them acquiring Netscape. It would not be considered anti-competitive. Now you and I know in our souls that that would be incredibly anti-competitive. But there aren't traditional anti-trust models that would have predicted that. So it's a very difficult problem to figure out when innovation is being enhanced—because you're concentrating resources, you're getting synergies, you're increasing efficiency—when innovation and competition are being stifled.

**Q:** *So how do you proceed?*

**A:** Very carefully. You tread very carefully. And you pay very close attention to what industry leaders are saying.

**Q:** *What's your view on Congress' role concerning these issues? If regulatory bodies like the FTC are slow, Congress is slower and more reactive to public opinion.*

**A:** Well, I think that privacy is breaking through as an issue on the Hill. In the last two-year session of Congress I think there were something like seven thousand bills, and one thousand of them had some sort of privacy provision. And about one hundred had some real significant level of privacy in them. So I think that the privacy issue is going to come up; I think that Congress is going to get pulled into encryption one way of the other. Probably kicking and screaming. There are also a lot of copyright issues, and Congress may have to get involved in those. But I think the legislative process will be very, very slow. To the extent that Congress sees immediate harm, or immediate political gain, then they'll enact legislation quickly. But I'm not sure that they see that in any of the areas I've identified.

**Q:** *What does that mean for the FTC?*

**A:** I think it means that Congress is looking to us to point out areas where we think they need to legislate. And they are also looking to us to provide some solutions. One of the models we've talked about is that we have issued "agency guidelines," which don't have the force of law, in the context of environmental advertising—they are called "Green Guides." So if a company is going to make a claim about being "environmental," we wrote guidelines—at the industry's request—that now have the force of law. And most of the mainstream players abide by those laws. To the extent that we see advertising that's not consistent with those rules, we often prosecute it as either deceptive, or fraudulent, or unfair. What it does, in effect, is create a safe harbor. It says, "If you play within these confines, you're okay." If you get outside of them, you're outside of them at your own peril.

We could conceivably do the same thing regarding kids' information collection practices, kids' advertising practices. But if we did it, we'd do it with the industry. We'd sit down at the table with who we consider to be the legitimate players, who are concerned about these issues, and try and help craft rules that make sense. The advantage is that the rules will be much more flexible than regulation, because you can change them constantly.

The other way we could go was something that happened a few years ago. Congress passed a law called the Telemarketing Fraud Act. And the act is like two paragraphs: it says telemarketing fraud is fraud. It costs us $40 million a year, it's illegal, it's prohibited, and the FTC should go write regulations. What we did, based on that law, was we sat down with the legitimate telemarketers—and there are some—and said, "Okay. What do you currently do?" And then we wrote rules that really reflected their practices. So we weren't putting an additional burden on Time Warner, which is a legitimate telemarketer trying to sell *Time Magazine*, but we created a framework that reflected the current best practices in legitimate industry. And the industry was very supportive.

Now we were able to do that because Congress told us to. It's very hard for us to enact regulation in the absence of a directive from Congress. We can do it, but it's burdensome, it's cumbersome, and it's lengthy. So presumably Congress can write a law that says, "Collection of information from children without their parents' knowledge or consent is reprehensible and shouldn't be done. FTC go write rules."

**Q:** *Those are two very flexible approaches.*

**A:** The latter is less flexible because, although it's stronger, it clearly outlines what's legal and what's illegal. That may be a good thing. The former is more flexible, and you could probably get it done quicker. And we may end up doing both.

**Q:** *It sounds like you're trying to use the power of the FTC without having to go through the long, arduous law-making process.*

**A:** Well, I wouldn't put it that way. I'd say we're extremely respectful of what's an appropriate role for Congress, and what's an appropriate role for the court, and what's an appropriate role for the regulatory agencies. And I think that sometimes a Federal Regulatory agency can step up to the plate and provide industry guidance with what the regulatory agency thinks is the best practice—maybe before it's right for the Congress to legislate it. Or maybe it will never be right for Congress to legislate it. Because maybe there won't be a problem.

**Q:** *You've been on the FTC since 1994. What's the most dramatic change in your own thinking?*

**A:** I guess I thought, back in 1994, that we should focus all our energy in the policy arena, and not much in law enforcement. Because I thought everybody on the Internet was sophisticated and smart, and I didn't think there would be that much garden-variety fraud. But I've been really astounded by the amount of fraud. Guess what: it's not only wizards on the Internet anymore. ■

# WORK IN PROGRESS
## *People & Projects at W3C*

## ROHIT KHARE
## *SECURITY MAVEN*

The W3C is arguably best known amongst Internet users for its nurture of the evolution of HyperText Markup Language. Perhaps less known in the public mind, but of singular interest to W3C leaders and members, is the Consortium's development and acceptance of technologies enabling secure communication and transactions across the Internet. Security issues have been so crucial to the W3C in fact, that in the eyes of departing security expert Rohit Khare, the disagreements which animated early discussions of standards helped to define the role the young organization would come to play as the Internet advanced.

"The mission was to harmonize conflicting standards to bring peace to the Web security wars," Khare says of those early days. He remembers the first W3C meeting was not over HTML but Internet security. "It became an acute need by the end of 1994." As you might expect from an organization in its infancy, when Khare joined the fray in 1995 he remembers no one had titles, business cards, or clear operating principles, the last being so important to an independent organization which presumes to orchestrate agreed upon technologies in a subject everyone knew would encourage the growth of a rich online marketplace we see emerging today.

All Khare knew is this was a fight worth entering his dog in. Knowing all course requirements for his degree were met, he left Caltech three months before graduation, seeing an opportunity to leverage his engineering skills from a premier university to make an impact in the construction of a new and robust marketplace unlike the world has ever seen. "In this area over security conflict, there was tremendous interest in what we would do. My role was to redefine the battleground." Without title or portfolio, he decided to call himself "Security Maven."

Those early battles frequently pitted one camp of technology giants against another in a war over different technical approaches to arriving at the same outcome: robust, reliable Internet security for confidential communication or electronic commerce. First, Netscape introduced Secure Socket Layer (SSL) technology while Terisa Systems weighed in with Secure HTTP (SHTTP).* "SSL and SHTTP were portrayed as competing technologies when they really weren't." To recap, SSL uses the TCPI/IP protocol to provide transaction security at the transport level; security properties are linked to the channel of communication between two parties. SHTTP provides transaction security at the document level; each document is designated as private by the sender. The way Khare saw it, each approach sought to provide answers to different questions. In the case of SSL: how do I keep the conversation or transaction within this channel private?

In the case of SHTTP: how do I authenticate and authorize Web transactions? Then he saw IBM and Mastercard arrayed against Visa and Microsoft as to how secure credit card transactions could be executed. "The difference was over irrelevant stuff," Khare says.

Out of these early disagreements the Joint Electronics Payment Initiative (JEPI) was born, an early test of W3C's growing influence as an impartial mediator and cultivator of consensus. The goal of JEPI was to bring industry players together to ensure that an array of transactions and payment protocols could operate effectively in Web applications while remaining neutral in the ensuing debate as to which one the marketplace should choose for a security solution. "What you can do is put a common hook into different payment schemes. It's like the decal on the store front that says we accept Mastercard *or* Visa," Khare says.

In Khare's estimation, JEPI gave the W3C the institutional confidence to announce an ambitious plan to resolve what it recognized as serious shortcomings of existing industry security frameworks. Entitled the Digital Signature Initiative (DSig), it is W3C's effort to confront issues of trust; that is, the end user's trust in object oriented applets compiled locally like Active X Controls or Java, and trust in the authenticity of documents, whether it be politi-

---

* TCP/IP, the internal communications protocol for all Internet applications (including email, Usenet, World Wide Web), uses an programming abstraction called a socket to implement reliable transport between two parties on the Internet. Secure Sockets Layer (SSL), developed by Netscape Communications, is a security enhanced abstraction of sockets that provides transaction security at the link or transport level. With SSL, security properties are attached to the link or channel of communication between two parties, not the documents themselves. Secure HTTP provides transaction security at a document level—each document may be marked as private and/or signed by the sender. Reference implementations of Secure HTTP in the form of Secure NCSA Mosaic and Secure NCSA httpd are available from EIT and currently deployed to the CommerceNet consortium.

cal messages, press releases presumed to be accurate by the media, or price lists of goods and services the consumer would make a buying decision from. DSig is charged with developing a framework such that users could be reasonably assured applets or plugins are not loaded with malicious code, nor are they being duped by someone who attributes a prank document to an individual who had no knowledge of its existence nor authorship. What distinguishes the DSig effort from all others in Khare's view is the W3C's aggressively taking the lead on the subject rather than reacting to the grievance of a technology company by just playing honest broker.

"The abiding interest in security has crystallized the operating principals of the W3C," Khare says placing it in the hothouse of Internet innovation while it continues to act like loving parents who avoid choosing a favorite amongst siblings. "We are now in the role of collaborative development, reaction to industry demand and we're also involved in "blue sky" development (the what if, experimental kind)," Khare says. As the solutions to aspects of security continue to emerge smoothly, the latest Greek drama which hit the stage is the <OBJECT> tag embedded in HTML documents. "The question is how do we design the general <OBJECT> tag for Web pages rather than choose between Active X or Java?" asks Khare rhetorically as a way to reiterate the W3C's neutrality in what he calls the turf wars over specific technology solutions. The wisdom and maturity the organization gained winning the "security wars" over the past three years should serve the organization, industry mem-

bers, and the larger Internet community well as they work to answer such questions.

*– John Berry*

# JIM GALVIN
## *BUILDING TRUST FROM THE GROUND UP*

James Galvin manages the Security and Trust technology portfolio at CommerceNet, an industry consortium that was established to jump-start Internet commerce. Initially in the Silicon Valley, CommerceNet now has offices around the world. Galvin draws upon his background in research and development in practical network security, his involvement with the Internet Engineering Task Force (IETF), as well as hands-on experience prototyping secure implementations for telnet, email, DNS, and routing. Part of coming on board at CommerceNet, one of his goals was to address "how we actually make things happen in such a way that it gets deployed." W3J interviewed Galvin in June 1997.

**W3J:** *Can you tell us about the origin and history of CommerceNet and how it recently reorganized into its current structure?*

**JG:** CommerceNet originally started [by Director Marty Tenenbaum] about three and a half years ago as part of a technology reinvestment program (TRP), funded by a number of agencies from the U.S. government. It was created back when electronic commerce was just a vision. Its mission for our three-year contract was to create electronic commerce.

During the third year, we asked ourselves, "do you declare success and go away or do you declare success and find a new problem and move on?" Obviously, since we're still here after three years, we chose to find a new problem and moved on. Now CommerceNet is positioning itself as an organization to accelerate Internet-based electronic commerce: the vision of the future is a totally integrated commerce system using the Internet as the base communication path.

Building vertical markets is probably the best way to think about our role in Internet-based ecommerce, and the real estate industry is one of the best ways to imagine how a vertically integrated market works. A number of different industries are involved. There's not only the buying and selling of your house—mortgage companies, home inspectors, termite inspections, credit reports, credit agencies, your local government, and insurance agencies are also involved.

**W3J:** *Jim, what exactly is the output of CommerceNet?*

**JG:** There are a couple of different ways we operate. For example, contrasting with W3C which develops specs and tools, our members receive research papers and white papers. CommerceNet picks a topic, finds an industry expert, and commissions a white paper in order to visit that particular topic and provide data back to our membership. A company joins a particular portfolio that you can think of as a mutual fund, for which they contribute membership fees.

We also create projects. As an organization CommerceNet actually has an exemption from the Federal Trade Commission, under the Research Act, which makes our activities exempt from anti-trust actions. This is very desirable, especially to commercial companies. Oftentimes companies want to work on something together but don't have a mechanism to do this without a number of exchanges, bilateral nondisclosure agreements, and so on.

We make that issue go away by bringing activities under our auspices—for example, we run pilot projects with groups of companies. Probably our most notable pilot project at the moment is the secure EDI over the Internet.

**W3J:** *So, in some ways a project is a group of companies working together on test implementations?*

**JG:** Yes. And it could also be a group of companies working together to develop agreements for how to do something. For example, we had a task force whose intent was to create baseline template legal agreements for interacting and working with a Certification Authority (CA).

**W3J:** *Isn't one of the pilot projects for the Social Security Administration?*

**JG:** Yes. This started a couple of weeks ago. The Social Security Administration contacted us to do a survey of strong authentication mechanisms as used on the Internet. This is in response to their attempts to distribute Personal Earnings Benefit Estimate Statements (PEBES) through the Web.

**W3J:** *What was the problem with distributing this information online?*

**JG:** Well, there are a couple of interesting things to note about the whole thing. Originally a user had to fill out a request, which was turned into their standard paper-processing backend. But in the last couple of months they changed it so you could also just fill out the same information on an online form to get access to your statement. Simson Garfinkel publicized the potential privacy holes in a front page *USA TODAY* story, which pointed out that in practice, name, address, and mother's maiden name isn't secret enough.

I suppose there's a part of me that agrees with him. But, on the other hand, I don't agree with the way all of this has turned out. It's interesting that the data SSA asks you for online in order to prove who you are, is actually more than what they would ask for if you walked into their office, presented them with a piece of paper, or just wrote them a letter asking for your statement.

It's a privacy issue. The concern is that the data SSA asked for on the Web form is, in theory, private data—though in practice we know that it's generally not. For example, the two most notable things are Social Security Number and mother's maiden name. Presumably these are private—a lot of people like to think that they are—but those of us who are technical folks recognize that this is just not true.

The fundamental issue in the case of the PEBES is that although they know a lot about you, they don't know how to authenticate you in a way that our societal infrastructure recognizes as being trusted. And this is where you get into the issue of Social Security Number, mother's maiden name, and other kinds of secrets. It's public knowledge for all practical purposes.

What's different in the physical world is a matter of velocity. I can only walk in as an individual so many times, to so many different tellers, and in so many offices and lie to get my statement. On the Internet I could lie thousands of times before anybody ever figures it out. And that's the issue for SSA.

The issue here is not whether Social Security did anything wrong, but that we fundamentally have a societal problem with what's private and what's not. We are holding Social Security, primarily because they're a U.S. government agency, up to a higher standard. I don't know whether that's good or bad.

**W3J:** *Well, it certainly is good for CommerceNet since it's the impetus for a very nice, high profile project; one that is quite important for the country.*

**JG:** Yes. So, we're going to do this survey and provide detailed feedback. Obviously, what the Social Security Administration wants is to reinstate the PEBES service. They actually have a whole set of services they would like to roll out as time goes on. But all that's on hold right now.

**W3J:** *Do we have solutions to the problem that we can't trust everybody online and that people will abuse the system?*

**JG:** What we were looking for specifically was how people used authentication and what authentication they were using. One of the things that we discovered was there are, for all practical purposes, two industry standards for authentication: one is login and password. If I establish a sufficient encryption tunnel I can use login and password underneath it—and that turns out to be a widely used industry standard. Much more so than I thought before I started conducting this survey.

The other industry standard people are using is public key-based systems. But they are very much a closed system and certainly are in the minority.

One of the conclusions that came from all of this was that Social Security has a unique problem: they need to accept queries from individuals with whom they, for all practical purposes, have no *a priori* relationship. And that's what sets them apart from the rest of the industry.

**W3J:** *They also have an extremely intimate relationship, which is the data at stake. It's an interesting paradox, based on the earnings history in the first place.*

**JG:** Yes, it is.

**W3J:** *So the basic problem is about trust— understanding who it is you're trusting and for what. How do explain the differences between "trust" and "security" to your business customers?*

**JG:** I generally start by defining trust and security, and what that means with where we're going. I regard security as a technical issue. To a very large extent, we do not have a technology problem securing the Internet. There's lots of technology out there as well as plenty of software and hardware providers.

But the issue is that we don't have individual applications to integrate the services. And the most significant issue, setting aside legal and policy questions and all of your export issues, is one of Trust Management. The fundamental problem is the lack of an integrated infrastructure for taking a certificate from its original form, validating it in such a way so I could apply some trust to it, and therefore approving the requested transaction.

The systems that have been rolled out today are closed systems. They work if you are a part of the system—you have to go through this process of entering the system, becoming a part of it, and subscribing to it. The model that we really want is one in which my identity will be valid irrespective of the context I use it in. Today, every time I want to use a new service or conduct a different kind of transaction, I have to join or subscribe to that service.

What's missing is Trust Management: the ability to recognize identities that are asserted by other entities so other communities can make use of them. The success of PGP (Pretty Good Privacy) showed us how a Web of Trust can work—but the reality is it really doesn't scale. You can build these huge Webs of Trust, and people do. But the further away a public key is from you—and the number of signatures you have to validate to decide if that a public key is trustworthy—the less trustworthy it is. But PGP did demonstrate that for relatively regional communities, as opposed to closed communities, you can build up quite a secure communication path. What we need is to formalize that same kind of system on a global scale.

**W3J:** *What kinds of identities will emerge? Closed, special purpose certificates or an open, general purpose PKI?*

**JG:** Let's put it this way. When an individual is born, he or she gets a name. That name is based on where and when you were born.

Imagine an ideal world where I get a public/private key pair and I get it stuck in a certificate with that identity. This key pair guarantees uniqueness throughout the world. What I really want is to have the authority to use the public/private key pair in particular contexts. Closed systems and closed certificates essentially do two things: one, they identify you and two, they authorize you to use the public/private key pair in that context.

Separating those issues simplifies things. Now I can have an identity that will always be valid and will always work. I can use that identity to say, "this is who I am." Then I can use other important criteria to receive a separate, opaque token.

Take the credit card industry. They give you a credit card number. On a gross conceptual level, it's an opaque token that gives me authorization to do a set of things. But my identity doesn't change because I went to

American Express versus Visa versus Master-Card. Only the token that I used in their context changed. That's the infrastructure that's missing today—the ability to have an identity infrastructure.

If we were to have that kind of open infrastructure, an open public key infrastructure which focused only on identity, that would be a win across the board.

**W3J:** *Who would provide it?*

**JG:** Well, one way is for local governments to issue a digital as well as a birth certificate. This gives us a nice hierarchical infrastructure that, in fact, applies for all practical purposes worldwide.

**W3J:** *The civil libertarians are worried about that.*

**JG:** There are a lot of reasons to worry—for instance, people believe that they will lose a certain amount of privacy. In some countries that's more true than it is in the U.S. But personally, I'm less concerned about the government than about the commercial world. With the exception of a few notable agencies, the U.S. government is an open book. We always have the right to reach in and look at our government. (Take, for example, what's happening with Social Security and PEBES.)

On the other hand, there is absolutely nothing to protect me from commercial service providers. Credit reporting agencies are the best example of that. You get a blip on your credit history and there is just no making it go away.

What about the financial services industries? The banks are really in the business of knowing who you are—they figure out who you are and then they base that relationship on an account number. But once they know who you are and they have that account number, think about what they do for you and how they act on your behalf. They are a trusted, multinational group: there are processes that have been in operation for a century or more, which deal with exchanging money, passing it around, and acting on your behalf. Why couldn't a bank be the source of issuing you an identity certificate?

Some members of the banking industry recognize this option. But because of how regulated it is, the banking industry is slow to move, and cautious. On the other hand, maybe that's one of the reasons why they would be good for this job.

**W3J:** *How is CommerceNet involved in any of this?*

**JG:** Well, trust is our most significant issue, and I think the goal here is to identify the projects that will address that fact. One such project involves cross-certification with Japan-Net and CommerceNet Japan, where we're trading up disjoint hierarchies, one over there and one over here.

This is interesting from the point of view that it's an international operation. We can have CA services in different countries and actually validate the signatures using certificates that we have issued respectively in our country. That's a step in helping to manage trust until we can roll out a global infrastructure. If I can't have a single sort of trusted hierarchy, I want to build it out of pulling together pieces of hierarchies that I know I can trust.

If we are going to have disjoint hierarchies in the United States, then let's talk about cross-certification. If we accept that there will be hundreds or thousands of certification hierarchies, how do we build up trusted relationships between them? Let's talk about minimum requirements for Certification Authorities so we can establish trust for a public key coming to us and a certificate from a hierarchy that is disjoint from our own.

**W3J:** *When we talk about trust it's really the fact that certain businesses know each other. One company has a business relationship with another, and so on. We work through those networks to establish the connections we need. But of course on the Net it's very easy to "go direct," eliminating some of the middle men. Is that a fair characterization?*

**JG:** Let me try and play that back a little differently. I think that the business-to-business world is very different than the consumer-to-business world. The business-to-business world has very well established processes and procedures for creating and establishing trust. The problems with rolling out any kind of security improvement to the consumer market are significant, and this will not be a straightforward process.

One of the reasons I believe there will be lots of disjoint hierarchies is because the business-to-business world is really based on bilateral agreements. So, if I'm an organization, why shouldn't I issue my own certificates? Then, when I decide I'm going to deal with you, we will simply exchange our "root certificates" and do business together from that point on. And why shouldn't that be the case? Why must businesses have a single global identity infrastructure? It isn't necessary. You end up building your global trust from the ground up, and I think it works in the business market. ■

*– Dale Dougherty*
*and Rohit Khare*

## Mathematical Markup Language Working Draft

**MAY 15, 1997**

The HTML Math Working Group, cochaired by Patrick Ion of AMS and Robert Miner of the NSF-sponsored Geometry Center at the University of Minnesota, announced the release of the Mathematical Markup Language Working Draft. The publication of this draft is the result of more than a year of in-depth study and experimentation. It was edited by Patrick Ion and Robert Miner; principal writers were Stephen Buswell, Angel Diaz, Nico Poppelier, Bruce Smith, Neil Soiffer and Stephen Watt. *[W3J expects to publish a stable edition of this specification in an upcoming issue.] http://www.w3.org/TR/WD-math/*

## White Paper on Joint Electronic Payment Initiative

**MAY 19, 1997**

This white paper documents lessons learned during JEPI Project Phase 1. Designed to offer an automatable payment selection process, Phase 1 was a joint project between W3C and CommerceNet, which ultimately enhances the user shopping experience while allowing the coexistence of multiple payment systems. This document, written by JEPI Project Manager Daniel Dardailler and Eui-Suk Chung, Visiting Engineer from Ericsson, details the long-term vision, technical problems and solutions, project management experiences, future plans, and more. *[This paper is included in the "W3C Reports" section of this issue.] http://www.w3.org/TR/NOTE-jepi.html*

## HTML Working Group Meeting

**MAY 20, 1997,** *Sophia-Antipolis, France*

 The former HTML Editorial Review Board was recently rechartered under the new W3C Process as the HTML Working Group. Its second meeting was arranged under the auspices of W3C's European host, INRIA. Chair Dan Connolly led discussions on several features to be included in the next version of HTML, codenamed "Cougar." Several public drafts are available from W3C on these issues, including frames, objects, internationalization, style sheets, forms, and images. *http://www.w3.org/MarkUp/*

## Amaya Source Code Public Release (1.0b beta)

**MAY 21, 1997,** *Grenoble, France*

Amaya is both a browser and an authoring tool specifically conceived to serve as a testbed client for new Web protocols and formats as well as new extensions to existing ones. Amaya was designed as an active client, but also works as an authoring tool that allows for creating new documents, editing existing ones, and publishing these documents on remote Web servers. The 1.0b is a milestone release. *http://www.w3.org/Amaya/*

## CSS & FP Working Group Meeting

**MAY 21, 1997,** *Sophia-Antipolis, France*

The Cascading Style Sheets & Formatting Properties Working Group was the second team spun out from the former HTML ERB. Chair Chris Lilley convened CSS implementors and other interested W3C members at INRIA to discuss positioning, printing, aural/visual rendering, accessibility, and fonts. *http://www.w3.org/Style/*

## Web Accessibility Initiative Working Group Meeting

**MAY 22, 1997,** *Sophia-Antipolis, France*

The first Technical Working Group of the Web Accessibility Initiative, chaired by Daniel Dardailler, met at INRIA to work on various issues including HTML, Cougar, XML, CSS and Aural extensions, HTTP content/feature negotiation, DOM, support for Math, certification, and labeling and rating with PICS. *http://www.w3.org/WAI/*

## Digital Signature Label Specification

**MAY 23, 1997**

A year's worth of investigations were capped off by the 1.0 release of a standard format for making digitally-signed, machine-readable assertions about a particular information resource. The goal of the DSig project is to provide a mechanism to make the following statement: "signer believes statement about information resource." The Working Draft, authored by Philip Des-Autels, Peter Lipp, Brian LaMacchia, and Yang-Hua Chu, describes a method of utilizing PICS 1.1 labels with extensions to meet this goal. *[This working draft is included in the "W3C Reports" section of this issue.] http://www.w3.org/TR/WD-DSIG-label.html*

## Synchronized Multimedia Working Group Meeting

**MAY 29-30, 1997,** *New York, New York*

The second meeting of the Synchronized Multimedia Working Group was held at Columbia University. The meeting focused on discussing requirements for a declarative format for describing synchronized multimedia presentations. The group agreed to come up with a strawman proposal for the format until the end of June. *http://www.w3.org/AudioVideo/*

## Mathematical Markup Working Group Meeting

**JUNE 1-2, 1997,** *Minneapolis, Minnesota*

The Mathematical Markup Working Group, cochaired by Robert Miner of the Geometry Center and Patrick Ion of AMS, met at the NSF-sponsored Geometry Center at the University of Minnesota. The Group addressed several follow-on issues not included in its initial MathML Working Draft through extension protocols—in particular, macros, input syntaxes, and machine communication. *http://www.w3.org/MarkUp/Math/*

## *Document Object Model Working Group Meeting*

**JUNE 2-3, 1997,** *Mountain View, California*

The third team spun out of the former HTML ERB focuses on automating and animating HTML resources. The Document Object Model (DOM) Working Group held its second meeting at Netscape's headquarters to discuss document representation, structural models, and scripting interfaces. Their initial investigations determined developers' needs for document navigation, content manipulation, and Document Type Definition (DTD) manipulation. *http://www.w3.org/ MarkUp/DOM/*

## *Federal Trade Commission Public Workshop on Consumer Information Privacy*

**JUNE 10-12, 1997,** *Washington, D.C.*

Tim Berners-Lee represented W3C at the Workshop on Online Privacy at the Federal Trade Commission [FTC] Public Workshop on Consumer Information Privacy. The P3 Project, approved by W3C Membership in late May, was publically announced in this forum. A P3 prototype was demonstrated to illustrate how both Web sites as well as users can easily describe their privacy practices and set policies about the collection and use of data. W3C members including IBM, AT&T, Microsoft, Netscape and the Direct Marketing Association will participate in the P3 Project. *http://www.w3.org/Press/P3, http://www.w3.org/Privacy/*

## *W3C Advisory Committee Meeting*

**JUNE 18-19, 1997,** *Tokyo, Japan*

Official Member representatives convened to hear updates from the W3C Director and Staff on various areas of activity and future plans. This meeting marked the debut of the newest W3C host institution, Keio University. *http://www.w3.org/pub/WWW/Consortium/Prospectus/* [Public], *http://www.w3.org/pub/WWW/Member/Meeting/97JuneAC* [Members only]

*The World Wide Web Consortium has been an active player in the Web Security debates since, or before, its inception. It has taken steps to enhance the security of passwords in HTTP, helped strengthen the privacy of "cookies," and proposed a larger HTTP Security Extension Architecture (SEA). In addition, the W3C has taken a leading role in fostering the creation of trusted applications with its members, including the Joint Electronic Payments Initiative (with CommerceNet) and the newly launched Platform for Privacy Preferences (P3). In this issue's "W3C Reports," we include the latest results from the effort to build a trusted Web.*

*In April 1996, W3C and its members evaluated the direction of their general purpose security plans. They agreed that privacy needs were largely addressed with transport layer encryption, through SSL and later TLS. The missing link was document authentication—particularly for mobile code. The Digital Signature Initiative grew out of our insight that signatures need to be combined with specific assertions to become general purpose, automatable tools.*

*DSig became a formal W3C project under the management of Philip DesAutels in Fall 1996. With a design team drawing on the talents of W3C, IBM, Sun, Microsoft, and several other Members, work proceeded quickly through the winter to yield a preliminary architecture by early January 1997. "Digital Signature Label Architecture" reflected the group's consensus at that point in time; though it will have been updated by the time this volume is in print, it provides a useful framework for the main course: "DSig 1.0 Signature Labels: Using PICS 1.1 Labels for Digital Signatures."*

*W3C eventually hopes to issue Member-approved Recommendations for a framework, protocol, and format to address the issues set forth in the Digital Signature Ininitiative; a sample code base to implement it; and an ongoing process for maintaining and extending the same (e.g., either W3C, IETF, ANSI, or some other body). W3C's MIT office also supports joint academic work on Trust Management applications of DSig, as discussed in the REFEREE paper in the "Technical Reports" section.*

*Another area ot security-related work at W3C focused on electronic commerce—specifically, the issues of competing payment systems and the resulting need to develop a single framework for selecting between them. A work in progress since January, 1996, the Joint Electronic Payment Initiative's goal was to develop a set of HTTP headers—much like the Visa and Master Card logos—for automatically negotiating available systems. The resulting white paper, "Joint Electronic Payment Initiative (JEPI)" is a summary of lessons learned a year into the project.*

# DSig 1.0 Signature Labels
## Using PICS 1.1 Labels for Digital Signatures

*Philip DesAutels, editor*

*Philip DesAutels, Peter Lipp, Brian LaMacchia, Yang-hua Chu*

### Abstract

*[W3C Working Draft; WD-DSIG-label-970605, June 5, 1997]*

*The W3C Digital Signature Working Group ("DSig") proposes a standard format for making digitally-signed, machine-readable assertions about a particular information resource. More generally, it is the goal of the DSig project to provide a mechanism to make the statement:* signer *believes* statement *about* information resource. *This document describes a method of utilizing PICS 1.1 labels with extensions to meet this goal.*

## Status of This Document

This is a W3C Working Draft for review by W3C members and other interested parties. It is a draft document and may be updated, replaced or obsoleted by other documents at any time. It is inappropriate to use W3C Working Drafts as reference material or to cite them as other than "work in progress". A list of current W3C working drafts can be found at *http://www.w3.org/pub/WWW/TR/*

**Note:** Since working drafts are subject to frequent change, you are advised to reference the above URL, rather than the URLs for working drafts themselves.

## DSig 1.0 Overview

This document describes a method of utilizing PICS 1.1 labels with extensions to meet the goal of making digitally signed, machine-readable assertions about a particular information resource. It also provides detailed usage guidelines for creating PICS 1.1 labels, which are valid DSig 1.0 Signature labels.

DSig 1.0 signature labels inherit both a means of transporting signature block data and a simple framework for making the machine-readable assertions from the underlying PICS framework. PICS compliant applications can syntactically parse DSig 1.0 signature labels; only cryptographic functions need to be added to PICS-aware applications in order to make use of the semantic content of a DSig signature.

In its simplest form, a DSig 1.0 signature label is a signed statement about an information resource. This document describes two DSig-specific extensions to standard PICS 1.1 labels: *resinfo* and *sigblock*. The *resinfo* extension is used to create cryptographic links between the signature label and the information resource described by the label. Typically this linkage is created through the use of one or more cryptographic hash functions. The *sigblock* extension contains one or more digital signatures of the other contents of the label.

In DSig 1.0, it is important to note the following:

- At no time does a DSig 1.0 signature label "wrap" the information resource it is signing

- The signature label can always be separated from the information resource

- DSig 1.0 Signature Labels provide a means of making assertions about resources with cryptographic integrity, but they do not protect the confidentiality the information resource referenced

The basic structure of a PICS 1.1 label is described below.

W3C recommendations and working drafts related to this document are listed in the "Reference" section of this document, and include:

- The "DSig Signature Label Architecture," available as a W3C working draft at *http://www.w3.org/pub/WWW/TR/WD-DSIG-label-arch.html*

- "PICS Label Distribution Label Syntax and Communication Protocols version 1.1," *http://www.w3.org/pub/WWW/TR/REC-PICS-labels-961031.html*

- "Rating Services and Rating Systems (and Their Machine Readable Descriptions) Version 1.1," *http://www.w3.org/pub/WWW/TR/REC-PICS-services-961031.html*

We assume familiarity with these documents.

At the core of DSig 1.0 is the PICS 1.1 label, so we begin by reviewing the PICS 1.1 architecture and illustrating how DSig 1.0 signature labels are built on top of PICS 1.1 labels.

# PICS Architecture

At the core of the PICS infrastructure is the rating service (Figure 1). The *rating service* either chooses an existing, or develops a new, *rating system* to use in labeling content. The *rating system*, described in a human readable form at the rating system URL is the range of statements that can be made. The rating service establishes criteria for determining who can label content using their name and how the labels must be applied. This combination of criteria and rating service are uniquely identified by the particular service URL. This service URL becomes the brand, if you will, of the rating service. At a minimum, the service URL will return a human readable form of the rating criteria and a link to the description of the rating system. The rating service is also responsible for delivering a service description file. This is a machine-readable version of the rating system with pointers to the rating system URL and the rating service. While not required, it is recom-

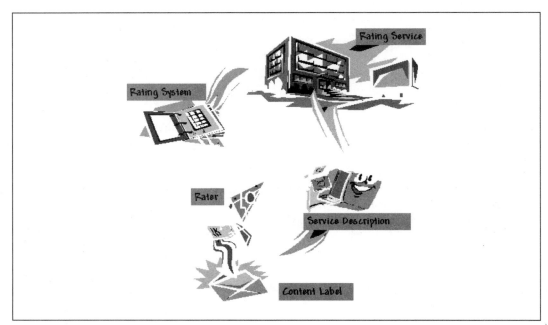

**Figure 1**     Elements of PICS infrastructure

*Web Security: A Matter of Trust*

mended that this be available automatically at the service URL.

A labeler, given authority by the rating service, uses the criteria established by them along with the rating system to label content. These *content labels* contain a statement about the content of the resource being labeled and contain a link back to the service URL. Content labels can come in the content itself, with the content or from a trusted third party such as a label bureau. Policies determine what actions are taken based on the specific statements in the content label. If a content label is based on an unknown service URL, it is a simple (and automatable) task to retrieve the appropriate *service description* file to understand what statements are being made in the label.

DSig 1.0 utilizes the PICS infrastructure as described above with a few exceptions:

- In DSig 1.0, the notion of content labels and labelers is somewhat different. Indeed, DSig 1.0 signature labels are content labels in that they are signed statements about content, but the entity that does the labeling may be different than those that signed the label. DSig 1.0 signature labels provide fields for storing information about both the label creator and the signer(s).

- Additional signatures can be added in parallel with existing signatures at any point in time.

- The PICS rating system referenced in the signature label is an *assertion system* in DSig. The statement in the label (made via the PICS ratings) is an assertion that the labeler is making about the referenced content.

- Additional resource reference information may be included within the DSig label to help disambiguate the subject of the label. The DSig *resinfo* extension is one way of including such information; it allows the label signer to provide cryptographic hashes of the labeled content. Other private extension types may also be defined and included

in accordance with the PICS 1.1 specifications.

- By signing a content label, the signer is explicitly stating that he believes the statements contained within the label. A signature does not necessarily indicate that the signer created the label, but only that he believes the statements contained within it to be valid.

## PICS 1.1 Labels and Label Lists

PICS labels are always transmitted as lists of one or more individual PICS labels ("label lists"); in common PICS practice PICS label lists usually contain exactly one label. Full details of PICS labels and label lists are available in [2], in the following sections:

- General Format of PICS Labels

- Semantics of PICS Labels and Label Lists

- Requesting Labels Separately

In DSig 1.0, each assertion about an information resource is given in a label. A label consists of the following components:

- Service identifier

- Options

- Extensions

- Assertion (in PICS 1.1 the assertion is called a rating)

The *service identifier* is the URL chosen by the rating service (see [1]) as its unique identifier. *Options* and *extensions* give additional properties of the label, the document being labeled and properties of the assertion itself. The *assertion* itself is a set of attribute-value pairs that describe a document along one or more dimensions. One or more labels may be distributed together as a list which allows for some data aggregation.

A PICS labels contains one or more service sections

```
(PICS-1.1
    <Service 1 section>
    <Service 2 section>
    <Service 3 section>)
```

where each service section contains options and labels:

```
<Service URL> <Service options for
        all labels in this
        section>
    labels <options for this label>
        ratings <rating for
        this label>
        <options for this label>
        ratings <rating for
        this label>
        ...
```

The general form for a label list (formatted for presentation, and not showing error status codes) is as follows:

```
(PICS-1.1
    <service 1 url> [service 1
        option...]
    labels [label 1 option...]
        ratings (<category>
        <value> ...)
        [label 2 option...]
        ratings (<category>
        <value> ...)
        ...
    <service 2 url> [service 2
        option...]
    labels [label 3 option...]
        ratings (<category>
        <value> ...)
        [label 4 option...]
        ratings (<category>
        <value> ...)
        ...
    ...)
```

Labels in a label list are grouped by service. Each service may have service options which are inherited by each label within the scope of the service; service options may be overridden by individual label options. When a new service is identified in the label list, the options from the previous service no longer apply. Thus, in the above example `label 4` could be equivalently represented as:

```
(PICS-1.1
    <service 2 url>
    labels [ service 2 options +
        label 4 option...]
        ratings (<category>
        <value> ...))
```

In DSig 1.0, we sign individual labels or portions thereof; the details of signing labels are presented below.

PICS defines two distinct types of labels, specific and generic:

- A *specific* label applies to a single resource. For example, if a labeled document is in HTML format, the label applies only to the HTML document itself and not to any other documents referenced via hyperlinks or <img> tags. This is the default label type.

- A *generic* label (identified by the use of the PICS *generic* option within the label) applies to any document with a URL that has a particular prefix (the prefix is specified via the PICS *for* option in the label). A generic label for a site or directory should be used only if it applies to all the documents in that site or directory. The DSig 1.0 *resinfo* extension is not meaningful within a generic label.

## PICS Options and DSig

### Semantics of Embedded Signature Blocks

By convention, a DSig signature block itself has the weakest possible semantics, namely

> the entity possessing the key that created this signature had access to the secret key used to generate the signature and the signed data at the same time

For DSig 1.0 signature labels, we want somewhat stronger semantics that also include the semantics of the ratings contained within the label. Thus, by definition, a PICS label which includes a DSig *sigblock* extension has the following semantics:

The entity possessing the secret key that digitally signed this PICS 1.1 label had access to the secret key and the label at the same time *and asserts that the statements made within the label are valid*

## Applying PICS to DSig

Following the format given in [2] we now review each of the PICS 1.1 options, giving appropriate usage rules for applying them within the context of DSig 1.0 Signature Labels.

PICS label options can be divided into three groups, which are described in the sections that follow. Options from the first group supply information about the document to which the label applies. Options from the second group supply information about the label itself. Options in the last group provides miscellaneous information.

### Information about the document that is labeled

at *quoted-ISO-date*

> The last modification date of the information resource to which this assertion applies, at the time the assertion was made. This can serve as a less expensive, but less reliable, alternative to the DSig 1.0 *resinfo extension.*

MIC-md5 "*Base64-string*"
-or- md5 "*Base64-string*"

> *This option is not used in DSIG 1.0.* If this option is present in a DSig 1.0 label, it should be ignored. Further, it should be removed from the label for the purposes of signing. This option has been superceded by the SDIG 1.0 *resinfo* extension.

### Information about the label itself

by *quotedname*

> An identifier for the person or entity who was responsible for creating this particular label. The contents of the by field are not restricted by the DSig 1.0 specification; it is common practice in PICS usage to include a name or email address in the string value of the *by* field. Within DSig 1.0, the *by* field is

considered informational only; the *by* option name need not be the same as that of the signer(s). The *sigblock* extension includes fields for the identity of the signer (in the *signature* section) and certificates (or references to them) identifying the signer(s) (within the *attribution information* section).

for *quotedURL*

> The URL (or prefix string of a URL) of the information resource to which this assertion applies. This option is required for generic labels and in certain other cases (see "Requesting Labels Separately," in [2]; it is optional in other cases. The *for* option is valid as both a service and label option in a label list.

generic *boolean*
-or- gen *boolean*

> If this option is set to true, the label can be applied to any URL starting with the prefix given in the *for* option. By default, this option is false. Set to true, it is used to supply ratings for entire sites or any subparts of sites. All generic labels must also include the *for* option. A generic label should not be created unless it can be legitimately applied to *all* documents whose URL begins with the prefix specified in the *for* option (even if a more specific label exists). If the generic option is used with a true value, the DSig 1.0 *resinfo extension* can not be used because there will not be a specific information resource to hash.

on *quoted-ISO-date*

> The date on which this label was created. This may be different than the date the label was signed (which may be included within the DSig 1.0 *sigblock* extension).

signature-RSA-MD5 "*Base64-string*"

> *This option is not used in DSig 1.0.* If this option is present in a DSIG 1.0 label it should ignored and removed from the label fooses of signing. This option has been

replaced with the DSig 1.0 *sigblock* extension.

until *quoted-ISO-date*
-or- exp *quoted-ISO-date*
> The date on which the label expires (how long the label is good for).

### Other information

comment *quotedname*
> Information for humans who may see the label; no associated semantics.

complete-label *quotedURL*
-or- full *quotedURL*
> Dereferencing this URL returns a complete label that can be used in place of the current one. The complete label has values for as many attributes as possible. This option is used when a short label is transmitted for performance purposes but additional information is also available. When the URL is dereferenced it returns an item of type application/pics-labels that contains a label list with exactly one label. In DSig 1.0 this option might be used if the initial label transmitted was an abbreviated version of the full label. The abbreviated version might contain minimal options and no signature. The client application could then dereference this URL to get the full, signed version of the label.

extension (optional *quotedURL data\**)
-or- extension (mandatory *quotedURL data\**)
> Future extension mechanism. To avoid duplication of extension names, each extension is identified by a *quotedURL*. It may be possible to dereferenced the URL to obtain a human-readable description of the extension. If the extension is *optional* then software which does not understand the extension can simply ignore it; if the extension is *mandatory* then software which does not understand the extension should act as though no label had been supplied. Each item of *data* must be one of a fixed set of simple-to-parse data types as specified in the

detailed syntax below. See *http://www.w3.org/PICS/extensions/* to find out what extensions are currently in use. The DSig 1.0 *resinfo* and *sigblock* extensions uses this mechanism (see the next extension for details).

## DSig Extensions

A DSig label "signs" an information resource. To do this in a secure fashion, the signed label must have a cryptographic connection to that resource. We create cryptographic links between a label and the labeled resource by including one or more hashes of the information resource within the signature label. Similar, albeit limited, functionality was accomplished in the PICS 1.1 specification via the *MIC-md5* (or *md5*) option. DSig 1.0 replaces this option with the *resinfo* extension, which permits a single label to include multiple hashes using multiple hash algorithms.

PICS 1.1 also specified a signature option, *signature-RSA-MD5*, but its functionality was similarly limited. DSig replaces *signature-RSA-MD5* with the *sigblock* extension. The *sigblock* extension may contain one or more signatures using any cryptographic algorithm; in addition, a sigblock may optionally include information in the form of certificates or links to certificates.

A DSig 1.0 Signature Label is a standard PICS 1.1 label. The DSig extensions *resinfo* and *sigblock* are both optional and can be used as needed. A PICS 1.1 label is only considered a DSig 1.0 Signature Label when it contains a *sigblock* extension.

### Resource Reference Information Extension

The goal of the resource reference information (*resinfo*) extension is to provide a cryptographic link between the signature label and an information resource. DSig 1.0's *resinfo* extension builds upon the PICS 1.1 *for*, *at* and *MIC-md5* options to provide this cryptographic link. Specifically, the *resinfo* extension provides a mechanism for including cryptographic checksums (hashes), in any named cryptographic algorithm, to the label. These hashes provide a means for the receiver of the label to determine if the information resource they have is the same as the one about which the assertion was made.

The *resinfo* extension is associated with a specific resource. This resource may be identified by the *for* option or may be implied by the context of the label (in the resource, delivered in the HTTP header with the resource, returned by a label bureau based on a request, etc.).

In the structure of a PICS label, the *resinfo* extension can be a *service* option and/or a *label* option. It functions identically to any other option with respect to inheritance within a service section from service option to label option. A single document can have many URLs; the URL used to retrieve a document may differ from the URL in the *for* option of a label that accompanies the document, but the document retrieved must be the same document or the hash(s) contained in the *resinfo* extension will not be valid.

Structurally, *resinfo* contains one or more hashes of the information resource; each hash includes a hash algorithm identifier, the actual hash of the resource and (optionally) the date the hash was computed:

```
("hash algorithm identifier"
    "base64-string of hash" "hash
    date")
```

The hash algorithm identifier is a quoted URL, it identifies the specific hashing algorithm by which the following hash was computed. The DSig 1.0 compliance document identifies several hash algorithms currently in common use and defines standard URLs for each. To ensure that no two hash algorithms use the same identifier, the identifier must be a valid URL. This in effect creates a distributed registry of unique names which can be created and shared by any community of interest.

Since the hash algorithm identifier is a URL, it can be resolved to retrieve a document (although it is not required that any document be accessible at a given URL). A document so referenced may be in any format, but we recommend that the following conditions are true:

- The document is in HTML format

- The document identifies the entity that created and maintains the identifier

- The document describes the specifics of the hashing algorithm, or provides a link to another document which does so

- The document is available in multiple languages, either through an existing negotiation mechanism or through links to alternate language versions

Any incompatible change in a hash algorithm should be accomplished by creating an entirely new hash algorithm identifier URL.

**Notes:**

- There can be at most one *resinfo* extension per label.

- A *resinfo* extension can contain multiple hashes of the information resource. Each must necessarily use a different hash algorithm; it is not valid to label multiple versions of a single document by including multiple, distinct hashes in one label.

- The *resinfo* extension can be either an "optional" or a "mandatory" extension. *Mandatory* implies that the software reading the label that contains the extension must understand an extension of type `http://www.w3.org/PICS/DSig/resinfo-1.0.html` or the entire label should be disregarded. *Optional* implies hat even if the processing software does not understand the extension, it should still process the label. These are powerful options that allow the author of the label wide latitude in affecting the processing policy of the client.

- The *resinfo* extension is not valid in a *generic* PICS 1.1 label. It is only valid within a *specific* (non-generic) PICS 1.1 label.

- *Resinfo* is not extensible: In DSig 1.0, if other disambiguating or differentiating information is needed, a separate extension will need to be created. We assume that the next version of DSig will allow for much richer and extensible resource reference information.

## Detailed syntax of the resinfo extension in a PICS 1.1 label

The following syntax of the *resinfo* extension (Example 1) is written in modified BNF. By convention, * indicates 0 or more instances of the token that precedes the special character, *1 indicates 0 or 1 instance of the token, and + indicates 1 or more instances of the token. The quoted strings are case-sensitive but other literal elements are case-insensitive.

Example 2 shows a valid DSig 1.0 *resinfo* extension with two hashes of the referenced information resource.

In Example 2, we begin with the *extension (optional* tokens which identify this extension as an optional extension to the PICS label within which it is contained. This declaration is followed by a *URL*, http://www.w3.org/PICS/DSig/ resinfo-1_0.html, which provides a unique name for the extension. Dereferencing the URL should provide human readable information on the extension. Finally we have two repeating sub-sections of the extension, each of which contain hash information. Here again, dereferencing the hash algorithm identifier URL would return a human readable description, this time of the hash algorithm. In Example 2, the first hash is of type

## Example 1

```
resinfo-extension ::='extension (' mand/opt
        '"http://www.w3.org/PICS/DSig/resinfo-1_0.html" resinfo-data+ ')'
mand/opt          ::= 'optional' | 'mandatory'
resinfo-data      ::='(' HashAlgoURL resource-hash hash-date*1 ')'
HashAlgoURL       ::= quotedURL
quotedURL         ::= '"' URL '"'
resource-hash     ::= '"base64-string"'
hash-date         ::= quoted-ISO-date
quoted-ISO-date   ::= '"'YYYY'.'MM'.'DD'T'hh':'mmStz'"'
        based on the ISO 8601:1988 date and time standard, restricted
        to the specific form described here:
        YYYY ::= four-digit year
        MM   ::= two-digit month (01=January, etc.)
        DD   ::= two-digit day of month (01 through 31)
        hh   ::= two digits of hour (00 through 23) (am/pm NOT allowed)
        mm   ::= two digits of minute (00 through 60)
        S    ::= sign of time zone offset from UTC ('+' or '-')
        tz   ::= four digit amount of offset from UTC
             (e.g., 1512 means 15 hours and 12 minutes)
        For example, "1994.11.05T08:15-0500" is a valid quoted-ISO-date
        denoting November 5, 1994, 8:15 am, US Eastern Standard Time
        Note: The ISO standard allows considerably greater
        flexibility than that described here.  PICS requires precisely
        the syntax described here -- neither the time nor the time zone may
        be omitted, none of the alternate formats are permitted, and
        the punctuation must be as specified here.
base64-string     ::= as defined in RFC-1521.
```

## Example 2

```
extension
    ( optional "http://www.w3.org/PICS/DSig/resinfo-1_0.html"
            ( "http://www.w3.org/PICS/DSig/SHA1.html" "base64-hash" )
            ( "http://www.w3.org/PICS/DSig/MD5.html" "base64-hash"
              "1997.02.05T08:15-0500" ) )
```

**SHA1**. This is followed by the actual hash data and followed by the date the hash was computed. The second clause uses the **MD5** hash algorithm.

## The Signature Block Extension

The DSig 1.0 Signature Block Extension (*sigblock*) provides cryptographic protection of the DSig 1.0 label by using digital signature techniques. It identifies the following:

- Who has signed the information resource

- Which parts of the label were signed (if not the entire label)

- Which algorithms were used to generate the signature

- The signature data itself

The *sigblock* extension can also contain certificates that can be used by a trust management system (TMS) to decide if the signature is trustworthy.

### Format specification

A Signature Block consists of Attribution Information, and one or more Signatures.

The Signature Block extension can be either an *optional* or a *mandatory* PICS 1.1 extension. We do not require that the extension be understood (mandatory) because the information contained within the label may be useful to applications that cannot understand the signature information. Whether information contained within an unsigned or unverified label should be used is a trust management question.

Here is a structural representation of the sigblock extension:

```
extension
    ( optional http://www.w3.org/
        PICS/DSig/sigblock-1_0.html
      <attribution info>
          <signature>* ) )
```

### Attribution information

The Attribution Information section contains self-verifiable information related to the creation of the digital signature on the label. In particular, cryptographic certificates asserting identity, authorization or other capabilities may be included here. Certificates may be directly embedded within the Attribution Information section of the *sigblock* extension, or URLs pointing to certificates may be included. Since Attribution Information is not required (i.e., this section of the extension may be empty), trust management systems must depend on other information sources when interpreting the label. Furthermore, the information provided herein may or may not be used by the trust management system in processing the label.

Attribution Information supports many certificate formats, and the types of certificates included will depend on the public key infrastructure used by the application. Certificate format is indicated by a unique URL identifier (like the hash identifier in the *resinfo* extension above); DSig 1.0 defines URLs identifying X.509v3 certificates and PGP style certificates, but also is open to new, emerging standards like [3] or [4]. These formats need not be registered, they must only be valid and unique URLs.

URLs identifying certificate families need not necessarily point to anything; the fact that they are unique is sufficient to distinguish between certificate formats. If a certificate family URL does dereference to a document, the resulting docu-

| Certificate Family | URL |
|---|---|
| X.509v3 | *http://www.w3.org/PICS/DSig/X509.html* |
| PGP | *http://www.w3.org/PICS/DSig/pgpcert.html* |

ment should provide a description of the format of certificates within the certificate family or pointers to other locations where such descriptions may be found. We strongly recommend that such format descriptions always be provided. In the future, we expect certificate family identifiers to point to downloadable active elements that are able to parse the certificate format.

None of the information contained within the Attribution Information section is signed by the label's signature because certificates themselves are expected to be self-verifying. (More precisely, none of the information within the entire *sigblock* extension, including the Attribution Information section, contributes to the hash of the label that is signed as part of the signature option.) Thus, applications may augment the contents of the Attribution Information section without invalidating the signature on the label (e.g. newly-discovered certificates may be included in the Attribution Information section as they are found, or an expired certificate may be replaced).

Here is an example Attribution Information section:

```
( "AttribInfo"
    ( "http://www.w3.org/PICS/
            DSig/X509.html"
        "base64-x.509-cert")
    ( "http://www.w3.org/PICS/
            DSig/X509.html"
      "http://ice-tel-ca/certs/DN/
            CN=Lipp,O=TU-
            Graz,OU=IAIK")
    ( "http://www.w3.org/PICS/
            DSig/pgpcert.html"
        "base64-pgp-signed-
            key")
    ( "http://www.w3.org/PICS/
            DSig/pgpcert.html"
```

```
      "http://pgp.com/certstore/
            plipp@iaik.tu-graz.
            ac.at" ) )
```

## Signatures

The Signature section of the *sigblock* extension contains the actual digital signature data. Each Signature section contains exactly one signature; multiple Signature sections may be included in the *sigblock* extension when multiple, parallel signatures are desired. The syntax of the a Signature section is:

```
( "Signature" SignatureSuite
    SigData*1)
```

Being crypto-neutral, DSig 1.0 does not prescribe the use of particular algorithms for generating hashes or digital signatures. DSig 1.0 also does not define any particular format for representing cryptographic information in the *sigblock*. Instead, we introduce the concept of "signature suites," which bundle together certain hashing algorithms, signature algorithms and representation format. Each digital signature includes a signature suite identifier that tells applications how the signature was generated and how it should be parsed.

Like hash and certificate family identifiers, the signature-suite element is a URL that uniquely identifies the signature-suite used for generating the associated signature. If dereferencing the URL yields a document, that document should provide all necessary details for parsing, interpreting, and verifying the signature data. If the signature-suite is proprietary (e.g., tied to a hardware token), the URL need not point to a specification document and serves only as an identifier.

The "DSig 1.0 Compatibility Document," a sibling to this specification, defines URL identifiers for some common, popular signature suites and defines minimum required support for those suites in DSig 1.0 compliant implementations. Of course, DSig 1.0 implementations are not restricted to using only these signature suites.

Each signature suite does the following:

- Specifies the algorithms that have been used for creating the signature

- Defines the content of any subsequent `Sig-Data`

Signature suites have complete control over the contents of the `SigData` immediately following the signature suite URL. The format of this data must satisfy the `SigData` portion of the BNF (basically, the data must be a single s-expression); beyond that requirement, the format of the data is also governed by the signature suite.

## Common SigData fields

Although each signature suite is free to specify its own format for signature data (`SigData`) fields, there are some types of information that are likely to be used by most signature suites. For example, signature suites need to include the actual cryptographic data that constitutes a digital signature. Signature suites will probably also wish to include information about the cryptographic keys used to generate and verify the signature. We now define some common `SigData` fields and their identifying string tokens (see `SigToken-String` in the BNF in Example 4). These string tokens are *reserved words* in the sense that any signature suite that uses `SigData` field identified by these tokens must do so in a manner consistent with this specification.

Mathematically, a digital signature only cryptographically guarantees that at a particular point in time some process had access to both the signing (secret) key and the text of the signed document. The `"Keyholder"`-type `SigData` fields of a signature provides information about the key that was used to create the corresponding signature. The key may be bound to some entity (such as a person, server, or organization) by various certificates. There are four common ways to uniquely specify a particular key; each has its own identifying token:

- Provide the public key directly (`"ByKey"`);

- Provide a hash (or fingerprint) of the public key (`"ByHash"`);

- Provide some *name* that is associated with the public key, such as an X.509 "distinguished name" or the UserID string of a PGP key (`"ByName"`)

- Provide the name of a certifying authority (CA) and information, which identifies the desired key to the CA (`"ByCert"`)

To be useful, the information identifying the signing key will lead the application to corresponding certificates in the Attribution Information section (if any) or provide the starting point for fetching certificates from remote sources.

The following subsections specify the content of the `SigInfo` fields associated with each of these tokens.

### "ByKey"

The token `"ByKey"` identifies the value that follows as the key that should be used to validate the signature (or sufficient information to generate that key locally).

```
( "ByKey" <Key-Value, Signature-
    Suite dependent> )
```

The format of the included key necessarily depends on the particular signature-suite used and must be specified in the signature-suite document. Here is an example use of `"ByKey"` within the Digital Signature Algorithm (DSA) signature suite:

```
( "ByKey"
  ( "P" "base64-encoded-modulus" )
  ( "Q" "base64-encoded-divisor" )
  ( "G" "base64-encoded-number" )
  ( "Y" "base64-encoded-public-key"
      ) )
```

### "ByHash"

The token `"ByHash"` identifies the value that follows as the hash of the key that should be used to validate the signature.

```
("ByHash" "base-64-encoded-hash-of-
    key" )
```

Details on how the hash for a key is generated is a property of individual signature suites.

## "ByName"

The token "`ByName`" identifies the value that follows as a name (or other reference) that may be used to identify the corresponding public key. The name that should be provided depends on the relevant public key infrastructure.

```
( "ByName" "Name-as-string-value" )
```

## "ByCert"

The token "`ByCert`" identifies the value that follows as containing the name of a certifying authority (CA) and the serial number a relevant certificate issued by that CA. The name given for the CA depends on the naming conventions of the relevant public key or certification infrastructure.

```
( "ByCert" ( "CA-Name-as-string-
    value" <CA-Serial-No.> ) )
```

## The "On" token: Time of Signature generation

The token "`On`" identifies the value that follows as the time the label's signature was generated. (This option is distinct from the PICS 1.1 label option "`on`" which indicates the time at which the label itself was created.) We recommend using this standard element in all signature suites.

The time that the signature was created is encoded as a *quoted-ISO-Date*. The format of a quoted-ISO-Date is defined in the PICS 1.1 specifications.

```
("on" quoted-ISO-Date)
```

Notice that the "`on`" time is advisory only to applications verifying the digital signature; as this section is part of the entire *sigblock* extension it is not cryptographically protected by the signature itself. (The contents of the *sigblock* do not contribute to the hash of the label that is signed by the signature.) If a cryptographically-protected date is desired, the correct way to implement it is to include the date within another PICS label extension; that extension may then contribute to the hash of the canonicalized label.

## The "include" and "exclude" tokens: modifying the canonicalized form of the label

If an application wishes to transmit both signed and unsigned information in a label the suggested method for doing so is to generate two labels (one signed, one unsigned) and send both labels as a PICS label list. However, some PICS 1.1 protocols, including the protocol for requesting labels from a PICS label bureau, require that exactly one PICS label be returned in response to a request, and thus it may be necessary for a signing application to sign only a subset of a PICS label. If the signature suite permits signatures over partial contents of labels, the "`include`" and **exclude** tokens provide that functionality:

```
( "exclude" field-list )
( "include" field-list )
```

The "`include`" and "`exclude`" SigData fields modify the default behavior of the label canonicalizer. Before a label is signed, it is put into canonical form; the section "Creating an equivalent standalone label" later in this paper describes, in detail, the canonicalization process. PICS labels have many semantically equivalent forms yet these forms yield distinct hashes, so it is important that signing and verifying applications canonicalize labels in the same way. After the equivalent standalone label has been generated following the default canonicalization rules, individual label options may be dropped if an "`include`" or "`exclude`" option is present. If an "`include`" option is present, any field not listed in the field-list is removed from the canonicalized label. If an "`exclude`" option is present, all fields listed in the field-list are removed from the canonicalized label. At most one "`include`" or "`exclude`"; field may appear; it is an error to have both an "`include`" and an "`exclude`" option.

The value associated with an "`include`" or "`exclude`" option (the "`field-list`") is a list of label fields to be included or excluded in the canonicalized form. There are three types of fields in PICS 1.1 labels: options, ratings transmit/

value pairs, and extensions. The format of a `field-list` is as follows:

```
field-list      ::= '(' 1option-
    list*1 ratings-list*1 extension-
    list*1 ')'
option-list     ::= '(' "options"
    <options>* ')'
ratings-list    ::= '(' "ratings"
    <ratings>* ')'
extension-list  ::= '(' "extensions"
    <quoted-URL>* ')'
```

A `field-list` is simply a collections of at most one of each an `option-list`, `ratings-list` and `extension-list`. An `option-list` is a list of PICS 1.1 label option names (e.g., `"for"` or `"by"`). A `ratings-list` is a list of PICS 1.1 ratings service transmit-names (e.g., `"suds"` in the example "Good Clean Fun" rating service). An `extension-list` is a list of quoted-URLs, where each quoted-URL uniquely identifies a particular PICS 1.1 label extension.

**NOTE**

The `"include"` and `"exclude"` SigData types exist in this specification strictly to overcome limitations in PICS 1.1 protocols. These limitations should disappear in the next revision of the PICS specifications, and thus the requirement for these fields will disappear. It is the intention of the DSig working group that `"include"` and `"exclude"` not be present in the DSig 2.0 specification, which will build on new version of PICS.

## The "SigCrypto" token: signature cryptographic data

The `"SigCrypto"` token identifies the `SigData` field that contains the cryptographic data that is the signature itself. The format and contents of this field are entirely specified by particular signature suites.

### Hashing

Correct hashing is the key to successful signing. DSig 1.0 therefore specifies how a PICS 1.1 label is converted into a unique, canonicalized form which does not include the *sigblock* extension (this process is explained in the "Signing" section, later in this paper). This canonicalized label is the input to the signature suite's signature algorithm. The signature algorithm may require or accept other inputs in addition to the contents of the equivalent standalone label. For example, the signature suite may pad the data in a particular way, or mix into the hash of the data information concerning the algorithms used to generate the hash and signature.

## *Parallel and Cascaded Signatures*

Multiple parallel signatures on the same PICS 1.1 label may be created simply by including several `"Signature"` fields within the *sigblock* extension. Cascaded signatures (signatures on signatures) are not supported within a single DSig signature label. To create a cascaded signature, a DSig signature label may be signed using another DSig signature label.

Example 3 shows a sample *sigblock* extension.

**Example 3**

```
extension (optional "http://www.w3.org/PICS/DSig/sigblock-1_0.html"
    ("AttribInfo"
        ("http://www.w3.org/PICS/DSig/X509.html" "base64-x.509-cert")
        ("http://www.w3.org/PICS/DSig/X509.html"
         "http://SomeCa/Certs/ByDN/CN=PeterLipp,O=TU-Graz,OU=IAIK")
        ("http://www.w3.org/PICS/DSig/pgpcert.html" "base64-pgp-signed-key")
        ("http://www.w3.org/PICS/DSig/pgpcert.html"
         "http://pgp.com/certstore/plipp@iaik.tu-graz.ac.at"))
    ("Signature" "http://www.w3.org/PICS/DSig/RSA-MD5.html"
```

**Example 3** *(continued)*

```
        ("byKey" (("N" "aba21241241=")
                  ("E" "abcdefghijklmnop=")))
        ("on" "1996.12.02T22:20-0000")
        ("exclude" ("extensions" "http://foo/badextension.html"))
        ("SigCrypto" "aba1241241==")))
    ("Signature" "http://www.w3.org/PICS/DSig/DSS.html"
        ("ByName" "plipp@iaik.tu-graz.ac.at")
        ("on" "1996.12.02T22:20-0000")
        ("SigCrypto" (("R" "aba124124156")
                      ("S" "casdfkl3r489")))))
```

## The ABNF syntax

Example 4 presents a formal syntax for the *sig-block* extension. It is written in modified BNF. By convention, * indicates 0 or more instances of the token that precedes the special character, *1 indicates 0 or 1 instance of the token; and + indicates 1 or more instances of the token. Quoted strings are case-sensitive but other literal elements are case-insensitive. Whitespace is ignored except in quoted strings. Multiple contiguous whitespace characters may be treated as though they were a single space character.

### NOTE

This extension is not a valid PICS 1.1 extension because Base64, as defined in RFC-1521, contains a /, which technically cannot be represented as a PICS 1.1 datum. Nonetheless, we believe that all parsers will support the grammar presented in the next example, and expect the problem to be solved in the next version of PICS.

## Example 4

```
SignatureExtension  ::= 'extension (' mand/opt SigBlockURL
                                 AttributionInfo Signature* ')'
Mand/opt            ::= 'optional' | 'mandatory'
SigBlockURL         ::= '"http://www.w3.org/PICS/DSig/sigblock-1_0.html"'
AttributionInfo     ::= '(' '"AttribInfo"' Certificate* ')'
Certificate         ::= '(' CertificateType CertificateData ')'
CertificateType     ::= quotedUrl
CertificateData     ::= quotedBase64String | quotedUrl
Signature           ::= '( "Signature"' SignatureSuite SigData* ')'
SigData             ::= '(' SigTokenString SigInfo*1 ')'
SigTokenString      ::= '"' quotedName '"'
SigInfo             ::= SigData | quotedURL | quotedBase64String |
                        quotedName | number | '(' SigInfo* ')'
SignatureSuite      ::= quotedUrl
quotedURL           ::= '"' URL '"'
URL                 ::= as defined by RFC-1738.
quotedBase64String  ::= '"' base64String '"'
base64String        ::= as defined in RFC-1521.
alpha               ::= 'A' | .. | 'Z' | 'a' | .. | 'z'
digit               ::= '0' | .. | '9'
quotedName          ::= '"' ( urlChar | ' ')+ '"'
urlChar             ::= alphaNumPM | '.' | '$' | ',' | ';' | ':'
                        | '&' | '=' | '?' | '!' | '*' | '~' | '@'
                        | '#' | '_' | '(' | ')' | '/' | '%' hex hex
```

**Example 4**     *(continued)*

```
                        ; Note: Use the "%" escape technique to insert
                        ; single or double quotation marks within a URL
alphaNumPM              ::= alpha | digit | sign
hex                     ::= digit | 'A' | .. | 'F' | 'a' | .. | 'f'
sign                    ::= '+' / '-'
number                  ::= [sign]unsignedInt['.' [unsignedInt]]
unsignedInt             ::= digit+
```

# Signing

Since even a single DSig 1.0 signature label must be represented as a PICS 1.1 label list, it is important to understand the structure of such a list. This is explained earlier in the section "PICS 1.1 Labels and Label Lists." Here again is a structural representation of a PICS 1.1 label list:

```
(PICS-1.1
        <service 1 url> [service 1
                option...]
        labels [label 1 options...]
                [label 1 signature]
                ratings (<category>
                        <value> ...)
                [label 2 options...]
                [label 2 signature]
                ratings (<category>
                        <value> ...)
                ...
        <service 2 url> [service 2
                option...]
        labels [label 3 options...]
                [label 3 signature]
                ratings (<category>
                        <value> ...)
                [label 4 options...]
                [label 4 signature]
                ratings (<category>
                        <value> ...)
                ...

        ...
    )
```

## *Signing a Label*

The process for signing a label is fairly straightforward, whether the label list containing the label is made up of a single label or a series of labels. First we create an *equivalent standalone label for the label to be signed.* Then the equiva-

lent standalone label is canonicalized (similar to canonicalizing a PICS label for transmission). Finally, a digital signature is generated, inserted into a *sigblock* extension, and that extension is placed in the label as a label extension. An equivalent standalone label can have at most one *resinfo* extension (which it may inherit from the service options) and one *sigblock* extension.

### Creating an equivalent standalone label

An equivalent standalone label is a PICS 1.1 label list containing a single label. The single label must be normalized to a form where all options are label options (this includes extension options) and the *sigblock* extension (if present) has been removed. From the example label list above, **label 4** could be reduced to the single label:

```
(PICS-1.1
        <service 2 url>
        labels [service 2 option...]
                + [label 4 option...]
                ratings ([label 4 ratings .
                        ..]))
```

This is not yet an equivalent standalone label. We still need to take into account any modifications denoted by "`include`" or "`exclude`" specifiers in the *sigblock* extension. (Obviously, if the signature is being created the application knows which fields it wants to include in or exclude from the equivalent standalone label. The "`include`" and "`exclude`" options convey this information to applications trying to verify the signature.) The resulting label list is the equivalent standalone label.

**Canonicalization of the equivalent standalone label for signing**

- For a given PICS 1.1 label, insert a whitespace character between any two tokens. PICS 1.1 tokens include left and right parenthesis, symbols, quoted-strings, and numbers. Symbols are case-insensitive and converted to lowercase. Tokens (?) or (?) in multivalue syntax are considered symbols. Do not insert whitespaces for either the leading left parenthesis the trailing right parenthesis of a PICS 1.1 label.

- A normalized DSig-1.0 label consists of three parts in order: the PICS 1.1 header, the options, and the ratings. The header part is the `pics-1.1` symbol followed by the *serviceURL*.

- The option part is headed by the label keyword `l`, followed by a set of PICS-1.1 options, including the extensions. The set of options, including the extensions, are determined by the `option-list` and the `extension-list` fields of the `exclude` or the `include` option in the signature suite. The options are sorted alphabetically by their shortest names (i.e., use `full` instead of `complete-label`, `exp` instead of `until`).

Extension options are sorted by the *extension URL*.

- The rating part is headed by the rating keyword `r`, followed by a set of transmit name and value pairs. The set of transmit-name and value pairs are determined by the `rating-list` field of the `include` or `exclude` option in the signature. Transmit names are sorted alphabetically.

- When the client computes the equivalent standalone label format described above, it will use all options available to it: both service and label options. This implies a constraint on the server when it decides what options to include in the transmitted set. The transmitted set must include all options necessary as either service or label options to create the same equivalent standalone label as was signed.

The following examples illustrate a step-by-step process to sign a PICS 1.1 label.

Example 5 shows Step 1: creating a PICS 1.1 label.

Example 6 shows Step 2: computing the hashes of the document, creating the *resinfo* extension, and inserting it in the label.

Example 7 shows Step 3: canonicalizing the label.

**Example 5**

```
(PICS-1.1 "http://www.gcf.org/v2.5"
   by "John Doe"
   labels
      for "http://www.w3.org/PICS/DSig/Overview.html"
      on "1994.11.05T08:15-0500"
      ratings (suds 0.5 density 0 color 1))
```

**Example 6**

```
(PICS-1.1 "http://www.gcf.org/v2.5"
   by "John Doe"
   labels
      for "http://www.w3.org/PICS/DSig/Overview.html"
      extension
         (optional "http://www.w3.org/PICS/DSig/resinfo-1_0.html"
            ("http://www.w3.org/PICS/DSig/SHA1.html">http://www.w3.org/PICS/
                DSig/SHA1.html</a>" "aba21241241=")
            ("http://www.w3.org/PICS/DSig/MD5.html">http://www.w3.org/PICS/DSig/
                MD5.html</a>" "cdc43463463="
              "1997.02.05T08:15-0500"))
      on "1994.11.05T08:15-0500"
      ratings (suds 0.5 density 0 color 1))
```

And last, Example 8 shows Step 4: signing the canonicalized form of the label and inserting it in the label.

We now have a valid DSig-1.0 label.

## Signing Notes

While PICS allows labels to be truncated to reduce their size, if this is done in DSig 1.0 after signing, the signature will no longer be valid. An alternative is to distribute an unsigned label with the *complete* option pointing to a full, signed label. Client software in need of a signed label can dereference the *complete* option's URL to retrieve a complete, signed label.

# Appendix 1: Service Resource Information

There is a security hole in the above proposal. The semantics of the assertions (ratings) in a PICS 1.1 label are defined by the rating service, and the only information about the rating service contained within the label itself is the service's URL. Since the human-readable description pointed to by that URL is what defines the rating semantics, it is possible under the current scheme for the rating service semantics to change *after* the label has been created without invalidating the label.

If this is a concern, a simple policy in the trust engine that evaluates signatures could be established to require a separate signature label on the service description file.

**Example 7**

```
( PICS-1.1 "http://www.gcf.org/v2.5" l by "John Doe" for
  "http://www.w3.org/PICS/DSig/Overview.html" extension ( optional
  "http://www.w3.org/PICS/DSig/resinfo-1_0.html" (
  "http://www.w3.org/PICS/DSig/MD5.html" "cdc43463463="
  "1997.02.05T08:15-0500" ) ( "http://www.w3.org/PICS/DSig/SHA1.html"
  "aba21241241=" ) ) on "1994.11.05T08:15-0500" r ( suds 0.5 density 0
  color 1 ) )
```

**Example 8**

```
(PICS-1.1 "http://www.gcf.org/v2.5"
   by "John Doe"
   labels
      for "http://www.w3.org/PICS/DSig/Overview.html"
      extension
         (optional "http://www.w3.org/PICS/DSig/resinfo-1_0.html"
            ("http://www.w3.org/PICS/DSig/SHA1.html">http://www.w3.org/PICS/
               DSig/SHA1.html</a>" "aba21241241=")
            ("http://www.w3.org/PICS/DSig/MD5.html">http://www.w3.org/PICS/DSig/
               MD5.html</a>" "cdc43463463="
         "1997.02.05T08:15-0500"))
      extension
         (optional "http://www.w3.org/PICS/DSig/sigblock-1_0.html"
            ("AttribInfo"
               ("http://www.w3.org/PICS/DSig/X509.html">http://www.w3.org/PICS/
                  DSig/X509.html</a>" "efe64685685=")
               ("http://www.w3.org/PICS/DSig/X509.html">http://www.w3.org/PICS/
                  DSig/X509.html</a>"
               "http://SomeCA/Certs/ByDN/CN=PeterLipp,O=TU-Graz,OU=IAIK")
               ("http://www.w3.org/PICS/DSig/pgpcert.html">http://www.w3.org/
                  PICS/DSig/pgpcert.html</a>" "ghg86807807=")
               ("http://www.w3.org/PICS/DSig/pgpcert.html">http://www.w3.org/
                  PICS/DSig/pgpcert.html</a>"
               "http://pgp.com/certstore/plipp@iaik.tu-graz.ac.at"))
            ("Signature" "http://www.w3.org/PICS/DSig/RSA-MD5.html">http://www.
               w3.org/PICS/DSig/RSA-MD5.html"                  .
               ("byKey" (("N" "aba212412412=")
                         ("E" "3jdg93fj")))
               ("on" "1996.12.02T22:20-0000")
               ("SigCrypto" "3j9fsaJ30SD="))
      on "1994.11.05T08:15-0500"
      ratings (suds 0.5 density 0 color 1))
```

# Appendix 2: Transporting DSig 1.0 Labels

DSig 1.0 labels are PICS 1.1 compliant and thus may be transported in the same way as PICS 1.1 labels. [2] identifies three ways that a PICS label can be transported:

- In an HTML document

- With a document transported via a protocol that uses RFC-822 headers

- Separately from the document

Labels may also exist on their own, referenced via a URL. When the URL is dereferenced it returns an item of type application/pics-labels that contains a label list.

The specifications for embedding a PICS label in an HTML document are well defined. It is possible to use DSig labels in document other than HTML. To do this, a specification for how the label is embedded in that document type and how the document is normalized for hashing into the label must be created. ∎

# Acknowledgments

| | |
|---|---|
| John Carbajal | *carbajal@ibeam.intel.com* |
| Rosario Gennaro | *rosario@watson.ibm.com* |
| Amy Katriel | *amygk@watson.ibm.com* |
| Rohit Khare | *khare@w3.org* |
| Paul Lambert | *palamber@us.oracle.com* |
| Jim Miller | *jmiller@w3.org* |
| Hemma Prafullchandra | *hemma@eng.sun.com* |
| Rob Price | *robp@microsoft.com* |
| Paul Resnick | *presnick@research.att.com* |
| Pankaj Rohatgi | *rohatgi@watson.ibm.com* |
| Andreas Sterbenz | *sterbenz@iaik.tu-graz.ac.at* |

## References

1. "Rating Services and Rating Systems and Their Machine Readable Descriptions," version 1.1, W3C Recommendation, *http://www.w3.org/pub/WWW/TR/REC-PICS-services-961031.html*

2. "PICS Label Distribution Label Syntax and Communication Protocols," version 1.1, W3C Recommendation, *http://www.w3.org/pub/WWW/TR/REC-PICS-labels-961031.html*

3. Simple Distributed Security Information (SDSI), *http://theory.lc5.mit.edu/~cis/sdsi.html*

4. Simple Public Key Infrastructure (SPKI), *http://www.clark.net/pub/cme/html/spki.html*

## Additional Resources

1. N. Borestein, N. Freed, "MIME (Multipurpose Internet Mai Extensions) Part One: Mechanisms for Specifying and Describing the Format of Internet Message Bodies," RFC 1521, 09/23/1993.

2. T. Berners-Lee, L. Masinter, M. McCahill, "Uniform Resource Locators (URLs)," RFC 1738, 12/20/94.

3. Digital Signature Label Architecture, *W3C Working Draft*, *http://www.w3.org/pub/WWW/TR/WD-DSIG-label-arch.html*.

4. R. Rivest, "The MD5 Message-Digest Algorithm," RFC1321, 04/16/1992.

# About the Authors

**Philip DesAutels**
Project Manager
W3 Consortium
MIT Laboratory for Computer Science
545 Technology Square
Cambridge, MA 02139, U.S.A.
*philipd@w3.org*

Philip DesAutels, located at MIT, is a project manager responsible for work on digital signatures and intellectual property rights. Philip holds an M.S. degree in industrial and management engineering from Rensselear Polytechnic Institute. He comes to W3C after working for IBM and John Hancock Insurance where he has been a project manager and management advisor. He also spent a year with the Peace Corps in Uzbekistan, where he helped to establish an electronic mail infrastructure, taught business computing courses at Namangan Polytechnic Institute and worked to develop other local industries.

**Peter Lipp**
Institute for Applied Information Processing and Communications
Klosterwiesgasse 32/I, A-8010
Graz, Austria
*plipp@iaik.tu-graz.ac.at*

Peter Lipp, born 1958, studied mathematics at the University of Technology, Graz, Austria, where he got his Masters and later his PhD. In 1982 he started working for the Institute for Information Processing, and later for the Institute for Applied Information Processing and Communications at the University of Technology, Graz, Austria. His main interests are computer and network security, especially World Wide Web security. He is responsible for the Institute's participation in the ICE-TEL-project and the Digital Signature Initiative.

**Brian LaMacchia**
AT&T Laboratories
180 Park Ave.
P.O. Box 971
Florham Park, NJ 07932-0971
*bal@research.att.com*

Brian LaMacchia received the S.B., S.M., and Ph.D. degrees from the Massachusetts Institute of Technology in 1990, 1991, and 1996, respectively. He is currently a member of the Public Policy Research group at AT&T Labs—Research in Florham Park, NJ. His research interests include cryptography and security, automated resource discovery, and the interactions between various legal regimes and the network. He is a member of Eta Kappa Nu, Tau Beta Pi, and Sigma Xi.

**Yang-hua Chu**
Technical Staff
W3 Consortium
MIT Laboratory for Computer Science
545 Technology Square
Cambridge, MA 02139, U.S.A.
Tel: +1.617.253.5884
*yhchu@w3.org*

Yang-hua Chu is currently a Master of Engineering student at the Massachusetts Institute of Technology majoring in Computer Science. His interests are in cryptography and network security.

# DIGITAL SIGNATURE LABEL ARCHITECTURE

*Rohit Khare*

## Abstract

*[W3C Working Draft; January 10, 1997; WD-DSIG-label-arch-970110]*

*This document presents the architecture and design rationale behind Digital Signature's (DSig) Label specifications. The overall goal is to use digitally signed labels to make authenticatable assertions about standalone documents or about manifests of aggregate objects. The three basic elements—digital signatures, assertions, and manifests—are each analyzed in terms of their design, operation, data format, and distribution strategy. These elements can be assembled today within a PICS label to make a signed assertion about an information resource, or if that resource is itself a manifest listing others, to make assertions about several resources.*

## Status of This Memo

This is a W3C Working Draft for review by W3C members and other interested parties. It is a draft document and may be updated, replaced or obsoleted by other documents at any time. It is inappropriate to use W3C Working Drafts as reference material or to cite them as other than "works in progress." A list of current W3C working drafts can be found at *http://www.w3.org/pub/WWW/TR.*[*]

## 1. Introduction

The Digital Signature Label team is chartered with the design of a signed assertion format that states "the *keyholder* believes *assertion(s)* about *information resource(s)*." This statement format satisfies the twin goals of the DSig project: to *identify* and *endorse* information resources. This team, in turn, has decomposed its goal into three subtasks:

- "The *Keyholder* believes" is a cryptographically authenticated statement encapsulated into a signature block (SigBlock). The functionality and design requirements for the digital signature cryptography are explained in section 3, "Signatures."

- "*assertion(s)*" is a systematic, machine-readable description which allows for automatable trust decisions. In particular, as described in section 4, "Assertions," we propose using signed PICS ratings.

- "about *information resource(s)*" is a mapping of the assertions to several related information resources. Each reference to a resource should also include integrity checks that make a secure link from the signed assertion to the final data stream(s). These requirements are discussed in section 5, "Manifests."

Each of these subtasks will result in the following interlocking technical specifications.

---

[*] *Editor's Note:* This document represents the general DSig architecture as envisioned by the Digital Signature Design team. Work in implementing this architecture along with interaction with other groups working on metadata related efforts (PICS-NG, XML, DSig Collections, etc.) has led to substantial changes in the way we now envision the DSig architecture. The document presented here is incongruous with the current DSig 1.0 Digital Signature specification and the planned direction for DSig 2.0 and thus is obsolete. A major revision of the DSig Architecture will be available by 1 July, 1997 at *http://www.w3.org/pub/WWW/TR/WD-DSIG-label-arch.html.*

- *Signature Block* describes the syntax of a generic signature syntax and a series of cryptosystem-specific formats. The result is a standalone data-signature block. (*Editor:* Peter Lipp).

- *Signature Label* describes the technical steps for encoding a signature block within a PICS-1.1 label and its applicability. The latter part describes when signed PICS-1.1 assertions are appropriate and some inherent risks (*Editors:* Brian LaMacchia and Paul Lambert).

- *DSig Common Manifest Format (DCMF)* describes how manifests can be constructed to make joint assertions about a package of interrelated referents, as well as a particular manifest format (*Editor:* Hemma Prafullchandra).

(Please consult the DSig Team pages [1] for detailed updates on the timeline and status of these specifications.)

Each of these components can be combined in several ways; this document provides the context on how they fit together.

### Design

Each component supports DSig's top-level design goals, such as international cryptography support, flexible assertion semantics, and so on. Each component has a role to play in proving the flexibility, portability, and integrity of the DSig system.

### Operation

Each component's expected uses and supported deployment scenarios are explained operationally and diagrammed.

### Format

Each component has existing competitors; one of DSig's competitive advantages is its technological simplicity when weighed against the alternatives. Though there are competitors for each (PKCS-7', freeform assertions, Cryptolopes, and so on), each

DSig specification promotes a single format in the end.

### Distribution

Each component can be distributed across the Web in several ways. This document explains which components can be used with or without other components; which transmission modes are expected; and concrete deployment recommendations (see Section 6).

For example, a typical DSig scenario combines the three components in a tree. The following list describes how an author might first package up an applet in a manifest declaring his or her ownership, then certify that the package, taken as a whole, is a safe and useful applet when used correctly:

1. Author creates several related resources (the applet, its documentation, and sample files)

2. Author creates a manifest that points at each resource, with the assertion "I created this" for each.

3. Author creates a separate label pointing to the manifest, saying it describes a "safe applet."

4. Author signs the label and embeds the resulting signature block into the label produced in number 3, above.

The recipient can reverse the process, verifying the author's signature and constructing a pathway of three hash values and two assertions between the label and the eventual applet data proving the author's own *identity* and *endorsement* of that applet. DSig's real power, though, is that a third party can come along and replace steps 3 and 4 above:

1. Reviewer comes along and rates the applet for usability and coolness, creating a new label of the manifest from step number 2, in the previous list.

2. Reviewer signs the new "This is cool" label and distributes it separately.

In this scenario, the end user's trust manager can seek out a reviewer's endorsement and make a similar induction chain from the reviewer to the "cool" applet. With DSig in place, the end user's trust policy can automate the decision process.

## 2. Mission Statement

As part of its deliberations, the SigLabel team crafted the following mission statement to define its design envelope:

> A Digital Signature Label is a *stand-alone, cryptographically protected* statement that "*keyholder* believes *assertion* about *information resource(s)*."

An expansion of some of the key terms will help define the scope of our effort:

*Standalone*

Unlike traditional security approaches that wrap signed content, SigLabels will be complete statements, separate from the resource itself. This will allow us to leverage the PICS label distribution methodology: i.e., embedded within content, alongside it (in online protocols), and from external sources.

*Cryptographically protected*

SigLabels will include digital signatures to prove the authenticity and integrity of the keyholder's statements. SigBlocks will support many different combinations of cryptographic processes without prejudice.

*Keyholder*

Mathematically, a digital signature expresses only that at some point some process had access to both a secret and the unmodified message text. SigLabels will separate out mechanisms to deduce principals (keyholders) from those keys—whether the keys are catalogued in a centralized identity-checking certification authority (X.509), or in an *ad hoc* personal Web of Trust (PGP) or even in a simple system where principals are keys alone, no more or no less (SDSI/SPKI). The central insight is to disintermediate the binding between the cryptographic calculations and the certification infrastructure.

*Assertion*

An assertion qualifies the act of signature, in this case by describing the content of the information resource. A SigLabel includes assertions according to machine-readable schema so they are *automatable*—they can assist users in making trust decisions. One kind of machine-readability already provided in PICS-1.1 is *numeric-vector rating*. Another style of machine-readable encoding is *text assertions from a fixed grammar*. These two examples are separate from nonautomatable, nonmachine-readable, free-form comments or extensions, which can also fit into current PICS content ratings.

*Information Resource*

In Web usage, any information resource (including aggregate objects) can be pointed at through a Universal Resource Identifier (URI) [1]. Many applications of SigLabels will in fact be assertions about such sets of resources. A *manifest* groups several *referents* together, including assertions about each of them. Since URI technology can also incorporate other naming schemes, standalone SigLabels can be applied to any named data.

In this document, we illustrate several of the concepts referred to above with the icons shown in Figure 1.

## 3. Signatures

This section describes the design, operation, format, and transmission of the DSig signature block. Our SigBlock is a general purpose, simply encoded, cryptographically neutral standalone signature, which neither relies on any particular certification/identification scheme, nor has any inherent semantics. The SigBlock establishes only that some process had access to the data and to a secret. This means that a SigBlock alone cannot say what the signer meant—that comes only from

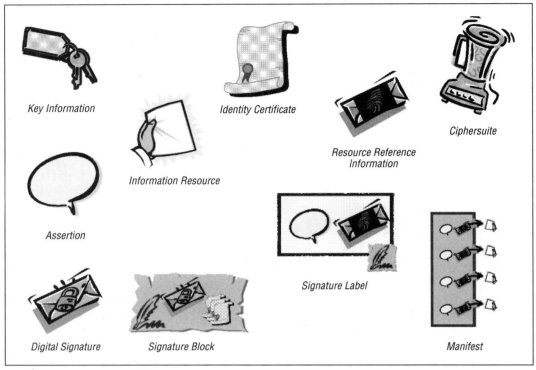

**Figure 1**    Icons referred to in this document

binding a SigBlock to an assertion within the overall SigLabel.

## 3.1 SigBlock Design

The SigBlock was identified as a separate design task very early on in the project. Signature systems such as PKCS-7' and PGP traditionally build upon a core data structure that represents the actual cryptography, and DSig is no exception. On the other hand, every signature system goes on to add idiosyncratic information to this structure: crytographic protection (padding, protection of algorithm identifiers), certification-authority dependence (naming, key serial numbers), content-dependent modification (how whitespace is hashed in), and mini-assertions (time of signature, whether signed in hardware/software). The result is then encoded in a particular format

(ASN.1, ASCII armor) and often used to wrap the whole signed data stream. The design goals for the DSig SigBlock, listed below, differentiate it from such approaches:

*General Purpose*

SigBlocks default to signing a fixed data stream, which means that any document or label can be signed. Conversely, a SigBlock can be used anywhere messages need to be signed (email, applets, etc). No SigBlock-dependent data modifes the document-signing process. This means that the *only* data being signed is the document—no SigBlock fields go into the computation by default. The document data is also separate from the SigBlock—we don't wrap protected data.

*Simple Encoding*

SigBlocks are encoded as ASCII text type-value S-expressions. This allows designers of new digital signature algorithms (ciphersuites) to use clean self-describing data structure, but does not preclude reuse of proprietary binary data with an appropriate type identifier. Using S-expressions sidesteps the complexity potentially affecting low-level type-length-value encoding problems. This makes it possible to use much simpler tools than traditionally associated with ASN.1, for example.

*Cryptographically neutral*

SigBlocks must be able to incorporate new cryptosystems without prejudice. This includes "black-box" tools that do not reveal internal steps like hashing. SigBlocks reuse the well-known concept of "ciphersuites" to refer to validated combinations of ciphers or hardware tokens.

*Self contained*

The SigBlock can contain all the data it needs to be verified. This implies it needs to be able to carry associated certificates as needed. It also follows that international deployment considerations require multiple, parallel signatures so that a standalone signed assertion can be evaluated against several ciphersuites—the end user just chooses a locally acceptable variant.

*Certification neutral*

Carrying certificates does not, on the other hand, imply normative dependence. There is nothing inherent in the cryptography of digital signature that requires certification chains, so SigBlocks, too, should be able to operate with opaque certificates. After all, certificates and other credentials exist only to establish trust in a key—a trust management problem, rather than a digital signature problem. Finally, since the first goal in the list implies that credentials are not "hashed into" any signatures, intermediaries can add and subtract credentials from the SigBlock as needed.

## 3.2 SigBlock Operation

To understand the SigBlock design, consider the signing processes shown in Figure 2 and Figure 3.

There are three basic structures of data in Figures 2 and 3, as described below:

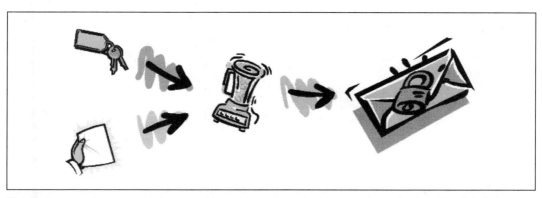

**Figure 2**    A document being signed by a ciphersuite and a key to produce a bright, shiny digital signature

**Figure 3**    The SigBlock itself with its pile of keyholder information, certificates and digital signature cryptography bits

*Document*

The data to be signed must be fixed to be signable. Typically, *a document must resolve to a unique hash through a computable function.* (Though the signature algorithm need not expose an explicit hash: A hardware token, for example, might not ever transmit the hash, just the signature. RSA Data Security's [2] software has the same effect through licensing restrictions.) For the purpose of discussing SigBlock, the Document can be any data, though DSig overall is concerned only with signed labels and manifests.

*Certificate*

The credential(s) associated with a signing key are used by a trust management system to establish the authenticity and validity of the signature. As far as the SigBlock is concerned, *a key must resolve to a keyholder though a certificate.* The SigBlock itself does *not* rely on this mapping, so it only acts as a carrier for certificates, not as a user. The `attribution-info` section of the SigBlock can include a set of certificates; the `signature-crypto` section can include some `keyholder-info` excepted from a certificate to establish the connection from signature block back up to the keyholder.

*Signature*

The digital signature cryptography itself binds (the hash of) the document and the signer's private key together. Thus, *a SigBlock resolves to a document through a keyed function.* For the user to find the right key, the SigBlock also needs some way to resolve which public key was used for the signature. Keyholder information has two roles: first to find the actual signature verification key, and second to find the keyholder and role so that the trust policy can evaluate the validity of the signature.

With these concepts in mind, here's the story:

A *user* controls her own *signing key* and *certificate.* Her software and hardware tokens implement a few *ciphersuites.* With a *document* and choice of *ciphersuite* in hand, the signature process runs through to completion to produce a bright, shiny chunk of `signature-crypto`. Along the way, the *signing key, date,* and *hash function name* may have all been inputs to the signing process and show up inside the `signature-crypto`. To make a complete, formatted SigBlock, though, a few more pieces of information have to be pieced together as discussed in Section 3.3.

There are a few more operations available to our user. She can proceed to attach additional parallel signatures of the same document. She may do this herself using several different algorithms so her recipients in other jurisdictions or in the future can verify her signatures against whichever ciphersuites they (still) trust. Other like-minded colleagues can also attach their signatures to the same statement to support policies that require *K-of-N* signatories to agree.[*] She cannot, however, cascade another signature to her own. The DSig design team has decided to support SigBlocks with parallel signatures, but not cascaded statements about a signature. Successive endorsements are still possible, though, by giving a SigLabel a name a producing another SigLabel about the first (see Section 4.4).

## 3.3 SigBlock Format

The SigBlock Format is a concrete representation of the various data elements required for a standalone signature. Broadly speaking, there are two levels at which we discuss the SigBlock format:

- The generic arrangement of attribution-information and signature data.

- The specific level of encoding choices for particular ciphersuites.

Figure 4 is a SigBlock data structure with examples of *http://w3.org/dsig/rsa/md5* and *http://rsalabs.com/PKCS-7/*—a structured set of bits versus an opaque ASN.1 blob.

At the generic level, a SigBlock needs to flesh out the `signature-crypto` with information about the signer. The first step is to pair the signature with `attribution-info`, a passive container for certificates and other credentials. This allows the trust management system to evaluate whether a certain keyholder is trusted and whether the key is valid. The second step is to make a link from the signature to the keyholder, by adding some `keyholder-info` to the signature itself.

There are several kinds of `keyholder-info` envisioned by DSig: the key itself, a digested fingerprint of the key, a Distinguished Name, a Certifying Authority (CA) and serial number, a role, etc. Each type serves to establish a path from the key to a credential (keyholder). Remember, the whole `attribution-info` section is optional material; the `keyholder-info` is the only normative link from a signature to a certification system. It's a critical disintermediating step because it allows the user to separately choose a CA infrastructure without changing the signature block format.

That's it for the generic level. By treating the cryptography as opaque, the only additional information required is keyholder identification. Within the cryptographic details, though, are a great number of critical, specific formatting decisions.

**Figure 4**

---

[*] In some systems, you need, for instance, three of five board members to sign a purchase order to make it effective. This is generally referred to as "K-of-N."

The `ciphersuite` is what defines the information found below it. For an existing format, like PKCS-7' (for RSA), all that's possible is to say "coming up, one blob of PKCS-7' data." DSig's preferred modes, though, encourage more trasnparency. The DSig ciphersuite for RSA, for example, is inspired by SDSI, with separate entries for the exponent, ciphertext, hash algorithm, signature time, and so on, burst out into an S-expression.

Note well the location of the signature-timestamp, as shown in section 3.1, the only cryptographically protected data is found within the customizable `signature-crypto`. If an implementation of RSA needs to sign its hash algorithm ID, it can do so on its own, rather than predicating that all DSig-usable ciphersuites must. For example, the U.S. government's Digital Signature Algorithm need not, since it is defined only in conjunction with SHA.

Of course, all this flexibility empowers any organization to issue a new ciphersuite. How can users trust that they are cryptographically safe combinations? Indeed, how will the DSig project validate its own recommendations? In the end, users and organizations will have to decide what makes sense for them. DSig will produce a small set of the most popular ciphersuites and work closely with leading cryptographers and organizations to vet its work. In particular, the Signature Label Implementation Team will include a user-driven review team that will cooperate with RSA Labs (holder of the PKCS [Public Key Cryptography Standards] specifications), the IETF, and IEEE 1363 in establishing its core set of DSig ciphersuites.

### 3.4 SigBlock Distribution

It is worth reiterating that the SigBlock is only a stepping-stone in our work. It is not deployable on its own for two reasons:

1. Technologically, because it does not have any pointer or connection to the data being signed—not even a document hash (since some signature ciphersuites do not expose an intermediate hash value).

2. Philosophically, because it does not include any assertions about the data being signed.

Deploying "naked" SigBlocks without associated assertions drags us back to circular question, "yes, but what does this signature *mean?*" In short, the DSig project supports only signed assertions, which translates into SigBlocks embedded in PICS labels or in a manifest. SigBlocks may later be embedded in other formats, which is why we have made the effort to separate out its definition—but even then, not without clear, automatable semantics in the new embedding.

The first implementation target is an embedding of SigBlocks into PICS 1.*x* labels, as discussed in section 4.4. In this case, signing PICS ratings imbues SigBlocks with stronger semantics particular to this context: "keyholder believes ratings are correct."

## 4. Assertions

While many signature projects have succeeded at proving the identity or provenance of an information resource, the DSig project breaks new ground because of its emphasis on *endorsement*, in the form of signed assertions that users can rely upon to make trust decisions automatable. The bedrock of this work is reducing generic "assertions" to concrete rating labels so we can have clear, machine-readable semantics to sign. In this section, we discuss the design of an assertion format, inspired largely by PICS-1.*x*.

Though there are several reasons to motivate the adoption of PICS—its distribution mechanisms, established user base, and rating organizations—this section discusses only the rating part of a label ensuring that the integrity of the binding to the eventual information resource is a critical function (as presented in section 5).

## 4.1 Assertion Design

DSig needs an assertion system designed to convey a clear meaning applied to almost any kind of content. This drives two sets of design criteria: one about the semantics of "assertable" statements and another about what can be labeled.

### Clear Semantics

The ultimate test of an assertion is its clear explanation to the end user. DSig assertions must be explained clearly. One kind of clear explanation is a *value judgment*, a policy statement like, "This movie is not for unaccompanied minors." It may be subject to interpretation, but it is clear. A more flexible platform is a *content description*: a statement that characterizes the content at hand with respect to an objective scale, "This movie contains adult language and graphic violence"—giving the end user facts upon which to make a local judgment.

Ratings along well known axes are clearly explicable concepts. PICS explicitly adopts this model for its ratings, and initial deployment reinforces the idea that parents can set policies in this idiom. The ratings need not be "*x* out of *y*" continuous values: the PICS spec [2] describes how to encode multivalue sets and other variants.

### Automatable Semantics

Trust management systems can make life easier for users and administrators by acting upon clearly stated assertions. Automatability requires assertions that are clear and mechanically interpretable. In another context, automatability requires access to the rating *schema*: the system behind the labels. PICS goes above and beyond this requirement by not only requiring fixed rating systems, but also requiring machine-readable schema descriptions.

Rating systems will be developed by many organizations for many purposes (such as Democrats for political press releases, ISVs for trustworthiness, and so on). The key to broad acceptance is clearly stated: objective scales and community support. Clarity is also a requirement for signable assertions: even more than for PICS rating, digitally signed, legally enforceable signed assertions need to be very defensible.

### Extensible Semantics

At the same time, there are many descriptions that won't fit into any fixed set of axes, numeric or otherwise. DSig assertions must support extensible, even arbitrary semantics. PICS' optional and mandatory extensions are a credible escape mechanism for this purpose, which allows for both signed and unsigned extensions.

DSig needs to apply assertions with those qualities to several different kinds of documents:

### Static Documents

Labeling static documents is trivial using hash functions to prove the integrity of the link. A document fingerprint in the label can prove that the label and labelled document are in sync. To support DSig's cryptosystem neutrality, labels must be able to include several hashes according to different algorithms. Other fields, like a last-modified date and properties of a document like color, type, size, etc. can be used for the same purpose (see section 5).

### Dynamic Documents

Many information resources are inherently dynamic: the current temperature in Oslo, chat rooms, live video cameras. This does not, however, preclude making assertions about them. A service provider may ensure that a chat room is chaperoned and sign an accompanying "no graphic violence" assertion. In this case, the link from the label to the resource is the name (URI) itself, along with some of the same document properties listed in the Static Document case, above.

*Novel Documents*

New kinds of documents and naming systems are always cropping up. What about an assertion regarding slides three through seven of a presentation? How about assertions about geographic areas? Here, we appeal to the universality of URIs and fragment identifiers that allow any motivated principal to both define new namespaces and new identifiers for subparts of a document. As a reminder, URIs, unlike URLs, don't have to include hostnames and are useful for online, as well as offline document identification.

Finally, there is a new consideration about the *heritability* of signed assertions. While it is technically correct to insist that ratings apply only to the particular information resource specified, typical Web client usage may trigger a whole series of actions when visiting a single "location": loading inline images, embedded applets, etc. So at one level, assertions need to precisely delineate what they apply to. Second, there is a mathematical question of how far to extend a network of linked objects. A SigBlock protects a label directly; the label points indirectly to a manifest; the manifest points indirectly to the target information resource; and so on. Even if each step of the way is verified by a document hash, how large can the tree grow with confidence that all of the links allow the top-level assertion to be inherited? DSig design guidelines are clear on this point as well. The conservative rule is that assertions only apply one level removed by default.

There are a number of additional considerations about working with collections of different resources, which are discussed at length in section 5.

## 4.2 Assertion Operation

A signature label combining an assertion, information about the referenced resource, and a digital signature block. If we zoomed in on the Sig-Label, a PICS 1.*x* label, it would contain a pointer-to-schema (URL), pointer-to-document

(URI), machine-readable rating, extended non-machine-readable rating comments, info-about-rating (on, by, generic flag), info-about-document (resinfo), and embedded SigBlock.

A rating assertion is a passive data structure that can be used to answer a series of questions, whether in the context of a simple content-filtering UI or a full-blown trust management system, as follows:

*What language is this rating written in?*

To understand the rating, you need to understand its schema, the rating system. The name of the rating systems is a URL—the location of the machine-readable rating system description file(s). A PICS rating system description, for example, identifies the sponsoring organization, the axes, icons and descriptions of points along each scale, the kind of scale it is, and so on. This file can be used to construct a user interface on the fly that presents the whole system to an administrator to set limits on acceptable ratings, for example. Several versions in different languages may be available at the same URL.

*What's the rating?*

The actual assertion is a rating vector according to some schema plus some optional extension information. Its meaning can be imputed back from the rating system description (schema) by presenting the comments, icons, and description of each point on each scale. The label can include additional metainformation about the rating itself: who made the rating and when; whether the rating applies only to the named resources or generically to any resources with a matching name.

*What document does this rating apply to?*

Within the label structure, we can extract fields for the name (URI) and optional fields like the hash, type, etc. Each piece of information about the resource can increase a user's confidence in the connection: name equivalence, the hash value, file type and length, and so on.

Of course, an assertion label alone cannot prove that a recipient should *believe* that assertion. A Trust Management (TM) system has to investigate several aspects of a signed label before making that decision. For example, the TM would have to establish the integrity of the connection of the label to the resource it's labeling. Particular pieces of resource information can be attacked, but taken together they can prove the integrity of the association between assertion and the resource. For example, providing the name alone is vulnerable to attacks on the Domain Name System; a cryptographic hash could be reverse-engineered or "birthday-attacked"; and a file length can be tampered with, but a TM system can check each of these.

All of this additional information, or *resinfo*, has its roots in PICS-1.1 usage, but expands the range of possible additional data and provides for its own extension mechanism. More details can be found in the specification for signing PICS 1.*x* labels by Brian LaMacchia. Paul Resnick, one of the original designers of PICS, made the following comment:

> I admit that the PICS-1.1 label format does not syntactically separate the components that describe the information resource (e.g., the URL, hash, and ratings) from those components that describe the label (e.g., expiration date, signature, by). The PICS designers' understanding of this separation idea evolved as we wrote the specs: in our text description of the fields in the spec, we divide them into those that describe the document and those that describe the label, but we didn't get so far as to make a syntactic distinction, in the labels themselves. It remains to be seen whether we can remedy this in PICS-1.2 or 2.0, but it is certainly an important design goal.

## 4.3 Assertion Format

We are proposing using the PICS rating label format with some expected modifications. Some are minor, like allowing full S-expressions as the value of an extension field (instead of only allowing strings). Others are more substantial, but already in discussion for PICS-1.2, such as string-valued ratings. As DSig implementation continues, we expect a dialogue with the PICS Working Group which will influence the evolution of both projects.

With respect to signing PICS rating labels, there is a concern about which PICS extension fields are included under the protection of the SigBlock. For now, we propose that the entire PICS label and all extension data must be signed together without exceptions.

Finally, it makes sense to provide default rating systems for basic signature applications, along the lines of "This is True" and "This is Mine." Just as the SigBlock is used to prove the identity and integrity of an assertion, these rating systems can be used to make signed testaments of the provenance and veracity of information resources themselves.

## 4.4 Assertion Distribution

One of the primary reasons DSig builds upon PICS for its label syntax is to reuse PICS's three label distribution mechanisms. Since SigLabels are just PICS labels with embedded SigBlocks, they can be sent in the following ways:

- *Embedded* in the information resource itself (e.g., using the HTML META tag)

- *Attached* to the information resource (e.g., using HTTP entity headers)

- *Detached*, possibly from third parties (e.g., using a "label bureau")

The first mode could be popular for many other trust management applications, such as embedding SigLabels into applets, fonts, and other protected resources. Especially for the latter two modes, though, there must be a reliable link to the actual information resource. As discussed in Section 4.2, labels must accommodate a range of additional resource information to vouch for the connection. Document hashes are a particularly effective way of proving the link even when the label and content are separated, but only for static documents. For dynamic data, such as a chat room or live video camera feed, other properties might be used.

Note that this assertion distribution strategy also fixes a SigBlock distribution strategy: embedded in rating labels. SigBlocks are only found embedded in PICS labels in this scenario. This makes the association of a SigBlock to its signed data extremely clear.

Finally, another implicit resource that must be distributed reliably with the assertions is the rating schema. Since rating systems can legitimately exist in several languages and compatible versions, it is not a simple task to protect the integrity of the reference to the rating system. DSig recommends that applications that are sensitive to this need should use manifests and include the exact rating system(s). In this case, a rating system is just one more information resource the overall package depends on, like a font or a configuration file.

# 5. Manifests

Many applications that call for the added security and integrity of digital signatures actually address sets of interrelated content rather than a single information resource. Several of the organizations participating in the DSig design phase arrived with proposals including proprietary manifest formats. This section presents common design considerations for using standalone manifest files and proposes a new intermediate, the DSig Common Manifest Format (DCMF).

## 5.1 Manifest Design

The critical difference between a set of singular signed assertions, as collected into a manifest and signed jointly, is the interrelationships between the elements. Manifests establish relationships the following ways:

- By the mere act of selection and grouping
- By rating components on the same scales
- Through additional resource information

Each entry in the manifest also needs to provide enough information about the target resource to unambiguously identify it. Finally, there can be additional goals for particular manifest formats, such as optimized data layout, real-time manifest generation, and user interface support.

The relationships between components can dramatically shade their meaning. A picture and a caption, for example, are strongly connected, and a different choice among alternative captions can shade the meaning of the picture dramatically. First, the act of preparing a manifest alone allows us to make statements about the aggregate as a whole. Different manifests can associate a picture with different captions. In a legal context, it can be essential to demonstrate that all parties are referring to the complete agreement (for example, a Will and its codicils). Second, the assertions about each entry in the manifest establish another kind of relationship, specific to the rating system at hand. A user could select components by label ("please show all the Impressionist pictures"). Third, additional resource information can clarify relationships like "32-bit-color-version-of" or "full-screen-sized."

Beyond clarifying the semantics of a package, a manifest file must unambiguously identify its components to legitimately stand in for signing each individual part. Operationally, manifests allow us to seal $N$ resources at once, which is more efficient than having to execute $N$ potentially expensive and time-consuming signature operations. To mathematically verify this aggregation, each referent must include verifiable information about the target resource, like its hash fingerprints. In fact, the entire *resinfo* mechanism presented in section 4.2 actually emerged from manifest discussions. The PICS-1.1 *resinfo* extension was created to emphasize the isomorphism between an individual label and an individual manifest referent.

Finally, there can be more specific design goals for particular manifest formats. Some applications may integrate the user interface of a package with the manifest itself. An HTML WebMap file can represent manifest referents *and* a visual hierarchy, multimedia descriptions, and more. Another example is signing streaming or dynamic data. For a real-time video stream, it may be essential to provide a new kind of hash tree for each video segment rather than a single hash value at the end. A dynamically generated Web page may have several components and use a manifest that first sends its table of contents, then its hash values. Such data layout considerations are discussed in section 5.3 and in the DCMF specification.

## 5.2 Manifest Operation

Figure 5 shows a SigLabel pointing at an aggregate object manifest rather than a single document.

As far as the signature label is concerned, a manifest is just another type of information resource. In turn, the manifest is just the collection of resource references; the cryptographic protection is inherited from the SigLabel and doesn't appear directly within the manifest. The induction chain from the SigBlock to the target resource is mediated by two assertions, one from the SigLabel that applies to the entire manifest and an optional assertion from the referent in the manifest.

The manifest itself provides several pieces of data for each referent: name, hash information, additional resource information, and a rating assertion. This is the same information provided for a reference in a singular PICS SigLabel, as well. The hash information, in particular, is the crux of the chaining argument that allows the top-level Sig-Block to "sign" the target data. In fact, the chain can extend further if the target is another aggregate subcomponent represented by a manifest.

There is a new operational concern about signing several assertions jointly. To protect the cryptographic hygiene of a signing key, it may be necessary to restrict which kinds of assertions it can

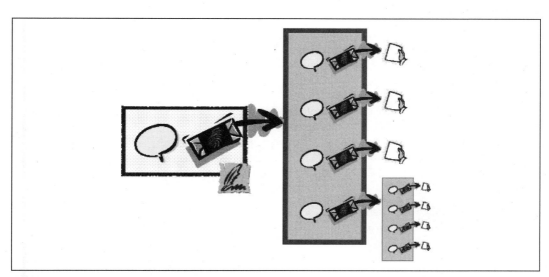

**Figure 5**

speak for. For example, it could be risky to use the same key to protect high value assertions about indemification and low value assertions about the color scheme.

## 5.3 Manifest Format

The data format for the manifest should be compact and allow for efficient access to data about each referent. In DCMF, "fixed" information like the selection of hash algorithms and the rating schemas are declared once, in a preamble. Then, several columns of data are available for each referent: the name (URI), ratings, several hash values (if applicable), and additional *resinfo*.

This abstract model of a manifest describes many formats, including Java JARchives, IBM's Cryptolope, a PICS label list, an HTML Web collection (Sitemap). Though a file in any of these formats could be signed with a SigLabel, and a Trust Management engine could parse all of them to establish links back to the target resources, DCMF alleviates compatiblity problems. DCMF's data layout is designed to be compact, streamable, easily decoded, extensible, and scalable—an evolutionary successor to many of these contenders.

## 5.4 Manifest Distribution

Since manifests are useful indexes quite separately from SigLabels, several distribution strategies should be supported. Standalone manifest files can be made available with the data, from third parties, or embedded directly into a package (e.g., a ZIP or TAR archive). The complexity is compounded by the additional options for distributing SigLabels. The SigLabel providing the integrity of a manifest might be embedded within it, sent with it over HTTP, or come from yet another third party.

As long as a manifest file is static (that is, it can be hashed itself) and as long as it can provide verifiable information about which resources it refers to, any of these distribution strategies will work. The mathematics can support an induction chain from any SigLabel through any manifest to any target resource, even through a cascaded chain of nested manifests.

## 6. Putting It All Together

Though we have separated the tasks into understanding how each of these three pieces work on their own, they are intended to work together. This section explains how the DSig project implementation will assemble these components to solve users' trust problems.

In general, the user starts with a single object or aggregate object to make an assertion about. The assertion is prepared as a PICS 1.*x* rating about the object or aggregate, and the label is then signed with a SigBlock. Indeed, several signatures can be included in parallel, starting from multiple endorsers using multiple ciphersuites. In the case of an aggregate object, the components are listed out in a manifest, optionally including assertions describing the role of each.

Many combinations of distribution strategies exist to reach the end user. One simple online scenario is a signed press release with a SigLabel in its HTTP entity headers. For an aggregate object distributed over the Web, a user could fetch the manifest over HTTP and receive the author's SigLabel with it before proceeding to fetch any of its components. In another example, a CD-ROM might include a manifest with an embedded SigLabel. Before running an applet found on the Internet, a user's trust engine could try to fetch a SigLabel from a third-party label bureau. Scenarios can be generated for every combination of information resource, speaker, format, and distribution technique.

## 7. Conclusions

Digital signature labels are assembled from three interlocking components. Signature blocks, assertions, and manifests have each been described in terms of their design, operation, format, and distribution. The initial deployment target is signed PICS rating labels applied to single information resources; manifests are a particular kind of information resource that can, in turn, be used to point at several more resources while maintaining cryptographic integrity of the signature label.

This architecture document serves as the context for several subsidiary technical documents specifying the exact syntax and semantics of the SigBlock, SigBlock embedding in PICS 1.*x*, and DSig Common Manifest Format (DCMF). Comments on this document should be directed to the author or any of the specification editors. The SigLabel design team has its own (closed) mailing list for discussing these issues at *w3c-dsig-label@w3. org*; W3C member organizations can send comments there directly. Members are also encouraged to join the DSig implementation phase to continue developing these specifications in products, or through our user-organization review teams. ■

## Acknowledgments

This document reflects a hard-won consensus among all the various players of the SigLabel team. Many of the ideas here came from different participants; my role is primarily to wrap it all together here in this architecture document. Kudos to all!

| John Carbajal | *carbajal@ibeam.intel.com* |
| Philip DesAutels | *philipd@w3.org* |
| Rosario Gennaro | *rosario@watson.ibm.com* |
| Jack Haverty | *jhaverty@oracle1.xo.com* |

| Brian LaMacchia | *bal@research.att.com* |
| Paul Lambert | *palamber@us.oracle.com* |
| Peter Lipp | *plipp@iaik.tu-graz.ac.at* |
| Jim Miller | *jmiller@w3.org* |
| Hemma Prafullchandra | *hemma@eng.sun.com* |
| Rob Price | *robp@microsoft.com* |
| Paul Resnick | *presnick@research.att.com* |
| Pankaj Rohatgi | *rohatgi@watson.ibm.com* |

### References

1. *http://www.w3.org/pub/WWW/Security/DSig/*
2. RSA's reference library of code. See also *http://www.rsa.com.*

## About the Author

**Rohit Khare**
*editor@w3j.com*

Rohit Khare is a member of the MCI Internet Architecture staff in Boston, MA, and is the Editor of the *World Wide Web Journal.* He was previously on the technical staff of the World Wide Web Consortium at MIT, where he focused on security and electronic commerce issues. He has been involved in the development of cryptographic software tools and Web-related technology development. He expects to join the Ph.D. program in Computer Science at the University of California, Irvine in fall 1997.

# JEPI
## Joint Electronic Payment Initiative

*Eui-Suk Chung, Daniel Dardailler*

### Abstract

*JEPI, a joint project of the W3C, CommerceNet, and a number of industry partners, explores the process that typically takes place after shopping on the Internet and before payment begins. It is at this point that the exact payment instrument—credit card, debit card, electronic check, electronic cash, and so on—is agreed upon between the browsing client and the merchant server. The development of HTTP extensions like PEP (Protocol Extension Protocol) and UPP (Universal Payment Preamble) has enabled JEPI phase 1 to offer an automatable payment selection process. This process not only enhances the user shopping experience, it also allows for the coexistence of multiple payment systems.*

*Our primary goal in writing this paper was to document everything we learned during JEPI phase 1 including the long-term vision, technical problems and solutions, project management experiences, and future plans. Each section of this paper is independent of the others; readers interested only in a particular aspect of the project are encouraged to read the relevent section(s) of the paper.*

## Introduction

The Internet is becoming an increasingly commercial arena in which payments are rendered for goods, information, and services. To support such commerce, various Internet payment protocols have been proposed and adopted by a variety of organizations. Most of these protocols are incompatible with each other, however, and the immediate future holds little prospet of their unification or abandonment.

In fact, the existence of different payment mechanisms is justified given the variety of needs that must be satisfied, as listed below:

- Cryptographic needs (strong, symmetric, exportable, importable, etc.)

- Latency of the transaction (micropayment must be *very* fast)

- Minimal and maximal amount for the transaction itself

- Minimal and maximal amount for the cost of the transaction

- Repudiation, notarization needs

- Involvement of financial institution

Some examples of payment protocols are:

- SET standard (being developed by Master-Card and VISA)

- CyberCash system

- GCtech's GlobeID

- CMU's NetBill

- First Virtual

- DigiCash's ECash

While the multiplicity of payment systems encourages healthy competition among players, it also introduces a greater level of complexity to end users such as consumers and merchants. The goal of phase 1 was to help consumers and merchants select, among the payment systems, one that is appropriate for both parties for any given transaction.

## Goals

W3C's role in the JEPI project is not to provide a new payment protocol or a way to convert dynamically between payment schemes; it is, rather, to provide an architecturally viable and neutral mechanism for automating the negotiation of payment instruments over the Web.

Indeed, the purpose of JEPI is to negotiate and select a single payment system for use in a particular transaction from the group of multiple payment systems installed on the client and server platform.

If, for instance, a server has installed payment systems *A* and *B*, and a client has installed Wallet *C* and *D*, JEPI will not help; no conversion functionality is provided. If, on the other hand, a server has installed payment systems *A*, *B*, and *C*, and a client has installed Wallet *C* and *D*, then JEPI should be able to select *C* as the appropriate method on behalf of both users.

JEPI should also allow end users to smoothly extend their arsenal of payment mechanisms with new payment systems and without interfering with already installed systems.

## Payment Negotiation

The following scenario shows an example of a complicated process that takes place in the real world:

> As you approach the cash register, you see decals indicating that the merchant will accept payment by MasterCard and Visa. (It is understood, of course, that you can pay in the local currency.) You ask whether the merchant will accept a check. She tells you she will not accept a check without a check guarantee card, which you do not own. You then ask if she will accept American Express. She admits that they do, but then reveals that she will give you 2% off if you use MasterCard or Visa, or 5% if you pay cash. You decide to pay cash, and ask if there is a discount for AAA members. She admits that there is, but not on top of the 5% cash discount. They *do*, however, offer United Airlines Frequent Flyer Miles. . .

Though this is admittedly a bit more complicated than usual for consumer payment, it is very similar to the negotiations that take place in inter-corporate purchasing arrangements. The JEPI project is intended to enable "automatable payment negotiation": a process in which the computers negotiate to find out what capabilities they have in common, and the user makes the final selection decision.

To demonstrate the advantages of using JEPI, we will show two online shopping scenarios, with and without JEPI.

Without JEPI, a merchant must allow the consumer to manually select payment options (via WWW pages), as described below:

> You visit a merchant's Web site. After browsing the catalog for some time, you find a few interesting items. You select the desired items and press the Submit button. The merchant acknowledges the order by sending you an invoice along with a list of payment systems he can accept. To accommodate his customer, the merchant includes a list of all 79 payment systems he can accept. After intensive browsing through the list and some head scratching, you select one payment system, and press the Pay button. The payment transaction starts. But you suddenly realize that you missed a significant discount offered to those customers paying with the merchant's favorite credit card. Too late . . .

This is the way commerce is usually conducted today, both in the electronic and the physical worlds. For example, it is not unusual to find a gas pump with 40 to 50 different decals. There are many limitations to this approach:

- The merchant must specify all choices up-front rather than silently accepting some of them without advertising them.

- The potentially long list of payment choices is cumbersome for the consumer.

- There is no way to automatically eliminate choices that can't work, like accepting a check in a foreign currency.

- There is no way to automatically apply payment preferences. For instance, you might want to use the micropayment method for all transactions under a certain amount of money if and only if the merchant accepts that method.

- There is no way for the consumer to counter-offer some other choice.

JEPI is designed to address these issues by providing automatable negotiation and selection of a payment system based on common capabilities and preferences of both the consumer and the merchant.

Here is the same scenario, but this time both the consumer and the merchant are JEPI-enabled:

> You visit a merchant's Web site. While browsing the catalog, your JEPI-enabled client software talks to your merchant server; it informs the server about your five preferred payment methods. You select your items and press the Submit button. The merchant acknowledges the order by sending you an invoice along with a list of payment systems he can accept. But this time, he sends only seven options; four of five methods suggested by you and three additional methods of his preference, including his favorite credit card to which a big discount is associated. To take advantage of the discount, you select the merchant's favorite credit card, and press the Pay button. The payment transaction starts.

In this scenario, the consumer is happy because she didn't miss the discount and was presented only with relevant payment choices. The merchant is also happy because he was able to use his favorite payment method.

# The JEPI Project

JEPI, a joint project of the W3C, CommerceNet, and a number of industry partners, explores the payment negotiation process as set forth earlier in the last section. Its milestones are shown in the following table:

| Date | Milestone |
| --- | --- |
| 1995/96 | JEPI phase 1 is launched by W3C and Commerce-Net |
| Mid-October 1996 | Protocol specification ready |
| Mid-October 1996 | JEPI Demonstrator |
| Late February 1997 | Executable demo implementation |
| March 1997 | JEPI whitepaper |
| April 1997 WWW6 Conference | JEPI presentation and demo |

As with all W3C activities, this project would not exist without industrial partners from our membership base or by invitation. (In the JEPI project, CommerceNet members were welcome as well.)

One of our first tasks with JEPI was to define specific roles in the context of an electronic commerce transaction; the companies in the following table stepped up to participate in the design and implementation phases:

| Activity | Participants |
| --- | --- |
| Payment systems | CyberCash, GCTech |
| Browser | Microsoft |
| Servers | IBM, Open Market |
| Merchants | Xerox, British Telecom, VendaMall |
| Specifications, Prototyping, Technical Management | W3C |

| Activity | Participants |
|---|---|
| Marketing | CommerceNet |
| Demonstrator, Engineering resource to W3C | Ericsson |

Notice that there is no bank or financial institution in the table. The reason is simple: in JEPI we rely on the payment system service providers to handle the connection/gateway to the financial world. This happens both on the client (wallet) and the server (cash register) sides.

# JEPI Architecture

## Overview

JEPI hinges around creating specifications for a pair of negotiation protocols, as described below.

- A general purpose negotiation protocol based on PEP (Protocol Extension Protocol). This allows a Web client and server to ask one another what extension modules they support, to negotiate parameters for these extensions, and to ask the other end to commence using an extension if possible. This

work is being folded into the specifications of HTTP through the IETF processes.

- A specific extension module, UPP (Universal Payment Preamble), used to negotiate over the payment instrument (check, credit card, debit card, electronic cash, etc.), brand (Visa, MasterCard, American Express, etc.), and payment protocol (SET, CyberCash, Globe-ID, etc.). This work is being done primarily as part of the JEPI project, but will probably be turned over to another party for formal standardization when the project is complete.

Figure 1 shows the overall architecture of JEPI, with the PEP and UPP layers acting as a stack on top of existing HTTP communication to perform a negotiation and selection of payments.

## The PEP Layer

The Protocol Extension Protocol (PEP) is a generic framework for describing extensions within HTTP. Each PEP extension represents new features to HTTP, and is associated with a URL. A PEP extension uses a few new header fields to carry the extension identifier and related informa-

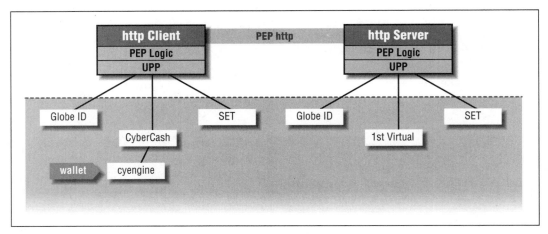

**Figure 1**

tion from HTTP clients, through proxies and intermediaries, to servers, and back again.

PEP has already been used by the PICS (Platform for Internet Content Selection) project for exchanging labels, and we expect it to be used whenever a negotiation of features is needed at the level of client/server communication on the Web. In JEPI, it forms the basis of UPP, which does the payment negotiation.

JEPI phase 1 uses the version of PEP from August 1996 [2] which defines four new headers:

- `Protocol:`
- `Protocol-Request:`
- `Protocol-Query:`
- `Protocol-Info:`

These headers allow for naming (identification of extension), initiation/request of a protocol usage, inquiries on protocol availability, and advertising (notification of usage). The newer version of PEP [3] is somewhat simpler.

Here is an example HTTP message extended with the PICS-1.1 protocol:

```
Server -> Client
   HTTP/1.0 200 OK
   Date: Thu, 30 Jun 1995 17:51:47
      GMT
   Last-modified: Thursday, 29-Jun-
      95 17:51:47 GMT
   Protocol: {PICS-1.1 {headers
      PICS-Label}}
   PICS-Label:
   (PICS-1.1 "http://www.gcf.org/
         v2.5" labels
      for "http://www.greatdocs.com/
         foo.html"
      ratings (suds 0.5 density 0
         color/hue 1))
   Content-type: text/html

   ...contents of foo.html...
```

## The UPP Layer

The Universal Payment Preamble (UPP) is the foundation of JEPI. It provides the semantics of the payment selection. It is based on PEP and therefore operates at the HTTP level.

In the UPP view of the world, some set of payment protocols are installed with the consumer software and a (possibly different) set of payment protocols are installed at the vendor. Each payment system is considered to be a PEP extension, identified by a URL. The *http://w3.org/UPP* protocol also exists, as well as a module implementing it.

UPP headers allow parties to negotiate payment alternatives at any point in shopping, until a final hand-off occurs to the chosen payment system. UPP provides two capabilities: payment service negotiation and initiation of the specific payment system. The payment service and initiation information are sufficient to smoothly bridge from shopping to payment and, if appropriate, from payment back to other customer-vendor interaction.

The Universal Payment Preamble is so called because it exchanges information that needs to be resolved *before* a particular payment system is entered, as well as providing an initiation message to enter the payment protocol.

In addition to allowing exchange of purchase information such as amount, currency, brand, etc., UPP also provides a way of transitioning to the next state depending on the result of the execution of the chosen payment system; either side can notify the other of success or failure, or cancel of the transaction.

The following code shows an example of UPP Flows [6]. First, the client requests the catalog:

```
Client -> Server
   GET http://www.arix.com/catalog.
      htm HTTP/1.1
```

Then, the server sends the catalog to the client along with a request to use the UPP protocol for the Submit button. The server also informs the client that he can accept Coin and GlobeID.

```
Server -> Client
    ....
    Content-Type: text/html
    Protocol-Request: {http://w3.org/
        UPP {str req}
                    {for
        /SubmitButton}}
    Protocol-Info:
        {http://CyberCash.com/Coin
            {for /*}},
        {http://GCTech.com/GlobeID
            {for /*}}
    Content-Length: 807
    ...
```

Next, the client presses the Submit button, and tells the server that it is using Coin. He also sends a series of payment information, such as the account number, expiration date, and the amount.

```
Client -> Server
    POST http://www.arix.com/
        SubmitButton HTTP/1.1
    Protocol:
        {http://w3.org/UPP {via http:/
            /CyberCash.com/Coin}}
        {http://CyberCash.com/Coin
            {params {account 12345}
                {expire 9/19/99}
                    {amount {usd 270}}}}
```

Last, the server executes the chosen payment system, and informs the client of three possible URLs to choose from depending on the result.

```
Server -> Client
    Content-Type: application/
        cybercash
    Protocol: {http://w3.org/UPP
        {params {success /worked}
            {failure /didnt}
            {cancel
                    /incomplete}}}
    Content-Length: 359
    ...
```

## Miscellaneous Issues

JEPI architecture itself does not address security issues. It is the specific payment system invoked—not PEP or UPP—that is responsible for the secure transmission of funds.

In JEPI phase 1, we implemented only credit card protocols. UPP, however, is more general and provides features to support other payment systems—UPP can carry payment protocol parameters such as brand names, for instance. This implicitly allows a fourth protocol layer on top of HTTP, PEP, and UPP, where protocol-specific information is carried via UPP. In this way, UPP claims to provide extensibility in order to meet the needs of other payment protocols.

## Current Status

The first phase of JEPI is based on a version of PEP specification from August 1996 [2]. Since then, PEP was revised and a new version was submitted to IETF for review [3]. When accepted by IETF, PEP will formally be a part of HTTP. As noted, however, the UPP specification is based on the PEP draft from August 1996, and has not yet been updated to meet the changes of PEP.

As of the writing of this document, we have an implementation of PEP and UPP available as extensions to Microsoft Internet Explorer 3.01 and IBM Web server on Windows NT. We also have a JEPI Demonstrator [5], provided by Ericsson, which is a set of Web pages that illustrate various shopping scenarios with and without JEPI. PEP/UPP messages transported in each step of a shopping scenario are described in detail.

So far, our pilot has been involved only with emulated transactions rather than real merchants' back-end systems. The next step in our project is to move into a real life experiment. Though we could extend the pilot to support a real merchant system based on the JEPI support we already have in the MS browser and the IBM server, it would be more desirable to define a simple predefined interface, and to build on top of it.

With the presentation and a live demo of the JEPI prototype at the Sixth International World Wide Web Conference in Santa Clara (April 1997), the first phase of JEPI is officially finished. We are now evaluating options for phase two (see the section entitled "Future Work").

# Lessons Learned

Here are a few lessons we learned while working on the first phase of the JEPI project.

## Project Management Issues

### Coping with the distributed project model

The JEPI project is quite different from a traditional industry project geared toward a specific product development by a dedicated team of developers. Its most notable characteristics are the following:

- Participants come from completely independent organizations (companies) spread over different geographical locations, all having different interests and expertise. We found that while diversification of *expertise* is good, diversification of *interest* can be harmful. We also found the different time zones (nine hours difference between Seattle and France) to present a challenge.
- The project leader neither holds a stick nor carrot; he must rely on participants' voluntary cooperation.

The coordination of a distributed project of this sort, which involved so many different participants, proved to be difficult and time consuming.

### Attacking a poorly understood problem

The scope of the JEPI project was limited to payment negotiation and selection. While this offered a good focus for the problem at hand, we were still too ambitious; we wanted to support back-and-forth negotiation, but didn't have any experience of the real demand for such negotiation. In the demo, we helped ourselves tremendously by limiting the scope to simple payment selection.

### Basing the project on unstable ground

The status of PEP, which was poorly documented and in design flux, was problematic. Specifically, both the server and browser support for UPP got caught up in the details of how to support PEP itself. In addition, UPP was not flexible enough for certain situations, especially where selection of payment brand was needed depending on conditions dictated by the merchant or client.

### Including non-technical participants in a technical project

Merchants are interested in completed solutions. Including them at the requirements development process level was a good idea, and we benefited from useful input. However, the merchants were neither interested in the technical design, nor did they want to be involved in a prototype. In addition, it was challenging to convince the merchants to invest in a demonstration that has no planned follow-up.

### Application of Demonstrator

The Demonstrator was extremely useful, not only as a way of illustrating the potential of JEPI, but also as a means of communicating between different participants in the projects. The PEP and UPP specifications describe the exact syntax and intent of their messages, but fail to describe how the protocols are supposed to be used in practice. The Demonstrator filled this gap, and was an efficient complement to the protocol specifications.

### Timing

JEPI is ahead of the real world demand for payment negotiation. We will see a proliferation of various electronic payment systems in the near future, and the need for JEPI's negotiation support will be obvious. Today, however, only a limited number of electronic payment systems are available. Most consumers and merchants support very few of these systems, and don't see the need for negotiation support.

# Technical Issues

Here are some of the technical issues that we encountered in the first phase of the JEPI project.

### Orientation to payment mechanism

As currently structured, UPP is oriented to select a payment mechanism (CyberCash, [7] GCTech [8], etc.), and within that mechanism, a brand (Visa, MC, etc.). Because today's consumers are usually familiar with brands rather than with mechanisms, this is a bad strategy. Consumers may not even care about the underlying mechanisms used to carry out the transaction—a fact that might point to a greater interest in negotiation over payment instruments (credit card brands, etc.) than over payment mechanisms.

On the other hand, situations do exist where consumers need to know about mechanisms. For example, the choice of mechanism could be directly related to consumer's rights, liability, cost, and so on. A system like JEPI should allow different payment models and operation modes to coexist.

### Distinguishing levels of negotiation

Implicitly, there were four levels of negotiation in the JEPI project, and we didn't do a good job of distinguishing them. Seen from the perspective of one participant in a PEP/UPP negotiation, we have the following cases to consider:

1. The peer may or may not support PEP.
2. The peer may or may not support UPP.
3. The peer may or may not recognize or be willing to use a given payment mechanism.
4. The peer may or may not recognize or be willing to use a specific aspect (e.g., a brand) associated with a particular payment mechanism.

In particular, PEP and UPP can't efficiently handle case, number 4, above. There's no easy way to say, "I reject brand $X$ for mechanism $Y$" versus "I reject mechanism $Y$," much less say, "I would accept brand $X$ and mechanism $Y$ but only under constraint $Z$."

### Maintaining state

HTTP is a stateless protocol. An HTTP transaction consists of a client's request for a resource, e.g., an HTML page and the server's reply; normally, nothing is remembered between multiple HTTP transactions. Payment negotiation, on the other hand, requires involved parties to remember previous negotiations in order to improve the offer next time.

Because PEP and UPP messages are basically HTTP messages, JEPI lacked good infrastructure for maintaining state. In JEPI the state was maintained in a limited manner, as parameters within UPP messages: in this way, the payment systems accumulate state within transactions. Because of these limitations, the JEPI team should have looked more closely at the issues surrounding state in an HTTP environment.

### Supporting multiple interfaces

At the server end of the JEPI project, we had four different interfaces, which made for a very complicated environment.

1. The PEP/UPP protocol messages exchanged with the browser.
2. The merchant server itself.
3. CyberCash's merchant support.
4. GC Tech's merchant support.

We significantly underestimated the time it would take to get these interfaces working together. The complexities of supporting multiple interfaces has been made simpler by using a common platform—Intel-based Windows NT. However, it required the porting of many already existing software components to the common platform, and left less time to focus on the protocol itself.

# Future Work

The discussions about the future of JEPI within W3C have already begun. A possible JEPI phase 2 encompasses several elements:

- Revising UPP in the context of the evolution of PEP, on top of which it is layered.

- Extending UPP to address issues arising from introducing smart cards, electronic checks, electronic cash, and micropayments as payment mechanisms that can be negotiated.

- Implementing all scenarios described in the UPP flows document (JEPI 1 focused on just one).

- Prototyping implementation using new payment systems like the ones derived from SET, micropayment, smart card, and so on.

- Extending HTML to address issues arising from micropayment, but not necessarily the other mechanisms.

- Specifying and implementing wallet and cash register APIs for connecting to payment systems, but at the participant's request. Ditto for APIs between wallet/cash register and browser/server.

We are in the process of receiving feedback from the industry regarding the priority of the above list. The pace at which we will pursue any activity will depend greatly on the market context. For one thing, the electronic market has been slower than expected to really take off, and working on any payment negotiation aspect in that context could be perceived by some as putting the cart before the horse. As a result, JEPI 2 has yet to be defined.

We still believe, however, that JEPI's negotiation over payment method is important, given the continuing growth of the number of protocols. As time goes on, the community is slowly acknowledging the depth of the problem, but JEPI still remains ahead of its time. ∎

## References

1. HTTP 1.1, *http://www.w3.org/pub/WWW/Protocols/rfc2068/rfc2068*

2. PEP version used in JEPI (from August 86), *http://www.w3.org/pub/WWW/TR/WD-http-pep-960820.html*

3. PEP latest version, *http://www.w3.org/pub/WWW/TR/WD-http-pep-970321.html*

4. UPP, *http://www.w3.org/pub/WWW/Payments/specs/upp.txt*

5. Demonstrator, *http://www.w3.org/pub/WWW/Payments/group/Demo/scenes/index.htm*

6. UPP flows document, *http://www.w3.org/pub/WWW/TR/WD-jepi-uppflow-970106.html*

7. CyberCash, *http://www.cybercash.com/*

8. GCTech, *http://www.gctec.com/*

# Acknowledgments

| | |
|---|---|
| Donald E. Eastlake 3rd | *dee@cybercash.com* CyberCash Contact Person Author of UPP specification |
| James M. Galvin | *galvin@commerce.net* CommerceNet Contact Person |
| Rick Johnson | *rickj@microsoft.com:* Microsoft Project Leader |
| Rohit Khare | *khare@w3.org* W3C staff Editor of PEP specification |
| Mark Linehan | *linehan@watson.ibm.com* IBM Project Leader |
| Jim Miller | *jmiller@w3.org* W3C Technology & Society Domain Leader |
| Frank Naranjo | *frank@agetech.net* IBM Server Implementation |
| Paul-Andre Pays | *pays@gctech.fr* GCTech Contact Person |
| Marc Whitman | *a-mwhit@microsoft.com* Microsoft Client Implementation |

| Jake Hill | *jah@alien.bt.co.uk* Author of earlier version of JEPI demonstrator |
|---|---|
| Peter van der Linden | *vdl@gctech.fr* GCTech Contact Person |
| Fabrice de Comarmond | *fdc@gctec.com* GCTech Contact Person |
| Win Treese | *reese@openmarket.com* OpenMarket Contact Person |
| Jim Davis | *jdavis@parc.xerox.com* |
| Scott Kelly | *kellys@ren.pcdocs.com* |

## About the Authors

**Eui-Suk Chung**
MIT
545 Technology Square
Cambridge, MA 02139
*euisuk@w3.org*

Eui-Suk Chung joined the W3C in August 96 on secondment from the Swedish telecom company Ericsson. Before joining W3C, he was working on query processing for object-oriented database systems at the MIT Laboratory for Computer Science on a grant from Sweden.

He is interested in most aspects of the Web, and is currently working on electronic commerce within W3C's Technology & Society domain. He is also interested in security, real-time audio/video, distributed computing, and mobile code.

**Daniel Dardailler**
2004, route des Lucioles—B.P. 93
06902 Sophia Antipolis Cedex
France
*danield@w3.org*

Daniel joined the W3C-Sophia team in July 1996 to work in the field of Technology and Society for Europe (e-commerce, security, etc). Prior to that, he was a Software Architect at the X Consortium, responsible for the Motif toolkit and other CDE components.

Daniel holds a Ph.D. in Computer Science from the University of Nice/Sophia-Antipolis.

*The technical papers in this section spiral outward from a central insight: we need to reach beyond cryptographic debates to understand the trust relationships embedded in the Web. The opening survey paper, "Weaving a Web of Trust" by Rohit Khare and Adam Rifkin, outlines this new approach to Web security issues. It will be constructed on the twin pillars of strong conventional security and new, automatable Trust Management (TM) tools. Those points are made, respectively, by Simson Garfinkel and Gene Spafford's "Cryptography and the Web" and "REFEREE: Trust Management for Web Applications" by Yang-Hua Chu et al.*

*The next twist is network infrastructure: the tools and protocols where these philosophies hit the wire. In many Web security primers, the lowest level is Secure Sockets Layer (SSL), which creates a private communications channel. Frederick Hirsch ably introduces it alongside the thorny practical issues of identity establishment, using a freeware toolkit in "Understanding SSL and Certificates Using SSLeay." Nevertheless, the secured infrastructure needs to reach deeper. Today's DNS is insecure, but fixing it could also help solve key-distribution for other applications as well. These prospects are explained in John Gilmore's "Security for the Domain Name System" and implemented as "Name Server Security Features in BIND 4.9.5," described by Cricket Liu. Finally, once the layers below HTTP are secured, we can return our focus to building sturdy interfaces to the Web. Authors Garfinkel and Spafford return to offer expert techniques for "Secure CGI/API Programming."*

*Turning the crank again, we see the fruits of all this planning for the other side of those interfaces: trustworthy Web applications. Electronic commerce, whether business-to-business or retail, hard goods or intellectual property, is always about contracts and other trust relationships. Moving those instruments onto the Web will drive the deployment of a common toolset for identifying customers, signing purchase orders, and a thousand and one other commercial relationships, as Mark Madsen and Andrew Herbert argue in "A Guide to Secure Electronic Business Using the E2S Architecture." There's more to life than money, though; a breach of contract can have redress, but inaccurate or insecure health records are another level of trusted application entirely. Medical Doctor and Web security expert Lincoln Stein paints a compelling vision in "Electronic Medical Records: Promises and Threats."*

*Moving this sort of extremely sensitive application to the Web brings us to the outermost layer: the intersection of technology and society. The consequences of reflecting our trust relationships on the Web raise urgent policy questions. What currency should digital signatures hold? Who can vouch for citizens' identities when they are reduced to public keys? Lawyer Brad Biddle argues that some states are taking the lead—in the wrong direction—in "Legislating Market Winners: Digital Signature Laws and the Electronic Commerce Marketplace." In fact, governments around the world want even more: many are planning back doors into citizen's conversations. An all-star team of eminent cryptographers and security experts raise a red flag in "The Risks of Key Recovery, Key Escrow, and Trusted Third-Party Encryption." The debate promises to be joined in force around the world, according to Clint Smith's "Government Promotion of Key Recovery Encryption: How Current Government Initiatives Will Impact Internet Security."*

# Weaving a Web of Trust

*Robit Khare, Adam Rifkin*

## Abstract

*To date, "World Wide Web Security" has been publicly associated with debates over cryptographic technology, protocols, and public policy. This narrow focus can obscure the wider challenge of building trusted Web applications. Since the Web aims to be an information space that reflects not just human knowledge but also human relationships, it will soon reflect the full complexity of trust relationships among people, computers, and organizations. Within the computer security community, "Trust Management" has emerged as a new philosophy for protecting open, decentralized systems, in contrast to traditional tools for securing closed systems. Trust Management is an essential approach because the Web crosses many trust boundaries that old-school computer security cannot even begin to handle.*

*In this paper, we consider how the Trust Management philosophy could be applied to the Web. We introduce the fundamental principles, principals, and policies of Trust Management, as well as Web-specific pragmatic issues. In so doing, we develop a taxonomy for how trust assertions can be specified, justified, and validated. We demonstrate the value of this framework by considering the trust questions faced by the designers of applications for secure document distribution, content filtering, electronic commerce, and downloadable-code systems. We conclude by sketching the limits to automatable Trust Management, demonstrating how trust on the Web will adapt to the trust rules of human communities, and vice versa.*

## 1. Motivation

Clara Customer fires up her favorite Web browser one morning and connects to her bank to pay her rent. The bank's computer duly opens up an encrypted session, and Clara fills out the payment form from her landlord. Later that morning Bob banker has to approve the transaction.

Should Bob move the money from Clara to her landlord? The bank uses Secure Sockets Layer (SSL) [26] or IETF Transport Layer Security (TLS) [16] to encrypt the whole conversation (to the strongest degree allowed by law), so no attacker can scramble Clara's payment order. Since the cryptography checks out, the transaction is secure, right?

Wrong. Although cryptography has been well studied [46] and well publicized, traditional secure applications use many other implicit rules as well. For example, we might assume that the

transaction can be initiated only from a secure location, such as an Automated Teller Machine (ATM). Or, we might assume that the authorized user has a unique physical token to establish her identity, such as an ATM card. Or, we might assume that the transaction takes place in real-time, rather than being faked later.

These implicit assumptions do not hold for a Web-based "virtual ATM." Although custom-built secure applications can enforce specific roles such as "Secret-level users should not be able to read top secret documents," the cryptography exists solely as a tool for verifying these assumptions.

Unfortunately, many users and designers behave as though strong cryptography can paper over security holes in the World Wide Web. The Web is powerful precisely because it is such a generic platform for developing applications such as this "virtual ATM" scenario. Often, intoxicated with the power and ease of building Web gateways, we overlook the consequences of the transition.

Since developers no longer control both ends of the connection as they did in traditional client-server systems, many implicit rules are invalidated by the shift to open Web clients.

Bob banker's job is actually much harder in the Web-wide world than it was in the world of ATM machines; for example:

- Nothing in the online encryption handshake necessarily establishes Clara's identity

- No recoverable signed document exists as a receipt for the transaction

- No verification exists that the landlord toted up the rent correctly

These are just some of the questions Bob faces before trusting Clara. As tough as they are, however, they pale in comparison to Clara's challenge of determining whether to trust the bank! After all, "How do [banks] convey trustworthiness without marble?" [18]

The key word in the previous sentence is "trust." Instead of asking the cryptographic question, "Has this instruction been tampered with?" we can learn more by asking the more appropriate question, "Does the bank *trust* this instruction?" In fact, the trust questions raised in this scenario are far more profound than the cryptographic ones:

- Why should Clara trust that she is really talking to her bank?

- Why should Clara trust the bank to present her landlord's bill?

- Why should Bob trust Clara to issue these payment instructions?

Cryptography cannot directly answer these "why" questions. Even the act of tinkering deep in the bowels of our favorite protocols cannot guide us to the right "why" questions, since they will depend on the semantics of the application itself. However, thinking carefully about the trust each party grants, we can translate them into the following "how" questions that cryptography *can*

answer (using encryption, certification authorities, and digital signatures):

- How can Clara be sure she is talking to a computer that is a legitimate arm of her bank? *[Encrypted messages from a certified bank server]*

- How can Clara and the landlord be sure the bank will represent the landlord's bill accurately? *[The landlord's digital signature]*

- How can the bank be sure that Clara is authorized to make these payments? *[Encrypted messages, digitally signed, with her bank account certificate]*

Since the bank's very *raison d'être* is to be a trusted broker for all parties, this banking scenario is actually fairly simple: the bank manages the trust. Suppose we venture into murkier territory:

> Sara Surfer hears about a whiz-bang new financial applet from Jesse Jester. She hops over to FlyByNight.Com and downloads their latest and greatest auto-stock-picker.

What is Sara's next move? Can she trust the applet to suggest good stock trades? Can she trust it to read her portfolio database? Can she trust it to make stock trades on her behalf? Can she be sure the applet will not maliciously reformat her hard drive? Can she be confident that the applet will not leak her private financial data to the world? Should she decide to run this applet because Jesse endorsed it, because she trusts *FlyByNight.Com*, or because some certifying agency claims *FlyByNight.Com* is a good developer? Can she even be sure an attacker has not modified the applet while she was downloading it?

Like the banking scenario, this financial applet scenario is about protecting computers and the data contained on them. Sara's private data can be recovered by keeping logs, running regular audits, and maintaining backups.

What if, instead, the trust scenario involved something that could not be undone? For example, suppose the trust question is, "Do I trust my child to see this content?" Matters of sex, religion, and violence are also Trust Management challenges on the World Wide Web. The Platform for Internet Content Selection (PICS) content-labeling system [44] represents just one credential in a complicated "trust calculation."*

Each of these scenarios revolves around assertions and judgment calls from several parties, rather than from cryptographic proofs alone. Welcome to the frontier of Trust Management [3], a relatively new approach to the classic challenges of computer security that generalizes existing access control list and capability-granting approaches. The philosophy behind Trust Management is accessible and powerful, whether one favors the new, generic authorization tools Trust Management proposes such as PolicyMaker [4] and REFEREE [11],† or whether one continues to build special purpose secure applications. Asking the basic question *"Who has to trust whom for what to take this action?"* will clarify security issues—not just for cryptographers, but for webmasters, application developers, businesspeople, and consumers.

In this paper, we consider the potential of Trust Management within the context of the World Wide Web. Because the Web is as much a social phenomenon as a technical one, it provides an ideal laboratory for several competing trust models. After all, *trust* relationships bottom out to *human* relationships, represented by *people, computers,* and *organizations.*

Section 2 maps out some of the fundamental *principles* for codifying trust; section 3 describes tools for vouchsafing the *principals* (people, computers, and organizations) concerned; section 4 discusses several common trust *policies*; and section 5 presents the *pragmatics* of managing trust in the Web. In section 6, we offer several

application areas that could potentially drive the deployment of Trust Management tools: secure document distribution, content filtering, electronic commerce, and downloadable-code systems. As more and more trust relationships are mirrored on the Web, we will run into the limits of Trust Managment and learn how real world relationships might change to adapt to those limits, as discussed in section 7. As we adopt this philosophy in designing Web security technology and new applications, we will weave a "Web of Trust" together, as summarized in section 8.

# 2. Principles

> *Oh! What a tangled web we weave,*
> *When first we practice to deceive . . .*
> —Sir Walter Scott

Perhaps we can learn as much about Trust Management from breaking trust as by establishing it: a "tangled web" blooms like cracks in shattered glass around the central lie. For example, "If Joe would lie to me about bumping my car in the lot, can I trust him to work up the departmental budget?" Although humans are naturally suspicious, our personal Trust Management schemes are often vague, which can foil our plans for security systems to be executed by our notoriously literal-minded assistants. Likewise, holistic judgments about integrity and honesty of character are not so easily conveyed to computers. On the other hand, digital Trust Management can be much more exacting and dogged about establishing the authority to take a certain action.

## 2.1 Be Specific

This leads us to the most fundamental principle behind Trust Management: *Be specific.* Who, precisely, is in the trusted group, and what exact actions do we trust them to take? Blanket statements such as "I trust my bank" are woefully

---

* With PICS, a Web browser can help a parent determine how appropriate a Web page is for his child. For instance, the page may be suitable because it is from a certain author, because it is rated above a certain threshold by some trusted agency, or because it is *not* on a "blacklist."
† Yang-Hua Chu's (*et al.*) "REFEREE: Trust Management for Web Applications" is featured later in this issue.

inadequate for useful analysis—real life bears that out because banks never offer such contracts! A direct deposit agreement, for example, specifies precisely the account into which the employer will forward funds, the times payment will be made, and the expected bank recourses in case of error. We are used to making broad claims such as, "I trust my husband absolutely"—but for what? To purchase the right groceries? To feed the cats? To remain faithful? Without specifically quantifying the bounds of our trust relationships, we cannot expect those bonds to be worth anything.

Admittedly, it is difficult to be specific with the crude tools available on the World Wide Web today. A typical HTTP server might offer to "protect" some URLs by requesting a username/password challenge before granting access. Even putting aside the absurd weakness of sending passwords in the clear for *basic* authentication in HTTP, this kind of access privilege is still too broad. It requires the server administrator to be vigilant about what content is in the "protected" and open areas; it does not typically restrict the range of methods available (GET, PUT, POST, and so on) in the protected area; and it does not establish the identity or credentials of each user.

Essentially, the only security policy we can talk about is the "form" of a request (that is, its method and URL), not the "substance," or contents of that request.

In the "virtual ATM" scenario in section 1, one can imagine that the legacy banking application would have detailed security instructions about viewing and modifying statements. If the Web server can only see CGI-generated HTML pages [30], it cannot secure them based on the information represented within the confines of the firewall.

Better yet, consider what happens on the client side. Web surfers eagerly swat aside the "Show alert each time unsecured data is sent?" dialog box. These surfers receive no guidance as to whether on the one hand the alert might be a vital warning prior to sending credit card data, but useless for other Web transactions. Such ambiguities force Web security experts to issue blanket warnings such as, "Think very carefully before accepting a digitally signed program; how competent and trustworthy is the signer?" [22].

It is often arduous to be specific with existing downloadable code systems [52]. The user might desire the functionality of the following statement:

> I trust the *Foolodex* applet to read and index *.foo* files on my disk, but never to write to my disk.

Unfortunately, however useful, one has little chance to enforce such a clause—today's typical ActiveX and Java environments do not expose such specific management interfaces. Although this particular effect could be simulated by a sandbox leveraging operating system–level file protection, it also compounds the room for error. A similarly unimplementable policy is,

> Jane is not allowed to access *.foo* files directly. She must use the *Foolodex* applet.

In fact, even the operating system–level "file read" permission might be too broad for comfort; a user may want his boss to be able to read only the work-related fields of his *Foolodex*, for example.

Given the difficulty of implementing specific rules with today's "security," the principle of specificity seems foolishly pedantic. However, when we understand Trust Management concepts, even with today's insufficient tools, the benefits of rigorous planning are evident:

- By segregating users into different categories and levels, and by separating differently secured information and functions into different URL-prefixes, a webmaster can implement site security reliably with HTTP servers.

- Deploying the improved Digest authentication scheme [25], HTTP/1.1 [24] can increase the server's confidence that it is conversing with an approved user with a fresh request, rather than a replay.

- Cutting edge certificate-based authentication and the "client-authenticate" modes of SSL and TLS can help webmasters manage groups of people and also help them delegate authority.

As Trust Management technology advances forward, specific trust declarations will become more useful.

Unfortunately, we are not used to factoring our actions into different sets and granting trust only to certain domains; the human mind does not perpetually ask the general "who/what/when" trust question, "Does $X$ have permission to do $Y$ during time period $Z$?" PolicyMaker and REFEREE, for example, make this compartmentalization explicit because the only question one can ask the system is, "Does $X$ have permission to do $Y$ to resource $Z$?" In other words, not "Do I trust this applet" but "Can I allow this applet written by this person to check my financial data for the rest of this month?" We will explore the general "who/what/when" trust question throughout the rest of this paper.

Note that another dimension of trust exists, which is difficult to specify for computers: that is, *confidence in the trust statement itself.* In reality, all forms of trust come in shades of gray. Unfortunately, computers cannot successfully bridge the gap between different shades; instead, computers view systems with several binary switches that yield discrete intermediate shades. For example, the PGP Web of Trust [27] is based on introductions from trusted friends. When a keyring accepts a friend's key, the keyring owner determines whether to always, sometimes, or never automatically trust introductions to strangers through that friend. Here, the fuzzy confidence we might have had in real life had to be reduced

to those three levels, and that confidence, in turn, spans two dimensions:

- Is your friend a reliable go-between?
- Is she computer-savvy enough to protect her own key?

## 2.2 Trust Yourself

All trust begins and ends with the self: *Trust no one but yourself!* This is a plea for existential philosophy—a mechanical constraint that tidies up loose ends. Any trust decision should logically be derived from the axioms you yourself believe. For example, even the simplest assertion that "My credit card number is *xxxx*" cannot be taken for granted as external truth. To be certain, you implicitly work backwards:

> I believe that CreditCorp told me that *xxxx* is my number; I believe CreditCorp is who it says it is because my bank stands behind them; and I trust that my bank said so because its public key matches the one I was given when I opened my account.

Although you may sometimes derive shaky axioms, those axioms are still *a priori* beliefs that belong to you. Over time, "My credit card number is *xxxx*" might become an axiom of its own as you use it a few times to buy widgets, thereby building confidence as an entry in and of itself.

A similar rationale holds for trusting Internet domain names: we do not blindly accept that *xent.w3.org* is bound to 18.29.0.61 because some deity has designated it from a mountaintop; rather, we trust the mapping because a sysadmin decided to trust the local Domain Name System server,* which in turn relies on other DNS servers up the line, ending in the root server authorized by the Internet Assigned Numbers Authority, care of Jon Postel. Working inexorably down the trust

---

* For more about Domain Name Systems and Secure DNS, see John Gilmore's article entitled "Security for the Domain Name System" in this issue.

chain, each Internet user must choose to trust Jon or not.

This principle was inspired by two recent public key management proposals that directly mandate it. To set the stage, recall that the basic role of a Public Key Infrastructure is to validate the binding of a principal's name to a key. Rather than require each user to maintain a vast table of name-key pairs for all other users, most Public Key Infrastructure (PKI) proposals allow *Certification Authorities* (CAs) to intermediate the table. The Telephone Company is a good analogy: we trust the White Pages as a name-to-phone number mapping because the company has validated each telephone user and stands behind the directory. We can also call directory service for up-to-date information if the directory becomes stale.

Unfortunately, most public key infrastructure proposals require users to trust some external, omnipotent deity to sit atop the pyramid of CAs. After all, which Telephone Company should we ultimately trust, and who gave *it* a unique name in the first place? Whether the legitimacy comes from a "root CA" (like the government), or from popular approval (see section 4), two recent proposals enshrine the rule that you have to be your own meta-root.

- In the Simple Distributed Security Infrastructure (SDSI) [38], each person is the root of his own namespace; users explicitly choose to delegate authority for identifying Credit-Corp employees to *Credit.Com*.

- The Simple Public Key Infrastructure (SPKI) [19] relies on explicit authorization chains that form directed cycles beginning and ending at the user. SPKI's Simple Public Key Certificates [20] help establish relationships by assigning authorization attributes to digital principals.

Work is currently underway to merge SDSI and SPKI into SDSI 2.0, providing a unified treatment of certificates, a coherent treatment of names for both individuals and groups, an algebra of tags for describing permissions and attributes, and a flexible way to denote cryptographic keys. Other solutions, like the PGP Web of Trust [27], have also been founded upon the principle of *trust yourself*.

## 2.3 Be Careful

> *Trust in haste, Regret at leisure.*
> —*poster on the wall of Mr. Lime's office at Information Retrieval in the motion picture* Brazil

We close out our triad of trust principles with some common sense: *Be careful*. Rigorously justify every single trust decision in your application. By logically proving each trust decision, you can automatically explain each action the application takes. Any time you short circuit that logic, the consequences can spread immediately; after all, permit just one Trojan Horse applet past the firewall and the security perimeter is toast. There is no substitute for careful planning and execution; without meticulous scrutiny, the most logical policies can be correctly implemented, yet still leave the system wide open for attack.

For example, the World Wide Web Consortium has three levels of protected access to its Web site: Public, Member, and Team. Digital Equipment Corporation is a Member, so every machine in the *Digital.Com* domain has Member access. One of them is *Scooter*, the Web spider that fetches documents for AltaVista's Web search index. Unfortunately, since *Scooter* is a Member, AltaVista ended up reporting search hits that revealed Member-only information to the Public! Even though W3C was quite specific about its policy—we trust each Member to disseminate Member information within the organization, but not to redistribute it to the public—without being careful, security holes can propagate. Our Web tools cannot implement the specific *not-for-redistribution* policy today, so sensitive information was exposed. In this case, "careful execution" required synchronizing policies in several completely different systems: our password database, file system, HTTP servers, and Robot Exclusion configuration file [36].

# 3. Principals

The three principles underlying Trust Management discussed in section 2 imply that each decision should be backed with a direct inference chain from the axioms all the way to the request. In this section we explore the three kinds of beads we can string together to create these rosaries: statements by *people, computers,* and *organizations.* People are represented by their *names,* and can make trust assertions using digital signatures. Computers and other devices can mechanically verify the integrity of data transmissions, thereby vouching for their *addresses.* And organizations can represent collections of people or computers by granting memberships and credentials with digitally signed *certificates* that intermediate the binding of *names* and *addresses.*

To make a trust decision to "run this ActiveX applet" using the original Microsoft Authenticode scheme [40], we rely on statements made by each type of *principal.* The first step is a machine-to-machine verification, for example:

> I got this applet from another, known computer and it arrived uncorrupted, encrypted under a random session key chosen by both.

Then, we find a digital signature attached, implying the approval of the author, which is a personal or corporate name. In this case, the personal name binding is intermediated by two Certifying Authorities—the VeriSign and Microsoft organizations—and their respective certificates.

The third and final step is dissecting the certificate granted by VeriSign for two credential bits: one bit flipped to indicate that the author has signed an Applet Publisher Pledge, the other bit flipped to the setting "author is a commercial enterprise." Thus, because Authenticode had a policy to run any commercial publisher's applet, permission is granted.

In the end, these three principals correspond to the three basic reasons for granting permission to take an action: it could depend on which person is asking, what computer is asking, or which organization vouches for the requestor.

## 3.1 People

> *I don't trust [Lando Calrissian] either, but he is my friend.*
> —Han Solo, *The Empire Strikes Back*

Ultimately, trust reflects our belief that someone will act in a certain way, based both on our past history and on the expectations of others. Trust is a faith placed in humans, even though sometimes this faith may be manifested so as to appear that we are only trusting some device. Even a bank ATM's failures are ultimately backed by a Board of Directors. Perhaps this observation is just a trivial converse of the fact that you can sue only people, not computers!

As a consequence, most computer security systems "bottom out" in defining human beings. People are ultimately accountable for the actions of computers because people have persistent identities as names that are meaningful in the real world. Although an application designer's first instinct is to reduce a noble human being to a mere account number for the computer's convenience, at the root of that account number is always a human identity. This has two implications:

- The name should be established as a permanent identifier outside any particular application.

- People are "born" as a *tabula rasa*—that is, people cannot be automatically trusted for anything.

The canonical mechanism for establishing a name is to issue a digital certificate. The beauty of public key cryptography, as compared to its predecessors, is the ease with which we can create and distribute these identities. We create a secret key, entrusted to a human user, and then immediately use it to sign a declaration that "Waldo has this public key." Then, as long as the user protects his secret key, he can speak as Waldo on the Internet. Of course, based on the principle "trust only yourself," Waldo is the only person who believes in his new identity so far! To convince other people that he speaks for Waldo, he must get them to trust his identity certificate. While the user can go around "door-to-door" (so to speak), organizations can simplify the acceptance process among the entire community of people who trust that organization (see section 3.3).

Organizations are also critical for assigning credentials to people. Another way of putting this is that people need to adopt a role within an application. For example, Clara Beekham has no privileges at the bank; indeed, there is not even any reason for the bank to believe her name is what she declares it to be! By contrast, when Clara Beekham reveals herself as Clara Customer (from section 1), she gains the privileges of a bank account holder. At some point in time, Clara and the bank may have set up another explicit, named identity to act as a proxy for the role of bank account holder: the bank account number. The bank agrees to set up an account number for her human identity under her signature; in the future, Clara, the bank, and merchants cashing her checks all agree to refer to the account number instead. Later, Clara can delegate this role with its specific capabilities—for example, she could entrust her lawyer to act as Clara Customer.

**NOTE**

There is a faction in the computer security community that disagrees with the notion that humans are principals. The alternative credo is *keys are principals*; that is, the most basic element is the private key, and nothing else can be reliably determined about the key holder. This is absolutely true, since the cryptography of a digital signature can prove only that "someone had access to the message and the secret key"—and not what the fingerprints or pen-and-ink signatures could say about a specific person.

Though this credo is very useful when formally verifying secure systems, we choose to set it aside in this paper; trust can be exchanged only among people, not between people and keys. Furthermore, pseudonymous identities are a clever compromise to reconcile these alternatives.

## 3.2 Computers

*Artoo Deetoo, you know better than to trust a strange computer!*
—See-Threepio, *The Empire Strikes Back*

Many of the ideas in this paper are fairly generic comments about the human social phenomenon of trust. The bank, for example, uses the same principals to safeguard its internal humans-and-paperwork procedures as it does for a Web-based virtual ATM. Computers alter this equation by substituting the explicit power of cryptography for the implicit power of psychology.

However, this does not address the fundamental question of how we can even trust computers. Or, in the terms of classical computer security, what is the Web's Trusted Computing Base (TCB) [17]?

Indeed, many of the challenges raised in section 1 stem from the fact that the bank used to control its own trusted hardware at the client: the ATM machine. Though the Web client replacing it is more appealing in terms of flexibility and accessibility, it's less powerful and should not be automatically trusted. Even without considering concerted, malicious attacks, there are too many operational points of failure on a random customer's personal computer, such as buggy operating systems, network sniffers, and viruses.

Naturally, we have well developed tools for establishing trust within the computing devices themselves. Although these mechanical principals cannot be sued in court, they can certainly establish a reliable identity through number crunching and cryptography. Various protocols exist to verify remotely that a correspondent computer has a working clock, a good random number generator [43], and a unique address. Building on these primitive operations, we entrust these devices to take some limited actions through their peripheral devices: print a document, place a phone call, dispense money, or fire a (supposedly therapeutic) X-ray beam at a patient [39]. Note that these examples—"irreversible" actions that affect the real world—happen to be the most sensitive and protected actions "computers" can take. Traditional security tools such as logging and auditing can be used to detect and roll back fraud "inside the box" after the fact, in lieu of the strict trust calculations that protect "out of the box" actions.

Many approaches to computer security do not distinguish between people and computers, since both can be considered as principals with associated public and private keys. As long as the human or device protects its secret, either can play the same roles in various cryptographic protocols.

From the perspective of Trust Management it is important to qualify precisely what you can ultimately trust a principal for. In our opinion, the potential legal and moral liabilities are the critical difference. No matter how many tests you inflict on a remote computer, you can trust it only *as a device*. You can trust that a computer is connected to a working X-ray beam, but you can never trust it to decide on its own to fire it: that is a decision best reserved to people (and organizations, as described in section 3.3).

"Cloned" cellular phone fraud is a classic example of conflating trust in computers with people. Today's cellular networks already use a "secure" challenge to identify each telephone in a network's coverage area based on its supposedly unique fingerprint (serial number). While this proves the device's address, the network allows calls to be placed (and billed) to the owner: the operators assume that this authentication sufficiently proves the subscriber's ownership. In fact, only a personal secret—a PIN—can prove a one-to-one owner relationship; without a PIN to close the loop with the subscriber, the system can fail as soon as the address-authentication is cracked.[*]

Checksums, channel security, clock-challenge authentication, and other related techniques can prove only that we are talking to a working device with a consistent *address*—an identity limited to the scope of the immediate application. People and their delegates have *names*—permanent identities of beings (*a la* René Descartes) that go on living beyond any particular application. Establishing an SSL connection, for example, creates a secret, ironclad connection between two endpoints, but only *as computers*, and only for this session. Today many Web applications make an implicit (and mistaken) assumption that an SSL connection is a secret between two people or organizations.[†] In fact, though SSL can prove that you are talking to one machine—perhaps even the same machine you were talking to a moment ago—nothing in SSL alone can prove you are talking to, say, AirlineCo. You have to separately establish trust that public key *P* is the sole property of AirlineCo—that *some computer* is really the authorized delegate of *some person*. As for proving *P* is AirlineCo's key, that remains the task of the last part of the principals triad, *organizations*.

---

[*] Unfortunately for the U.S. cellular industry, this proved all too easy for some moderately skilled hackers. When the Europeans led the development of the General System for Mobile (GSM) phones as a successor to the U.S.-led Analog Mobile Phone Standard (AMPS), they designed authentication to reach beyond the phone to a "smart card" inserted into the unit by the owner [8]. A smart card establishes the proper trust in the subscriber because its address can substitute for the subscriber's name—it really is a unique, unclonable physical token.

[†] For more information about SSL, see the article "Introducing SSL and Certificates Using SSLeay," by Frederick Hirsch.

## 3.3 Organizations

*Badges? We don't need no steenkin'
badges!*

*—Blazing Saddles*

Just as people are separate from computers because their human identities have wider and more permanent scopes than transient devices, organizations are a third force because their existences have even larger scope. Organizations are critical to the trust relationships in our everyday lives and on the Web, precisely because they outlive their individual members. Western legal systems even institutionalized this notion through the process of incorporation, literally transforming the incorporeal body into a legal entity in the eyes of the court. In fact, in many technical ways, organizations are treated exactly like people: they both use the same kinds of certificates and they both need to protect their private keys.

The critical difference between organizations and people is that organizations can issue credentials that tie together people and computers—with enough scale and a high enough level of abstraction to make the world manageable. Imagine what a nightmare it would be if a user had to set up pairwise mutual authentication with every possible telephone caller with whom he or she might ever speak. The Telephone Company makes the entire enterprise possible because it brokers the transaction. Both the caller and the callee trust the Telephone Company to correctly connect their calls, to protect the integrity of their addresses (phone numbers), and to protect the binding of people to phones. In one fell swoop, $N$-factorial one-to-one trust relationships collapse to $2N$, thanks to this organization. This materially reduces the effective *transaction cost* of making a call—the same Nobel-prizewinning economic insight that justifies the existence of any organization. Life is easier, cheaper, and faster with intermediaries. Would anyone rather buy a 747 from the thousands of parts manufacturers instead of one-stop-shopping from Boeing?

Credentials issued by organizations are powerful because the whole is more than the sum of its parts. Driver's licenses, black belts, Consumer Reports scores, and bond ratings are all familiar credentials, trusted precisely because they are backed by universal standards that presumably are not subject to the whims of individuals. Look no further than the trust placed in sovereign governments as it compares with the trustworthiness of individual politicians.

Establishing unbroken trust chains between people and devices requires credentials to link them together. The cell-phone smart card that prevents fraud works only because the Telephone Company stands behind the unique link between the card and the subscriber. By issuing a smart card, the credential takes a physical form, which in turn elevates the computer-to-computer trust between components of the phone system ("This is the unique phone") into person-to-organization trust ("This call is billable to a known subscriber").

Of course, individuals can also grant credentials to other people and devices. In fact, there may be a legion of such structures that make sense only to that individual for bookkeeping within their own trusted environment ("I trust my dog to bring back the right newspaper").

As soon as one person has to share these facts with another, the seed of an organization has been planted. Settling a dispute with the neighbors may rely on the newspaper's subscriber label to establish ownership, and a service center may need to attest that your system is virus-free. As soon as more than one person or computer has to share trust, organizations will surely follow. As soon as we scale up to community identity, the very nature of the actor changes from person to organization, which completes our triad of principals.

# 4. Policies

*Our policy is, when in doubt, do the right thing.*
—Roy Ash, *Director of the Office of Management and Budget under Richard Nixon*

We can decide to permit or deny various actions by stringing together a proof from several principals' statements. For each action, there are specific *policies* that govern which statements suffice as justification. Trust Management engines like PolicyMaker and REFEREE literally take a subject, action, statements about the subject, and a policy controlling the action as input. Some policies are simple ("Approve the loan if any officer above the rank of branch manager says so"), whereas others are not ("Approve the loan only if the assets are above $A$, debt is below $B$ percent, returns are $C$ percent after taxes"), and some are just too ethereal to be expressed mechanically ("Approve the loan if the applicant is the manager's secret high school sweetheart"). In the realm of computer security, Trust Management tools are restricted to the former kinds of policies: automatable rules about chaining together statements from principals.

In many computer security applications, the rules are compiled in, so they are harder to recognize. The initial release of Microsoft Authenticode, as described in section 3, had a built-in policy that requires the various cryptographically proven "facts" about each principal to be combined into a sentence of a certain form. While it is easier to verify the correct implementation of a hardcoded policy ("Does this code ever leak top secret information to secret users?"), that inflexibility can be harmful in the market—as Microsoft learned with its policy sentences that favored commercial software publishers.

Since the Web encompasses such a wide range of applications, we should expect to see many, many different kinds of security policies. Sometimes a user will be in control, as when deciding what types of applets to execute; other times a publisher will be in control to enforce intellectual property rights (for example, "Do not display this font without a digitally signed proof-of-purchase"). Nevertheless, we can take a stab at systematizing a framework for thinking about policies, and categorizing the most popular approaches from traditional computer security.

A textbook treatment of authorization control centers around a simple table with the principals along one axis, objects along the other, and permissible actions at the intersections. Rather than transmit the fully expanded table in all its exponential glory, the first step in designing a security system is collapsing this treatment along one axis, as illustrated by a bank example in Table 1. This represents one specific bank management policy, which can be expressed in many equivalent ways by focusing on the principals, objects, or actions in it.

Though the complete table represents one specific way to manage a bank, it can be expressed in several equivalent ways, as described below.

*Principals*

> We can characterize the privileges granted to individual users and groups of users by explicitly listing each of the actions those individuals are permitted to apply to each object. A typical way to implement this is by labeling the principals with a strictly ordered security classification, and then labeling each object and action by the minimum- or maximum-level authorized user.

*Objects*

> By focusing on the individual information resources, we can label each permissible action with an explicit list of authorized users. This popular approach attaches an access-control list (ACL) to each object of interest.

*Actions*

> We can choose to manage the actions taken within the system. "Capability security"

labels each action or group of actions with a token. Then principals and objects are granted specific capabilities, which may or may not be further delegated. Several programming environments enforce this style of security.

These three ways of expressing policies also define three styles for determining policies. Choosing a language also influences your trust model: authorization based on *who you know*, *what you have*, or *what you can do*, respectively. The next three subsections explain the ramifications of these choices, including possible policies for the bank in Table 1.

## 4.1 Principal-Centric Policies

In popular culture, principal-centric security is far and away the most dramatic (and dramatically fallible) way to protect secrets. Spy novel conventions have familiarized us all with the model of sorting characters into "confidential," "secret," and "top secret" bins and compartmentalizing all information on a need-to-know basis. Agents could then read information at a lesser or equal clearance level, but write reports only at their own level.* This model can be extended to many more actions than read or write; for example, we can require minimum or maximum clearances for entering locked rooms or firing nuclear weapons.

In the mid-1970s, computer security theorists began to formalize this model and proved many of the basic insights of the field. Dorothy Denning [14] rigorously analyzed the flow of information in such systems to prove that, for instance, top secret information could never leak out though a secret report. Such proofs are possible as long as there is a well formed lattice—a kind of hierarchy—among all the clearances [15]. Around the same time, Bell and LaPadula published their famous model of secure computing systems along these lines [2]. Over the years, these principles were enshrined in the U.S. Department of Defense's requirements for trusted computer systems, as well as many other countries'. Real operating systems evolved along with the theory, from Bell and LaPadula's original work with Multics to the 1980s *Orange Book* certified A1-level secure computers [17] and the 1990s revised standards [42].

In our banking scenario in Table 1, we can easily identify a few levels of clearances. The *Branch Manager* has the combined power of the *Teller* and the *Guard* plus others. These are three separate roles because the principle of least privilege suggests that each role should be restricted to the minimum authority to do its job.

To summarize, the bank that chooses an identity-centric model tends towards a policy that *only certain people can be trusted*, and enforces it by checking the clearance of each principal proposing some action on an object.

## 4.2 Object-Centric Policies

A locked vault represents a simple security policy: without a guard to check clearances or limit the actions of entrants, anyone who has the combination has free reign. In this case, trusted access to one object depends on control of another, or sometimes a set of other objects, as in the case of a safe deposit box that requires two

**Table 1**     A Secure Access Authorization Matrix

|  | *Credit Line* | *Savings Account* | *Vault* |
|---|---|---|---|
| Branch Manager | Create, Read/Write | Create, Read/Write | Deposit, Withdraw |
| Teller | Read | Read/Write | Deposit |
| Guard | None | None | Withdraw |

---

* Or above their level, which leads to the comic consequence of not being cleared to read one's own reports.

separate keys, turned simultaneously by the customer and the bank.

With cryptography we move beyond the physical realm by substituting numbers for keys—even if those numbers are stored on smart cards. The principle remains the same, though. Consider the savings account in Table 1. An object-oriented security policy might require one key to access any particular account and another key to create one in the first place. The overall security policy is enforced by giving the former key to tellers and managers, but reserving the latter key for managers alone.

Sometimes the objects are neither unique nor even secrets. In the PGP Web of Trust, personal aquaintances sign each others' keys to establish identity within their own *ad hoc* community. When a random correspondent sends you a PGP message for the first time, you must establish trust that the signature key belongs to the person claiming to be the owner—the standard identity certification problem discussed in section 3.1. The default PGP policy is to rummage through your pile of (already trusted) friends' keys (that is, the objects you have) to construct an unbroken path ("Bob vouches for Clara; Clara vouches for Sara"); if this path construction is successful, it then has one more new binding to store away.

Finally, access to an object does not always mean free reign. The vault, for example, could have a deposit-only slot within a door, each with separate keys. Microsoft's Common Object Model (COM) [10] is an example that implements a similar situation in software. The savings account, if implemented as an ActiveX object, could have two interfaces—one for creation and another for read/write operations. Rather than using a generic pointer to the memory where the account data is stored, COM uses *handles* indicating which interfaces' actions are accessible. These handles are then passed between program components as needed; any part of the program that has the handle can take those actions on the target object (see section 4.3 for further discussion).

Handles, keys, and combinations are the essence of object-centric security policies. With this approach, security managers invest trust in and control distribution of a small number of objects. In the case of a bank, with its vaults and locked ledgers, the policy is that *only certain objects are trusted*. This is enforced by checking that a principal has an object representing permission to execute actions on another object.

## 4.3 Action-Centric Policies

The Community Boating program in Boston will let anyone who can swim 75 yards borrow a sailboat and take their chances on the muddy Charles. Oh, there is a membership fee, classes, and additional certification for solo ratings and particular craft, but the basic offer illustrates the nature of action-centric policies. In this case, the ability to swim out of harm's way is seen as sufficient to entrust a principal with access to a boat.

A closer look, however, tells us that swimming is not one of the actions traditionally applied to boating. What about tests in tying knots, basic physics, and navigation? Those activities are all actions one performs on a boat, just as reading and writing deposit entries and cash management are activities associated with a bank. Just as principal-centric policies ascribe trust levels to each user and object-centric policies ascribe trust policies to each artifact, one would imagine that action-centric policies should attach a list of trusted users and applicable objects to each and every action.

On closer inspection, though, identity-based policies evolved immediately into labeled compartments that grouped together many similar principals. Object-centric policies are most reasonable to manage where there are a few types of objects with many instances (for example, one key to access the ledgers for a thousand accounts). By extension, action-centric policies make the most sense when the myriad actions in a table can be simplified to a handful of broad capabilities. In fact, as discussed in section 4.4, the choice of policy approach depends mainly on the ease of abstraction along each axis for the application at hand.

Our bank could collapse its actions in Table 1 into three categories:

- Account bookkeeping

- Account creation

- Vault access (which might also be split into deposit and withdraw access)

Bookkeeping is the ability to read and write transactions to the ledger for an account—either savings or a credit line. Account creation, naturally, would cover the means for creating any account; this kind of generalization is especially useful as the list of objects changes over time (say, by adding checking accounts). The security manager would take the care to assign these capabilities in the right combinations to each principal, and also configure each object to demand evidence of the same before executing an action. This model represents a policy that *only certain actions are trusted*, and enforces it by checking the permissibility of any action by any principal to any object.

While this may work fine for our bank, it still does not explain how a swimming test proves seaworthiness (or Charlesworthiness as the case may be). Even Community Boating would admit that the ability to swim does not directly justify any of the skills of sailing. Policy, however, is in the eye of the beholder. In this case, it may not be obvious at first glance that CB's policy is not one that ensures members can sail, but one that ensures that members will not be injured. To fulfill the latter policy, proving the ability to swim across the Charles eliminates most risk; thus, CB will grant trusted access to boats.

On the other hand, CB might entrust you with a boat, but you might not trust yourself without those additional sailing-related capabilities—a small reminder that in any security analysis, several principals' policies may be at work. To safely entrust yourself at the helm, you might also take

some free classes and qualify for that solo rating. This demonstrates how often secure systems confuse capabilities with organizational credentials. Board-licensed beauticians, doctorates in computer science, and chartered public accountants can all testify to the value of a trusted credential. Sometimes, however, the trust may have more to do with the clout of the issuing organization, as would be the case with computer science departments or the local electricians' union.

These examples all illuminate the philosophy of action-centric security: execution privileges independent of the particular principal or object involved. Sometimes it can be difficult to differentiate a *capability* from the two other kinds of permissions assigned to principals or objects. The ability to purchase and consume alcohol is not assigned to individual people, since there is no registration process. It also is not a property of alcoholic beverages themselves, because bottles do not have any access controls.

### 4.4 Implementing Policies

As different as these three styles of policymaking can seem, they are equally powerful. The implementation details of any particular system usually drive designers toward one of the three approaches. Before considering the Web and its limitations, let's walk through one more real-world example of Trust Management: that is, entrusting people to hurtle through long narrow spaces at high speed, cocooned in explosive devices aimed at each other—driving an automobile. Consider these scenarios:

1. Angela wants to let only certain people drive her car. Angela's car is labeled with an access-control list of people's names or categories of approved people from a hierarchy (friends, coworkers, and in-laws). Angela's car has an ignition with a driver's license reader and fingerprint scanner to prove identity.

2. Brenda will let anyone drive her car. She might carefully check people out before

handing over her keys, but the car itself does not care who turns the ignition.

3. Carol is a member of the Wyoming Citizen's Car Collective. WC3 owns all of the cars in the state; it takes only a valid license and insurance policy in the smart card slot to drive off with one of these cars.

Because of the pragmatic details of car ownership and operations, Angela and Carol's policies are fantasies. Brenda's world reflects society's best balance of privacy, flexibility, and safety in view of the implementation costs. While Angela uses centralized identity registration and complex programmable car computers, she still permits unsafe drivers (since she uses only the license as an identity token). Carol's state does not have private cars, but the system is quite flexible (if there is a car to be found!) and safe because she uses licenses as capabilities. Brenda's system, however, is the simplest to implement: each car comes with a key, and that is that. She can delegate the car to anyone she wants to at any time, including unsafe drivers. Society complements her policy with its own rules (and police) to check safety and to recover stolen cars.

Precisely because each of the three policy approaches can yield different flavors of trusted systems, implementation concerns are the deciding factor favoring a primary policy framework for an application. The goal is to write the simplest, most compact policies, since they are easiest to validate and extend as the system evolves. This often means choosing policies along the simplest axis.

Our bank has a myriad of products and processes, but only a few levels of trusted personnel; hence, an identity-centric policy may be cheapest to implement and audit. Consider, too, which axis needs to be most dynamic, and avoid that one; driving access is extended to many principals, but the target is a single class of object, a car. A third concern is efficiency: it takes less effort to do an on-the-spot swimming test than an exhaustive background check, so Community

Boating opts for an action-centric policy. Conversely, the police's action-centric policy does not assess driving talent during a traffic stop; it checks the validity of a capability token (license) that was "precomputed" during a drivers test.

Real organizations with real policies are not so simple. Since policy is not the access matrix alone, but rather, the reasons *why* those decisions were made, two equivalent systems can be described using radically different policies. The identity-centric policies "any manager can approve a credit line" and "any Mormon can approve a credit line" might work for Bob the Mormon manager, but the former would be more directly responsive to the bank's mission than the latter. Occam's Razor slices in favor of the policy that best upholds the principles outlined in section 2.

For a bank with an identity-centric scheme, *be specific* implies precisely labeling all people, objects, and actions with their proper clearances and specifically checking identity on each access. Trouble often lurks when policy styles overlap: a hotel chain was once rebuked by a credit card company for using its cards (which merely prove the ability to pay) to open hotel door locks (incorrectly using it as proof of identity). Returning to a previous example, the bank's policy must trust only the bank's own clearances and controls. Finally, the bank's operations must be carefully audited and enforced in depth. After all, even a manager still needs a unique key to open a vault and can withdraw money only under video surveillance.

Even today's state-of-the-art HTTP servers do not have the full expressive range described in this section. They are limited to identity-centric access controls that sort humans and computers into groups by their passwords or IP addresses, respectively. These groups are then permitted certain actions (for example, GET but not DELETE) for certain objects (for instance, "only the */Drafts/* directory"). Web servers inherited this model from their underlying operating systems' file protections. The classic computer security solution for this was to have users log in, use those user IDs to label ownership of files, and then label each file with permitted actions (for example, "only the owner can write"). As a result, today's Web does not have the rich semantics for action- or object-centric security. When every transaction looks like a POST to program in the */cgi-bin/* directory, it is difficult to separate the capability to deposit from the capability to transact a withdrawal. When every resource is just an opaque stream of bits, it is difficult to protect "all files containing next year's budget figures." Soon, though, the Web will evolve beyond its roots as a file transfer tool and cast off such pragmatic limits.

# 5. Pragmatics

*Doveryay, no proveryay . . .*

*Trust, but verify.*
> —Ronald Reagan, *on signing the 1987 Intermediate Nuclear Forces Treaty, quoting a favorite phrase of Gorbachev and Lenin*

The mechanics of Web security are complicated by the open, distributed nature of its (un)trusted computing base. The topological shift away from a single secure node to a network of separately administered domains is driving the development of innovative Web-specific Trust Management protocols, format, and tools, as follows:

- Hierarchically administered Public Key Infrastructure (PKI) schemes will face competition from decentralized alternatives.

- Proprietary or obscure security related labels embedded in secure systems will have to adapt to an emerging Web metadata format.

- The wide range of trusted applications deployed over the Web will require a diverse base of policy languages.

- The complexity of establishing trust in this environment will justify unified, automated Trust Management tools.

These efforts will result in facilities for efficient, automatable trust calculations—worldwide!—thanks to common programming interfaces, which in turn will affect how we identify principals, assign labels to resources on the Web, and codify policies to manage both.

## 5.1 Identifying Principals

The first step in constructing a secure system is usually to identify the system's users, authorized or otherwise. In a few rare systems, we can forego this step by presuming physical security instead, but by default, we identify those principals' names or addresses with cryptographic secrets. Passwords are a common solution for closed systems, such as login programs. Public key cryptography is a far more secure way of managing such secrets, but the Web's radically decentralized trust model is catalyzing new systems for identifying the people, computers, and organizations holding such keys.[*]

A *digital certificate* [35] ensures the binding between cryptographic keys and its owner as a signed assertion. It is the missing link between the mathematics, which computers can verify, and the principals, who are controlled by policy. The challenge is in deciding who should sign that assertion and why. The traditional answer is that a Certificate Authority (CA) vouches for the binding, after investigating all of the germane details. With a certificate declaring "Joe Doaks' public key is 19, signed, UC Irvine," anyone else who also trusts UC Irvine will trust that messages encrypted by 19 are Joe Doaks'. Someone outside of the UC Irvine community could instead consult the next level of verification, searching for a Certificate Authority assertion declaring "The state of California trusts UC Irvine, whose public key is 23, to certify students' identities." The

---

[*] For more information on cryptography and the Web, see the article of the same name by Simson Garfinkel and Gene Spafford in this issue.

result is a classical hierarchical pyramid of CAs, an approach promoted by ISO's X.509 certificate format, X.400 addressing, and X.500 directory service.

The utility of a Certificate Authority is directly proportional to its *reach*: the size of the community willing to trust that CA. Climbing up the pyramid, CAs have ever greater reach, but with less specificity. UC Irvine can certify students, but the state of California may be able to certify only generic "citizens." This increases the CA's liability, as discussed below, leading to the reductionist nomination of sovereign governments as top-level CAs, with bilateral international cross-certification.

There is an opposite alternative: what if everyone just certified themselves ("self-signed certificates"), and others introduced themselves one-on-one, just like in real life? The PGP Web of Trust is a living example of such an anarchic certification system. The same pitfall resurfaces in a complimentary guise; in this case, the absence of a central trusted broker makes it very difficult to scale to large user groups such as "all UC Irvine students."

These scalability concerns are inevitable because general purpose identity certification violates the principles of Trust Management (see section 2). Without knowing the application at hand, a person or organization vouching for Joe Doaks' identity cannot *be specific* about the degree of trust involved. Does it mean that we can trust that anyone using the key 19 can now check out a library book, enter a locked dormitory, or accept a student loan? If someone tricks the certifier, who is liable—and for how much?

Second, relying on hierarchical CAs weakens the principle of *trusting yourself*, since it requires blanket trust in very large scale CAs, with corresponding conflicts of interest. If an MCI-er wants to talk privately to a Bell-head without being overheard by a Sprint-ee, he would be stuck constructing a certificate chain routed through some common parent CA such as VeriSign. This might be acceptable even if all three companies are VeriSign's clients, but what if VeriSign is a competitor?

Third, the logistical challenges of centralized certification make it difficult to *be careful* using these certificates. To verify any certificate, a validator must rummage through every CA's Certificate Revocation Lists (CRL) to be sure the key has not been cracked or canceled. As the number of certified users scales upward, the frequency of changes to the database, of invalidated keys, and so on, will increase, too, creating a logistical bottleneck.

As discussed in section 2.2, the two new decentralized PKI proposals, SDSI and SPKI, are better suited to the Web, and they respect the principles of Trust Management. As a result, they may be able to scale alongside the Web for the following reasons:

- They use application-specific certificates that identify exactly for what each key is authorized.

- Both systems literally construct a trust chain that must loop back to the user, instead of being diverted to some omnipotent CA—in fact, these systems directly inspired the *trust yourself* principle. The path might hop between individuals, like PGP, or between organizations, like X.509, but the final link must lead back directly to the user.

- Both systems offer simple, real-time certificate validation, which makes perfect sense for an online Web. This decision also leverages the shift toward online directory services for locating users in the worldwide haystack, such as the Lightweight Directory Access Protocol (LDAP) [32].

Moving to the decentralized Web will have other pragmatic implications for managing principals. The sheer scale of some applications, combined with the insecurity of client operating systems, may force the deployment of smart cards or biometric sensors such as fingerprints or voiceprints to protect keys. Of course, the Web can assimilate these innovations only if popular standards emerge as a common denominator for representing keys, certificates, and identities. The Web's key evolutionary advantage is that we can recursively invoke it to describe these artifacts using labels, as we will see in the next section.

## 5.2 Labeling Resources

The second step in constructing a secure system is describing the authorization matrix given in Table 1. As described in section 4, three primary styles are available. Principal-centric implementations label each principal with its clearance level, and label every object and action with its maximum or minimum clearance. Action-centric and object-centric implementations similarly label each with the required capability or access key. Whichever style of policy we choose, every element in the system ends up associated with *security metadata* that enforces access limits.

Traditionally secure computing systems wire these critical bits directly into data structures and files. For example, in UNIX-like operating systems with principal-centric policies, every running process is limited to the privileges of the owners recorded in the process table. Every file on disk is stamped with its user and group ownership, as well as an access control list declaring users' read, write, and execute permissions. Today's Web servers are a thin wrapper around these underlying security tools (see section 4.4).

According to the principle of specificity (section 2.1), we often need to label Web resources more explicitly than these tools allow. Rather than accepting an identity certificate *per se*, we may need to restrict it to a particular role. Rather than just offering blanket "execute" access, an applet may have particular restrictions attached to its runtime environment (see section 6.4). In addition, rather than implicitly grouping protected objects by their place in the file system's directory hierarchy, we may want to directly label "medical records" wherever they may lurk.*

While we could build mission-specific Web clients and servers with embedded classification bits, a more flexible solution would be to use separate security labels with general purpose label handling. Each of the conditions just mentioned could be captured as a separate statement bound by URL to a Web resource. Furthermore, the conditions themselves could be categorized into a systematic scale that is readable by machines. The result then seems indistinguishable from our null hypothesis: more mission-specific classification bits, except now they are pulled out into a label.

Three critical differences indicate that security labels are better suited to the Web than are traditional security attributes. First, the label can be considered a Web resource of its own: the label has a name, and thus it can be made available in several ways. The original resource's owner can embed a label within the resource, send it along with a resource, or obtain labels from entirely separate third parties. Second, the scales, or rating schemas, can reflectively be considered a Web resource. That is to say, the grammar of a machine-readable label can itself be fetched from the Web for use. It, in turn, can be further described by hypermedia Web documents, bridging the gap between machine-readable and human-readable information. Finally, labels are a safe choice because even though the security attributes are "floating around" separately from the resources, labels can be securely bound to Web resources by name and by hash. As a result of these three differences, labels are an excellent tool for Trust Management systems [33] [5].

Security labels must, however, address several pragmatic pitfalls to adapt to the Web. These concerns motivate convergence on a single metadata platform for a range of related Web applications. For example, language-negotiation and content-

---

* Medical records privacy is discussed in the article "The Electronic Medical Record: Promises and Threats," by Lincoln Stein.

negotiation can affect which variant of a Web resource a user receives. It may be acceptable to ignore this effect to rate "pages from *Playboy. Com* have sexual content," but a digitally signed assertion "© 1997 Playboy Enterprises" requires an exact digital hash of the a particular page, English or French, JPEG or PNG. W3C and its partners are developing a common link syntax for specifying such variants based on the eXtensible Markup Language (XML) [6].* Another benefit of reusing a common metadata format is its support for collections of labels, such as a combined manifest declaring copyright on all four page variants at once.

XML is also an excellent choice for generic metadata because it embodies the philosophy of self-description. Just as PICS labels can be described in terms of their schemas, XML tags are part of a Document Type Definition (DTD). Rather than emboldening a part number, for example, XML purchase orders could use the `<PART>` tag and explain what that tag means elsewhere. The strategy of interleaving machine-readable self-documentation and human-readable policy background is an excellent solution for encouraging automatable assertions and policies.

A key factor for this success is Web documentation of the Web itself. The need for self-reference is most acute at the boundaries of machine understanding, where the human judgment of policies comes into play.

## 5.3 Codifying Policies

The final step in implementing a secured system is populating the security access-matrix with authorization decisions according to some policy. This stage is the least amenable to standardization in practice, because Web design philosophy upholds the credo famously enshrined by the X Consortium: *Mechanism, Not Policy.* As a generic platform, the Web should be flexible enough to accommodate a wide range of applications with varying trust policies. One way to achieve this is to isolate policy decisions as local "black boxes." Using this strategy, Trust Management tools are an effective way to adapt to different policies, especially to integrate policies set by different sources.

The three policy styles discussed in section 4— principal-centric, object-centric, and action-centric—are only broad outlines. In practice, policies can recombine elements from all three, as well as incorporate completely independent criteria like the time of day. We can also expect policies to be codified in a variety of languages. One PICS filtering policy may be a simple numerical gamut; another may weigh the opinions of several ratings in different systems; a third may incorporate a Turing-complete content analyzer.

Language independence is only one half of achieving our Mechanism, Not Policy credo. The other key to preserving the flexibility of Web tools is to exchange assertions rather than policy on the wire. For example, in the payment-selection system developed for the Joint Electronic Payment Initiative (JEPI), both sides exchange lists of payment instruments they could accept or will reject. Both merchants and consumers have their own policies for their payment preferences: lower commissions on one, frequent flier miles with another, and no purchases above two dollars with a third. The alternative JEPI design would have been to exchange preference lists (that is, policies); this solution is more restrictive since it requires classifying all possible axes of preference in advance, permanently constraining the range of policies. JEPI's actual implementation is more verbose, but it can adapt to any rules that eventually emerge for electronic commerce. †

The REFEREE Trust Management system incorporates these lessons. Rather than using a single policy language, users load interpreters for as many languages as needed. This mix-and-match

---

* XML is the subject of the Fall 1997 issue of the *World Wide Web Journal.*
† See the article entitled "JEPI: Joint Electronic Payment Initiative" in the "W3C Reports" section of this issue.

approach works because there is a single, unified API for all trust decisions: given a pile of facts, a target, a proposed action, and its policy, we can determine if it is always, sometimes, or never allowed.

Another benefit of an integrated policy engine is the ease of composing policies for multiple authorities. For instance, a publisher, a child's parents, her school, and even the government may all be involved in deciding whether a Web page is appropriate for the child.[*]

## 5.4 Automating the World Wide Web of Trust

Trust Management provides an opportunity to return more control to the user—depending on your policy, you can seek out, collect, and manipulate all kinds of data. Rather than using a closed content selection system like Antarctica Online's policy ("All our content is okay, trust us"), users have the full power of PICS labels, from multiple sources, according to different systems, with personalized policies. Decentralized principal identification, the integration of security attributes with the Web metadata, and policy flexibility all advance the goal of automatable Trust Management through machine-readable assertions.

All of these projected shifts will justify developers' investments to make verifiable, quantifiable, machine-readable trust assertions. Tools like PolicyMaker and REFEREE reflect the "mechanized" vision of Trust Management that will move us forward. In the next section, we investigate some applications that will make this vision possible.

# 6. Applications

*In theory, there is no difference between theory and practice, But, in practice, there is.*

—Jan L.A. van de Snepscheut

A new wave of secure applications highlights the need for Trust Management on the Web, as a supplement to conventional cryptography. These applications, traditionally supported within closed, secure environments, must now cope with an open, distributed Web. There is also an accompanying shift away from closed, known user communities to open, publicly accessible service models, exacerbating the security analysis. In contrast, the Web is portrayed as a passive "library" of information for this new generation of "trusted" applications promises to move malls, banks, and city halls onto the Web, as well.

In the following sections, we discuss four kinds of applications that are already capturing the imagination of Web developers. By extending these archetypal systems to the Web, developers will also have to work further up the value chain to convince end users that these will be trustworthy systems. This places a premium on usability: developers must make their built-in security policies comprehensible to end users. These examples also provide a compelling argument to implement a unified Trust Management interface.

Web-based Trust Management is changing peoples' perception, both by clarifying relationships and by pointing to new technology. Web applications must leap across tall organizational trust boundaries when they become open. As a result, as systems grow outward, we need to establish interdependent trust in system components for citizens, parents, customers, and end users. This fosters a symbiotic coevolution between systems and their clients.

## 6.1 Secure Document Distribution

The publication of a presidential press release is nearly as complicated as how a bill becomes a law. First, a proposal is drafted by the press secretary's staffers. Secrecy is of paramount importance; even the *existence* of possible activity on an issue is a sensitive matter. An ongoing editing

---

[*] Christine Varney, FTC Commissioner, talks about children, the Web, and tools for blocking inappropriate pages in the Interview.

cycle can draw, *ad hoc*, upon the entire White House staff. Once it has the secretary's approval, a final draft is reviewed by other cabinet-level officials. Finally, the press release is made available on *www.whitehouse.gov*, but only after the president has affixed his digital signature.

This is a classic secure application: a controlled set of principals with different access levels—in this case viewing and editing—acting on a long list of protected documents. While the old process might have been implemented on a single mainframe system using operating system–level security, it is not flexible, scalable, or rich enough to handle today's document production cycle. At first glance, replacing it with a secured Web server seems like an excellent alternative; it offers more accessible clients, better collaboration tools, and an expressive format for linking it all together.

A closer look at using the Web as a secure authoring environment reveals many complications. At the very minimum, there is an open-systems integration challenge of replacing the old monolithic username/password database with an interoperable public key certificate infrastructure. On top of that, extending the trusted computing base to all those staffers' desktop PCs adds the potential risks of leaked documents left behind in users' caches, weak points for eavesdropping viruses and insecure key management.

The marginal benefit of editing a position paper from a cybercafe instead of a hardwired terminal in the office hardly seems worth the risk. The real benefit is that the Web of Trust surrounding these documents expands outward from authoring to distribution, access, and readers' evaluation. As the Web is used to cross those organizational boundaries, from White House to newspaper to ISP to citizen, it can leverage a common Trust Management infrastructure to identify speakers and to make assertions.

Within the White House, secured Web Distributed Authoring and Versioning (WebDAV) [48] servers are already slated to include metainforma-

tion management components for labeling documents, tracking revisions, and managing workflow among team members. These components must then tie into existing identity infrastructures for HTTP, such as White House smart cards and digital certificates. With these in place, a few hours before public release, the White House can pass an embargoed copy to the newspapers' distribution network. Unlike the old closed system, the trust boundary must now include a commitment from the newspapers to not redistribute the information before the stated time.

The newspapers need to operate their own trusted meshes of cache and mirror sites to bring the data nearer to their users for the big night. Or consider the newsstand, which is trusted by both parties to sit in the middle and shuffle bits around an efficient cache tree. Now a new kind of trust role emerges because of *intermediation*. We trust intermediation companites such as *ZippyPush. Com* to work on behalf of its subscribers to get fresh, safe copies of tasty bits within a reasonable amount of time. We also trust *ZippyPush.Com* to work on behalf of its publishers to get their copies out on time and collect subscription fees. We do not normally think of "trusted" news agents, but that is only because it is so expensive to fake a story in the real word; after all, too many trees would be wasted in the process.

The next step in the chain is access. People need to trust their servers; with a subscription model, there is mutual authentication of many, many people. As a result, there is significant need for a scalable PKI to identify principals, e-commerce issues such as payment protocols, and proof of privacy (see section 6.3). Tools like SSL can help in the establishment of *computer-to-computer* trust.

Ultimately, the publishers have to keep the subscribers happy; this requires readers to believe the integrity of published information as well as the meaning of the information. Whether for the president or the publishers, this whole process is valuable only if it increases the public's trust in the "official word" (and the words of supporters, opponents, and so on, helping to establish trust in Web content in general). In today's world of spoofable systems, it may take a while to discover false identities. In the future, especially with the malleability of digital media (such as hackable video, photographs, and even entire Web sites), digital signatures and assertions will become vastly more important.

This all culminates in very practical social consequences: how can we trust what our officials say? Worse, how can we trust *any* public document? Consider the infamous video of the Rodney King beating: when we surf over to *CNN.Com* and download the DVD stream, how can we articulate our outrage at the LAPD? And if we believe that the LAPD beat up a drunk driver, perhaps the Zapruder film is not so farfetched;[*] in this way, trust can easily be diffused. These critical questions *cannot* be addressed by any single one of the classic computer security solutions with their fixed trust templates. Each citizen has the right to establish trust in his or her own way. Some trust their neighbors (*community filtering*), some their religious leaders, some get tidbits from family, and so on. Some will trust the King tapes because of the identity of the cameraman (perhaps he's a former fraternity brother), because of the quality of his camera (perhaps we trust the manufacturer), or because of an organization (perhaps the U.S. government accepts it as legal evidence; more chillingly, perhaps a private corporation such as CNN declares its verity). Note that in all cases, trust is established through principles—via a person, computer, or organization.

The benefit of the Trust Management philosophy is its ability to dig beyond the traditional knee jerk reaction of "we need encrypted and authenticated server access" to ask *why* we actually need these things. The answer might be "so the public can trust what it reads"—and yet still come to trust information on its own terms. In essence, we are widening the scope of trust by redrawing the box around "trusted systems," and creating a synergy across the entire value chain, from authoring to publishing to distributing to accessing to reading.

## 6.2 Content Filtering

Selecting appropriate content from the Internet is yet another kind of trust question: "Do I trust my nine-year-old to visit *Playboy.Com*?" Asking that question across the entire universe of network-accessible information requires developing intermediated trust relationships; no closed system can hope to assess the exponentially growing Web on its own.

Many vendors today try to do just that, though. Blacklist screening software can consult a database of "bad" URLs and rules such as "ban URLs with xxx in them." Church, state, and citizen's groups have historically supported and enforced such schemes in traditional media by targeting the few trusted agents at the top: broadcasters, publishers, and filmmakers. The Web's distributed control and rapid growth continuously obsoletes such lists. Those factors also make it difficult to maintain whitelists of known "good" sites. Online services promise to be kid-safe by merely linking to a small set of resources. With URLs advertised on buses and fortune cookies these days, users are aware of many more safe sites than an organization can catalog. We therefore end up with either high false-negative or false-positive blocking rates. Furthermore, these two schemes can only handle the most clear-cut judgment calls: if .*edu* is fine, and sex is verboten, what does this imply about *sex.edu*?

To tackle a problem expanding as rapidly as the Web, we must harness it. After all, for every "fact" on the Web, there is an equal and opposite opinion—just codify and distribute them. The label pragmatics such as those afforded by PICS (see section 5.2) can scale because labels can be put on objects by the author or by a third party. The key is bootstrapping the meaning of each label.

---

[*] This was the film of the JFK assassination.

Machine-readable metadata labels themselves can leverage the Web through self-description—in fact, this ratings cycle is the key specificity, by offering a measurable, concrete rating that other trust calculators can then reuse.

Those calculators embody the *trust yourself* principle. Instead of a closed black- or whitelist system approach, each user's tools can decide to grant access depending on the opinions of several services (see section 5.3). We also need more flexibility regarding where these filters are placed within the network. In a traditional end-to-end security mindset, such filtering belongs exclusively at the periphery because there are only two players: publisher and reader. To properly represent the trust relationships in this application, we must account for entire households, schools, libraries, offices, and governments who have a say in what constitutes acceptable content. Filtering technology must be available within the network, controlled by administrators of such organizations.

Sometimes, though, the trust relationships are reversed: the publishers of intellectual property need to select who can access their resources. The same labeling infrastructure can be built into client software to, say, block the use of fonts that haven't been paid for. Rights management and privacy labels could be the basis for a new kind of purely electronic commerce in information goods, as described in the next section.

## 6.3 Electronic Commerce

Electronic commerce, contrary to media reports, is not a new idea. Many of the whiz-bang issues being debated today would be quite familiar to Richard Sears at the dawn of mail-order catalog sales over a century ago. Establishing trust in an invisible merchant, committing transactions over an insecure medium, individualized customer service, privacy, and taxation policy are not new risks; they merely exemplify the kind of factors free economies account for in stride.

The news about e-commerce is its scale, not in terms of business volume but in the size of businesses.* This round of making commerce more efficient is creating small, fast, disintermediated components. The *fin-de-siècle* "virtual corporations" are outsourcing their R&D, marketing, and production departments, even leasing back their own employees. We believe that the cause for this turnabout is that distributed, secure systems make it easier to whittle away at the "critical mass" of a trusted operation. Advertising, for example, was formerly kept within a firm's trust umbrella as an integral department in the age of paper. Today secure email, courier services, and electronic information systems for billing and bidding have obsoleted in-house advertising departments.

Electronic commerce systems are inspired by the tenets of classical computer security: closed systems with implicit rules built in to the system. When WalMart wants to integrate its suppliers' manufacturing capacity forecasts with its seasonal sales data, it has to actively manage access to a centralized data warehouse in Bentonville, Arkansas [9]. It might be acceptable to offer login IDs for a handful of partners, but the resulting Trust Management mushrooms in complexity. After all, WalMart's goal of automating restocking orders highlights the risk of asking suppliers how much of their product to buy. The result is a laundry list of small, focused electronic commerce collaboration tools. Vertical market acceptance of Electronic Data Interchange reflects a similar growth pattern. EDI purchase orders and invoices were foisted on the 50,000-odd firm automotive supplier chain under pressure from the Big Three. The result is "point-to-point" e-commerce, where EDI is used precisely for reducing paperwork.

Moving business relationships onto the Web opens the prospect of more intimate cooperation

---

* See the article "A Guide to Secure Electronic Business Using the E2S Architecture," by Mark Madsen and Andrew Herbert, for more on this topic.

on a broader scale. By merely deploying the Web as an information service, businesses can reduce their paperwork for publishing catalogs, soliciting bids, and providing technical support. Furthermore, escalating to "transactional" Web services will deliver even greater benefits. For example, collaborative product development is facilitated when a team whose members come from multiple companies can conveniently toss up a "virtual war room" with secure access for team members, and not other parts of the same companies—a common paradox in today's coop-etitive industries.

Whereas EDI today can deliver trusted purchase documents only across a single organizational boundary, tomorrow's distributed e-commerce systems will offer trusted collaboration tools, shared information services, secure payment, and settlement systems, which are expressly designed to knit a single trusted enterprise from separate parts. Consider CommerceNet's southeastern chapter real estate pilot project: it aims to seamlessly integrate the experience of buying a home by drawing on separate buyers' and sellers' agents, mortgage brokers, appraisers, and termite inspectors.[*]

Trust is much more central to the retail consumer experience because business-to-business trust is often a matter among equals. The "little guy" has the most to lose in dealing with the big company, which is more vested in brands, guarantees, and solidity.

Consumers' fears are being addressed on several fronts. Electronic payments players are migrating today's familiar tools to the Web, including e-checks, e-credit cards, and e-debit cards. The World Wide Web Consortium is working with CommerceNet to build Web-integrated solutions using JEPI. The key to such solutions is, again, reliable metadata: by labeling a Web site in exactly the way that today's storefronts are labeled with Mastercard, Visa, and American Express decals.

Another hot button is consumer privacy, currently being investigated by the W3C with the Internet Privacy Working Group (IPWG). TRUSTe and BBBonline are trying to license the use of a logo to businesses commercially, and W3C's Privacy Preferences Platform is based on specific, trusted labels of site policy. The latter can be automated in software screens, and it can be made available from third parties. This essentially puts the trust decision in the hands of the user, a clear victory for Trust Management thinking over the traditional closed-system thinking.

Finally, one of the most exciting frontiers for retail electronic commerce, intellectual property distribution will also drive Trust Management tools and infrastructure. Articles, songs, and movies all offer content for the e-commerce market, and the foundations for "pay-per-view" reside in cryptographic innovation: new watermarking algorithms, hiding license information in the content (*steganography*), packaging together multiple contents in a lockbox, and integrating content with trusted hardware and secure coprocessors [12]. However, since e-commerce involves fostering an agreement between a buyer and a seller, each of whom are masters of their own domains, the issues of this problem become much clearer if it is approached as a Trust Management challenge.

The market for finite-use intellectual property will not be enabled by a magic way of metering each original sale; rather, it will require an ongoing trust relationship in which the buyer agrees to not redistribute the content, or agrees not to use the content more than a specified number of times without paying more. For example, Corel is implementing its entire WordPerfect Suite in Java, with the hope that people eventually will be able to download an application from the Web and use it for a paid amount of time. Enforcement of this policy requires a significant trust relationship between Corel and the users downloading its code.

---

[*] Jim Galvin discusses CommerceNet's real estate pilot project in "Work in Progress" in this issue.

## 6.4 Downloadable Code

*The moral is obvious. You cannot trust code that you did not totally create yourself.*

—Ken Thompson,
*Turing Award Lecture* [50]

According to the media hype about the Web, perhaps the only phenomenon more wondrous, dangerous, and novel than "electronic commerce" is "mobile code." The risks of trusting downloadable code represent more back-to-the-future experiences to computer security experts. Once again, the critical difference is the shift from closed to open environments. Within secured systems, the primary threat was malfunctioning or malicious code; as a result, no code even entered a system without both a review and an administrator's explicit authorization. The advent of mobile code does not particularly exacerbate execution risks, as many of the security precautions mentioned below are unmodified from their original formulations. What it did ignite, though, was a wave of executable programs hopping across organizational trust boundaries. While doing nothing more serious than surfing to some random Web page, your browser might take the opportunity to download, install, and execute objects and scripts from unknown sources.

What is the matter here? This "ready, fire, aim" approach violates all three Trust Management principles we have discussed! If the truth be known, users themselves were never explicitly expected to trust new applets. Once invoked, however, applets have wide open access, because there are no specific limits on their trust. Worse, the initial tools shipped without either care to log and audit the activity of the downloaded code, or to defend against simple "system bugs" such as self-modifying virtual machines, unprotected namespaces, and loopholes in file-system access. The risks were evident right off the bat, triggering the wave of press hysteria that continues unabated. Let's take a look at some popular solutions to the problem of trusting code across organizational barriers.

As discussed in section 2.1, Microsoft does not have any runtime limits on its ActiveX components; in fact, the only control a user has is the initial decision to install it. Naturally, as the largest commercial consumer software publisher in the world, Microsoft is interested in offering some security policy to users. To that end, their Authenticode provides identity-centric policy based on VeriSign publisher certificates. Java, on the other hand, is a bytecode-interpreted language with wider scope for "sandboxing." JavaSoft and Netscape both promote policies based on granting or denying such capabilities. Their systems encourage developers to declare exactly what type of access they require, by analogy to some common models users might be familiar with: none (draw, no disk), video-game (draw, access just a few files), and word processor (full access) are a few examples.

In practice, no single security policy will suffice for safely using downloaded code, any more than a single policy can capture an entire household's morals for content filtering. Even the earliest secure operating systems, like Multics, had the foresight to combine identity and capability limits for executing code. Managing the trust placed in downloadable components will draw on the same list of Trust Management tools suggested throughout this paper: identity certification of authors and endorsers; machine-readable metadata about the trustworthiness of principals, objects, and actions; and flexible Trust Management engines that can compose the policies of end users, administrators, and publishers.

Deploying a common base of Trust Management tools seems like a goal that won't be achieved in the near future, but the intense industrial interest in the area will accelerate the development of standards. W3C's Digital Signature Initiative has worked to ensure industry consensus over the last year because it anticipated this interest.* As a result, the Consortium was able to harness the energy surrounding the "Java vs. ActiveX safety debate" [22] to propose and promote reusable, general purpose tools. The very title of the Digital Signature project is a good indication: W3C frames the problem as "helping users decide what to trust on the Web," and focuses not just on downloadable code. The initial target is a digitally signed PICS labels, which forms the technological foundation for any of the applications in this section.

# 7. Limits of Trust

> *The problem is not trust . . . the problem is how he will implement what has been agreed upon.*
>
> —Yasir Arafat *on Benjamin Netanyahu's trustworthiness, in* Newsweek, *June 19, 1997*

Even with the best of intentions, the interleaved elements of Trust Management still weave quite a tangled web. It seems much simpler merely to protect our information services in the name of Web Security and leave these "trust" decisions in their original (human) hands. In the long run, though, the Web to its descendents will evolve into a mirror of our communities in the real world. Trust relationships are the essence of human community, so automatable Trust Management in its many guises will become an integral part of those systems. By considering the ultimate limits of trust, it also becomes clear that not only will the Web need to adapt to today's social organizations; society will surely have to adapt to the Web as well. We need to work together as developers, webmasters, businesspeople, users, and citizens, to explore and settle this new frontier.

## 7.1 Limits of Web Security

> *"Pone seram, cohibe."*
> *Sed quis custodiet ipsos custodes? Cauta est et ab illis incipit uxor.*
>
> *"Bolt her in, keep her indoors."*
> *But who is to guard the guards themselves? Your wife arranges accordingly and begins with them.*
> —Juvenal *(c. 60–130* A.D.*),* Satires

Amid the headlong rush toward new protocols, ciphers, patches, and press releases to which the Web security industry seems addicted, it is easy to lose sight of the fact that conventional security technology, even if implemented perfectly, does not add up to Trust Management. If we narrowly protect Web transactions by securing them in a closed system we will never realize the full potential of the Web and integrate its users' trusted applications. Certainly, the Web of Trust will be built atop conventional Web security (see [45]), exploiting its services to the hilt: signatures, certificates, secure channels, and so on. Nevertheless, Web security alone, in the form of crypto-savvy servers and clients, cannot match the criteria set forth in this paper.

Fundamentally, the limitations of Web security depend entirely on the weaknesses of the individual services themselves. The Web as an information system does not publish political press releases, corrupt youth, sell books, or reprogram computers. It is just a request-response protocol for importing and exporting bags of bits from exotic locations across the network. If you draw a circle around Web clients and servers, you actually capture very little of the value people are deriving from the Web, since so much of the Web's power is hidden behind the curtains: CGI-BIN fill-in-the-form handlers, content databases, filesystems, caches, and ever-expanding browsers. "Securing a Web transaction" proves only that a pile of bits has moved from one machine to another without anyone peeking.

---

* See the specifications "DSig 1.0 Signature Labels: Using PICS 1.1 Labels for Digital Signatures" and "Digital Signature Label Architecture," for more about W3C's digital signature initiative.

We can protect Web transactions at three levels:

- In the Transport layer underlying HTTP
- Within the HTTP messages themselves
- In the content exchanged atop HTTP [34]

The Transport layer can provide only a secure channel; it cannot be used to reason about the protection of individual "documents" or of different HTTP "actions," since it is oblivious to them. Those decisions are properly part of the Application layer, driving the development of security within the HTTP messages. Finally, application developers can circumvent Web security entirely, and build their own end-to-end solutions, by using HTTP as a black box for exchanging files.

In the Transport layer, SSL and its successor TLS can provide channel security only between two processes. A temporary session key is set up for each cryptographic handshake between any client and server. The emphasis, however, is on "any": the only way to be sure that the device on the other end speaks for some person or organization is through patches that exchange X.509 hierarchical identity certificates. These protocols alone cannot further establish trust in those principals, because it is an "out-of-band" certification problem. Also, these protocols do not respect the trust topology, as evidenced by their ability to be spoofed with man-in-the-middle attacks [23].

At the Application layer, where such decisions ought to reside, security features are even weaker. With the lukewarm market acceptance of Secure HTTP (S-HTTP), today's developers have few options for securing Web semantics. Only recent fixes address the trust topology, authenticating to proxies in between as well as to original servers and clients. However, many desirable security mechanisms are still needed. For example, S-HTTP was able to cloak entire transactions, but with its passing, there is no longer a way to hide URLs.

Above the Application layer, security is flexible, but its gains are minimal without its underlying layers being secure. Similar problems occur with other "generic" tools; for example, firewalls and tunnels to form Virtual Private Networks cannot overcome security loopholes in the underlying infrastructure.

Web servers exhibit many potential security weaknesses with respect to the trust taxonomy we have outlined in this paper:

*Principles*

Web servers often disobey all of the principles set forth in section 2. Servers are often too broad and they have difficulty fully establishing trust in any action because they use the Web only as a carrier of information. HTTP servers cannot *be specific* because they cannot accurately identify the particular privileges that different groups might have.

Also, if you do not know the who, how, and what, you cannot *trust yourself*: Web servers often outsource work to the operating system, which is quite risky in and of itself. Furthermore, such outsourcing makes Web servers overly reliant on other subsystems' security, causing them to be vulnerable at multiple points of entry: the corruptible filesystem can be clobbered on the FTP, telnet, and email channels; viruses can make the operating system miserable; and poor extensibility features such as servlets might unintentionally reveal security flaws as well.

Adding insult to injury, Web servers have trouble *being careful*, too. Their logging features are rudimentary (that is, they flood the client with information, without any intelligent anomaly detection). Rollback is virtually nonexistent, due to the loose coordination with information sources; in response, WebDAV is attempting to retrofit the server with rollback in *one* aspect: versioning content.

*Principals*

Web servers cannot reliably identify any of our three types of principals. Worse, we rely on very weak security when Web servers need to make assertions today: passwords for users are often crackable, IP addresses spoofable, and DNS entries corruptible.

Sometimes we do have the right tool for determining principals but the implementation is in the wrong layer entirely: SSL client authorization does not propagate up, and passwords for one-time logins have to be reaffirmed for every (stateless) transaction.

*Policies*

Web servers offer very little flexibility in policy. As discussed in section 4.4, the security policies implementable in today's secure Web servers have difficulty obeying the principles set out in section 2.

Likewise, Web clients manifest many unsafe characteristics:

*Principles*

Web browsers have difficulty *being specific*; they work exactly the same for all of the locations in Web space. Users do not get to set policies specifically based on the subject of their conversations, although Microsoft has started providing very primitive "zones" in Internet Explorer 4.

Also, Web clients behave the same way for all active content, with no specific limits on the capabilities of components. At the very best, you have a little unbroken key icon, which contains nothing specific about the company to whom you are talking, as we have today with corporate logos and buildings. The net result is that tools offer no means by which to *trust yourself*. In fact, Web browsers often put us at the mercy of the trust of others: if *BigSWPub.Com* thinks its 0.99 beta is trusted to ship, you have no choice but to trust that the code is intact and ready to run. Users cannot actively establish trust with any of the sites with which they regularly correspondend.

Web browsers cannot *be careful*, again because clients are not integrated with hosts, so the potential is great for subsystems leaks. And we haven't even mentioned caches possibly sharing information with other "users," bugs in the so-called sandboxed virtual machines, and difficulties with logging activities.

*Principals*

User machines often have no idea of principals. Regarding *humans*, for example, Windows 95 has a weak concept of a uniquely identifiable user, and user IDs were easily cracked in early Windows NT.

Identifying *computers* is difficult, too, since the user interface often hides what little location cues there are, leading to spoofer sites [23] that complete the illusion by using JavaScript to disable the parts of the user interface that indicate with which computer the browser is talking.

In fact, the same attack works to subvert users' ability to identify *organizations*: today, spoofing seems to depend more on realistic counterfeit GIF images than anything else. Legitimate DNS battles over trademark status also cause confusion, such as the fight for the Web site *peta.org* between People for the Ethical Treatment of Animals and People Eating Tasty Animals.

*Policies*

Web clients can barely even claim to having security policies: often what little protection there is, is compiled in and not user-configurable. As discussed in section 4.4, the results violate all three principles we have discussed.

Recapitulating the security lessons of the last twenty years is not a very ambitious mark for the Web. We can do better and we *must* do better, because computers are not islands any more. Instead, the Web seamlessly interweaves computers with our "real world" activities: production (business), assembly (politics), and friendship (socializing). Web computing, whether we like it or not, is becoming an increasingly important element in the social contract of trust.

## 7.2 Trust as a Social Contract

*Trust is the result of a risk successfully survived.*

—Andy Gibb

Trust is not a decision; it is an ongoing process. Sara Surfer will have to try out her new auto-stock-picker and test its recommendations. Community Boating will have a word or two with you if you capsize a sailboat. Clara Customer can sue the bank for a penny out of place. In real life, principals build up trust over time, learning from shared experiences; for example, during the time you have read this paper, we, the authors, have been building trust with you, the reader. These relationships can then be codified as formal and informal contracts on specific issues, with their own measures for success and redress. Finally, communities can emerge from principals who share a trust relationship, ranging from a basketball team to a multinational corporation like MCI. As society coevolves with the Web, Trust Management tools must also automate the learning process, and not just the decisions.

Studying the process of trust-building would seem to be as sticky a tar pit as the philosophy or morality of trust. In fact, however, mathematicians and economists have been studying formal models of trust-building in the field of Game Theory, ever since von Neumann invented it in the 1940s [51]. Through simulation and analysis of game trees, we can begin to quantify how trust compares favorably to suspicion, how players discover trust, and how communities that trust each other can emerge.

Consider the classic Prisoner's Dilemma, in which two noncommunicating principals decide whether to reveal to the police that the other one mastermind the crime. If neither principal talks to the police (that is, they trust each other to cooperate without communicating), they both get light jail sentences because the police have no evidence but lots of circumstantial data. If both principals talk to the police (that is, they do not trust each other enough to cooperate without communicating), they both get heavy sentences because the police have lots of evidence of premeditated conspiracy. If one principal talks and the other does not, the one who talks gets out of jail free, while the other one gets an extremely heavy sentence because the freebird is willing to take the stand to convict him. The "dilemma" comes from each party wondering if he can trust the other party without direct communication.

Each player should independently choose to defect from the trust relationship to avoid being sold out by the other in exchange for freedom. They might even believe that they are better off trusting each other (thus securing light jail sentences for both). But since the situation is a one-shot trial, double- and triple-think leads back to a greedy defector's end* and a heavy jail sentence. When the economics theorists add a twist—such as, what if the "game" continued every day indefinitely so the participants had to play many times—we discover that trust emerges as a viable option. However, to glean trust the game must be perceived as ongoing and without foreseeable end: if the cops tell the prisoners they will interrogate them for only a week, the prisoners can look ahead, work backwards, determine that it is in their best interests to squeal, and still always defect.

If the situation is ongoing, however, a whole new pattern emerges: cooperation can become stable (*the discovery of trust!*). Axelrod added a second twist [1]: what if you were playing this "game" against a community of other people, one at a time? He proposed a competition of different behaviors: pitting a wide-eyed cooperator, a cynical defector, and a host of in-between strategizers in a multiround competition. The clear victory of one strategy proved a final point: *An entire community can slowly learn to trust each over over time.* The winning strategy was, in fact, tit-for-tat: I will do whatever the last person did to me. This

---

* Thanks to the principle *trust yourself!*

strategy was a *universal* winner over every other. So there we have it, the duality between cooperation and retaliation. Apparently learning comes from positive *and* negative feedback, after all.

The balance between cooperation and defection is what leads to the abstraction of *trust as a contract*. Rather than accept the full risk of cooperating while others defect, we rely on effective redress to define the limits of trust (thereby defining trust as a process derived through its contracts). This is not the classical definition of trust: in computer security or Web security, trust is a decision you get by inserting facts and policy and turning the crank. Note that in the real world, *transactions are never based on brittle, infinite trust*: for example, because of the airlines' practice of overbooking, you are never absolutely guaranteed an airline seat, and your bank account statement is never final in case errors are discovered. We have the following two ways to mechanically implement these limits:

- *Auditing* (that is, logging and analyzing the outcomes of each trust decision) lets us detect intruders and identify buggy programs, among other things. Both ActiveX and Java code security use this technique, for registering each foreign applet loaded and for tracking their behavior (logging for COM; sandboxing for Java).

- *Rollbacks*, which executable code systems do not have access to. An effective redress for a trust violation is undoing its effects as far as possible. For example, in some cases, it may be fine to let anyone write to the server as long as there are backups. If a bank check clears into the wrong account, there is a window to roll it back (three days in the U.S.). Sometimes rollback is only approximately achieved: fraudulent credit card use costs the holder only $50 in the U.S., but the bank must absorb any losses due to fraudulent charges above and beyond that amount.

Sometimes the best way to build trust is *not* to have rollback—for example, notarized documents. Surety Technologies is licensing a very clever and simple way of entangling your document notarization signature with that of everyone else in the world who notarizes a document in the same time window [31], yielding a single number at the top of the CA pyramid, which is published in the *New York Times*. Here, the only way to forge the timestamp is to get *everyone else* in on your lie; so even if you do not trust some of the individuals in the tree, you can still trust the entire tree. In general, though, if your trust is violated without redress (such as refunding your money), society calls it a crime: libel, theft, even murder.

Thus, to model trust fully within the Web, we need to acknowledge that trust is a social contract, a learning process. Our Web of Trust has to work precisely the same way. With respect to filtering objectionable content, we need to learn from our friends, neighbors, and organizations what is and is not acceptable. Machine readable ratings make this learning possible, because we can both fetch the facts from many people, and learn metainformation from these facts because they are machine-readable. We want downloadable-code managers that track which ways programs fail or cause security holes, and dynamically remove those programs or patch those holes. We also need to learn in redundant ways; for example, we may need to check out a new game against several policies. Is it virus-free? Is it above three-stars on the *PCPundit* rating scale? Is is not too violent or sexual? The result of learning may be dynamic, self-modifying policies for taking various actions. This is another good reason for developing a common Trust Management API: PolicyMaker and REFEREE have already demonstrated power of policies written in many languages (see section 5.3).

Representing this rich and subtle model of trust will help us contain the Pandora's box of complexity we have unleashed. In the conventional security world, generations of eunuchs worked to define the security perimeter of an application as narrowly as possible and to make mechanical trust decisions. Now, we insist that the Web of Trust supports all manner of applications that reach out of the box, intertwining many parties' trust concerns. It is not enough to distribute a document securely. We need to build confidence that the client and server computers are sending documents with integrity and privacy, that the author was trusted to speak for the organization, and that the reader can trust the author's words. In embracing the messy real-world nature of trust, we naturally encounter the limitations to Trust Management. As we automate the real-world, we can automate only those trust decisions that we can ultimately audit and/or roll-back: we will need people in the loop if we are going to bring our communities onto the Web.

## 7.3 Trust in the Mirror

*A Mirror World is some huge institution's moving, true-to-life mirror image trapped inside a computer—where you can see and grasp it whole. The thick, dense, busy subworld that encompasses you is also, now, an object in your hands.*

—David Gelernter
Mirror Worlds [29]

With each new home page, mailing list, and transaction, another community finds its reflection on the World Wide Web. Soon, their trust relationships—the very essence of community—will be automated onto the Web, too. As the Web and its descendents evolve into a Mirror World, they will need to adapt to the human trust relationships, but just as inevitably, human trust relationships will have to adapt to digital management. Mirror Webs will distort the nature of trust—and thus, communities—by creating new kinds of agreements and by shattering old ones.

Consider the changes wrought upon one very large community being reflected onto the Internet: people who use money. Currencies represent a community of customers, merchants, citizens,

and bankers who choose to have trust it—after all, even the Almighty Dollar is inscribed, "In God We Trust." There are myriad payment systems atop each currency: checks, credit cards, debit cards, and so on. The race is on to find their electronic equivalents, but not their clones. The root of the difference is that in cyberspace, cryptography has to substitute for atoms: gone are the old certainties of pen-and-ink signatures, fingerprints, and the physical truth that if I spend a dollar, I cannot keep it.

The new risks of the electronic world—sniffers instead of snipers—have catalyzed a slew of competing electronic payment systems [47]. Each is a dance with the same four dancers: payer, payee, and their respective banks, but with different steps. The resulting combinations of information flows, trust relationships, and risk allocations rewrite the social contracts establishing banks, credit card associations, and other financial communities. Their foundations reside in the trust required to accept risks, but instead of holding a mirror to today's money, the Internet has become more like a kaleidoscope.

The Mirror Web also magnifies latent flaws in existing trust relationships. Consider the U.S. Social Security Administration's ill-fated attempt to put its records on the Web.[*] Each American worker has a trust relationship with the SSA regarding his pensions, sealed by the "secrecy" of his social security number, mother's maiden name, and birth state. For decades, those were the keys to obtaining one's Personal Earnings and Benefit Estimate Statement (PEBES). When the exact same interface was reflected on the Web, nationwide outrage erupted over the perceived loss of privacy, resulting in a hurried shutdown and "reevaluation" [28].

In this case, fast and easy HTTP access has raised the potential for large-scale abuse not present in the original, postal system. The SSA is stuck with a trust relationship that is not represented by a

---

[*] See the "Works in Progress" interview of Jim Galvin for more information.

corresponding secret, so cryptography cannot solve their problem. The irony, though, is that they do share one secret record with each worker: that worker's earnings history—which is why workers request a PEBES in the first place!

In the end, there will have to be a more secure way of accessing such records—perhaps with a digital identity certificate corresponding to today's Social Security Card. Such precautions may even strengthen how the "traditional" paper system works, demonstrating one kind of distortion from the Mirror Web. Cryptography can offer much stronger proof than traditional means, so trust relationships will tend to be cemented with shared secrets that enable those protocols, such as PIN numbers, shared keys, and credentials. A second distorting consequence of the Mirror Web is that making trust easier to establish, audit, and revoke will increase the number of boundaries and trust relationships in society. If the transaction costs of creating and maintaining trusted communities (such as corporations) fall, the inevitable result will be smaller communities. If economic downsizing is not a distorting enough aspect of the Mirror Web, consider an Information Society where fringe groups can "drop out" of the mainstream and stay that way through narrowcasting. Even non-fringe groups can have an impact: until the Chinese uphold intellectual property rights or India recognizes process patents, no level of cryptography can force their PCs to do so.

## 8. Weaving a Web of Trust

*We believe in the interconnectedness of all things.*

—Douglas Adams,
*Dirk Gently's Holistic Detective Agency*

Rather than changing existing technology, adopting the philosophy of Trust Management changes our *attitudes* on how to apply that technology. To summarize, the components include the following:

*Principles*

When deciding to trust someone to take some action with some object, it is absolutely critical to *be specific* about the privileges granted, to *trust yourself* when vouchsafing the claim, and to *be careful* before and after taking that step.

*Principals*

The decision to grant trust is constructed from a chain of assertions, leading to permission. Three kinds of actors are making the assertional links based on their particular identity lifetimes: *people* make assertions with broad scope, bound to their long-lived *names*; *computers* make narrow proofs of correct operation from their limited-scope *addresses*; and *organizations* make assertions about people and computers because they have the widest scope of all. *Credentials* describe each kind of principal and its relationships, such as membership and delegation.

*Policies*

There are rules about which assertions can be combined to yield permission. Broadly speaking, policies can grant authority based on the *identity* of the principal asking, the *capability* at issue, or an *object* already in hand. In other words, you might be trusted based on *who you are*, *what you can do*, or *what you have*.

*Pragmatics*

Deploying a Trust Management infrastructure across so many administrative boundaries on the open, distributed Web requires adapting to pragmatic limitations. Since objects can live anywhere on the Web, so can their security labels. Furthermore, such labels should use a common, machine-readable format that recursively uses the Web to document its language. The real benefits of Trust Management come from tying all of these details together within a single Trust Management engine. This will drive a handful of standard protocols, formats, and APIs for representing principals and policies.

We note, however, that Trust Management is no silver bullet. It will be a long struggle to weave a Web of Trust out of the scattered parts invented in our quest for Web security. There is a lot going for the always-cheaper, always-simpler, head-in-the-sand approach of merely securing Web transactions, instead of attempting to secure Web communities. Everyone has a role to play in bringing this vision to fruition:

### Web developers

The people and organizations ultimately responsible for reducing Web standard formats, protocols, and APIs to practice in software and hardware should be committed to developing Trust Management technologies. They should become engaged in the current standardization debates surrounding public key infrastructure (the SPKI/SDSI working group at the IETF), digital signatures (in the legislatures and courts as well as IETF and W3C), and formats for adding security and trust metadata to the Web (at W3C). Looking further ahead, they should be aware of the latest research in this new approach to computer security, such as the 1996 DIMACS Workshop on Trust Management [7].

### Web users

Users have the power to make developers follow this agenda: this is the power of the purse. Web users should be aware of the laundry list of trust decisions confronting them every day: whether they are talking to the right organization, whether they should run an applet, or whether to allow their children to access a site. They are in the best position to demand that client and server toolmakers help automate these judgments.

### Application designers

The businesspeople, programmers, and regulators responsible for creating and controlling new, secure Web applications should use the concepts described in this paper to identify and control security risks. Upholding the principles of Trust Management, identifying principals, constructing policies, and integrating these principles with the Web are not just a cryptographer's problems. Each party of applications development process should think carefully about whom they are trusting, in what roles, to permit what action, for what time period.

### Citizens

The emergence of the Web as a social phenomenon will even affect people who do not use the Web. As informed citizens, we have to consider the impact of automating trust decisions and moving our human bonds into WebSpace. Trust Management tools allow communities of people to define their own world views—but should we allow the KKKnet to exclude the truth about the Holocaust? What are the social consequences of fragmenting our trust communities?

If we all work together, automatable Trust Management could indeed weave a World Wide Web of Trust, spun from the filaments of our faith in one another. ∎

## Acknowledgments

A broad survey paper springboards from the minds of innumerable correspondents. "Weaving a Web of Trust" is based on over two years' experience working with the Web security community. Particular plaudits go to colleagues at the World Wide Web Consortium, including Jim Miller, Phill Hallam-Baker, and Philip DesAutels; W3C's Security Editorial Review Board, including Ron Rivest, Butler Lampson, Allan Schiffman, and Jeff Schiller; the AT&T-centered team behind the "Trust Management" concept, including Joan Feigenbaum, Yang-Hua Chu, and Brian LaMacchia; and fellow Web security researchers Carl Ellison and Mary Ellen Zurko. We also thank Ross Anderson and Megan Coughlin for their suggestions to improve this document.

# References

1. Axelrod, Robert. *The Complexity of Cooperation: Agent-Based Models of Competition and Collaboration*, Princeton University Press, 1997. Available at *http://pscs.physics.lsa.umich.edu/Software/ComplexCoop.html*

2. Bell, David E. and L.J. LaPadula. "Secure Computer Systems: Unified Exposition and Multics Interpretation," MTR-2997 Revision 1, MITRE Corporation, Bedford, MA, March 1976.

3. Blaze, Matt, Feigenbaum, Joan, and Jack Lacy. "Decentralized Trust Management," *Proceedings of the 1996 IEEE Symposium on Security and Privacy*, IEEE Computer Society Press, Los Alamitos, 1996, pp. 164–73. Available as a DIMACS Technical Report from *ftp://dimacs.rutgers.edu/pub/dimacs/TechnicalReports/TechReports/1996/96-17.ps.gz*

4. Blaze, Matt, Feigenbaum, Joan, and Jack Lacy. "The PolicyMaker Approach to Trust Management," DIMACS Workshop on Trust Management in Networks, South Plainfield, NJ, September 1996. (1996b) Available at *http://dimacs.rutgers.edu/Workshops/Management/Blaze.html*

5. Blaze, Matt, Feigenbaum, Joan, Resnick, Paul, and Martin Strauss. "Managing Trust in an Information-Labeling System," *European Transactions on Telecommunications*, 1997. Available as AT&T Technical Report 96.15.1, *http://www.research.att.com/~presnick/papers/bfrs/*

6. Bray Tim, and C.M. Sperberg-McQueen. "Extensible Markup Language (XML): Part I. Syntax," World Wide Web Consortium Working Draft (work in progress), March 1997. Available at *http://www.w3.org/pub/WWW/TR/WD-xml-lang.html*

7. Brickell, Ernie, Feigenbaum, Joan, and David Maher. DIMACS Workshop on Trust Management in Networks, South Plainfield, NJ, September 1996. Available at *http://dimacs.rutgers.edu/Workshops/Management/*

8. Brookson, C. "GSM Security: A Description of the Reasons for Security and the Techniques, IEEE Colloquium on Security and Cryptography Applications to Radio Systems," 1994, pp. 1–4. Available at *http://btlabs1.labs.bt.com/bookshop/papers/4720987.htm*

9. Caldwell, Bruce. "Wal-Mart Ups The Pace," *Information Week*, December 9, 1996, pp. 37–51.

10. Chappell, David. *Understanding ActiveX and OLE*, Microsoft Press, 1996.

11. Chu, Yang-Hua, Feigenbaum, Joan, LaMacchia, Brian, Resnick, Paul, and Martin Strauss. "REFEREE: Trust Management for Web Applications," *Proceedings of the Sixth International World Wide Web Conference*, Santa Clara, CA, April 1997. Available at *http://www6.nttlabs.com/HyperNews/get/PAPER116.html* and in this issue of the *World Wide Web Journal*.

12. Cox, Brad. *Superdistribution: Objects as Property on the Electronic Frontier*, Addison-Wesley, 1996.

13. Dean, Drew, Felten, Edward W., and Dan Wallach. "Trust Management In Web Browsers, Present and Future," DIMACS Workshop on Trust Management in Networks, South Plainfield, NJ, September 1996. Avaliable at *http://dimacs.rutgers.edu/Workshops/Management/Felten.html*

14. Denning, Dorothy E. "A Lattice Model of Secure Information Flow," *Communications of the ACM*, vol. 19, no. 5, May 1976, p. 236–43.

15. Denning, Dorothy E. *Cryptography and Data Security*, Addison-Wesley, 1982.

16. Dierks, Tim, and Christopher Allen. "The TLS Protocol," version 1.0, Internet Draft (work in progress), May 1997. Available at *ftp://ietf.org/internet-drafts/draft-ietf-tls-protocol-03.txt*

17. Department of Defense/NCSC. "Trusted Computer System Evaluation Criteria" ("The Orange Book"), DoD 5200.28-STD, 1985. Available at *http://www.radium.ncsc.mil/tpep/library/rainbow/5200.28-STD.html*

18. The Economist. "Tremble, Everyone," *Economist Survey on Electronic Commerce*, May 10 1997, p. 10.

19. Ellison, Carl. "SPKI Certificates," DIMACS Workshop on Trust Management in Networks, South Plainfield, NJ, September 1996. Available at *http://dimacs.rutgers.edu/Workshops/Management/Ellison.html*; see also the SPKI page at *http://www.clark.net/pub/cme/html/spki.html*

20. Ellison, Carl, Frantz, Bill, Rivest, Ron, and Brian M. Thomas. "Simple Public Key Certificate," Internet Draft (work in progress), April 1997. Available at *http://www.clark.net/pub/cme/spki.txt*

21. Electronic Privacy Information Center. "Surfer Beware: Personal Privacy and the Internet," June 1997. Available at *http://www.epic.org/reports/surfer-beware.html*

22. Felten, Edward W. "Security Tradeoffs: Java vs. ActiveX," April 1997. Available at *http://www.cs.princeton.edu/sip/java-vs-activex.html*

23. Felten, Edward W., Balfanz, Dirk, Dean, Drew, and Dan S. Wallach. "Web Spoofing: An Internet

Con Game," Princeton University Technical Report 540-96 (revised), revised February 1997. Available at *http://www.cs.princeton.edu/sip/pub/spoofing.html*

24. Fielding, Roy, Gettys, Jim, Mogul, Jeff, Frystyk, Henrik, and Tim Berners-Lee. "Hypertext Transfer Protocol—HTTP/1.1," RFC 2068, January 1997. Available at *http://www.w3.org/Protocols/rfc2068/rfc2068* and in the Fall 1996 issue of the *World Wide Web Journal.*

25. Franks, John, Hallam-Baker, Phill, Hostetler, J., Leach, P., Luotonen, A., Sink, E., and L. Stewart. "An Extension to HTTP: Digest Access Authentication," RFC 2069, January 1997. Available at *http://www.w3.org/Protocols/rfc2069/rfc2069* and in the Fall 1996 issue of the *World Wide Web Journal.*

26. Freier, Alan O., Karlton, Philip, and Paul C. Kocher. "The Secure Sockets Layer Protocol," version 3.0, Internet Draft (work in progress), November 1996. Available at *ftp://ietf.org/internet-drafts/draft-ietf-tls-ssl-version3-00.txt*

27. Garfinkel, Simson. *PGP: Pretty Good Privacy*, O'Reilly & Associates, 1994.

28. Garfinkel, Simson. "Few Key Bits of Info Open Social Security Records," *USA Today*, May 12, 1997, p. A1.

29. Gelernter, David. *Mirror Worlds: The Day Software Puts the Universe in a Shoebox . . . How it Will Happen and What it Will Mean*, Oxford University Press, 1991.

30. Gundavaram, Shishir. *CGI Programming on the World Wide Web*, O'Reilly & Associates, 1996.

31. Haber, Stuart, and W. Scott Stornetta. "How to Time-Stamp a Digital Document," *Journal of Cryptology*, vol. 3, no. 2, 1991, pp. 99–112.

32. Howes, T., and M. Smith. "The LDAP Application Program Interface," Internet Draft (work in progress), RFC 1823, August 1995. Available at *ftp://ietf.org/internet-drafts/draft-howes-ldap-app-00.txt*

33. Khare, Rohit. "Using PICS Labels for Trust Management," DIMACS Workshop on Trust Management in Networks, South Plainfield, NJ, September 1996. Available at *http://dimacs.rutgers.edu/Workshops/Management/Khare.html*

34. Khare, Rohit. "Security Extensions for the Web," RSA Data Security Conference, 1996. (1996b) Available at *http://www.w3.org/pub/WWW/Talks/960119-RSA/*

35. Kohnfelder, Loren M. "Towards a Practical Public-Key Cryptosystem," B.S. thesis supervised by Len Adleman, May 1978.

36. Koster, Martijn. "A Method for Robots Control," Internet Draft (work in progress), *draft-koster-robots-00.txt*, December 1996. Available at *http://info.webcrawler.com/mak/projects/robots/norobots-rfc.html*

37. Lampson, Butler, Abadi, Martin, Burrows, Michael, and Edward Wobber. "Authentication in Distributed Systems: Theory and Practice," Digital SRC Research Report 83, February 1992. A nice mathematical treatment of trust, available at *http://gatekeeper.dec.com/pub/DEC/SRC/research-reports/abstracts/src-rr-083.html*

38. Lampson, Butler, and Ron Rivest. "SDSI—A Simple Distributed Security Infrastructure," DIMACS Workshop on Trust Management in Networks, South Plainfield, NJ, September 1996. Available at *http://dimacs.rutgers.edu/Workshops/Management/Lampson.html*; see also the SDSI page at *http://theory.lcs.mit.edu/~cis/sdsi.html*

39. Leveson, Nancy G., and C.L. Turner. "An Investigation of the Therac-25 Accidents," *IEEE Computer*, July 1993. Also appears as Appendix A of Leveson, Nancy G., *Safeware: System Safety and Computers*, Addison Wesley, 1995.

40. Microsoft. Microsoft Authenticode Technology, 1997. Available at *http://www.microsoft.com/security/tech/misf8_2.htm*

41. Neumann, Peter G. *Computer-Related Risks*, Addison Wesley, 1995.

42. NIST/NSA. "Federal Criteria for Information Technology Security," vols 1 and 2, version 1.0, December 1992. Federal Information Processing Standard (FIPS) to replace the NCSC's "Orange Book."

43. Park, Steve, and Keith Miller. "Random Number Generators: Good Ones Are Hard to Find," *Communications of the ACM*, vol. 31, no. 10, October 1988, pp. 1192–1201.

44. Resnick, Paul, and Jim Miller. "PICS: Internet Access Controls without Censorship," *Communications of the ACM*, vol. 39, 1996, pp. 87–93. Available at *http://www.w3.org/pub/WWW/PICS/iacwcv2.htm*

45. Rubin, Avi, Geer, Dan, and Marcus Ranum. *Web Security Sourcebook*, John Wiley and Sons, 1997. Available at *http://www.clark.net/pub/mjr/websec/oview.htm*

46. Schneier, Bruce. "Applied Cryptography: Protocols, Algorithms, and Source Code in C," 2d edition, John Wiley and Sons, 1996. Available at *http://website-1.openmarket.com/techinfo/applied.htm*

47. Sirbu, Marvin A. "Credits and Debits on the Internet," *IEEE Spectrum*, February 1997, pp. 23–29.

48. Slein, J.A., Vitali, F., Whitehead, E. Jim Jr., and D.G. Durand. "Requirements for Distributed Authoring and Versioning on the World Wide Web," Internet Draft (work in progress), May 1997. Available at *ftp://ietf.org/internet-drafts/draft-ietf-webdav-requirements-00.txt*

49. Stein, Lincoln D. "The World Wide Web Security FAQ," version 1.3.7, May 1997. Available at *http://www-genome.wi.mit.edu/WWW/faqs/www-security-faq.html*

50. Thompson, Ken. "Reflections on Trusting Trust," *Communication of the ACM*, vol. 27, no. 8, August 1984, pp. 761–63. Available at *http://www.acm.org/classics/sep95/*

51. von Neumann, John, and Oskar Morgenstern. *Theory of Games and Economic Behavior*, 2d edition, Princeton University Press, 1947.

52. Wallach, Dan S., Balfanz, Dirk, Dean, Drew, and Edward W. Felten. "Extensible Security Architectures for Java," Princeton University Technical Report 546-97, April 1997. Available at *http://www.cs.princeton.edu/sip/pub/extensible.html*

## About the Authors

### Rohit Khare

*editorial@w3j.com*

Rohit Khare is a member of the MCI Internet Architecture staff in Boston, MA. He was previously on the technical staff of the World Wide Web Consortium at MIT, where he focused on security and electronic commerce issues. He has been involved in the development of cryptographic software tools and Web-related standards development. Rohit received a B.S. in Engineering and Applied Science and in Economics from California Institute of Technology in 1995. He expects to join the Ph.D. program in computer science at the University of California, Irvine in Fall 1997.

### Adam Rifkin

*adam@cs.caltech.edu*

Adam Rifkin received his B.S. and M.S. in Computer Science from the College of William and Mary. He is presently pursuing a Ph.D. in computer science at the California Institute of Technology, where he works with the Caltech Infospheres Project on the composition of distributed active objects. His efforts with infospheres have won best paper awards both at the Fifth IEEE International Symposium on High Performance Distributed Computing in August 1996, and at the Thirtieth Hawaii International Conference on System Sciences in January 1997. He has done Internet consulting and performed research with several organizations, including Canon, Hewlett-Packard, Griffiss Air Force Base, and the NASA-Langley Research Center.

# CRYPTOGRAPHY AND THE WEB

W3J

*Simson Garfinkel with Gene Spafford*

## Abstract

*Encryption is the fundamental technology that protects information as it travels over the Internet. Although strong host security can prevent people from breaking into your computer—or at least prevent them from doing much damage once they have broken in—there is no way to safely transport the information that resides on your computer to another computer over a public network without using encryption. Encryption is fundamental to World Wide Web security. This article, excerpted from Web Security & Commerce (O'Reilly & Associates, 1997), discusses the many different cryptographic techniques that keep information secure.*

There are many cryptographic techniques, each addressing a different need. In some cases, the differences between encryption systems represent technical differences—after all, no one solution can answer every problem. Other times, the differences are the result of restrictions resulting from government controls, as we'll describe in this article.

## Cryptography and Web Security

Security professionals have identified four key-words that are used to describe all of the different functions that encryption plays in modern information systems. The different functions are these:

*Confidentiality*

Encryption is used to scramble information sent over the Internet and stored on servers so that eavesdroppers cannot access the data's content. Some people call this quality "privacy," but most professionals reserve that word to refer to the protection of personal information (whether confidential or not) from aggregation and improper use.

*Authentication*

Digital signatures are used to identify the author of a message; people who receive the message can verify the identity of the person who signed them. They can be used in conjunction with passwords or as an alternative to them.

*Integrity*

Methods are used to verify that a message has not been modified while in transit. Often, this is done with digitally signed message digest codes.

*Nonrepudiation*

Cryptographic receipts are created so that an author of a message cannot falsely deny sending a message.

Strictly speaking, there is some overlap among these areas. For example, when the DES encryption algorithm is used to provide confidentiality, it frequently provides integrity as a byproduct. That's because if an encrypted message is altered, it will not decrypt properly. In practice, however, it is better engineering to use different algorithms that are specifically designed to assure integrity for this purpose, rather than relying on the byproduct of other algorithms. That way, if the user decides to not include one aspect (such as encryption) because of efficiency or legal reasons, the user will still have a standard algorithm to use for the other system requirements.

Before describing the cryptographic systems at work on the Web today, the following sections reveiw the basics of cryptography on which many secure Internet protocols are based.

# Basics of Cryptography

Cryptography is a collection of techniques for keeping information secure. Using cryptography, you can transform written words and other kinds of messages so that they are unintelligible to unauthorized recipients. An authorized recipient can then transform the words or messages back into a message that is perfectly understandable.

For example, here is a message that you might want to encrypt:

```
SSL is a cryptographic protocol
```

And here is the message after it has been encrypted:

```
Ç'^ @%[»FÇ«$TfiPÂ|x¿EÛóõÑ‰ß+ö˜•ÖaÜ˝BÆuâw
```

Even better, with cryptography you can transform this gibberish back into the original easily understood message.

## Terminology

Modern cryptographic systems consist of two complementary processes:

*Encryption*

A process by which a message (the *plaintext*) is transformed into a second message (the *ciphertext*) using a complex function (the *encryption algorithm*) and a special *encryption key*.

*Decryption*

The reverse process, in which the ciphertext is transformed back into the original plaintext using a second complex function and a *decryption key*. With some encryption systems, the encryption key and the decryption key are the same. With others, they are different.

Figure 1 illustrates how these two processes fit together.

The goal of cryptography is to make it impossible to take a ciphertext and reproduce the original plaintext without the corresponding key and to raise the cost of guessing the key beyond what is practical. Many modern cryptographic systems now easily achieve this goal. Indeed, cryptographic algorithms that have no known flaws are readily available today.

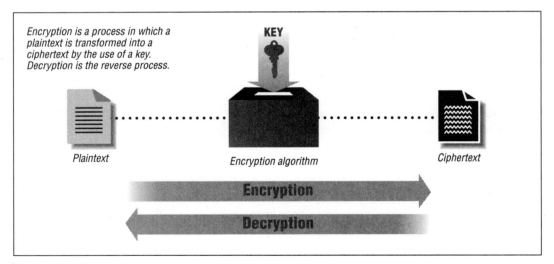

Encryption is a process in which a plaintext is transformed into a ciphertext by the use of a key. Decryption is the reverse process.

KEY

Plaintext          Encryption algorithm          Ciphertext

Encryption

Decryption

**Figure 1**

## Cryptographic Algorithms and Functions

There are two basic kinds of encryption algorithms in use today:

*Symmetric key algorithms*

> With these algorithms, the same key is used to encrypt and decrypt the message. The DES algorithm discussed earlier is a symmetric key algorithm. Sometimes symmetric key algorithms are called secret key algorithms and sometimes they are called private key algorithms. Unfortunately, both of those names cause confusion with public key algorithms, which are unrelated to symmetric key algorithms.

*Public key algorithms*

> With these algorithms, one key is used to encrypt the message and another key to decrypt it. The encryption key is normally called the *public key* because it can be made publicly available without compromising the secrecy of the message or the decryption key. The decryption key is normally called the *private key* or *secret key.*
>
> Public key systems are sometimes (but rarely) called *asymmetric key* algorithms.

Symmetric key algorithms are the workhorses of modern cryptographic systems. They are generally much faster than public key algorithms. They are also some what easier to implement. Unfortunately, symmetric key algorithms have a problem that limits their use in the real world: for two parties to securely exchange information using a symmetric key algorithm, those parties must first securely exchange an encryption key.

Public key algorithms overcome this problem. People wishing to communicate create a public key and a secret key. The public key is published. If Sascha wants to send Wendy a confidential message, all he has to do is get a copy of Wendy's public key (perhaps from her Web page), use that key to encrypt the message, and then send it along. Nobody but Wendy can decrypt the message, because only Wendy possesses the matching secret key.

Public key cryptography is also used for creating *digital signatures** on data, such as electronic mail, to certify the data's origin and integrity. In the case of digital signatures, the secret key is used to create the digital signature, and the public key is used to verify it. For example, Wendy could write a letter to Sascha and sign it with her digital key. When Sascha receives the letter, he can verify it with Wendy's public key.

Public key algorithms have a significant problem of their own: they are incredibly slow. In practice, public key encryption and decryption runs betweeen 10 and 100 times slower than the equivalent symmetric key encryption algorithm. For that reason, there is a third kind of system:

*Hybrid public/private cryptosystems*

> With these systems, slower public key cryptography is used to exchange a random *session key*, which is then used as the basis of a private (symmetric) key algorithm. (A session key is used only for a single encryption session and is then discarded.) Nearly all practical public key cryptography implementations are actually hybrid systems.

Finally, there is a new class of functions that have become popular in recent years and are used in conjunction with public key cryptography:

*Message digest functions*

> A message digest function generates a unique (or nearly so) pattern of bits for a given input. The digest value is computed in such a way that finding an input that will exactly generate a given digest is computationally infeasible. Message digests are often regarded as fingerprints for files.

---

* For more information on digital signatures see the "DSig 1.0 Signature Labels" specification in the "W3C Reports" section of this issue.

The following sections look at all of these classes of algorithms in detail.

## Symmetric Key Algorithms

Symmetric key algorithms are used for the bulk encryption of data or data streams. These algorithms are designed to be very fast and (usually) have a large number of possible keys. The best symmetric key algorithms offer near-perfect secrecy: once data is encrypted with a given key, there is no way to decrypt the data without possessing the same key.

Symmetric key algorithms can be divided into two categories: block and stream. *Block algorithms* encrypt data one block at a time, while *stream algorithms* encrypt byte by byte.

There are many symmetric key algorithms in use today. Some of the algorithms that are commonly encountered in the field of Web security are summarized in the following list:

*DES*

The Data Encryption Standard was adopted as a U.S. government standard in 1977 and as an ANSI standard in 1981. The DES is a block cipher that uses a 56-bit key and has several different operating modes depending on the purpose for which it is employed. The DES is a strong algorithm, but it is conjectured that a machine capable of breaking a DES-encrypted message in a few hours can be built for under $1 million. Such machines probably exist, although no government or corporation officially admits to having one.

*DESX*

DESX is a simple modification to the DES algorithm that is built around two "whitening" steps. These steps appear to improve the security of the algorithm dramatically, effectively rendering key search impossible. Further information about DESX can be found on the RSA Data Security "Cryptogra-

phy FAQ," at *http://www.rsa.com/rsalabs/ newfaq/*.

*Triple-DES*

Triple-DES is a way to make the DES at least twice as secure by using the DES encryption algorithm three times with three different keys. (Simply using the DES twice with two different keys does not improve its security to the extent that one might at first suspect because of a theoretical kind of known plaintext attack called "meet-in-the-middle," in which an attacker simultaneously attempts encrypting the plaintext with a single DES operation and decrypting the ciphertext with another single DES operation, until a match is made in the middle.) Triple-DES is currently being used by financial institutions as an alternative to DES.

*IDEA*

The International Data Encryption Algorithm (IDEA) was developed in Zurich, Switzerland, by James L. Massey and Xuejia Lai and published in 1990. IDEA uses a 128-bit key and is believed to be quite strong. IDEA is used by the popular program PGP to encrypt files and electronic mail. Unfortunately, wider use of IDEA has been hampered by a series of software patents on the algorithm, which is currently held by Ascom-Tech AG in Solothurn, Switzerland.

*RC2*

This block cipher was originally developed by Ronald Rivest and kept as a trade secret by RSA Data Security. This algorithm was revealed by an anonymous Usenet posting in 1996 and appears to be reasonably strong (although there are some particular keys that are weak). RC2 is sold with an implementation that allows keys between 1 and 2048 bits. The RC2 key length is often limited to 40 bits in software that is sold for export.[*]

---

[*] A 40-bit key is vulnerable to a key search attack.

### RC4

This stream cipher was originally developed by Ronald Rivest and kept as a trade secret by RSA Data Security. This algorithm was also revealed by an anonymous Usenet posting in 1994 and appears to be reasonably strong. RC4 is sold with an implementation that allows keys between 1 and 2048 bits. The RC4 key length is often limited to 40 bits in software that is sold for export.

### RC5

This block cipher was developed by Ronald Rivest and published in 1994. RC5 allows a user-defined key length, data block size, and number of encryption rounds.

## Public Key Algorithms

The existence of public key cryptography was first postulated in print in the fall of 1975 by Whitfield Diffie and Martin Hellman. The two researchers, then at Stanford University, wrote a paper in which they presupposed the existence of an encryption technique with which information encrypted with one key could be decrypted by a second, apparently unrelated key. Robert Merkle, then a graduate student at Berkeley, had similar ideas, but due to the vagaries of the academic publication process Merkle's papers were not published until the idea of public key encryption was widely known.

Since that time, a variety of public key encryption systems have been developed. Unfortunately, there have been significantly fewer developments in public key algorithms than in symmetric key algorithms. The reason has to do with the way that these algorithms are designed. Good symmetric key algorithms simply scramble their input depending on the input key; developing a new symmetric key algorithm simply requires coming up with new ways for performing that scrambling reliably. Public key algorithms tend to be based on number theory. Developing new public key algorithms requires identifying new mathematical problems with particular properties.

The following list summarizes the public key systems in common use today:

### Diffie-Hellman key exchange

A system for exchanging cryptographic keys between active parties. Diffie-Hellman is not actually a method of encryption and decryption, but a method of developing and exchanging a shared private key over a public communications channel. In effect, the two parties agree to some common numerical values, and then each party creates a key. Mathematical transformations of the keys are exchanged. Each party can then calculate a third session key that cannot easily be derived by an attacker who knows both exchanged values.

### RSA

RSA is a well-known public key cryptography system developed by (then) MIT professors Ronald Rivest, Adi Shamir, and Leonard Adleman. RSA can be used both for encrypting information and as the basis of a digital signature system. Digital signatures can be used to prove the authorship and authenticity of digital information. The key may be any length, depending on the particular implementation used.

### ElGamal

Named after its creator Taher ElGamal, this is a public key encryption system that is based on the Diffie-Hellman key exchange protocol. ElGamal may be used for encryption and digital signatures in a manner similar to the RSA algorithm.

### DSS

The Digital Signature Standard was developed by the National Security Agency (NSA) and adopted as a Federal Information Processing Standard (FIPS) by the National Institute for Standards and Technology (NIST). DSS is based on the Digital Signature Algorithm (DSA). Although DSA allows keys of any length, only keys between 512 and 1024 bits are permitted under the DSS FIPS. As specified, DSS can be used only for digital signatures, although it is possible to use DSA implementations for encryption as well.

## Message Digest Functions

Message digest functions distill the information contained in a file (small or large) into a single large number, typically between 128 and 256 bits in length. This is illustrated in Figure 2. The best message digest functions combine these mathematical properties:

- Every bit of the message digest function is influenced by every bit of the function's input.

- If any given bit of the function's input is changed, every output bit has a 50 percent chance of changing.

- Given an input file and its corresponding message digest, it should be computationally infeasible to find another file with the same message digest value.

Message digests are also called one-way *hash functions* because they produce values that are difficult to invert, resistant to attack, mostly unique, and widely distributed.

Many message digest functions have been proposed and are in use today. Here are just a few:

*HMAC*

The Hashed Message Authentication Code, a technique that uses a secret key and a message digest function to create a secret message authentication code. The HMAC method strengthens an existing message digest function to make it resistant to external attack, even if the message digest function itself is somehow compromised. (See RFC 2104 for details.)

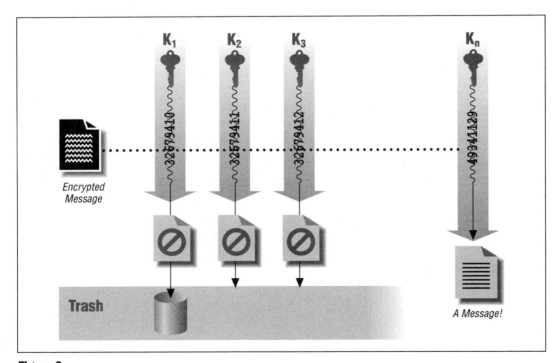

**Figure 2**

### MD2

Message Digest #2, developed by Ronald Rivest. This message digest is the most secure of Rivest's message digest functions, but takes the longest to compute. It produces a 128-bit digest.

### MD4

Message Digest #4, also developed by Ronald Rivest. This message digest algorithm was developed as a fast alternative to MD2. Subsequently, MD4 has been shown to be insecure. That is, it is possible to find two files that produce the same MD4 codes without requiring a brute force search. MD4 produces a 128-bit digest.

### MD5

Message Digest #5, also developed by Ronald Rivest. MD5 is a modification of MD4 that includes techniques designed to make it more secure. Although widely used, in the summer of 1996 a few flaws were discovered in MD5 that allowed some kinds of collisions to be calculated. As a result, MD5 is slowly falling out of favor. MD5 produces a 128-bit digest.

### SHA

The Secure Hash Algorithm, developed by the NSA and designed for use with the National Institute for Standards and Technology's Digital Signature Standard (NIST's DSS). Shortly after the publication of the SHA, NIST announced that it was not suitable for use without a small change. SHA produces a 160-bit digest.

### SHA-1

The revised Secure Hash Algorithm, also developed by the NSA and designed for use with the NSA's DSS. SHA-1 incorporates minor changes from SHA. It is not known if these changes make SHA-1 more secure than SHA, although some people believe that it does. SHA-1 produces a 160-bit digest.

# Today's Working Encryption Systems

Although encryption is a technology that will be widespread in the future, it is already hard at work on the World Wide Web today. In recent years, more than a dozen cryptographic systems have been developed and fielded on the Internet.

Working cryptographic systems can be divided into two categories. The first group are programs and protocols that are used for encryption of email messages. These programs take a plaintext message, encrypt it, and either store the ciphertext or transmit it to another user on the Internet. Such programs can also be used to encrypt files that are stored on computers to give these files added protection. Some popular systems that fall into this category include the following:

- PGP

- S/MIME

The second category of cryptographic systems are network protocols used for providing confidentiality, authentication, integrity, and non-repudiation in a networked environment. Such systems require real-time interplay between a client and a server to work properly. Some popular systems that fall into this category include the following:

- SSL

- PCT

- S-HTTP

- SET and CyberCash

- DNSSEC

- IPsec and IPv6

- Kerberos

- SSH

All of these systems are summarized in Table 1 and are described in the sections that follow.

**Table 1**      Comparison of Encryption Systems Available on the Internet Today

| System | What is it? | Algorithms | Provides |
|---|---|---|---|
| PGP | Application program for encrypting electronic mail | IDEA, RSA, MD5 | Confidentiality, authentication, integrity, nonrepudiation |
| S/MIME | Format for encrypting electronic mail | User-specified | Confidentiality, authentication, integrity, nonrepudiation |
| SSL | Protocol for encrypting TCP/IP transmissions | RSA, RCZ, RC4, MD5, and others | Confidentiality, authentication, integrity, nonrepudiation |
| PCT | Protocol for encrypting TCP/IP transmissions. | RSA, MD5, RCZ, RC4, and others | Confidentiality, authentication, integrity, nonrepudiation |
| S-HTTP | Protocol for encrypting HTTP requests and responses | RSA, DES, and others | Confidentiality, authentication, integrity, nonrepudiation; however, it's obsolete |
| SET and CyberCash | Protocols for sending secure payment instructions over the Internet | RSA, MD5, RC2 | Confidentiality of credit card numbers, but nothing else; integrity of entire message; authentication of buyer and seller; nonrepudiation of transactions |
| DNSSEC | Secure Domain Name System | RSA, MD5 | Authentication, integrity |
| IPsec and IPv6 | Low-level protocol for encrypting IP packets | Diffie-Hellman and others | Confidentiality (optional), authentication, integrity |
| Kerberos | Network security service for securing higher-level applications | DES | Confidentiality, authentication |
| SSH | Encrypted remote terminal | RSA, Diffie-Helman, DES, Triple-DES, Blowfish, and others | Confidentiality, authentication |

## PGP

One of the first widespread public key encryption programs was Pretty Good Privacy (PGP), written by Phil Zimmermann and released on the Internet in June 1991. PGP is a complete working system for the cryptographic protection of electronic mail and files. PGP is also a set of standards that describe the formats for encrypted messages, keys, and digital signatures.

PGP is a hybrid encryption system, using RSA public key encryption for key management and the IDEA symmetric cipher for the bulk encryption of data.

Referring to the four basic encryption keywords mentioned at the beginning of this article, PGP offers confidentiality, through the use of the IDEA encryption algorithm; integrity, through the use of the MD5 cryptographic hash function; authentication, through the use of public key certificates; and nonrepudiation, through the use of cryptographically signed messages.

PGP is available in two ways, as a standalone application and as an integrated email program available from PGP, Inc. The standalone program runs on many more platforms than the integrated system but is more difficult to use. PGP, Inc., is also developing plug-ins for popular email systems to allow them to send and receive PGP-encrypted messages.

A problem with PGP is the management and certification of public keys. PGP keys never expire: instead, when the keys are compromised, it is up to the keyholder to distribute a special PGP key revocation certificate to everyone with whom he or she communicates. Correspondents who do not learn of a compromised key and use it weeks, months, or years later to send an encrypted message do so at their own risk. As a side effect, if you create and distribute a PGP public key, you must hold onto the secret key for all time because the key never expires.

PGP public keys are validated by a *web of trust.* Each PGP user can certify any key that he or she wishes, meaning that the user believes the key actually belongs to the person named in the key certificate. But PGP also allows users to say that they *trust* particular individuals to vouch for the authenticity of still more keys. PGP users sign each other's keys, vouching for the authenticity of the key's apparent holder.

Another way that PGP public keys are distributed is by the PGP public key servers located on the Internet.

## S/MIME

The Multipurpose Internet Mail Extensions (MIME) is a standard for sending files with binary attachments over the Internet. Secure/MIME extends the MIME standard to allow for encrypted email. Unlike PGP, S/MIME was not first implemented as a single program, but as a toolkit that was designed to be added to existing mail packages. Because this toolkit comes from RSA Data Security and includes licenses for all necessary algorithms and patents, and because the major companies selling email systems already have a business relationship with RSA Data Security, it is

possible that S/MIME will be adopted by many email vendors in preference to PGP.

S/MIME offers confidentiality, through the use of user-specified encryption algorithms; integrity, through the use of user-specified cryptographic hash function; authentication, through the use of X.509 v3 public key certificates (see the sidebar); and nonrepudiation, through the use of cryptographically signed messages. The system can be used with strong or weak encryption.

To send people encrypted mail with S/MIME, you must first have a copy of their public keys. It is expected that most S/MIME programs will use X. 509 v3 public key infrastructures such as those being built by VeriSign and other certification authorities.

## SSL

The Secure Socket Layer (SSL) is a general purpose cryptographic protocol for securing bidirectional communication channels.* SSL is commonly used with the TCP/IP Internet protocol. SSL is the encryption system that is used by Web browsers such as Netscape Navigator and Microsoft's Internet Explorer, but it can be used with any TCP/IP service.

SSL connections are usually initiated with a Web browser through the use of a special URL prefix. For example, the prefix "https:" is used to indicate an SSL-encrypted HTTP connection, whereas "snews:" is used to indicate an SSL-encrypted NNTP connection.

SSL offers confidentiality through the use of user-specified encryption algorithms; integrity, through the use of user-specified cryptographic hash function; authentication, through the use of X.509 v3 public key certificates; and nonrepudiation, through the use of cryptographically signed messages.

---

* For more information on SSL see the article entitled "Introducing SSL and Certificates Using SSLeay" in this issue.

## The X.509 v3 Certificate

The X.509 v3 certificate is a popular standard for public key certificates. X.509 v3 certificates are widely used by many modern cryptographic protocols, including SSL. (X.509 certificates are not used by the PGP email encryption program versions 2.0 through 4.5, but it is possible that future versions of PGP will support X.509 v3.)

Each X.509 certificate contains a version number, serial number, identity information, algorithm-related information, and the signature of the issuing authority.

The industry has adopted X.509 v3 certificates, rather than the original X.509 certificates, because the X.509 v3 standard allows arbitrary name/value pairs to be included in the standard certificate. These pairs can be used for many purposes. Microsoft's Internet Explorer will display some of the fields if you choose the Properties option while looking at a secure document.

## PCT

PCT is a transport layer security protocol similar to SSL that was developed by Microsoft. Reportedly, the acronym has had several expansions: the current favored one is Private Communications Technology. PCT was developed in response to problems with SSL 2.0; these problems were also addressed in SSL 3.0.

Although Microsoft is supporting SSL 3.0 and TLS, the new Transport Layer Security model, Microsoft intends to continue supporting PCT because it is being used by several large Microsoft customers on their corporate intranets.

## S-HTTP

S-HTTP is a system for signing and encrypting information sent over the Web's HTTP protocol. (The "S" stands for Secure.) S-HTTP was designed before SSL was publicly released. It includes some nifty features, such as the ability to have presigned documents reside on a Web server. But S-HTTP is largely a dead protocol because Netscape and Microsoft have failed to implement it in their browsers.

## SET

SET is a cryptographic protocol designed for sending encrypted credit card numbers over the Internet. Unlike the other protocols described here, it is still under development.

There are three parts to the SET system: an "electronic wallet" that resides on the user's computer; a server that runs at the merchant's Web site; and the SET Payment Server that runs at the merchant's bank.

To use the SET system, you must first enter your credit card number into the electronic wallet software. Most implementations will store the credit card number in an encrypted file on your hard disk or in a smart card. The software also creates a public and a secret key for encrypting your financial information before it is sent over the Internet.

When you want to buy something, your credit card number is encrypted and sent to the merchant. The merchant's software digitally signs the payment message and forwards it to the processing bank, where the Payment Server decrypts all of the information and runs the credit card charge. Finally, a receipt gets sent back to both the merchant and you, the customer.

Banks that process credit cards are excited about SET because it keeps credit card numbers out of the hands of the merchants. That should cut down on a lot of fraud, because it is merchants (and their employees), and not teenage hackers, who are responsible for much of the credit card fraud in the world today.

SET offers confidentiality for credit card numbers, as they are encrypted using the RSA algorithm. But it does not offer confidentiality (and thus privacy) for the other elements of a user's transaction: this was a compromise necessary to gain approval to export the SET software without restriction. SET does provide for integrity, authentication, and nonrepudiation through the use of message digest functions and digital signatures.

## CyberCash/CyberCoin

CyberCash is an electronic payment protocol, similar in purpose to SET, that allows conventional credit cards to be used over the World Wide Web. The CyberCoin is an adaptation of the technology for small-value transactions. Instead of issuing a credit card charge, the CyberCash server can be thought of as a debit card.

Before using CyberCash, the consumer must download special software from the CyberCash Web site, *http://www.cybercash.com/*. The software, called the "CyberCash wallet," maintains a database of a user's credit cards and other payment instruments.

To use a credit card with the CyberCash system, the credit card must be enrolled. To create a CyberCoin account, a user must complete an online enrollment form. The current CyberCash implementation allows money to be transferred into a CyberCoin account from a credit card or from a checking account using the Automated Clearing House (ACH) electronic funds transfer system. Money that is transferred into the Cyber-Coin account from a checking account can be transferred back out again, but money that is transferred into the account from a credit card must be spent. CyberCash allows the user to close his or her CyberCoin account and receive a check for the remaining funds.

The CyberCash wallet registers itself as a helper application for Netscape Navigator and Micro-

soft's Internet Explorer. Purchases can then be initiated by downloading files of a particular MIME file type.

When a purchase is initiated, the CyberCash wallet displays the amount of the transaction and the name of the merchant. The user then decides which credit card to use and whether to approve or reject the transaction. The software can also be programmed to automatically approve small-value transactions.

If the user approves the transaction, an encrypted payment order is sent to the merchant. The merchant can decrypt some of the information in the payment order but not other information. The merchant adds its own payment information to the order, digitally signs it, and sends it to the CyberCash gateway for processing.

The CyberCash gateway receives the payment information and decrypts it. The gateway checks for duplicate requests and verifies the user's copy of the invoice against the merchant's to make sure neither has lied to the other. The gateway then sends the credit card payment information to the acquiring bank. The acquiring bank authorizes the transaction and sends the response back to CyberCash, which sends an encrypted response back to the merchant. Finally, the merchant transmits the CyberCash payment acknowledgment back to the consumer.

The CyberCash payment is designed to protect consumers, merchants, and banks against fraud. It does this by using cryptography to protect payment information while it is in transit.

All payment information is encrypted before it is sent over the Internet. But CyberCash further protects consumers from fraud on the part of the merchant: the merchant never has access to the consumer's credit card number.

## DNSSEC

The Domain Name System Security (DNSSEC) standard is a system designed to bring security to the Internet's Domain Name System (DNS).* DNS-SEC creates a parallel public key infrastructure built upon the DNS system. Each DNS domain is assigned a public key. A domain's public key can be obtained in a trusted manner from the parent domain or it can be preloaded into a DNS server using the server's "boot" file.

DNSSEC allows for secure updating of information stored in DNS servers, making it ideal for remote administration. Working implementations are available for free download from Trusted Information Systems (*http://www.tis.com/*) and CyberCash (*http://www.cybercash.com/*).

## IPsec and IPv6

IPsec is a cryptographic protocol designed by the Internet Engineering Task Force to provide end-to-end confidentiality for packets traveling over the Internet. IPsec works with IPv4, the standard version of IP used on today's Internet. IPv6, the "next-generation" IP, includes IPsec.

IPsec does not provide for integrity, authentication, or nonrepudiation, but leaves these features to other protocols. Currently, the main use of IPsec seems to be as a multivendor protocol for creating virtual private networks (VPNs) over the Internet. But IPsec has the capacity to provide authentication, integrity, and optionally, data confidentiality for all communication that takes place over the Internet, provided that vendors widely implement the protocol and that governments allow its use.

## Kerberos

Kerberos is a network security system developed at MIT and used throughout the United States. Unlike the other systems mentioned in this chapter, Kerberos does not use public key technology. Instead, Kerberos is based on symmetric ciphers and secrets that are shared between the Kerberos server and each individual user. Each user has his own password, and the Kerberos server uses this password to encrypt messages sent to that user so that they cannot be read by anyone else.

Support for Kerberos must be added to each program that is to be protected. Currently, "Kerberized" versions of Telnet, FTP, POP, and Sun RPC are in general use. A system that used Kerberos to provide confidentiality for HTTP was developed but never made it out of the lab.

Kerberos is a difficult system to configure and administer. To operate a Kerberos system, each site must have a Kerberos server that is physically secure. The Kerberos server maintains a copy of every user's password. In the event that the Kerberos server is compromised, every user's password must be changed.

## SSH

SSH is the secure shell. It provides for cryptographically protected virtual terminal (Telnet) and file transfer (rcp) operations. Noncommercial versions of SSH are available for many versions of UNIX. SSH is available for UNIX, Windows, and the Macintosh from Data Fellows (*http://www.datafellows.com/*).

# Cryptography and U.S. Export Control Law

Under current U.S. law, cryptography is a munition, and the export of cryptographic machines (including computer programs that implement cryptography) is covered by the Defense Trade Regulations (formerly known as the International Traffic in Arms Regulation—ITAR). As of late December 1996, to export a program that includes cryptography, you need a license from the U.S. Commerce Department (prior to that

---

* DNSSEC is described in John Gilmore's article entitled "Security for the Domain Name System," in this issue.

date the U.S. State Department issued the licenses).*

In 1992, the Software Publishers Association and the State Department reached an agreement that allows the export of programs containing RSA Data Security's RC2 and RC4 algorithms, but only when the key size is set to 40 bits or less. These key sizes are not secure. Under the 1992 agreement, the 40-bit size was supposed to be periodically reviewed and extended as technology improved. No review ever took place.

In early 1996, the Clinton Administration proposed a new system called "software key escrow." Under this new system, companies would be allowed to export software that used keys up to 64 bits in size, but only under the condition that a copy of the key used by every program had been filed with an appropriate "escrow agent" within the United States, so that if law enforcement so wanted, any files or transmission encrypted with the system could be easily decrypted.

In late 1996, the Clinton administration replaced the software key escrow with a new proposal entitled "key recovery." Reasoning that the main objection to the previous "key escrow" proposals was the fact that businesses did not wish to have their secret keys escrowed, the new proposal was based on a new idea. Under the key recovery system, every encrypted document or communication is prefaced by a special key recovery data block. The key recovery data block contains the session key used to encrypt the message, but the session key is itself encrypted with the public key of a federally registered key recovery service. In this way, the key recovery service can recover the session key by decrypting that key with the service's private key.

The key recovery proposal is different from the key escrow proposal in two important ways:

- Because the key recovery service does not hold any user's private key, that key cannot be leaked to compromise all of the user's messages.

- On the other hand, if the key recovery service's private key is leaked, then many, many users will have all of their messages compromised.

Although some businesses seemed to be interested in the key recovery approach by late 1996, the key recovery proposal did not address the really hard problems created by any key escrow or key recovery regime. Some of those questions include:

- What happens when a foreign government asks for the keys for a U.S. corporation that is in strong competition with a company that just happens to be based in the foreign country? (That is, what happens when France asks for Boeing's keys? What keeps the information learned from decrypting Boeing's communications from being transmitted to Airbus, Boeing's chief rival?)

- What happens when a rogue government asks for an escrowed key?

- What happens when foreign governments ask for the escrowed copies of signature keys. (What purpose could there be to requesting a signature key except to create fraudulent evidence?)

## Foreign Restrictions on Cryptography

The primary way that cryptography is restricted within the United States is through the use of export controls. There are many reasons for this peculiar state of controls:

- It is widely believed that any direct restrictions on the use of encryption within the United States would be an unconstitutional

---

* See the article by Clint Smith entitled "Government Regulation of Encryption: How Policy Will Impact Security on the Web," as well as "The Risks of Key Recovery, Key Escrow, and Trusted Third-Party Encryption" for more on this topic.

violation of the First Amendment, which forbids Congress from making laws restricting the freedom of speech or the freedom of association.

- The United States has a history of both openness and governmental abuse of investigative power. Nevertheless, the current policy has allowed the federal government to claim that it has no interest in restricting cryptography used within the United States.

- Nevertheless, restricting the cryptography technology that can be placed in software for export effectively limits the cryptography technology that can be placed in software that is used domestically, because most companies are loath to have two different, and incompatible, versions of their software.

- Fortunately for the federal government, the argument of how restrictions on foreign software impact domestic software are so complicated that they go over the heads of most sound bite-oriented Americans.

But other countries do not have a First Amendment, and many have already passed laws to regulate or prohibit the use of strong cryptography within their borders. Some are also pressing for world nongovernmental organizations, such as the OECD, to adopt policy statements on the regulation of cryptography. Not surprisingly, the strongest advocates for such worldwide regulation of cryptography are within the U.S. Government itself.

There are many surveys that attempt to compare the laws with respect to cryptography in different countries. Unfortunately, many of the surveys currently have contradictory findings for many countries.

A rather comprehensive document comparing the various surveys on cryptography laws was completed by Bert-Jaap Koops in October 1996 and updated in March 1997. The survey can be found on the World Wide Web at the location *http://cwis.kub.nl/~frw/people/koops/lawsurvey.htm.* Between October 1996 and March 1997, many more countries had imposed export, import, and domestic restrictions on cryptography. This trend is likely to continue. ■

## About the Authors

**Simson Garfinkel**
P.O. Box 4188
Vineyard Haven, MA 02568
*simsong@vineyard.net*

Simson Garfinkel is a computer consultant, science writer, and columnist for both *The Boston Globe* and *HotWired, Wired Magazine*'s online service. He is the author of *PGP: Pretty Good Privacy* (O'Reilly & Associates, 1994) and the coauthor of *Practical UNIX & Internet Security* (O'Reilly & Associates, 1996). Mr. Garfinkel writes frequently about science and technology, as well as their social impacts. The recently released *Web Security and Commerce* (O'Reilly & Associates, 1997) is his sixth book.

**Euguene H. Spafford**
Purdue University
Department of Computer Science
W. Lafayette, IN 47907-1398
*spaf@cs.purdue.edu*

Eugene H. Spafford is on the faculty of the Department of Computer Sciences at Purdue University. He is the founder and director of the Computer Operations, Audit, and Security Technology (COAST) Laboratory at Purdue. Professor Spafford is an active researcher in the areas of software testing and debugging, applied security, and professional computing issues. He is the coauthor of *Practical UNIX & Internet Security* (O'Reilly & Associates, 1996). He was the consulting editor for *Computer Crime: A Crimefighters Handbook* (O'Reilly & Associates, 1995), and has also coauthored a widely praised book on computer viruses.

# REFEREE
## TRUST MANAGEMENT FOR WEB APPLICATIONS

*Yang-Hua Chu, Joan Feigenbaum, Brian LaMacchia, Paul Resnick,*
*Martin Strauss*

### Abstract

*Digital signatures provide a mechanism for guaranteeing integrity and authenticity of Web content but not more general notions of security or trust. Web-aware applications must permit users to state clearly their own security policies and, of course, must provide the cryptographic tools for manipulating digital signatures. This paper describes the REFEREE trust management system for Web applications; REFEREE provides both a general policy evaluation mechanism for Web clients and servers and a language for specifying trust policies. REFEREE places all trust decisions under explicit policy control. In the REFEREE model every action, including evaluation of compliance with policy, happens under the control of some policy. That is, REFEREE is a system for writing policies about policies as well as policies about cryptographic keys, PICS label bureaus, certification authorities, trust delegation, or anything else.*

*In this paper, which is reprinted with the permission of the WWW6 committee, we flesh out the need for trust management in Web applications, explain the design philosophy of the REFEREE trust management system, and describe a prototype implementation of REFEREE.*

## Introduction

Web surfing is a dangerous sport. Downloaded software may contain viruses. Materials that appear to come from one source may in fact be spoofs provided by another source. Eavesdroppers may overhear credit card numbers or other sensitive information. Personal information may be collected legitimately but then used to violate one's privacy.

One way to approach these problems is to attempt to eliminate dangers. For example, the Java applet interpreter tries to provide an execution environment in which programs can only perform "harmless" actions. The PCC system (for "proof carrying code") requires mobile programs to prove to potential hosts that they are "harmless" [1] [2]. A wealth of cryptographic protocols attempt to eliminate dangers by enforcing secrecy or authenticity.

A complementary approach focuses on trust. To trust is to undertake a potentially dangerous operation *knowing that it is potentially dangerous.* A user might prefer to have *proof* of harm-lessness, but weaker forms of evidence may also be sufficient. A recommendation from a close friend may convince someone to trust that a piece of software is virus-free. Someone may trust an insecure channel for transmission of a credit card number if the credit card company assumes liability for any fraudulent uses of the number.

*Credentials* and *policies* are the raw materials for making trust decisions. A credential is a statement, purportedly made by some speaker. A policy determines the conditions under which a particular action is allowed.

Following [3], we use the term *trust management* to refer to the problem of deciding whether requested actions, supported by credentials, conform to policies. Just as a database manager coordinates the input and storage of data and processes queries, a trust manager coordinates the collection and storage of policies and credentials and processes requests for trust decisions. We refer to the processing of such a request as "evaluating compliance with a policy."

In current Web applications, the prototypical credential is a PICS label [4], which states some properties of an Internet resource (e.g., executable code has been virus-checked). An important idea of [3] that we use in this work is that of "programmable credentials." Rather than simply making unconditional statements, programmable credentials can examine statements made by other credentials and fetch information from the network before deciding which statements to make. For example, a credential may examine existing statements, ask `GoodMouseClicking` (see "Sample Policy 4") whether the authors of those statements are reliable, and then decide whether the statements are trustworthy.

In its simplest form, a policy sets rules about which credentials must be present in order to permit an action. In the course of deciding whether a requested action conforms to a policy, however, it is often necessary to perform potentially dangerous operations. In particular, it may be useful to fetch credentials over the network. For example, if one wants to know a particular reviewer's opinion about a video clip before deciding whether to watch it, it will be necessary to consult a server that distributes that reviewer's opinions. One danger is that information will leak out unintentionally during the fetching process. Another danger is that spoofed credentials may be retrieved. Yet a third danger is that, since credentials are programs, running credentials retrieved over the network exposes us to the full gamut of risks from running unknown programs.

Because we are interested in managing trust, rather than in eliminating danger, we permit these dangerous actions but put them under policy control. Policies state when to fetch credentials. Policies also determine which statements must be made about a credential before it is safe to run it. For example, credentials written in some (safe) programming languages may always be permitted to execute, while credentials written in other languages may be executed only if vouched for by some trusted party. Finally, policies determine whether and how credentials are to be authenticated before the statements they create are deemed to be trustworthy. For example, some kinds of statements may be used only if the credentials were signed using a particular cryptographic key.

Our trust management system is called REFEREE. The name is an acronym: Rule-controlled Environment For Evaluation of Rules, and Everything Else. It is an environment for evaluating compliance with policies (rules), but the evaluation process itself may involve dangerous actions and hence is under policy control. The "Everything Else" refers to credentials, whose evaluation (execution) also needs to be under policy control. In placing everything under policy control, REFEREE differs from *PolicyMaker*, the trust management system described in [3]. In particular, PolicyMaker does not permit policies to control credential-fetching or signature-verification; it assumes that the calling application has gathered all of the relevant credentials and verified all digital signatures before calling the trust management system.

Within the World Wide Web Consortium, the PICS Working Group and Digital Signature Initiative [7][*][†] are experimenting with REFEREE as a possible common platform for trust management in content selection and digital signature applications. Yang-hua Chu has implemented an early design of REFEREE as part of his masters' thesis research, and this paper reflects that early design.

We begin by presenting the REFEREE calling conventions for invocable programs (both policies and credentials). Next, we describe a simple language, called the `profiles-0.92` language, for writing policies and describe several other pro-

---

* See also the "DSig 1.0 Signature Label" specification in this issue.
† The PICS specifications—"Rating Services and Rating Systems (and Their Machine-Readable Descriptions)" and "Label Syntax and Communication Protocols"—are available at the W3C site and in the Fall 1996 (Vol. 1, No. 4) issue of the WWW Journal.

grams, including one that fetches PICS labels and converts them into REFEREE's internal statement format and one that verifies cryptographic hashes. Third, we present sample policies, expressed as REFEREE programs. This is followed by an execution trace of a sample policy that retrieves a set of PICS labels that are sufficient to authorize the requested action. The execution trace is taken from a working policy evaluator that can be accessed and exercised on the Web. Finally, we give a conclusion.

## REFEREE

There are three primitive data types in REFEREE:

- Programs
- Statement lists
- Tri-values

A *tri-value* is one of true, false, or unknown. A statement list is a collection of assertions expressed in a particular format, described later. Each program takes an initial statement list as an input and may also take additional arguments. A *program* may invoke another program during the course of its execution.

Intuitively, a policy governing a particular action is a program that returns true or false, depending on whether the available statements are sufficient to infer compliance or noncompliance with a policy, or returns unknown if no inference can be made.

Intuitively, a credential is a program that examines the initial statements passed to it and derives additional statements. This generalizes the usual notion of a credential as directly supplying statements: The new statements supplied by a credential may be conditional on the initial statements or other environmental factors, such as the amount of space available on the local hard disk.

Actually, REFEREE allows both policies and credentials to return tri-values and statement lists. It is useful for policies to return a justification, which can be expressed as a list of statements,

along with a tri-value answer. For example, a policy may reject downloading of code and provide statements indicating the following:

- Whether the code is known to be malicious
- Whether the local machine is currently too heavily loaded to permit downloads

It is also useful for credential programs to indicate whether the execution was successful (a tri-value) in addition to returning a list of statements. Thus, in REFEREE, *every* program returns both a tri-value and a list of statements. However, we will continue to observe the distinction between policies and credentials in this paper, for purposes of exposition.

Applications running on a Web server, a proxy server, or a personal computer may invoke REFEREE. When an application program invokes REFEREE, it provides a database of available programs, provides an initial statement list (that may be empty), designates a particular program (policy) to run, and optionally provides additional arguments to the designated program.

### The Logic of Tri-Values

Notions of true and false are familiar from Boolean logic. When asking, however, about authorization of a particular action (for example, "Should the following purchase order be approved?"), there are typically three possible outcomes:

1. "Yes, the action may be taken because sufficient credentials exist for the action to be approved."

2. "No, the action may not be taken because sufficient credentials exist to deny the action."

3. "The trust management system was unable to find sufficient credentials either to approve or to deny the requested action."

In the third case, the value returned by the trust management system is neither true nor false, but unknown, for the policy that was in force during the evaluation was not able to make a determination about the requested action. It is up to the application calling the trust management system to decide what action (if any) should be taken when the trust management system returns "unknown."

An alternative approach using only Boolean values would be to extend the definition of "false" to include requests with insufficient credentials to make a trust management decision. That is, an answer of false from the system would indicate "the action may not be taken either because sufficient credentials exist to deny the action or because sufficient credentials could not be found either to permit or to deny the action." Notice, however, that this solution intrinsically biases the trust management system against affirming questions asked of it, which may force users to ask questions in twisted forms to gain the desired mode of operation. This bias is often considered appropriate, particularly in "high security" applications. Because many Web applications do not fit easily into traditional "high security paradigms," we have chosen to avoid this bias in REFEREE. For a thorough discussion of the difficulties caused by allowing the trust management system to return a value of "unknown," see [5, Section 4]. Further, it may be counter-productive to hide the fact that a decision could not be reached under the current policy from calling applications, especially when the policy is invoked as a subprogram of another policy, which may have alternative policies for dealing with a lack of credentials.

## Statement Lists

A REFEREE statement is a two-element structure consisting of some *content* and a *context* for that content. The context and the content of a statement are each arbitrary s-expressions; the context determines how the content is to be interpreted, and the interpretation of the context itself is subject to agreement between the calling application and REFEREE. Statement lists are simply unordered lists of REFEREE statements.

## Invocations

The ability for one policy to call another policy is central to REFEREE for two reasons:

- Policies in general often defer judgment on some point to other policies: Bob may choose to allow his children to view any Web page that Alice allows her children to view.

- Evaluation of a particular request may require dangerous activity (such as network access), and invocations allow such dangerous actions to be executed from within REFEREE policies.

Thus, dangerous activity is controlled by policy, which is one aspect of REFEREE's central tenet of "everything is under policy control."

All programs that can be invoked by a REFEREE program must conform to the REFEREE calling conventions. The required input to a program is a statement list defining the current evaluation context; programs may also accept additional arguments (either required or optional). The output of an invocation is a REFEREE expression value: a tri-value and a statement list. Typically, a program will append returned statements to one of its own statement lists.

Note that once a REFEREE program invokes another program, control of the REFEREE engine is transferred to that program until it chooses to exit. Thus, invocation is inherently dangerous because the invoking program has no way to monitor or interrupt execution of the invoked program. It is important, therefore, to think carefully about whether it is acceptable to invoke a program before actually doing so.

## Installation

The REFEREE environment is extensible—it permits addition of new programs as long as they conform to the calling conventions. Thus, if a new cryptographic hash function is defined, a new hash-checking program can be added without reworking other components of a policy. Programs can even be downloaded and installed dynamically during execution. Once a callable program is downloaded over the Web a trust management decision must be made regarding whether the controlling REFEREE policy should allow the downloaded module to be invoked. REFEREE requires that a program explicitly *install* the invocable program into the database of named programs before it can be called. Thus, the addition of a new, callable program to REFEREE is controlled by the currently running policy.

Installations are not persistent across multiple calls to REFEREE unless the calling application explicitly takes action to make them so. That is, the calling application would need to record the new program and pass it in as part of the initial program database in future calls to REFEREE. Within an execution of REFEREE, installations have dynamic scope; a program can by default only install new functionality for itself and other programs it calls, not the programs that called it. Particular programs are free to override this default within their own scope, effectively enabling installations to have global scope.

## The Profiles-0.92 Language

W3C's PICS [6] and DSig (Digital Signature) [7] working groups are designing a language for expressing the most common policies involving PICS labels and digital signatures. The current incarnation, `profiles-0.92`, has four important features:

- Appending of statements returned by invoked programs
- The *Load-labels* invocable program
- Tri-value combinators and operators
- Statement-list pattern matching

`profiles-0.92` includes a language construct, *invoke*, for calling another REFEREE program. Programs are called using REFEREE's underlying mechanism. The name of the invoked program is prepended to the context portion of each returned statement; the statements are then appended to the initial statement list that was passed to the invoked program. In this manner, a program can invoke a subprogram to generate additional statements but keep track of which program generated them. The execution trace section provides a concrete example.

A `profiles-0.92` program can invoke the load-labels program to look for PICS labels, either embedded in documents or retrieved over the network from a label bureau. Once found, the labels are parsed and written as REFEREE statements, which are returned.

`profiles-0.92` provides tri-value generalizations of the Boolean operators AND, OR, and NOT. For example, (AND true false) evaluates to false, but (AND true unknown) evaluates to unknown. In addition, the operators *true-if-unknown* and *false-if-unknown* coerce tri-values into conventional Boolean values.

Finally, `profiles-0.92` provides a pattern matcher that examines the statement list for statements of a particular form.

The next section describes the features of the language.

## Sample Policies

We now present example policies written for REFEREE and explained in English. They illustrate the following three features of REFEREE:

- REFEREE can process and resolve conflicting information from multiple sources.
- Evaluation of policy itself may involve dangerous actions. REFEREE gives the user control over this.
- REFEREE allows a user to defer trust—to authorize privileged credentials to decide the acceptability of another credential.

Some of the following examples use a hypothetical PICS rating service called musac, with two dimensions, `sax` and `violins` (abbreviated `s` and `v` in PICS labels), and values 0, 1, and 2 along each dimension. Other examples use hypothetical rating services `"http://www.e-trust.org/privacy-descriptions"` and `"http://w3.org/privacy"` whose dimensions and values will be explained as needed. Throughout this section, we use the policy language `profiles-0.92` at the top level.

## Sample Policy 1

In Sample Policy 1 (Example 1), we view any URL with a PICS label in the musac system with `s < 2`.

We are worried about excessive use of saxophones in music distributed over the Internet. We trust publishers and all others to honestly declare the number of saxophones used; we want to check this number before browsing the URL.

This policy has two steps. First, we invoke `"load-label"` to find and download labels for the given URL; any labels found will be put on the statement list. We then run a pattern-matcher over the now-modified statement list, looking for any label using the rating service from `"http://www.musac.org/"`, with an `s` rating less than 2. If the matcher finds no musac label with an `s` dimension, it returns `unknown`; if it finds such a label, it returns `true` or `false` depending on whether the associated value is less than 2. The line `false-if-unknown` has the effect of converting a returned value `unknown` to `false`; this is a policy decision regarding semantics to give to three-valued logic—specifically about the meaning of `unknown`. The overall effect is to allow viewing of any document for which we can find at least a single label with a `musac-s` rating less than 2.

The following examples will build on this policy template.

## Sample Policy 2

In Sample Policy 2 (Example 2), we view URLs only if all PICS labels in the musac system for the URL say `s < 2`.

This policy is almost identical to Sample Policy 1 above, except that the restriction operator within the pattern matcher is `<!` instead of `<`. The `!`-ending restriction operators require every matching statement that is tested against the operator to satisfy the operator. The effect is that *all* labels from all sources that indicate a sax level must indicate a low sax level. Thus a user can choose this policy instead of the previous one, depending on how the user wants to resolve simultaneous reception of a label from Alice saying `musac-s level` 1 and a label from Bob saying `musac-s level` 2.

An alternative way to handle conflicting labels is to specify the rater(s) we recognize. For example, the variant in Example 3 tells the matcher to insist on labels from Alice.

**Example 1**

```
(invoke "load-label" STATEMENT-LIST URL "http://www.musac.org/" (EMBEDDED))
(false-if-unknown
 (match
  (("load-label" *)
   (* ((version "PICS-1.1") *
       (service "http://www.musac.org/") *
       (ratings (RESTRICT < s 2)))))
  STATEMENT-LIST))
```

**Example 2**

```
(invoke "load-label" STATEMENT-LIST URL "http://www.musac.org/" (EMBEDDED))
(false-if-unknown
 (match
  (("load-label" *)
   (* ((version "PICS-1.1") *
       (service "http://www.musac.org/") *
       (ratings (RESTRICT <! s 2)))))
   STATEMENT-LIST))
```

**Example 3**

```
(invoke "load-label" STATEMENT-LIST URL "http://www.musac.org/" (EMBEDDED))
(false-if-unknown
 (match
  (("load-label" *)
   (* ((version "PICS-1.1") *
       (service "http://www.musac.org/") *
       (by "mailto:alice")
       (ratings (RESTRICT < s 2)))))
   STATEMENT-LIST))
```

## Sample Policy 3

In Sample Policy 3 (Example 4), we combine simple filters and use a label bureau. This time we are not worried about the content of URLs but instead about what a remote host will do with information we submit. We therefore consult PICS labels in rating services that rate URLs according to the site's treatment of private information submitted by users. In Example 4, a value less than 2 in the **data-exchange** dimension of `"http://www.e-trust.org/privacy-descriptions"` indicates that the remote host gives no user-submitted data to anyone else. A value of 0 in the **personal-data-collected** dimension of

`"http://w3.org/privacy"` indicates that no information at all is retained.

This policy uses labels from two services. In the first step, we load labels for URL by invoking `"load-label"` twice, once for each rating service; `"load-label"` adds statements to the statement-list. We then search the returned statements for labels using two rating services, E-Trust and *w3.org*'s privacy service. Each pattern match uses criteria specific to one rating service, and the results of those two pattern-matches are then combined using **and**. Thus, in order for the policy to be satisfied, there must be labels in both rating services.

**Example 4**

```
(invoke "load-label" STATEMENT-LIST URL
        "http://www.e-trust.org/privacy-descriptions" ("http://labels.com"))
(invoke "load-label" STATEMENT-LIST URL
        "http://w3.org/privacy" ("http://labels.com"))
(false-if-unknown
 (and
  (match
   (("load-label" *)
    (* ((version "PICS-1.1") *
        (service "http://www.e-trust.org/privacy-descriptions") *
```

**Example 4**        *(continued)*

```
        (ratings (RESTRICT < data-exchange 2)))))
  STATEMENT-LIST)
 (match
  (("load-label" *)
   (* ((version "PICS-1.1") *
       (service "http://w3.org/privacy") *
       (ratings (RESTRICT = personal-data-collected 0)))))
  STATEMENT-LIST)))
```

In the previous examples, the requested document was downloaded and scanned for embedded labels, which would be used to decide whether to display the document. In a privacy application, what is at stake is our private information that could be passed to the remote host, including the fact that we accessed the site at all. For this reason, the user here has decided not to scan the document for labels (which would involve connecting to the remote site), but only to request labels separately from the document (from the bureau `"http://labels.com"`, which the user trusts for this purpose). Using this policy, we won't even connect to the originally-requested remote site unless we've first decided that it is safe.

## Sample Policy 4

In Sample Policy 4 (Example 5), we defer trust to GoodMouseClicking.

The alternate in Sample Policy 2 explicitly trusted a single rater of content, Alice. A more likely situation is that we would trust a single auditor (or a small number of auditors) and accept only labels from raters unknown to us but endorsed by the auditor. In Example 5, we assume that the user trusts GoodMouseClicking to endorse raters. The user sets a policy of trusting reviews from those reviewers for which GoodMouseClicking vouches.

The module `endorse-label` is a separate program that handles requests for deferral of trust. It takes a rater and a label bureau as arguments and contacts the label bureau to request labels from the specified rater that vouch for the author of each of the statements on STATEMENT-LIST. When GoodMouseClicking is found to vouch for a statement's author, GoodMouseClicking's identifier is added to the beginning of that statement, and the new statement is returned, to be added to the caller's STATEMENT-LIST. As in the previous examples, the *match* expression then searches the statement list, in this case for a statement added by the `endorse-label` program that begins with `"mailto:GoodMouseClicking@w3.org"`.

## Example 5

```
(invoke "load-label" STATEMENT-LIST URL
        "http://www.musac.org/v1.0" ("http://labels.com/"))
(invoke "endorse-label" STATEMENT-LIST
        "mailto:GoodMouseClicking@w3.org" ("http://labels.com/"))
(false-if-unknown
 (match
  (("endorse-label" *)
   (* "mailto:GoodMouseClicking@w3.org" *
    ((version "PICS-1.1") *
     (service "http://www.musac.org/v1.0") *
     (ratings * (RESTRICT < v 2) * )))))
  STATEMENT-LIST))
```

The same principle can be used to insist on signed labels, in case we are worried about forgeries. Instead of invoking `endorse-labels`, we could invoke a module that checks a digital signature or performs other types of cryptographic checks.

## Sample Policies Summary

These examples shown above illustrate three key features of the referee system. First, in Sample Policy 2 we saw how REFEREE can process and resolve conflicting information from multiple sources, by indicating whether all labels must agree or the existence of a single label of the desired type carries the decision. In Sample 3, we saw that the very process of deciding when a URL is acceptable may involve similar trust decisions; REFEREE puts the entire process under policy control. Finally, in Sample 4, we saw how REFEREE can easily adapt to new cryptographic algorithms and new paradigms for security (deferral of trust).

# An Execution Trace

In Examples 6–11, we present an execution trace extracted from a working REFEREE demo. An on-line version of this demo is available [8].

The policy used in this section extends Sample Policy 4 to include checking of hash functions. Here we emphasize the way different modules interact with each other as well as the data flow. There are four modules used here:

- `profiles-0.92`
- `load-label`
- `check-hash`
- `endorse-label`

The `profiles-0.92` module is the top-level module called by the REFEREE invoker to interpret the policy as described above, the `check-hash` module verifies hash values in PICS labels, and the `load-label` and `endorse-label` modules are explained in the previous section. When the caller invokes REFEREE with this policy and the URL `http://www.w3.org/pub/WWW/Overview.html` of interest, `profiles-0.92` first invokes `load-label`. `load-label` actually gets one label from the label bureau `http://labels.com` and returns the contents of Example 7. The module `load-label` returns true, because a label is found. The statement list contains a single statement describing the PICS label. The context of the statement is empty, because it is produced by the module itself. The caller `profiles-0.92` records this statement by prepending the name of the called module, "load-label," onto each context and appending the result shown in Example 8 onto its local copy of `STATEMENT-LIST`.

### Example 6

```
(invoke "load-label" STATEMENT-LIST URL
        "http://www.musac.org/v1.0" ("http://labels.com/"))
(invoke "check-hash" STATEMENT-LIST)
(invoke "endorse-label" STATEMENT-LIST
        "mailto:GoodMouseClicking@w3.org" ("http://labels.com/"))
(false-if-unknown (match (("endorse-label" "check-hash" *)
                   (* "mailto:GoodMouseClicking@w3.org" *
                     ((version "PICS-1.1") *
                      (service "http://www.musac.org/v1.0") *
                      (ratings * (RESTRICT < v 2) * ))))
                 STATEMENT-LIST))
```

## Example 7

```
tri-value = true
statement-list = ((()
                    (("load-label" "http://www.w3.org/pub/WWW/Overview.html"
                                   "http://labels.com/")
                  ((version "PICS-1.1")
                   (service "http://www.musac.org/v1.0")
                   (original
                       (PICS-1.1 "http://www.musac.org/v1.0"
                                 labels by "alice@rater.org"
                                        md5 "7A2B1a2bA72BxyzyplehJQ=="
                                        ratings (s 1 v 0)))
                   (by "alice@rater.org")
                   (md5 "7A2B1a2bA72BxyzyplehJQ==")
                   (ratings (s 1) (v 0))))))
```

Now `profiles-0.92` proceeds to the second line to check MD5 with the parsed statement above. The module `check-hash` is passed the above statement-list and, assuming the hash is good, returns

```
tri-value = true
```

and the same statement list it was passed. The caller, `profiles-0.92`, prepends `"check-hash"` onto each context and appends the statement in Example 9 to its copy of STATEMENT-LIST:

The presence of `"check-hash"` in the *context* of the statement indicates the hash verification. Now `profiles-0.92` proceeds to the third line, invoking the module `endorse-label` to check for an endorsement. Assuming the endorsing label is found, `endorse-label` returns a statement-list that gets `"endorse-label"` prepended to the context, resulting in Example 10.

Again, the string `"endorse-label"` is added to the context of this statement to indicate that the rater of this PICS label statement is approved by `endorse-label` policy. The passed content is wrapped in an expression containing `"mailto:GoodMouseClicking@w3.org"` (the name of the endorser).

Finally, `profiles-0.92` proceeds to the last line to check ratings. The match looks for a context with both `"endorse-label"` and `"check-hash"`—if either is missing, the match fails. Because the match succeeds, `profiles-0.92` returns to the application a tri-value of true and a statement-list of the statements produced by the form in Example 11, the *match*.

## Example 8

```
statement-list = ((("load-label")
                    (("load-label" "http://www.w3.org/pub/WWW/Overview.html"
                                   "http://labels.com/")
                  ((version "PICS-1.1")
                   (service "http://www.musac.org/v1.0")
                   (original (PICS-1.1 ...))
                   (by "alice@rater.org")
                   (md5 "7A2B1a2bA72BxyzyplehJQ==")
                   (ratings (s 1) (v 0))))))
```

**Example 9**

```
statement-list = ((("check-hash" "load-label")
                   (("load-label" "http://www.w3.org/pub/WWW/Overview.html"
                                  "http://labels.com/")
                    ((version "PICS-1.1")
                     (service "http://www.musac.org/v1.0")
                     (original (PICS-1.1 ...))
                     (by "alice@rater.org")
                     (md5 "7A2B1a2bA72BxyzyplehJQ==")
                     (ratings (s 1) (v 0))))))
```

The returned values say the action should be taken (tri-value is true), and it is justified by the rater-endorsed, hash-checked PICS label in the statement-list. They are returned to the caller application (such as a browser), and it interprets the action appropriately (by displaying the URL on the screen).

### Execution Trace Summary

This execution trace demonstrates that a typical decision about viewing a URL may involve (at least) the following tasks:

- Fetching credentials

- Authenticating credentials

- Deciding which credentials are trustworthy

Users may want to customize their policies for these tasks individually, and REFEREE allows a user to express each policy in a separate module.

The modules communicate via a common API that consists of passing statements in the convenient context-content format and returning both a true/false/unknown result and a justification in the form of additional statements.

## Conclusion

The most important feature of REFEREE is that it places all dangerous operations under policy control, rather than making arbitrary decisions to accept certain dangers and avoid others. For example, it might seem natural to avoid the danger of spoofed labels by requiring that the authenticity of all labels be verified by checking digital signatures. The likelihood of spoofed labels and their negative consequences, however, depends on the context. REFEREE makes it possible to write a policy that requires signature checking, one that does not, or one that does only in certain circumstances.

**Example 10**

```
tri-value = true
statement-list =
    ((("endorse-label" "check-hash" "load-label")
      ("mailto:GoodMouseClicking@w3.org"
       (("load-label" "http://www.w3.org/pub/WWW/Overview.html"
                      "http://labels.com/")
        ((version "PICS-1.1")
         (service "http://www.musac.org/v1.0")
         (original (PICS-1.1 ...))
         (by "alice@rater.org")
         (md5 "7A2B1a2bA72BxyzyplehJQ==")
         (ratings (s 1) (v 0)))))))
```

**Example 11**

```
tri-value = true
statement-list =
    ((("endorse-label" "check-hash" "load-label")
     ("mailto:GoodMouseClicking@w3.org"
      (("load-label" "http://www.w3.org/pub/WWW/Overview.html"
                      "http://labels.com/")
       ((version "PICS-1.1")
        (service "http://www.musac.org/v1.0")
        (original (PICS-1.1 ...))
        (by "alice@rater.org")
        (md5 "7A2B1a2bA72BxyzyplehJQ==")
        (ratings (s 1) (v 0))))))))
```

The Web will benefit greatly from a common platform for trust management because different organizations will be able to develop component programs. REFEREE is a promising candidate platform: its calling conventions impose minimal requirements on component programs while ensuring that they interoperate. As new safety features are desired, they can be added as installable programs, without rewriting all the other features. ■

### References

1. G. Necula, "Proof-Carrying Code," to appear in *Proceedings of the 1997 ACM Symposium on Principles of Programming Languages.*

2. G. Necula and P. Lee, "Safe Kernel Extensions without Run-time Checking," in *Proceedings of the 1996 Usenix Symposium on Operating System Design and Implementation*, pp. 229–243.

3. M. Blaze, J. Feigenbaum, and J. Lacy, "Decentralized Trust Management," in *Proceedings of the 1996 IEEE Symposium on Security and Privacy*, pp. 164–173. Also available as a DIMACS Technical Report from *ftp://dimacs.rutgers.edu/pub/dimacs/TechnicalReports/TechReports/1996/96-17.ps.gz.*

4. P. Resnick and J. Miller, "PICS: Internet Access Controls without Censorship," *Communications of the ACM*, 39 (1996), pp. 87–93. Also available as *http://www.w3.org/pub/WWW/PICS/iacwcv2.htm.*

5. M. Blaze, J. Feigenbaum, P. Resnick, and M. Strauss, "Managing Trust in an Information-Labeling System," to appear in *European Transactions on Telecommunications*. Available as AT&T Technical Report 96.15.1 and from *http://www.research.att.com/~presnick/papers/bfrs/.*

6. A working policy evaluator can be found online in *http://www.w3.org/pub/WWW/PICS/TrustMgt/demo/Overview.html.*

7. The PICS Working Group home page is *http://www.w3.org/PICS/.* The Digital Signature Initiative home page is *http://www.w3.org/pub/WWW/Security/DSig/.*

8. The online version of the demo is available at *http://www.w3.org/pub/WWW/PICS/TrustMgt/demo/Overview.html.* The REFEREE home page is at *http://www.w3.org/pub/WWW/PICS/TrustMgt/.*

## Acknowledgments

We thank Jonathan Brezin of IBM, Mary Fernandez and Kathleen Fisher of AT&T, and Rohit Khare and Jim Miller of W3C for helpful discussion on the early development of the Profiles language and the REFEREE system.

## About the Authors

**Yang-Hua Chu**
MIT/W3C
545 Technology Square
Cambridge Massachusetts 02139
*yhchu@mit.edu*

Yang-hua Chu is currently a Master of Engineering student at the Massachusetts Institute of Technology majoring in Computer Science. His interests are in cryptography and network security.

**Joan Feigenbaum**
AT&T Laboratories
180 Park Ave.
P.O. Box 971
Florham Park, NJ 07932-0971
*jf@research.att.com*

Joan Feigenbaum received a BA in Mathematics from Harvard and a PhD in Computer Science from Stanford. She is currently a Technology Consultant in the Algorithms and Optimization Department of AT&T Labs Research in Florham Park, NJ. Her interests are in security and cryptology, computational complexity theory, and algorithmic techniques for massive data sets. Within the security area, she is now working on systems to manage trust relationships in large, heterogeneous electronic marketplaces. She is on the editorial board of the *SIAM Journal on Computing* and recently became the Editor-in-Chief of the *Journal of Cryptology.*

**Brian LaMacchia**
AT&T Laboratories
180 Park Ave.
P.O. Box 971
Florham Park, NJ 07932-0971
*bal@research.att.com*

Brian LaMacchia received the S.B., S.M., and Ph.D. degrees from the Massachusetts Institute of Technology in 1990, 1991, and 1996, respectively. He is currently a member of the Public Policy Research group at AT&T Labs—Research in Florham Park, NJ. His research interests include cryptography and security, automated resource discovery, and the interactions between various legal regimes and the network. He is a member of Eta Kappa Nu, Tau Beta Pi, and Sigma Xi.

**Paul Resnick**
AT&T Laboratories
180 Park Ave.
P.O. Box 971
Florham Park, NJ 07932-0971
*presnick@research.att.com*

Paul Resnick received a Ph.D. in computer science from MIT in 1992. He is a Senior Technical Staff Member at AT&T Labs—Research. He also chairs the PICS Working Group at the World Wide Web Consortium. His research focuses on systems for sharing recommendations and reputations.

**Martin Strauss**
AT&T Laboratories
180 Park Ave.
P.O. Box 971
Florham Park, NJ 07932-0971
*mstrauss@research.att.com*

Martin Strauss is a senior technical staff member at AT&T Labs in Florham Park, New Jersey. He holds an A.B. degree from Columbia University and a PhD from Rutgers University, both in mathematics, and did a year of post-doctoral research at Iowa State University before joining AT&T. He has written several articles on complexity theory and computer security.

Homepages for the authors' organizations are *http://web.mit.edu/, http://www.w3.org/,* and *http://www.research.att.com/.* Send email to the authors at *yhchu@mit.edu, {jf, bal, presnick, mstrauss}@research.att.com.*

# Introducing SSL and Certificates Using SSLeay

*Frederick J. Hirsch*

## Abstract

*Security is important on the Web. Whether sharing financial, business, or personal information, people want to know with whom they are communicating (authentication), they want to ensure that what is sent is what is received (integrity), and they want to prevent others from intercepting what they are communicating (privacy). The Secure Sockets Layer protocol [13] provides one means for achieving these goals and is the subject of this article.*

*We introduce SSL by reviewing cryptographic techniques and by discussing certificates. We then describe SSL and packages for implementing SSL. We conclude with examples of how to use SSLeay, the free implementation of SSL by Eric Young. We use the SSLeay toolkit to create a Certificate Authority, as well as server and client certificates.*

## Introduction

An introduction to SSL, this article is aimed at readers who are familiar with the Web, HTTP, and Web servers, but are not security experts. It is not intended to be a definitive guide to the SSL protocol, nor does it discuss specific servers, techniques for managing certificates in an organization, or the important legal issues of patents and import and export restrictions.* Rather, this article guides users in implementing SSL, and pulls together various concepts, definitions, and examples as a starting point for further exploration.

## Cryptographic Techniques

Understanding SSL requires an understanding of cryptographic algorithms, message digest functions, and digital signatures. These techniques are the subject of entire books [8], and provide the basis for privacy, integrity, and authentication.

## Cryptographic Algorithms

Suppose Alice wants to send a message to her bank to transfer some money. Alice would like the message to be private, since it will include information such as her account number and transfer amount. One solution is to use a cryptographic algorithm, a technique that would transform her message into an encrypted form, unreadable except by those it is intended for. Once in this form, the message may only be interpreted through the use of a secret key. Without the key the message is useless: good cryptographic algorithms make it so difficult for intruders to decode the original text that it isn't worth their effort.

There are two categories of cryptographic algorithms: conventional and public key.

- *Conventional cryptography*, also known as symmetric cryptography, requires the sender and receiver to share a key: a secret piece of

---

* Our investigations make use of the fact that patent issues may be avoided in non-commercial experimentation, and export issues may be avoided by using weaker cryptography. The SSL 3.0 specification provides some information on U.S. export regulations. We do not address patent or export regulations here, other than to say you should be aware of them, observe them, and consult an attorney. There are a number of surveys of the issues available [6]. In addition, a brief explanation of export control law can be found in Simson Garfinkel's article, "Cryptography and the Web," in this issue.

information that may be used to encrypt or decrypt a message. If this key is secret, then nobody other than the sender or receiver may read the message. If Alice and the bank know a secret key, they may send each other private messages. The task of privately choosing a key before communicating, however, can be problematic.

- *Public key cryptography,* also known as asymmetric cryptography, solves the key exchange problem by defining an algorithm that uses two keys for encrypting a message. If one key is used to encrypt a message then the other must be used to decrypt it. This makes it possible to receive secure messages simply by publishing one key (the public key) and keeping the other secret (the private key). Anyone may encrypt a message using the public key, but only the owner of the private key will be able to read it. In this way, Alice may send private messages to the owner of a key-pair (the bank), by encrypting it using the public key. Only the bank will be able to decrypt it.

## Message Digests

Although Alice may encrypt her message to make it private, there is still a concern that someone might modify her original message or substitute it with a different one, in order to transfer the money to themselves, for instance. One way of guaranteeing the integrity of Alice's message is to create a concise summary of her message and send this to the bank as well. Upon receipt of the message, the bank creates its own summary and compares it with the one Alice sent. If they agree then the message was received intact.

A summary such as this is called a *message digest,* or *one-way hash.* Message digests are used to create short, fixed-length representations of longer, variable-length messages. Digest algorithms are designed to produce unique digests for different messages. This design makes it almost impossible both to determine the message from the digest and to find two different messages which create the same digest—thus eliminating the possibility of substituting one message for another while maintaining the same digest.

Another challenge that Alice faces is finding a way to send the digest to the bank securely; when this is achieved, the integrity of the associated message is assured. One way to do this is to include the digest in a digital signature.

## Digital Signatures

When Alice sends a message to the bank, the bank needs to ensure that the message is really from her, so an intruder does not request a transaction involving her account. A *digital signature,* created by Alice and included with the message, serves this purpose.[*]

Digital signatures are created by encrypting a digest of the message, and other information (such as a sequence number) with the sender's private key. Though anyone may *decrypt* the signature using the public key, only the signer knows the private key. Including the digest in the signature means the signature is only good for that message; it also ensures the integrity of the message since no one can change the digest and still sign it. To guard against the interception and reuse of the signature by an intruder at a later date, the signature contains a unique sequence number. This protects the bank from a fraudulent claim from Alice that she did not send the message—only she could have signed it (non-repudiation).

## Certificates

Although Alice could have sent a private message to the bank, signed it, and ensured the integrity of the message, she still needs to be sure that the

---

[*] For more information on digital signatures see the "DSig 1.0 Signature Labels" specification in the "W3C Reports" section of this issue.

**Table 1**     Certificate Information

| | |
|---|---|
| Subject | Distinguished Name, Public Key |
| Issuer | Distinguished Name, Signature |
| Period of Validity | Not Before Date, Not After Date |
| Administrative Information | Version, Serial Number |
| Extended Information | |

bank owns the public key. Similarly, the bank also needs to verify that the message signature really corresponds to Alice's signature. If each party has a certificate which validates the other's identity, confirms the public key, and is signed by a trusted agency, then they both will be assured that they are communicating with whom they think they are. Such a trusted agency is called a *Certificate Authority*, and certificates are used for authentication.

## Certificate Contents

A certificate associates a public key with the real identity of an individual, server, or other entity, known as the subject. As shown in Table 1, information about the subject includes identifying information (the distinguished name) and the public key. It also includes the identification and signature of the Certificate Authority that issued the certificate, and the period of time during which the certificate is valid. It may have additional information (or extensions) as well as administrative information for the Certificate Authority's use, such as a serial number.

A distinguished name is used to provide an identity in a specific context—for instance, an individual might have a personal certificate as well as one for their identity as an employee. Distinguished names are defined by the X.509 standard [2], which defines the fields, field names, and abbreviations used to refer to the fields (Table 2).

A Certificate Authority may define a policy specifing which distinguished field names are optional, and which are required. It may also place requirements upon the field contents, as may users of certificates. For example, a Netscape browser requires that the Common Name for a certificate representing a server matches a regular expression for the domain name of that server, such as *.opengroup.org*.

The *binary format* of a certificate is defined using the ASN.1 notation [1] [4]. This notation defines how to specify the contents, and encoding rules define how this information is translated into binary form. The *binary encoding* of the certificate is defined using Distinguished Encoding

**Table 2**     Distinguished Name Information

| Field | Abbreviation | Description | Example |
|---|---|---|---|
| Common Name | CN | Name being certified | CN=Frederick Hirsch |
| Organization or Company | O | Name is associated with this organization | O=The Open Group |
| Organization Unit | OU | Name is associated with this organization unit, such as a department | OU=Research Institute |
| City/Locality | L | Name is located in this City | L=Cambridge |
| State/Province | SP | Name is located in this State/Province | SP=Massachusetts |
| Country | C | Name is located in this Country (ISO code) | C=US |

Rules (DER), which are based on the more general Basic Encoding Rules (BER). For those transmissions that cannot handle binary, the binary form may be translated into an ASCII form by using base64 encoding. This encoded version is called PEM encoded, when placed between the following lines:

```
-----BEGIN CERTIFICATE-----
-----END CERTIFICATE-----
```

## Certificate Authorities

By first verifying the information in a certificate request, the Certificate Authority assures the identity of the private key owner of a key-pair. For instance, if Alice requests a personal certificate, the Certificate Authority must first make sure that Alice really is the person the certificate request claims.

### Certificate chains

A Certificate Authority may also issue a certificate for another Certificate Authority. When examining a certificate, Alice may also need to examine the certificate of the issuer, for each parent Certificate Authority, until reaching one which she has confidence in. She may decide to trust only certificates with a limited chain of issuers, to reduce her risk of a "bad" certificate in the chain.

### Creating a root level certificate authority

As noted earlier, each certificate requires an issuer to assert the validity of the identity of the certificate subject, up to the top-level Certificate Authority. This presents a problem: who vouches for the certificate of the top-level authority, which has no issuer? In this unique case, the certificate is "self-signed," so the issuer of the certificate is the same as the subject. As a result, one must exercise extra care in trusting a self-signed certificate. The wide publication of a public key by the root authority reduces the risk in trusting this key—it would be obvious if someone else publicized a key claiming to be the authority. Browsers are preconfigured to trust well-known certificate authorities.

A number of companies such as VeriSign [11] have established themselves as certificate authorities. These companies perform the following services:

- Verifying certificate requests
- Processing certificate requests
- Issuing and managing certificates

It is also possible to create your own Certificate Authority. Although risky in the Internet environment, it may be useful within an Intranet where the organization can easily verify the identities of individuals and servers.

### Certificate management

Establishing a Certificate Authority is a responsibility that requires solid administrative, technical, and management framework. Certificate Authorities not only issue certificates, they also manage them—that is, they determine how long certificates are valid, they renew them, and they keep lists of certificates that have already been issued but are no longer valid (certificate revocation lists, or CRLs). Say Alice is entitled to a certificate as an employee of a company. Say, too, that the certificate needs to be revoked when Alice leaves that company. Since certificates are objects that get passed around, it is impossible to tell from the certificate alone that it has been revoked. When examining certificates for validity, therefore, it is necessary to contact the issuing Certificate Authority to check CRLs—this is not usually an automated part of the process.

### NOTE

If you use a Certificate Authority that is not configured into browsers by default, it is necessary to load the Certificate Authority certificate into the browser, enabling the browser to validate server certificates signed by that Certificate Authority. Doing so may be dangerous, since once loaded, the browser will accept all certificates signed by that Certificate Authority.

# SSL

The Secure Sockets Layer protocol (SSL) is a protocol layer that may be placed between a reliable connection-oriented network layer protocol (TCP/IP) and the application protocol layer (HTTP). SSL provides for secure communication between client and server by allowing mutual authentication, the use of digital signatures for integrity, and encryption for privacy.

The protocol is designed to support a range of choices for specific algorithms used for cryptography, digests, and signatures. This allows algorithm selection for specific servers to be made based on legal, export, or other concerns, and also enables the protocol to take advantage of new algorithms. Choices are negotiated between client and server at the start of establishing a protocol session.

There are a number of versions of the SSL protocol, as shown in Table 3.

As noted in Table 3, one of the benefits in SSL 3.0 is that it adds support of certificate chain loading. This feature allows a server to pass a server certificate along with issuer certificates to the browser. Chain loading also permits the browser to validate the server certificate, even if Certificate Authority certificates are not installed for the intermediate issuers, since they are included in the certificate chain. SSL 3.0 is the basis for the Transaction Layer Security [14] protocol standard, currently in development by the Internet Engineering Task Force (IETF)

## Session Establishment

The SSL session is established by following a *handshake sequence* between client and server, as shown in Figure 1. This sequence may vary, depending on whether the server is configured to provide a server certificate or to request a client certificate. Though cases exist, where additional handshake steps are required for management of cipher information, this article summarizes one common scenario: see the SSL specification for the full range of possibilities.

### NOTE

Once an SSL session has been established it may be reused, thus avoiding the performance penalty of repeating the many steps needed to start a session.

The elements of the handshake sequence, as used by the client and server, are listed below:

1. Negotiate the Cipher Suite to be used during data transfer

2. Establish and share a session key between client and server

3. Optionally authenticate the server to the client

4. Optionally authenticate the client to the server

The first step, Cipher Suite negotiation, allows the client and server to choose a Cipher Suite sup-

**Table 3**    Versions of SSL

| Version | Source | Description | Browser Support |
|---------|--------|-------------|-----------------|
| SSL 2.0 | Published by Netscape [12] | Original protocol | Netscape 3.0, Internet Explorer 3.0 |
| SSL 3.0 | Expired Internet Draft [13] | Revisions to prevent specific security attacks, add ciphers, and support certificate chains | Netscape 3.0 Internet Explorer 3.0 |
| TLS 2.0 | IETF Draft [15] | Revision of SSL 3.0 | None |

portable by both of them. The SSL 3.0 protocol specification defines 31 Cipher Suites. Each Cipher Suite is defined by the following components:

- Key exchange method

- Cipher for data transfer

- Message digest for creating the Message Authentication Code (MAC)

These three elements are described in the sections that follow.

## Key exchange method

The *key exchange method* defines how the shared secret symmetric cryptography key used for application data transfer will be agreed upon by client and server. SSL 2.0 uses RSA key exchange, while the SSL 3.0 supports a choice of key exchange algorithms including the RSA key exchange when certificates are used, and Diffie-Hellman key exchange for exchanging keys without certificates and without prior communication between client and server [5].

One variable in the choice of key exchange methods is digital signatures—whether or not to use them, and if so, what kind of signatures to use. Signing with a private key provides assurance against a man-in-the-middle-attack during the information exchange used in generating the shared key [8, p. 516].

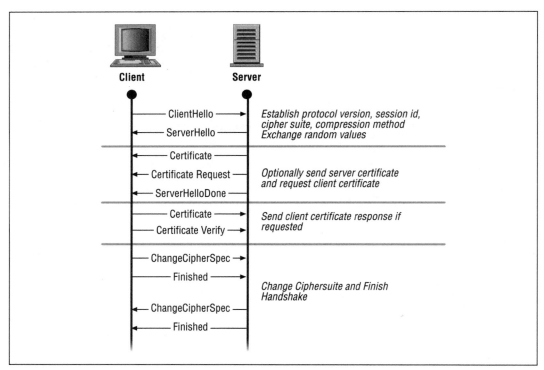

**Figure 1**     Simplified handshake sequence

## Cipher for data transfer

SSL uses the conventional cryptography algorithm (symmetric cryptography) described earlier for encrypting messages in a session. There are nine choices, including the choice to perform no encryption:

- No encryption
- Stream Ciphers
  - RC4 with 40-bit keys
  - RC4 with 128-bit keys
- CBC Block Ciphers
  - RC2 with 40 bit key
  - DES40, DES, 3DES_EDE
  - IDEA
  - Fortezza

"CBC" refers to Cipher Block Chaining, which means that a portion of the previously encrypted cipher text is used in the encryption of the current block. "DES" refers to the Data Encryption Standard [8, Chapter 12], which has a number of variants (including DES40 and 3DES_EDE). "Idea" is one of the best and cryptographically strongest available algorithms, and "RC2" is a proprietary algorithm from RSA [8, Chapter 13].

## Digest function

The choice of digest function determines how a digest is created from a record unit. SSL supports the following:

- No digest (Null choice)
- MD5, a 128-bit hash
- Secure Hash Algorithm (SHA), a 160-bit hash designed for use with the Digital Signature Standard (DSS) [5]

The message digest is used to create a Message Authentication Code (MAC), which is encrypted with the message to provide integrity and to prevent against replay attacks.

## Handshake Sequence Protocol

The handshake sequence uses three protocols:

- The "SSL Handshake Protocol," for performing the client and server SSL session establishment.
- The "SSL Change Cipher Spec protocol," for actually establishing agreement on the Cipher Suite for the session.
- The "SSL Alert Protocol," for conveying SSL error messages between client and server.

These protocols, as well as application protocol data, are encapsulated in the "SSL Record Protocol," as shown in Figure 2. An encapsulated protocol is transferred as data by the lower layer protocol, which does not examine the data. The encapsulated protocol has no knowledge of the underlying protocol.

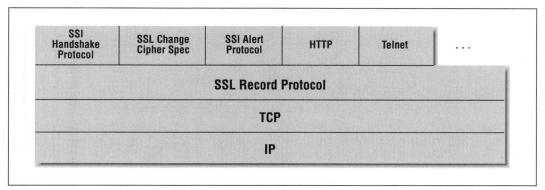

**Figure 2**    SSL protocol stack

The encapsulation of SSL control protocols by the record protocol means that if an active session is renegotiated the control protocols will be transmitted securely. If there were no session before, then the NULL Cipher Suite is used, which means there is no encryption and messages have no integrity digests until the session has been established.

## Data Transfer

The SSL Record Protocol, shown in Figure 3, is used to transfer application and SSL control data between the client and server, possibly fragmenting this data into smaller units, or combining multiple higher level protocol data messages into single units. It may compress, attach digest signatures, and encrypt these units before transmitting them using the underlying reliable transport protocol.

## Securing Web HTTP Communication

One common use of SSL is to secure Web HTTP communication between a browser client and a Web server. This case does not preclude the use of non-secured HTTP. The secure version uses URLs that begin with https rather than http, and a different server port (by default, 443). The browser will maintain client certificate private keys when they are generated, and display an indicator if a secure connection is being used.

# Implementing SSL

Although one might write an SSL implementation from scratch following the specification, it is much easier to use one of the existing SSL toolkit libraries. In addition, because of patents, it is usually necessary to license some of the cryptography libraries, at least in the United States. SSL toolkits include encryption, message digest, and

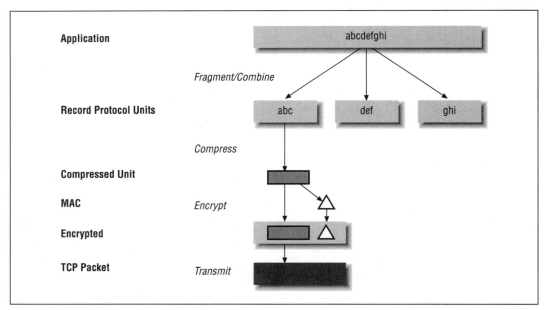

**Figure 3**    SSL record protocol

certificate management routines. Each also requires the use of a licensed public key package in the United States from Security Dynamics.[*]

There are two prominent RSA public key packages available:

*RSARef*

The RSA Reference implementation, an unsupported source code toolkit from RSA, may be used for freeware and non-commercial applications. Consensus Development Corporation used to market a license for commercial use but will no longer do so. [17]

*BSAFE3.0*

Commercial implementation of RSARef. [16]

These two public key implementations include a complete toolkit of public key algorithms (including RSA encryption and Diffie-Hellman key exchange), symmetric encryption algorithms, and digest functions. They may be used with SSL Toolkits, the most prominent of which include the following:

*SSLRef*

Sample SSL 3.0 implementation from Netscape Communications Corporation. [19]

*SSLPlus*

Commercial source code toolkit available from Consensus Development Corporation, an enhancement of SSLRef3.0. It requires BSAFE3.0 (from RSA) for use. [20]

*SSLava*

SSL 3.0 compliant toolkit written in Java from Phaos Technology. [18]

*SSLeay*

SSLeay-0.6.6 [21] is a free, non-commercial implementation of SSL 2.0 (support for 3.0 is under development). It includes a public key implementation that may be used outside the United States. In the United States, RSARef or BSAFE3.0 must be used due to patent requirements. SSLeay offers an inexpensive way to get started with SSL, and is the subject of the next section.

# SSLeay Examples

This section offers examples for creating a Certificate Authority, as well as request, sign, and use certificates using SSLeay. The Appendix offers brief instructions for installing SSLeay, establishing the SSLeay certificate environment, information on the SSLeay configuration file, and sample HTML pages and CGI scripts.

SSLeay 0.6.6 supports SSL 2.0, although support for SSL 3.0 should be available soon. SSL 2.0 is widely implemented and interoperation is easier than with SSL 3.0; we use SSLeay with SSL 2.0 in the examples that follow.

## Creating a Self-Signed CA Certificate

The first step in creating a Certificate Authority (apart from designing the management, administrative, and legal framework) is to create a *self-signed certificate* for the Certificate Authority. This is done in SSLeay by running the *req* command (see Example 5 in the Appendix). This command produces a certificate file (*CAcert.pem*) and key file (*CAkey.pem*). The CA certificate and key files must remain in *$SSLDIR/private*, which is where SSLeay will look for them by default (as specified in the *ssleay.cnf CA default* section), both when acting as a certificate authority, and also when used by the server to implement SSL and validate client certificates signed by the CA.

Install the self-signed certificate in a browser so the browser will recognize server certificates signed by the Certificate Authority. Installing a CA certificate in a browser is somewhat dangerous, unless you trust that certificate and the security of the Certificate Authority. Once installed, the browser accepts any certificate signed by that authority.

---

[*] Originally available from the Public Key Partners [RFC1170] and then from RSA, which was acquired by Security Dynamics [17].

To install the CA certificate, load it using HTTP Content-Type `application/x-x509-ca-cert.` To do this in a manner that does not depend on the server, use the CGI script (Example 6 in the Appendix), or save the certificate in a file with a *cacert* suffix and define this suffix in the server configuration file to correspond to the `application/x-x509-ca-cert` MIME type. For the Apache server, for example, add the line `AddType application/x-x509-ca-cert cacert` to *srm.conf.* The certificate and key files must also remain available to SSLeay for the server to be able to use the public key, and for the certificate authority to use the private key.

## Creating a Server Certificate

A *server certificate* authenticates the server to the client. To make a server certificate, create a certificate request, sign it with the self-signed CA certificate, and then install the certificate as follows:

1. Use the *req* command to create a new certificate request with SSLeay (see Example 8 in the Appendix). This command creates files containing a certificate request, and the private key.

2. Sign the request using the *ca* command (see Example 11 in the Appendix). This will produce a file containing the certificate.

3. Copy the certificate and key files to the server certificate directories:
   ```
   cp newcert.pem $certdir/sitecert.pem
   cp newkey.pem $certdir/sitekey.pem
   ```

4. Create hashes for the certificates in the server directory:
   ```
   cd $certdir
   ln -s sitecert.pem `$SSLDIR/bin/
       x509 -noout -hash < sitecert.pem`.0
   ```

5. Create DER format server certificate file:
   ```
   $SSLDIR/bin/x509 -in CAcert.pem
       -out CAcert.der -outform DER
   ```

6. Update the server configuration file to specify that this is the server certificate to use.

In order to easily find certificates, SSLeay uses hashes of the certificate subject names. Thus, when looking for the certificate of a certificate issuer, it looks for a file named with the hash value of the issuer name. This avoids opening files and examining certificates to find a match. The SSLeay *x509* command may be used to manipulate certificates; one option is to create a hash of the subject name.

Once these steps have been completed, an SSL connection may be established if the server does not require client certificates.

## Creating a Client Certificate

A *client certificate* is used to authenticate a client to a server. Creating and installing a client certificate is more difficult than creating a server certificate because the client must generate a key-pair, keep the private key to itself, and send the public key to the certificate authority to be incorporated into a certificate request. Once a signed certificate has been created using the Certificate Authority, this client certificate must be installed in the client so that the client may present it when needed.

Different clients such as Netscape Navigator 3.01 Gold and Microsoft Internet Explorer 3.02 support different mechanisms for creating client certificates [10, 9]. In this section, we demonstrate a technique for creating and installing a client certificate for each, using SSLeay certificate routines to sign certificate requests.[*]

The procedure for creating a client certificate involves HTML forms; these forms include client specific features such as special tags or JavaScript programs, and Perl CGI scripts that call SSLeay certificate handling applications. The procedures do not rely on special server features, other than the ability to run Perl CGI scripts. The examples completely automate the process, and enable a

---

[*] Back up the Windows NT registry before creating client certificates with Internet Explorer.

client certificate to be installed once the request form is submitted. (In a production environment, the Certificate Authority would need to perform validation instead of automatically issuing the certificate.)

The general steps for creating a client certificate are as follows:

1. User requests HTML page that displays form on client

2. User enters identification information

3. Submission of the form causes the following sequence to occur:

    a. Browser generates a key pair (public and private key)

    b. Private key is stored in browser

    c. Public key is sent with identification information to the server

    d. Server CGI script creates certificate and loads it into the client

The HTML form includes fields (containing defaults) for the different distinguished name attributes to be used in the client certificate, information allowing the browser to generate a key-pair, and a hidden field used to return this information to the CGI script. This hidden information is browser dependent.

In Netscape Navigator, the form contains an additional FORM tag, the <KEYGEN> tag. This tag creates a key pair, and causes the public key to be returned as a form value when the form is submitted (see Example 13 in the Appendix for source of a sample form). The <KEYGEN> tag causes the browser to display a choice of security grades, depending on the version of Navigator. All of the form information is used by the CGI script to create a certificate request, and this request is used to create a client certificate (see Figure 4).

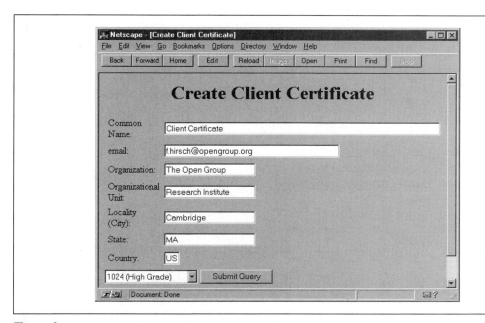

**Figure 4**    Sample Netscape Navigator user certificate form

The Microsoft Internet Explorer HTML form in Figure 5 is more complicated, because Internet Explorer requires a JavaScript (or Visual Basic) program in the page to use an ActiveX control to generate a key pair and create a certificate request. The JavaScript program is downloaded with the HTML page, and called when you press the Submit form button. The program calls the GenReqForm method of the certenr3 ActiveX control, passing to it the distinguished name values from the form. The certificate request produced by the control is then loaded into a hidden field of the form, and returned with the form values of the server CGI script (see Example 15 in the Appendix for a sample HTML page).

Both Netscape Navigator and Microsoft Internet Explorer present a sequence of dialogs as part of the key-pair creation. If this sequence is sucessfully completed then the form will cause the server CGI script to be called with the data from the form. Examples 13 and 15 in the Appendix present two CGI scripts, one for each browser, since the processing is different.

The CGI script for Netscape Navigator (Example 14 in the Appendix) creates a file containing the distinguished name values returned by the form, and a special SPKAC value for the "Signed Public Key And Challenge" generated by Navigator. The *ca* command is called with this file as an argument to generate a client certificate. If successful, this is returned by the CGI script as an `application/x-x509-user-cert` HTTP Convent-Type. Navigator recognizes this type and prompts the user for the remainder of the steps required to install the user certificate in the browser.

The CGI script for processing the Internet Explorer (Example 16 in the Appendix) request is more complicated. It takes the certificate request returned by the form and reformats it to conform to lines of length 72, and then uses the SSLeay *ca* command to create a signed user certificate based on this request. It then takes the client certificate and combines it with the SSLeay certificate revocation list (CRL) to create a PKCS#7 certificate using the SSLeay *crl2pkcs7* utility. The CGI Perl

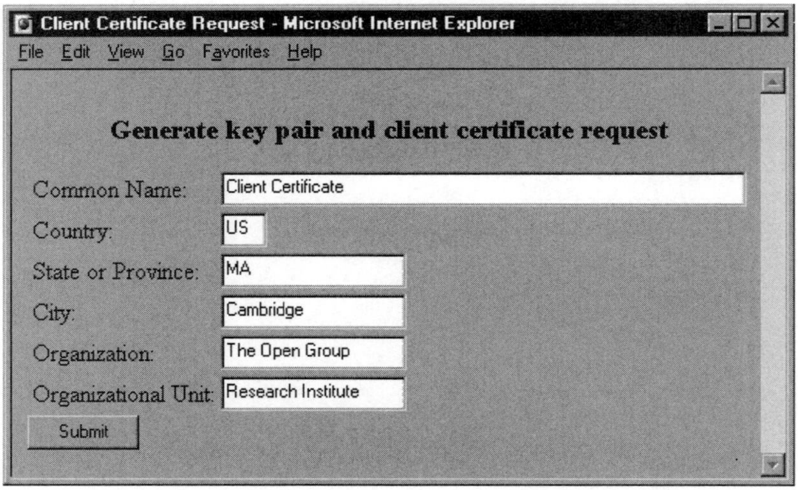

**Figure 5**     Sample Internet Explorer user certificate form

script then dynamically creates an HTML page which includes a JavaScript program to call the AcceptCredentials method of the `certenr3` ActiveX control to install the PKCS#7 certificate. This page is designed to take advantage of the JavaScript `onLoad` method, to automatically call the JavaScript program when the page is loaded, so that the certificate is immediately installed without user interaction. (In a production system, such automatic installation may not be desired.)

**NOTE**

Although I was able to establish an SSL connection using client certificates with Netscape Navigator, and establish an SSL connection with a VeriSign client certificate and the VeriSign client certificate test page,[*] I was unable to establish an SSL client-certificate connection using my client certificate with Microsoft Internet Explorer. The reason for this discrepancy will require more research or additional information from Microsoft.

Once the HTML forms and CGI scripts have been written, and the ActiveX control installed, the process of creating client certificates using SSLeay is simple for users.

## Configuring a Server and Establishing an SSL Connection

The server must have a server certificate installed, and the server's CA certificate must have been installed in the browser. The server will only requesta client certificate from the browser if it is required in the server configuration file. Apache uses the following directive in *httpd.conf:*

```
# Set SSLVerifyClient to:
# 0 if no certicate is required
# 1 if the client may present a
#   valid certificate
# 2 if the client must present a
#   valid certificate
```

```
# 3 if the client may present a
#   valid certificate but it is not
#   required to
#   have a valid CA
SSLVerifyClient 0
```

An SSL connection is established by requesting a URL from the browser of the form *https://example.opengroup.org/*, where the domain refers to the server which supports SSL.

## Conclusion

SSL uses encryption, message digests, digital signatures, and certificates to implement a protocol layer for providing privacy, integrity, and authentication to application protocols such as HTTP. This is valuable in the Web since it will allow a much greater degree of secure communication than is available without SSL. A number of toolkits exist for implementing SSL, including SSLeay. These toolkits also provide the facilities for creating one's own Intranet Certificate Authority and managing certificates. Many issues exist with respect to certificates, including those of certificate revocation and expiration, as well as management issues. Undoubtedly, the remaining issues involved in the management of certificates and Web security will be addressed, but an implementation of SSL using SSLeay permits much more confidence in Web communications .

## Appendix

This appendix offers a number of examples for certification management using SSLeay. The CGI scripts assume you are using Apache (tested with 1.2b7). If you have trouble it might be due to a *CGI.pm* version issue. The scripts in these examples also assume that the server installation directory includes the following subdirectories:

- *htdocs* (standard document root)

- *cgi-bin* (standard CGI directory)

- *certs* (new directory for certificate processing)

---

[*] *http://www.verisign.com/products/sites/job_demo/index.html*

When the scripts operate they create files containing certificate requests and certificates.

## SSLeay Installation

We have experimented using SSLeay and RSARef on UNIX, with the Secure Domain Gateway, a special SSL Web server that interfaces with the Distributed Computing Environment (DCE). We have also experimented using Apache-SSL (`apache_1.2b10+ss1_1.6.tar`). The following examples assume that you are building SSLeay under UNIX (e.g., HP-UX), but it is possible to build SSLeay on other platforms such as Windows NT. The SSLeay-0.6.6 distribution is obtained as a *tar* file (*SSLeay-0.6.6.tar*). A patch file (*SSLeay-0.6.6.patch1*) must also be obtained. Extracting from the *tar* file will create a new directory, *SSLeay-0.6.6*, in which SSLeay is built.

The following examples assume you are working in the *SSLeay-0.6.6* directory. Change to this directory, apply the patch (*patch < SSLeay-0.6.6.patch1*), and then build SSLeay following the directions in the *INSTALL* file. The examples assume that the results of building SSLeay are installed in *$SSLDIR* (e.g., */opt/dev/ssl* ).

SSLeay uses a configuration file (*ssleay.cnf*) that supports named sections, so one configuration file may be used for several purposes. We have modified this file, and show some of these modifications in the examples that follow. Subsequent descriptions in this document show various relevant sections of the log file.

Note that the addition of SSL to the server requires rebuilding the server to include the SSL toolkit and public key sources, and modifying the server configuration to support SSL.

## The SSLeay Certificate Environment

Before using SSLeay, create an environment for managing certificates, update the SSLeay configuration file, and update the server configuration file. Establish the SSLeay certificate management environment using the sequence in Example 1.

## The SSLeay Configuration File

The SSLeay configuration file (*ssleay.cnf*) has multiple sections. These configuration sections must be updated before the certificate authority may be used, especially the **dir** specification in the certificate authority configuration shown in Example 2. The **dir** specification value should be the same as $SSLDIR (e.g., */opt/dev/ssl*).

The **req** section of the configuration file is used when creating certificate requests, and supplies defaults and length limits for the various distinguished name fields. In our examples it has the configuration as shown in Example 3.

The **policy** section of the configuration file is used to define different certificate request signing policies. The examples here include the most lenient policy (**policy_anything**) as well as a stricter policy (**policy_match**) for restricting the values of certificate fields. The purpose of a policy is to guide processing of a certificate request.

**Example 1**   Establishing the SSLeay Certificate Environment

```
mkdir ${SSLDIR}/certs
mkdir ${SSLDIR}/crl
mkdir ${SSLDIR}/newcerts
mkdir ${SSLDIR}/private
echo "01" > ${SSLDIR}/serial
touch ${SSLDIR}/index.txt
```

**Example 2**    SSLeay Configuration File: ca Section

```
####################################################################
[ ca ]
default_ca      = CA_default      # The default ca section

####################################################################
[ CA_default ]

dir              = /opt/dev/ssl             # Where everything is kept
certs            = $dir/certs               # Where the issued certs are kept
crl_dir          = $dir/crl                 # Where the issued crl are kept
database         = $dir/index.txt           # database index file.
new_certs_dir    = $dir/newcerts            # default place for new certs.

certificate      = $dir/private/CAcert.pem  # The CA certificate
serial           = $dir/serial              # The current serial number
crl              = $dir/clr/crl.pem         # The current CRL
private_key      = $dir/private/CAkey.pem   # The private key
RANDFILE         = $dir/private/.rand       # private random number file

x509_extensions        = x509v3_extensions  # The extentions to add to the cert
default_days           = 365                # how long to certify for
default_crl_days= 30                        # how long before next CRL
default_md             = md5                # which md to use.
preserve               = no                 # keep passed DN ordering

# A few difference way of specifying how similar the request should look
# For type CA, the listed attributes must be the same, and the optional
# and supplied fields are just that :-)
policy           = policy_match
```

In Example 4, **match** means that the value of the field in the request must match the value in the CA certificate, or the request will not be signed.

**optional** means the field need not be present, while **supplied** means that it must be present in the certificate request.

**Example 3**    SSLeay Configuration File: Request Section

```
[ req ]
default_bits            = 512
default_keyfile         = privkey.pem
distinguished_name      = req_distinguished_name
attributes              = req_attributes

[ req_distinguished_name ]
countryName                     = Country Name (2 letter code)
countryName_default             = US
countryName_min                 = 2
countryName_max                 = 2

stateOrProvinceName             = State or Province Name (full name)
stateOrProvinceName_default     = MA
```

**Example 3**     SSLeay Configuration File: Request Section *(continued)*

```
localityName                    = Locality Name (eg, city)
localityName_default            = Cambridge

organizationName                = Organization Name (eg, company)
organizationName_default        = The Open Group

organizationalUnitName          = Organizational Unit Name (eg, section)
organizationalUnitName_default = Research Institute

commonName                      = Common Name (eg, YOUR name)
commonName_default              = example.osf.org
commonName_max                  = 64

emailAddress                    = Email Address
emailAddress_max                = 40

[ req_attributes ]
challengePassword               = A challenge password
challengePassword_min           = 4
challengePassword_max           = 20
```

## Creating a Self-Signed CA Certificate

The SSLeay *req* command creates a self-signed certificate when the *-x509* switch is used. The certificate is placed in the file *CAcert.pem*, and the private key in *CAkey.pem*. This command prompts for the password (e.g., caKEY) for the private key, and is used as shown in Example 5.

The SSLeay configuration file specifies the location of the CA certificate and key files using the following directives in the ca section:

```
# The CA certificate
certificate   =
  $dir/private/CAcert.pem
```

```
# The private key
private_key   =
  $dir/private/CAkey.pem
```

The Apache-SSL server *httpd.conf* file specifies the CA certificate and key files as follows:

```
#  Set the CA certificate
# verification path (must be PEM
# encoded).
SSLCACertificatePath /opt/dev/ssl/
    private
```

```
# Set the CA certificate
# verification path (must be PEM
# encoded).
SSLCACertificateFile /opt/dev/ssl/
    private/CAcert.pem
```

**Example 4**     SSLeay Configuration File: Policy Section

```
# For the CA policy
[ policy_match ]
countryName             = match
stateOrProvinceName     = match
localityName            = match
organizationName        = match
organizationalUnitName  = match
commonName              = supplied
emailAddress            = optional
```

**Example 4**     SSLeay Configuration File: Policy Section *(continued)*

```
# For the 'anything' policy
# At this point in time, you must list all acceptable 'object'
# types.
[ policy_anything ]
countryName             = optional
stateOrProvinceName     = optional
localityName            = optional
organizationName        = optional
organizationalUnitName  = optional
commonName              = supplied
emailAddress            = optional
```

## Loading a CA certificate into a browser using a CGI script

Load the CA certificate into the browser by accessing an HTML form like that in Example 6. This form calls a CGI script to load the certificate using the `application/x-x509-ca-cert` MIME type as the Content-Type.

Example 7 shows the *loadCAcert.pl* script.

Install the Certificate Authority certificate in the server certificate database as well as the browser,

so the server is able to locate the public key and validate certificate signatures signed by the certificate authority

## *Server Certificates*

### Creating a certificate request

The SSLeay *req* command is used to create a PKCS#10 (Public-Key Cryptography Standards [3]) certificate request. It also generates a key pair

**Example 5**     Creating a Self-Signed CA Certificate

```
$SSLDIR/bin/ssleay req -new -x509 -keyout ${SSLDIR}/private/CAkey.pem
     -out ${SSLDIR}/private/CAcert.pem  -config /opt/www/lib/ssleay.cnf

Using configuration from /opt/www/lib/ssleay.cnf
Generating a 512 bit private key
writing new private key to '../private/CAkey.pem'
Enter PEM pass phrase:
Verifying password - Enter PEM pass phrase:
-----
You are about to be asked to enter information that will be incorperated
into your certificate request.
What you are about to enter is what is called a Distinguished Name or a DN.
There are quite a few fields but you can leave some blank
For some fields there will be a default value,
If you enter '.', the field will be left blank.
-----
Country Name (2 letter code) [US]:
State or Province Name (full name) [MA]:
Locality Name (eg, city) [Cambridge]:
Organization Name (eg, company) [The Open Group]:
Organizational Unit Name (eg, section) [Research Institute]:
Common Name (eg, YOUR name) [example.osf.org]:Example CA
Email Address []:f.hirsch@opengroup.org
```

**Example 6**      HTML Form to Request CA Certificate to Load into Browser

```
<HTML><HEAD><TITLE>Load CA Certificate</TITLE></HEAD><BODY>
<H1>Load Certificate Authority Certificate</H1>

<FORM ACTION="http://example.osf.org/cgi-bin/loadCAcert.pl" METHOD=post>
<TABLE>
<TR>
<TD>Netscape Browser (PEM Format):</TD>
<TD><INPUT TYPE="RADIO" NAME="FORMAT" VALUE="PEM" CHECKED></TD></TR>

<TR><TD>Microsoft Browser (DER Format):</TD>
<TD><INPUT TYPE="RADIO" NAME="FORMAT" VALUE="DER"></TD></TR>
</TABLE>

<INPUT TYPE="SUBMIT" VALUE="Load Certificate">
</FORM>
</BODY></HTML>
```

when –new is specified, and may indicate the length of time the certificate is valid with the –days switch. SSLeay prompts for a new password for this certificate (call it siteKEY). A certificate request may be created as shown in Example 8.

Example 9 shows the results in a certificate request being created in *newreq.pem* (in this paper certificates and keys are truncated).

Example 10 shows a private key for the certificate being created in *newkey.pem*.

**Example 7**      Perl CGI Script to Load CA Certificate into Browser

```
#!/usr/local/bin/perl -T

require 5.003;
use strict;
use CGI;

my $cert_dir = "/opt/dev/ssl/private";
my $cert_file = "CAcert.pem";

my $query = new CGI;

my $kind = $query->param('FORMAT');
if($kind eq 'DER') { $cert_file = "CAcert.der"; }

my $cert_path = "$cert_dir/$cert_file";

open(CERT, "<$cert_path");
my data = join '', <CERT>;
close(CERT);
print "Content-Type: application/x-x509-ca-cert\n";
print "Content-Length: ", length($data), "\n\n$data";

1;
```

**Example 8**     Using SSLeay to Create Certificate Request

```
cd $SSLDIR/bin
./ssleay req  -new -keyout newkey.pem -out newreq.pem  -days 360
       -config /opt/www/lib/ssleay.cnf

Using configuration from /opt/www/lib/ssleay.cnf
Generating a 512 bit private key
writing new private key to 'newkey.pem'
Enter PEM pass phrase:
Verifying password - Enter PEM pass phrase:
-----
You are about to be asked to enter information that will be incorperated
into your certificate request.
What you are about to enter is what is called a Distinguished Name or a DN.
There are quite a few fields but you can leave some blank
For some fields there will be a default value,
If you enter '.', the field will be left blank.
-----
Country Name (2 letter code) [US]:
State or Province Name (full name) [MA]:
Locality Name (eg, city) [Cambridge]:
Organization Name (eg, company) [The Open Group]:
Organizational Unit Name (eg, section) [Research Institute]:
Common Name (eg, YOUR name) [example.osf.org]:
Email Address []:f.hirsch@opengroup.org

Please enter the following 'extra' attributes
to be sent with your certificate request
A challenge password []:
An optional company name []:
```

## Signing a certificate request

A server certificate is created by signing the certificate request using the SSLeay *ca* command. The `-policy` switch specifies the section of the SSLeay configuration file that defines which distinguished name fields are required, and the order of the fields. As an example, our test configuration file specifies the `policy_anything` section, which makes all the listed distinguished name fields optional.

When this command is executed, it prompts for the certificate authority password, as shown in Example 11.

The server certificate is created in the file *newcert.pem* as shown in Example 12 (linebreaks are added for `issuer` and `subject`).

**Example 9**     Sample Certificate Request

```
-----BEGIN CERTIFICATE REQUEST-----
MIIBXTCCAQcCAQAwgaMxCzAJBgNVBAYTAlVTMQswCQYDVQQIEwJNQTESMBAGA1UE
...
Aty7AlcmN9XNwxUk1w0H3hk=
-----END CERTIFICATE REQUEST-----
```

**Example 10**    Sample Private Key

```
-----BEGIN RSA PRIVATE KEY-----
Proc-Type: 4,ENCRYPTED
DEK-Info: DES-EDE3-CBC,21F13B37A796482C

XIY0c7gnv0BpVKkOqXIiqpyONx8xqW67wghzDlKyoOZt9NDcl9wF9jnddODwv9ZU
...
QxS2zwfKG1u+YqS1c2v5ecBgqW78DQLvxMkpYU8+xge7vDeoYKE14w==
-----END RSA PRIVATE KEY-----
```

The Apache-SSL *httpd.conf* file must be modified to specify the server certificate and key files as follows:

```
# Point SSLCertificateFile at a PEM
#  encoded certificate.
SSLCertificateFile /opt/www/lib/
    certs/sitecert.pem

# If the key is not combined with
# the certificate, use this
# directive to
# point at the key file. If this
# starts with a '/' it specifies
# an absolute
# path, otherwise it is relative to
# the default certificate area.
# That is,
# it means "/private/".
SSLCertificateKeyFile /opt/www/lib/
    certs/sitekey.pem
```

**Example 11**    Signing a Certificate Request to Create Server Certificate

```
cat newreq.pem newkey.pem > new.pem
./ssleay ca  -policy policy_anything -out newcert.pem
        -config /opt/www/lib/ssleay.cnf -infiles new.pem

Using configuration from /opt/www/lib/ssleay.cnf
Enter PEM pass phrase:
Check that the request matches the signature
Signature ok
The Subjects Distinguished Name is as follows
countryName            :PRINTABLE:'US'
stateOrProvinceName    :PRINTABLE:'MA'
localityName           :PRINTABLE:'Cambridge'
organizationName       :PRINTABLE:'The Open Group'
organizationalUnitName:PRINTABLE:'Research Institute'
commonName             :PRINTABLE:'example.osf.org'
emailAddress           :IA5STRING:'f.hirsch@opengroup.org'
Certificate is to be certified until May 12 15:39:33 1998 GMT (365 days)
Sign the certificate? [y/n]:y

1 out of 1 certificate requests certified, commit? [y/n]y
Write out database with 1 new entries
Data Base Updated
```

## Client Certificates

### Form to create Netscape client certificate request

Netscape returns a "Signed Public Key And Challenge" (SPKAC) public key when the <KEYGEN> form element is encountered. The form in

Example 13 returns this in the SPKAC hidden field. The CGI script then accesses this field and passes the SPKAC value to SSLeay using the *-spkac* switch to the *ca* command. (See *ns-ca.doc* in the *doc* directory in the SSLeay distribution.)

**Example 12**    Sample Server Certificate

```
issuer :/C=US/SP=MA/L=Cambridge/O=The Open Group/OU=Research Institute/
        CN=Example CA/Email=f.hirsch@opengroup.org
subject:/C=US/SP=MA/L=Cambridge/O=The Open Group/OU=Research Institute/
        CN=example.osf.org/Email=f.hirsch@opengroup.org
serial :01

Certificate:
    Data:
        Version: 0 (0x0)
        Serial Number: 1 (0x1)
        Signature Algorithm: md5withRSAEncryption
        Issuer: C=US, SP=MA, L=Cambridge, O=The Open Group,
                OU=Research Institute,
                CN=Example CA/Email=f.hirsch@opengroup.org
        Validity
            Not Before: May 12 15:39:33 1997 GMT
            Not After : May 12 15:39:33 1998 GMT
        Subject: C=US, SP=MA, L=Cambridge, O=The Open Group,
                OU=Research Institute,
                CN=example.osf.org/Email=f.hirsch@opengroup.org
        Subject Public Key Info:
            Public Key Algorithm: rsaEncryption
                Modulus:
                    00:a1:41:0b:0c:15:53:a5:a5:c4:37:a8:48:f5:79:
                    39:9f:18:2d:f4:bf:43:34:36:21:23:03:48:a5:65:
                    cb:e2:f8:97:af:9c:7d:df:1e:9b:54:e2:ad:21:e3:
                    41:3e:54:9a:ce:dc:66:4d:61:59:fb:83:11:36:bf:
                    9c:3b:47:20:fb
                Exponent: 65537 (0x10001)
    Signature Algorithm: md5withRSAEncryption
        63:77:e7:f8:aa:0b:90:5e:13:9e:4b:57:f1:0f:22:f9:4c:e3:
        7a:aa:ff:a7:8a:2e:3c:1c:a2:92:07:bc:9f:22:3f:2f:13:3f:
        60:62:57:a7:74:12:35:28:82:b1:00:2a:36:54:de:67:cd:a2:
        9e:24:3e:98:be:14:4e:35:b7:7f

-----BEGIN CERTIFICATE-----
MIICLTCCAdcCAQEwDQYJKoZIhvcNAQEEBQAwgZ4xCzAJBgNVBAYTAlVTMQswCQYD
...
Ij8vEz9gYlendBI1KIKxACo2VN5nzaKeJD6YvhRONbd/
-----END CERTIFICATE-----
```

**Example 13**     Sample Form to Request Netscape Client Certificate

```
<HTML><HEAD><TITLE>Create Client Certificate</TITLE></HEAD><BODY>
<CENTER><H1>Create Client Certificate</H1></CENTER>

<FORM NAME="GenerateForm" ACTION="http://example.osf.org/cgi-bin/ns_key.pl">
<TABLE>
<TR><TD>Common Name:</TD><TD>
<INPUT TYPE="TEXT" NAME="commonName" VALUE="Client Certificate" SIZE=64>
</TD></TR>
<TR><TD>email:</TD><TD>
<INPUT TYPE="TEXT" NAME="emailAddress" VALUE="f.hirsch@opengroup.org" SIZE=40>
</TD></TR>
<TR><TD>Organization:</TD><TD>
<INPUT TYPE="TEXT" NAME="organizationName" VALUE="The Open Group">
</TD></TR>
<TR><TD>Organizational Unit:</TD><TD>
<INPUT TYPE="TEXT" NAME="organizationalUnitName" VALUE="Research Institute">
</TD></TR>
<TR><TD>Locality (City):</TD><TD>
<INPUT TYPE="TEXT" NAME="localityName" VALUE="Cambridge">
</TD></TR>
<TR><TD>State:</TD><TD>
<INPUT TYPE="TEXT" NAME="stateOrProvinceName" VALUE="MA">
</TD></TR>
<TR><TD>Country:</TD><TD>
<INPUT TYPE="TEXT" NAME="countryName" VALUE="US" SIZE="2">
</TD></TR>
</TABLE>
<!--
' keygen is Netscape specific and will be ignored in
' internet explorer
-->
<KEYGEN NAME="SPKAC" CHALLENGE="challengePassword">

<INPUT TYPE="SUBMIT" NAME="SUBMIT">
</FORM>
<P><HR></BODY></HTML>
```

## Perl script to process Netscape client certificate request

Example 14 shows a Perl script used to create a client certificate for Netscape Navigator, as discussed in the section "Creating a Client Certificate."

The CGI script for Netscape Navigator creates a file containing the distinguished name values returned by the form, and a special SPKAC value for the Signed Public Key And Challenge (SPKAC) generated by Navigator. This file contains the information which would be in a certificate request, and is used to generate the certificate.

The SSLeay *ca* command is called with this file as an argument to generate a client certificate, as follows (see also *ns-ca.doc* from the SSLeay documentation) :

```
$SSLDIR/bin/ca -spkac $req_file \
    -out $result_file -days 360 \
    -key $CAPASS \
    -config /opt/www/lib/
        ssleay.cnf 2>errs
```

This example shows the command after some of the Perl processing to create the command has been performed. The *$req_file* variable contains the name of a unique file in the *certs* directory,

**Example 14**     Sample Perl Script to Process Netscape Client Certificate Request

```perl
#!/usr/local/bin/perl

require 5.003;
use strict;
use CGI;

use File::CounterFile;                 # module to maintain certificate
                                       # request counter
my $doc_dir = $ENV{'DOCUMENT_ROOT'};   # apache specific location for storage
unless($doc_dir) {
    print "<HTML><HEAD><TITLE>Failure</TITLE></HEAD>";
    print "<BODY>DOCUMENT_ROOT not defined</BODY></HTML>";
    exit(0);
}

my $base_dir = $doc_dir;
$base_dir =~ s/\/htdocs//;

my $SSLDIR = '/opt/dev/ssl';           # define where SSLeay files are located
my $CA = "$SSLDIR/bin/ca";
my $CONFIG = "/opt/www/lib/ssleay.cnf";
my $CAPASS = "caKEY";

my $query = new CGI;                    # get a handle on the form data

my $key = $query->param( SPKAC );       # this will fail if not Netscape browser
unless($key) { fail("No Key provided $key. Netscape required"); }

my $counter = new File::CounterFile("$base_dir/.counter", 1);
unless($counter) { fail("Could not create counter: $!"); }
my $count = $counter->inc();

my $certs_dir = "$base_dir/certs";
my $req_file = "$certs_dir/cert$count.req";          # certificate request filename
my $result_file = "$certs_dir/cert$count.result";    # certificate filename

# Explicitly list form fields we must have for certificate creation to work.
my @req_names = ('commonName', 'emailAddress', 'organizationName',
                 'organizationalUnitName', 'localityName',
                 'stateOrProvinceName', 'countryName', 'SPKAC');


# build the request file
open(REQ, ">$req_file") or fail("Could not create request $req_file: $!");

my $name;
foreach $name (@req_names) {
    my $value = $query->param("$name");
    $value =~ tr/\n//d;
    print REQ "$name = $value\n";
}
close(REQ);
# make sure we actually created a request file
```

**Example 14**    Sample Perl Script to Process Netscape Client Certificate Request *(continued)*

```perl
unless(-f $req_file) { fail("request missing: $req_file"); }

unless(-e $CA) { fail("command missing"); }      # ensure that ca command will run

# command for processing certificate request, without password
my $cmd = "$CA -config $CONFIG -spkac $req_file -out $result_file -days 360"
my $rc = system("$cmd -key $CAPASS 2>errs");
if($rc != 0) { fail("$cmd<P>rc = $rc", "errs"); }

open(CERT, "<$result_file") or fail("Could not open $result_file<P>$!");

# send the client certificate to the browser
print "Content-Type: application/ x-x509-user-cert\n";

my $result = join '', <CERT>;
close CERT;

my $len = length($result);
print "Content-Length: $len\n\n";
print $result;

exit(0);

sub fail {
    my($msg, $errs) = @_;

    print $query->header;
    print $query->start_html(-title => "Certificate Request Failure");
    print "<H2>Certificate request failed</H2>$msg<P>";
    if($errs) {
            if(open(ERR, "<errs")) {
                while(<ERR>) {
                        print "$_<BR>";
                }
                close ERR;
            }
    }
    print $query->dump();
    print $query->end_html();
    exit(0);
}

1;
```

used to contain the certificate request information obtained from the CGI form data. The *$result_file* variable contains the name of a unique file in the *certs* directory, used to contain the certificate. The $CAPASS Perl variable contains the CA key.

If the *ca* command is successful, then the certificate is returned by the CGI script as an *application/x-x509-user-cert* HTTP Content-Type. Navigator recognizes this type, and prompts the user for the remainder of the steps required to install the user certificate in the browser.

## Form to create Microsoft client certificate request

Example 15 shows the HTML form used to generate a certificate request from Microsoft Internet
Explorer, as discussed in the section "Creating a
client certificate."

**Example 15**    Sample HTML Form with JavaScript and ActiveX to Request IE Client Certificate

```
<HTML><HEAD><TITLE>Client Certificate Request</TITLE></HEAD><BODY>

<!-- Use the Microsoft ActiveX control to generate the certificate -->
<OBJECT CLASSID="clsid:33BEC9E0-F78F-11cf-B782-00C04FD7BF43"
        CODEBASE=certenr3.dll
            ID=certHelper>
</OBJECT>

<!-- JavaScript or Visual Basic will work. -->
<SCRIPT LANGUAGE="JavaScript">
<!---

// this is from JavaScript: The Definitive Guide, since
// Microsoft implementation of Math.random() is broken
//
function random() {
    random.seed = (random.seed*random.a + random.c) % random.m;
    return random.seed/random.m;
}
random.m = 714025; random.a = 4096; random.c = 150889;
random.seed = (new Date()).getTime()%random.m;

function GenReq ()
{
    var sessionId              = "a_unique_session_id";
    var reqHardware            = 0;
    var szName                 = "";
    var szPurpose              = "ClientAuth";
    var doAcceptanceUINow      = 0;
    var doAcceptanceUILater    = 0;
    var doOnline               = 1;
    var keySpec                = 1;

    szName = "";

    if (document.GenReqForm.commonName.value == "")
    {
        alert("No Common Name");
        return false;
    }
    else
     szName = "CN=" + document.GenReqForm.commonName.value;

    if (document.GenReqForm.countryName.value == "")
    {
        alert("No Country");
        return false;
```

```
}
else
    szName = szName + "; C=" + document.GenReqForm.countryName.value;

if (document.GenReqForm.stateOrProvinceName.value == "")
{
    alert("No State or Province");
    return false;
}
else
    szName = szName + "; S=" + document.GenReqForm.stateOrProvinceName.value;

if (document.GenReqForm.localityName.value == "")
{
    alert("No City");
    return false;
}
else
    szName = szName + "; L=" + document.GenReqForm.localityName.value;

if (document.GenReqForm.organizationName.value == "")
{
    alert("No Organization");
    return false;
}
else
    szName = szName + "; O=" + document.GenReqForm.organizationName.value;

if (document.GenReqForm.organizationalUnitName.value == "")
{
    alert("No Organizational Unit");
    return false;
}
else
    szName = szName + "; OU="+document.GenReqForm.organizationalUnitName.value;

/* make session id unique */
sessionId = "xx" + Math.round(random() * 1000););

sz10 = certHelper.GenerateKeyPair(sessionId, reqHardware, szName,
                                  0, szPurpose, doAcceptanceUINow,
                                  doOnline, keySpec, "", "", 1);

/*
 *
 * The condition sz10 being empty occurs on any condition in which the
 * credential was not successfully generated. In particular, it occurs
 * when the operation was cancelled by the user, as well as additional
 * errors. A cancel is distinguished from other unsuccessful
 * generations by an empty sz10 and an error value of zero.
 *
 */
```

```
    if (sz10 != "")
    {
        document.GenReqForm.reqEntry.value = sz10;
     document.GenReqForm.sessionId.value = sessionId;
    } else {
        alert("Key Pair Generation failed");
        return false;
    }
}


//--->
</SCRIPT>

<CENTER><H3>Generate key pair and client certificate request</H3></CENTER>

<FORM METHOD=POST ACTION="http://example.osf.org/cgi-bin/ms_key.pl"
    NAME="GenReqForm"  onSubmit="GenReq()">
<TABLE>
<TR><TD>Common Name:</TD><TD>
<INPUT TYPE=TEXT NAME="commonName" VALUE="Client Certificate" SIZE=64>

</TD></TR><TR><TD>Country:</TD><TD>
<INPUT TYPE=TEXT NAME="countryName"  VALUE="US" SIZE=2>

</TD></TR><TR><TD>State or Province:</TD><TD>
<INPUT TYPE=TEXT NAME="stateOrProvinceName" VALUE="MA">

</TD></TR><TR><TD>City:</TD><TD>
<INPUT TYPE=TEXT NAME="localityName" VALUE="Cambridge">

</TD></TR><TR><TD>Organization:</TD><TD>
<INPUT TYPE=TEXT NAME="organizationName" VALUE="The Open Group">

</TD></TR><TR><TD>Organizational Unit:</TD><TD>
<INPUT TYPE=TEXT NAME="organizationalUnitName" VALUE="Research Institute">

</TD></TR></TABLE>

<INPUT TYPE=HIDDENNAME="sessionId">
<INPUT TYPE=HIDDENNAME="reqEntry">

<INPUT TYPE="SUBMIT" name="SUBMIT">
</FORM>

</BODY></HTML>
```

## Perl script to process Microsoft client certificate request

Example 16 shows a Perl script used to create a client certificate for Microsoft Internet Explorer, as discussed in the section "Creating a client certificate." This script uses JavaScript and an ActiveX control to install the certificate into Internet Explorer.

**Example 16**     Sample Perl Script to Process Internet Explorer Client Certificate Request

```perl
#!/usr/local/bin/perl

require 5.003;
use strict;
use CGI;

use File::CounterFile;              # module to maintain certificate request counter

my $SSLDIR = '/opt/dev/ssl';
my $CA = "$SSLDIR/bin/ca";
my $CRL2PKCS7 = "$SSLDIR/bin/crl2pkcs7";
my $CONFIG = "/opt/www/lib/ssleay.cnf";
my $CRL = "$SSLDIR/crl/crl.pem";
my $CAPASS = "caKEY";

my $doc_dir = $ENV{'DOCUMENT_ROOT'};          # apache specific location for storage
unless($doc_dir) {
    print "<HTML><HEAD><TITLE>Failure</TITLE></HEAD>
    <BODY>DOCUMENT_ROOT not defined</BODY></HTML>";
    exit(0);
}
my $base_dir = $doc_dir;
$base_dir =~ s/\/htdocs//;

my $query = new CGI;

my $req = $query->param('reqEntry');

unless($req) { fail("No Certificate Request Provided"); }

my $counter = new File::CounterFile("$base_dir/.counter", 1);
unless($counter) { fail("Count not create counter: $!"); }
my $count = $counter->inc();

my $certs_dir = "$base_dir/certs";
my $req_file = "$certs_dir/cert$count.req";
my $result_file = "$certs_dir/cert$count.result";
my $key_file = "$certs_dir/$count.key";
my $debug_file = "$certs_dir/$count.debug";
my $pkcs7_file = "$certs_dir/cert$count.pkcs";

#process request
$req =~ tr/\r//d;
$req =~ tr/\n//d;

# save the certificate request to a file, as received
open(REQ, ">$req_file") or fail("Could no save certificate request to file");

print REQ "-----BEGIN CERTIFICATE REQUEST-----\n";
my $result = 1;
```

```perl
while($result) {
    $result = substr($req, 0, 72);
    if($result) {
        print REQ "$result\n";
        $req = substr($req, 72);
    }
}
print REQ "-----END CERTIFICATE REQUEST-----\n";
close(REQ);

unless(-e $CA) { fail("$CA command missing"); }

my $cmd = "$CA -config $CONFIG -in $req_file -out $result_file -days 360 -policy
    policy_match";
my $rc = system("$cmd -key $CAPASS 2>errs <<END\ny\ny\nEND");

my $session = $query->param('sessionId');
my $cn = $query->param('commonName');

if($rc != 0) { fail("Certification Request Failed</h2>$cmd<P>rc = $rc<P>\
                    sessionID = $session<BR>req = $req<BR>", "errs"); }

my $cmd = "$CRL2PKCS7 -certfile $result_file -in $CRL -out $pkcs7_file";
my $rc = system("$cmd 2>errs");

open(CERT, "<$pkcs7_file") or fail("Could not open $pkcs7_file<P>$!");

my $certificate = "";
my $started = 0;
while(<CERT>) {
    if(/BEGIN PKCS7/) {
        $started = 1;
        next;
    }
    if(/END PKCS7/) {
        last;
    }

    if($started) {
        chomp;
        $certificate .= "$_";
    }
}
close(CERT);

open(MSG, ">msg") or fail("Could not generate message");

print MSG <<_END_TEXT_;
<HTML><HEAD><TITLE>Finish Client Certificate Installation</TITLE>

<!-- Use the Microsoft ActiveX control to install the certificate -->
<OBJECT CLASSID="clsid:33BEC9E0-F78F-11cf-B782-00C04FD7BF43"
```

```
          CODE=certenr3.dll
          ID=certHelper>
</OBJECT>

<SCRIPT LANGUAGE="JavaScript">
<!--
function InstallCert (subject, sessionId, cert)
{
    if( sessionId == "") {
           alert("No Session id");
           return;
    }

    if(cert == "") {
           alert("No Certificate");
           return;
    }

    var doAcceptanceUILater = 0;

    result = certHelper.AcceptCredentials(sessionId, cert, 0,
                                    doAcceptanceUILater);


    if(result == "") {
        var msg = "Attempt to install " + subject + " client certificate failed";
        alert(msg);
        return false;
    } else {
           var msg = subject + " client certificate installed";
           alert(msg);
    }
}
-->
</SCRIPT>
</HEAD>

<BODY onLoad="InstallCert('$cn', '$session', '$certificate');">
Installing client certificate for $cn<BR> session: $session<BR>
</BODY>
</HTML>

_END_TEXT_

close(MSG);

open(RD, "<msg") or fail("Could not open msg file");
my $msg = join '', <RD>;
close(RD);

my $len = length($msg);

print "Content-Type: text/html\n";
```

```
print "Content-Length: $len\n\n";
print $msg;

exit(0);

sub fail {
    my($msg, $errs) = @_;

    print $query->header;
    print $query->start_html(-title => "Certificate Request Failure");
    print "<H2>Certificate request failed</H2>$msg<P>";
    if($errs) {
        if(open(ERR, "<errs")) {
            while(<ERR>) {
                print "$_<BR>";
            }
            close ERR;
        }
    }
    print $query->dump();
    print $query->end_html();
    exit(0);
}

1;
```

It is more complicated than the Netscape Navigator CGI script because it must create an HTML page containing JavaScript, which calls an ActiveX control in order to install the client certificate. The CGI script does the following:

1. Validates and reformats the certificate request passed in the hidden field

2. Calls the SSLeay *ca* command to create a certificate from the request

3. Combines the certificate with a certificate revocation list to create a PKCS#7 certificate

4. Dynamically generates an HTML form containing the certificate

5. Sends the HTML form to the browser to install the certificate

The script takes the certificate request generated by Internet Explorer from a hidden form field, and reformats it so that each line in the request is 72 characters long. It then passes this certificate request to the SSLeay *ca* command to generate a certificate, as follows:

```
$SSLDIR/bin/ca -in $req_file -out \
    $result_file -days 360 -policy \
    policy_match \
    -config /opt/www/lib/
        ssleay.cnf
    -key $CAPASS 2&gt;errs
```

This example shows the command after some of the Perl processing to create the command has been performed. The `$req_file` variable contains the name of a unique file in the certs directory used to contain the reformatted certificate request (the file is useful for debugging). The `$result_file` variable contains the name of a unique file in the certs directory used to contain the certificate. The `$CAPASS` Perl variable contains the CA key.

Once the certificate has been successfully generated, the SSLeay *crl2pkcs7* utility is used to combine the certificate with the SSLeay certificate revocation list (CRL) to create a PKCS#7 certificate. This is done using the *crl2pkcs7* command as follows:

```
$SSLDIR/bin/crl2pkcs7 -certfile \
    $result_file -in $CRL -out \
    $pkcs7_file 2>errs
```

This example shows the command after some of the Perl processing to create the command has been performed. The `$result_file` variable contains the name of a unique file in the certs directory used to contain the certificate. The `$pkcs7_file` Perl variable contains the name of a unique file in the certs directory used to contain the result PKCS#7 certificate. The `$CRL` Perl variable contains *$SSLDIR/crl/crl.pem*, the file containing the Certificate Authority certificate revocation list.

A certificate revocation list may be created using SSLeay as follows:

```
$SSLDIR/bin/ca -gencrl -config \
    /opt/www/lib/ssleay.cnf -out \
    $SSLDIR/crl/crl.pem
```

Once the PKCS#7 certificate has been successfully generated, an HTML page is dynamically generated. This page contains JavaScript code which calls an ActiveX control to install the certificate in the browser. The page in this example is designed to automatically load the certificate once the page has loaded into the browser, by using the JavaScript *onLoad* command. In a production system such automatic installation may not be desired. ∎

## Acknowledgments

Many thanks to Eric Young for creating SSLeay, Tim Hudson for his SSLeay work, and Jeff Barber for modifying it to work with Netscape client certificates.

Thanks to Rick Cormier, Ed Frankenberry, Scott Meeks, Tom Titchner, David Weisman, and Mary Ellen Zurko for reviewing this article and providing many useful suggestions and insights. Thanks to Doug McEachern for reviewing the Perl code.

## References

1. CCITT. Recommendation X.208: Specification of Abstract Syntax Notation One (ASN.1). 1988.

2. CCITT. Recommendation X.509: The Directory—Authentication Framework. 1988.

3. Kaliski, Burton S., Jr., "An Overview of the PKCS Standards," An RSA Laboratories Technical Note, revised November 1, 1993. *http://www.rsa.com/rsalabs/pubs/PKCS/*

4. Kaliski, Burton S., Jr., "A Layman's Guide to a Subset of ASN.1, BER, and DER," An RSA Laboratories Technical Note, revised November 1, 1993. *http://www.rsa.com/rsalabs/pubs/PKCS/*

5. Kaufman, Charlie, Radia Perlman, and Mike Speciner, *Network Security: PRIVATE Communication in a PUBLIC World*, Prentice Hall, 1995.

6. Koops, Bert-Jaap, "Crypto Law Survey," version 8.2, May 1997. *http://cwis.kub.nl/~frw/people/koops/lawsurvy.htm*

7. Phaos, SSL Resource Center, *http://www.phaos.com/sslresource.html*

8. Schneier, Bruce, *Applied Cryptography*, 2nd Edition, Wiley, 1996. See *http://www.counterpane.com/* for various materials by Bruce Schneier.

9. Microsoft Certificate Specifications, "Installing Certificates and Root Keys in Microsoft Internet Explorer 3.0 and IIS," *http://www.microsoft.com/intdev/security/csa/enroll.htm*

10. Netscape Certificate Specifications, *http://www.netscape.com/eng/security/certs.html*

11. VeriSign Digital Id FAQ, *http://digitalid.verisign.com/id_faqs.htm*

12. SSL 2.0, *http://www.netscape.com/newsref/std/SSL_old.html*

13. SSL 3.0 Internet Draft, *http://www.consensus.com/ietf-tls/tls-ssl-version3-00.txt*

14. TLS Working Group (IETF), *http://www.consensus.com/ietf-tls/*

15. TLS2.0, *http://www.consensus.com/ietf-tls/tls-protocol-02.txt*

16. BSAFE3.0, *http://www.rsa.com/rsa/prodspec/bsafe/bsafe_3_0_f.htm*

17. RSARef, *http://www.consensus.com/RSAREF/rsaref_toc.html*

18. SSLava, *http://www.phaos.com/solutions.html*

19. SSLRef, *http://www.netscape.com/newsref/std/sslref.html*

20. SSLPlus, *http://www.consensus.com/SSLPlus/*

21. SSLeay FAQ, *http://www.psy.uq.oz.au/~ftp/Crypto/*

## Additional Resources

1. Elgamal, Taher, Jeff Treuhaft, and Frank Chen, "Securing Communications on the Intranet and Over the Internet," Netscape Communications Corporation, July 1996. *http://www.go-digital.net/whitepapers/securecomm.html*

2. Flanagan, D., *JavaScript—The Definitive Guide*, O'Reilly & Associates, 2nd Edition, 1997.

3. Laurie, Ben, and Laurie Peter, *Apache—The Definitive Guide*, O'Reilly & Associates, 1997.

4. RSARef-FAQ, *http://www.consensus.com/RSAREF/rsaref-faq.html*

5. Stein, Lincoln D., *How to Set Up and Maintain a Web Site*, 2nd Edition, Addison-Wesley, 1997.

6. SSL-Talk FAQ, *http://www.consensus.com/security/ssl-talk-faq.html*

7. SSLeay-0.6.6, *ftp://ftp.psy.uq.oz.au/pub/Crypto/SSL/* (*SSLeay-0.6.tar.gz, SSLeay-0.6.tar.patch1*)

8. Wall, L., Christiansen, T., Schwartz, R., *Programming Perl*, O'Reilly & Associates, 1996.

9. *World Wide Web Journal*, "Advancing HTML," Winter 1997, Vol. 2, No. 1.

# About the Author

**Frederick J. Hirsch**
The Open Group Research Institute
11 Cambridge Center, Room 418
Cambridge, MA 02142
*f.hirsch@opengroup.org*

Frederick J. Hirsch is a Principal Research Engineer at The Open Group Research Institute.

His interests include human-computer interaction, artificial intelligence, and marketing. He is currently working on software to add functionality and ease of use to the Web by extending browsers, filtering HTTP streams, and implementing server plugins.

Before joining the Open Group Research Institute he wrote software for security trading at the MacGregor group and for network analysis at Bolt, Beranek and Newman (BBN). Prior to that, he worked on the Datakit local network at AT&T Bell Laboratories. He has an MBA from Boston University, a Master's in Computer Engineering from Stanford University, and a Bachelor of Science in Computer Science and Electrical Engineering from MIT.

# SECURITY FOR THE DOMAIN NAME SYSTEM

*John Gilmore*

## Abstract

*The Domain Name System (DNS) provides the Internet with human-readable names for email, Web sites, and other functions. It was designed in the "research" days of TCP/IP, when security against malicious attacks was of minimal concern. Secure DNS retrofits cryptographic integrity checking into the existing Domain Name System, allowing the Internet to continue operation while gradually upgrading its ability to withstand attack. It provides some additional benefits such as the ability to publish keys for other secure applications. It is being deployed in stages. Your site can benefit from this deployment by installing modern releases of the free BIND software.*

## Introduction

The Domain Name System provides translations between domain names like *www.w3.org* and numeric Internet addresses such as 18.23.0.22. It has become a largely invisible part of the Internet infrastructure, something that we all take for granted. We click on a link and the page comes up; it's so fast and reliable that we usually don't notice that DNS as well as HTTP was involved.

But behind the scenes, DNS is a high-performance, globally distributed, locally published, redundant, high reliability database system.

## DNS Overview

The structure of the DNS database is very similar to the structure of files on a hard disk. Each host on the network has a unique name, which contains information about the host. This information may include IP addresses, information about mail routing, and so on. The whole database can be pictured as an inverted tree, with the root at the top. Each node in the tree represents part of the overall database, called a domain. As with files, every domain has a short name (such as *www*), which can be used when you're "nearby." To describe a domain that's not local, use its full domain name—the sequence of names from the domain to the root, with a period (.) separating

them, such as *www.w3.org*. (The order that we write domain names is backwards from how we write filenames, where top-level directories come first instead of last.)

The top-level domains divide the Internet domain space organizationally. There are four generic top-level domains:

*.com* Commercial organizations, like Hewlett-Packard (*hp.com*), Sun Microsystems (*sun.com*), and IBM (*ibm.com*)

*.edu* Educational organizations, like U.C. Berkeley (*berkeley.edu*) and Purdue University (*purdue.edu*)

There are also top-level domains for United States governmental and international organizations:

*.gov* Government organizations, like NASA (*nasa.gov*) and the National Science Foundation (*nsf.gov*)

*.mil* Military organizations, like the U.S. Army (*army.mil*) and Navy (*navy.mil*)

*.net* Networking organizations, like NSFNET (*nsf.net*)

*.org* Noncommercial organizations, like the Electronic Frontier Foundation (*eff.org*)

*.int* International organizations, like NATO (*nato.int*)

In addition, a top-level domain exists for each country. Their domain names follow ISO 3166, an international standard defining a two-letter abbreviation for every country in the world. Examples are *.au* for Australia and *.in* for Indonesia.

The creation of additional top-level domains is currently under study, and it's likely that half a dozen or more new domains (like *.web*) will be created in the near future.

### Resource Records

The data associated with domain names are contained in resource records (RRs).[*] DNS manages a huge hierarchical set of resource records of many types, such as:

*SOA*
Start of authority. Indicates authority for the domain data.

*NS*

Name server. Lists a name server for the domain.

*A*

Address. Name-to-IP-address mapping.

*PTR*
Pointer. IP-address-to-name mapping.

*CNAME*
Canonical name (for aliases).

*TXT*
Textual information.

*RP*
Responsible person.

### Bind Overview

BIND, the Berkeley Internet Name Daemon, is the main implementation of the Domain Name System protocols. Its distribution includes *named*

(the *name* daemon), *libresolv* (the *name* resolution library), and various small tools such as *nslookup* and *dig*. Paul Vixie of the Internet Software Consortium maintains BIND. Until a year or two ago, it was the only real implementation of the Domain Name System, and it is still the most popular.

## Security

The Domain Name System was designed when security was not an issue on the Internet. The hard part was to get the Internet working at all; securing it could wait for later. The DNS protocol has been gradually clarified and improved, and the integrity checking in BIND has been tightened up a lot over the last few years, preventing the propagation of obviously incorrect information.[†] But there's a more fundamental issue: in the DNS protocol, there is no reliable way to determine the difference between correct information from the owner of a domain versus incorrect information maliciously supplied in order to attack the owner of a domain. If an attacker could convince part of the Internet to believe that *www.amazon.com* or *president@whitehouse.gov* was at a bogus network address, the attacker could impersonate a trusted Web site, monitor purchase transactions, receive email not intended for them, and so on.

To be trustworthy in tomorrow's Internet, the DNS protocol has been retrofitted with cryptographic integrity checking. The new protocol uses public-key cryptography in a very classic way. Each domain (or DNS "zone") generates a public key and matching private key, and uses the private key to digitally sign each group of resource records it publishes. Recipients use the domain's public key to check the signature on incoming resource records, to make sure they came from the owner of the domain. These keys

---

[*] Portions of the "DNS Overview" and "Resource Records" sections in this article are excerpted from the O'Reilly publication *DNS and BIND*, by Paul Albitz and Cricket Liu (2nd edition, 1997). See the *DNS and BIND* book for a complete list of resource records.
[†] See also the article entitled "Name Server Security Features in BIND 4.9.5," in this issue, by Cricket Liu.

and signatures go into new resource records, called KEY and SIG records.

Each domain's public key is also signed by its parent domain; for example, the public key for *www.w3.org* is signed by *w3.org*; the key for *w3. org* is signed by *org*; and the key for *org* is signed by the "root key," the key for the very highest domain—the "root" of the domain hierarchy. This cross-domain signing makes it tough for an impostor to just invent a new public key and claim that it belongs to someone else's existing domain. Because the chain of key signatures matches the hierarchy of the Domain Name System, it's relatively easy to determine who should sign the authentic public key for a given domain name, clarifying its validity. Each signed domain key (a combination of one or more KEY records and SIG records) corresponds to a "certificate" in other public-key systems, and the whole system amounts to a certification hierarchy that exactly follows the hierarchy of Domain Name delegation.

Each signature contains its own expiration date; even a clever attacker cannot "replay" old signed records after they have expired. The expiration period is set by the domain owner, choosing their own tradeoff between convenience and security. Short expiration periods provide higher security against replays of old data, but require that the zone be resigned more frequently even when the information hasn't changed.

Secure DNS also provides a convenient infrastructure for the publication of keys or certificates for use in other protocols. For example, X.509 certificates, PGP keys, and keys used by IP-Security encrypting firewalls can all be published and accessed this way. It's a relatively simple change to allow application programs to look up keys in the Domain Name System. This may be the easiest way to provide these applications with automated retrieval from a global key database.

The DNS Security architecture permits off-line generation of keys as well as offline signing of DNS resource records, for very high security. If the machine that contains the domain's private key is not on the net, it's difficult to break in and steal the private key, without physically breaking into the room where it resides. The signed resource records can then be moved to an on-net system for publication through the domain's primary BIND server. In a low security or prototype operation, key generation and record signing can take place on a machine on the Internet; however, there is a higher risk that the private key will be compromised.

The signature process takes a standard DNS ASCII zone file as input and produces a standard DNS ASCII zone file as output, which contains the original zone plus new SIG and NXT records. Therefore, only minimal changes in system administration are needed to secure your domain.

(Full details on Secure DNS are available in RFC 2065 [2]. Additional information is also available from the DNS Security Working Group [3] of the Internet Engineering Task Force [4], which developed Secure DNS.)

## Implementation and Availability

There are two current releases of BIND from the Internet Software Consortium [5], both of which contain partial DNS security support:

- BIND versions 4.9.5 and 4.9.6 can handle KEY and SIG records in parsing, printing, queries, and zone transfers.

- BIND version 8.1 does everything that version 4.9.6. does, plus handles the new NXT records. BIND 8 is where all future development will occur. Full cryptographic validation of resource records will be merged into a later BIND 8 release.

One common problem with deploying cryptographic security is that some governments have misguided regulations that treat cryptographic programs as contraband, or restrict their export. Governments get upset because people can use cryptography to hide information, thus potentially disabling them from secret wiretapping. I do not expect this to be a problem with Secure DNS; rather than hiding information, it only proves the authenticity of the already published information.*

The existing BIND releases do not contain any cryptography, and I believe them to be completely unaffected by export controls. They do not cryptographically validate their resource records, nor do they contain code for the cryptographic generation of KEY or SIG records—these facilities will be added in future releases. The prototype Secure DNS release from Trusted Information Systems does, however, include cryptography. With the exception of five or six completely embargoed countries, Secure DNS has already been examined and passed for worldwide export by the U.S. State and Commerce Departments. Official BIND releases will always be exportable.

DARPA, the U.S. military's long-range research organization, has funded several years of work aimed at securing our underlying computing and communication infrastructure against malicious attacks [6]. One small part of this program is the Internet Infrastructure Protection work done at Trusted Information Systems (TIS) [7]. DARPA funded TIS to write a prototype cryptographic Secure DNS implementation, which is now freely available worldwide from [8].

## Secure Dynamic Updates

Until recently there was no protocol defined for dynamic updates of Domain Name System resource records; records were modified by manually editing an ASCII text file. Recent work in the DNSIND working group [9], however, has produced proposed standards for a dynamic update protocol (see RFC 2136 [10]) and for defining how to secure the dynamic update protocol (see RFC 2137 [11]).

In order to prevent potential problems caused by unauthorized and malicious intruders trying to update your domain records, the secure update protocol requires the use of Secure DNS.

## How to Secure Your Own Domain Names

There are three steps involved with deploying Secure DNS at your site:

- First, you must deploy a modern version of BIND on all primary and secondary name servers. Once you add the KEY or SIG records to one of your zones (e.g., your main domain), your zone will fail to transfer to older secondaries (with a cryptic error message to *syslog*, probably ending up in */var/adm/messages*). If you run into this kind of problem, you can find more detailed error messages by running the *name* daemon (*named*) in debug mode; they will appear in files under */usr/tmp/xfer.ddt*.* This error will show up as an "unknown type" of DNS record; the cure will be to run a later version of BIND, or to remove the KEY and SIG records from the zone at the primary site until you can upgrade.

  Having deployed a modern version of BIND, you will be able to publish your users' public keys for upcoming application programs that know how to obtain them from the Domain Name System. For example, by adding a KEY record to the domain, users could publish their PGP or X.509 key to accept encrypted email. ("Flag bits" in the KEY record indicate whether a key is being published for secure email, for signing DNS records, and so on.)

- Second, use cryptographic program to generate experimental keys and signatures. Check the current version of BIND to see whether it includes this feature. If not, KEY

---

* Discussions about government policy on this issue can be found in the article "Government Regulation of Encryption: How Policy Will Impact Security on the Web" as well as the report "The Risks of Key Recovery, Key Escrow, and Trusted Third-Party Encryption."

and SIG records can be created using Trusted Information Systems' prototype cryptographic Secure DNS implementation, available worldwide from [12]. See the README file for instructions.

- Third, the top-level domains (TLDs) and the root domain must generate their own KEY records and start signing the resource records in their domains. They also must accept KEY records from the owners of their subdomains, sign them, and publish them (as with NS and glue records). This allows DNS clients to validate that the subdomain's signed DNS records have been issued by the entity to which the name space was delegated. (An example would be to verify that resource records from *usenix.org* are really from the party assigned the "usenix" name by the "org" domain's administrator.)

This third step may actually occur before your organization has deployed its own Secure DNS—some top-level domains will already publish their keys and sign their resource records before their subdomains do, helping to prevent attacks on high-level domains even before individual subdomains are secured.

Once the third step is complete, you will be able to depend on Secure DNS for production validation of name server records. Before completion, you will still be able to deploy Secure DNS within your own operations and sign those zone keys that you have a close relationship with. However, you will not be able to prove to the general public that your domain records are from the officially delegated source.

In conclusion, the first step in protecting your domain names is to install a modern version of BIND on each of your name servers. Along with closing up several security problems from older versions of BIND (which will help your security in the short term), it will allow you to add Secure DNS KEY and SIG records to your domain whenever your organization is ready to take advantage of them. ∎

## References

1. RFC1035, "Domain Names: Implementation and Specification," *http://globecom.net/ietf/rfc/rfc1035.shtml*

2. RFC 2065, "Domain Name System Security Extensions," *ftp://ds.internic.net/rfc/rfc2065.txt*

3. *http://www.ietf.org/html.charters/dnssec-charter.html*

4. *http://www.ietf.org*

5. *http://www.vix.com/isc/bind.html*

6. *http://www.ito.darpa.mil/ResearchAreas/Information_Survivability.html*

7. *http://www.tis.com/docs/research/network/iip.html*

8. *ftp://ftp.tis.com/pub/DNSSEC/*

9. *http://www.ietf.org/html.charters/dnsind-charter.html*

10. RFC 2136, "Dynamic Updates in the Domain Name System (DNS UPDATE)," *ftp://ds.internic.net/rfc/rfc2136.txt*

11. RFC 2137, "Secure Domain Name System Dynamic Update," *ftp://ds.internic.net/rfc/rfc2137.txt*

12. *ftp://ftp.tis.com/pub/DNSSEC/*

## Additional Resources

1. RFC 1034, "Domain Names—Concepts and Facilities," *ftp://ds.internic.net/rfc/rfc1034.txt*

2. Albitz, Paul, and Cricket Liu, *DNS and BIND*, O'Reilly & Associates, Inc., Second Edition, 1997.

# About the Author

**John Gilmore**
P.O. Box 170608
San Francisco, California  94117
*gnu@toad.com*
*http://www.cygnus.com/~gnu/*

John Gilmore is an entrepreneur and civil libertarian. He was an early employee of Sun Microsystems, and cofounded Cygnus Solutions, the Electronic Frontier Foundation, the Cypherpunks, and the Internet's *alt* newsgroups. He has twenty-five years of experience in the computer industry, including programming, hardware and software design, and management. He is also a significant contributor to the worldwide free software development effort. His advocacy efforts on encryption policy aim to improve public understanding of this fundamental technology for privacy and accountability in open societies.

# Name Server Security Features in BIND 4.9.5

*Cricket Liu*

## Abstract

*BIND (Berkeley Internet Name Domain) is by far the most popular implementation of DNS today. It has been ported to most flavors of UNIX and even to Microsoft's Windows NT. BIND is now maintained by Paul Vixie under the auspices of the Internet Software Consortium.*

*This article, excerpted from the second edition of DNS and BIND (O'Reilly & Associates), introduces security mechanisms in BIND 4.9.5. such as credibility checking, limiting queries your server answers, and restricting zone transfers from your server.*

BIND, the main UNIX implementation of the Domain Name System, was developed when the Internet—or really the ARPANET—was a small, clubby place. Early versions of BIND, therefore, didn't have much in the way of security features. The purpose of a naming service, after all, was to make names and addresses public, and to advertise them as widely as possible.

Today, the Internet is a rougher neighborhood. Spoofing attacks against name servers are becoming more common. Miscreants transfer whole zones of data from name servers to plot their next targets. BIND has had to adapt to work in this new environment.

The IETF's working group on DNS Security, DNSSEC, has begun the work of enhancing DNS to use secure hash algorithms to digitally sign the resource records that name servers store and return.[*] While not on a par with the cryptographic authentication of DNSSEC, BIND 4.9.5 introduces several useful security mechanisms. Some of these are configurable by the server administrator: the *secure_zone* TXT record, and the *xfernets, options no-recursion*, and *bogusns* boot file directives. Others are internal mechanisms, such as BIND's additional data and credi-

bility checking. Let's start by taking a closer look at the internal mechanisms.

## Under the Hood

### Internal Additional Data Checking

BIND spoofing attacks are unfortunately becoming more and more common. These attacks typically take advantage of trusting name servers by injecting spurious data into their caches, that they later use. BIND 4.9.5-P2 (patch level 2) introduces stronger checking of the "additional data" section of DNS reply packets your name server receives.[†] (The "additional data" section is where a hacker would probably tuck spoofed resource records.) P2 checks that the domain names in the "additional data" section relate to records in the earlier sections of the reply—the "answer" and "authority" sections. For example, if the "authority" section includes an NS record for the domain *acmebw.com* pointing to the name server *tarmac.acmebw.com,* then the "additional data" section of the packet might reasonably include the address *tarmac.acmebw.com*. There's no reason it should either include the address *back. acmebw.com,* or any PTR records, however.

---

[*] DNSSEC is described in John Gilmore's article entitled "Security for the Domain Name System," in this issue.
[†] You can pick up a copy at *ftp://ftp.isc.org/isc/bind/src/cur/bind-4/*.

This checking is important for any name server, regardless of role. If you run a name server connected to the Internet, you should upgrade to BIND 4.9.5-P2, if not BIND 8.1, which also includes these checks.

### Credibility Checking

Another good mechanism for controlling which records a response you accept—and which you reject—is *credibility*. Credibility is completely internal: there are no boot file directives or resource records to control its behavior. There are *no user serviceable parts inside.* Credibility allows a BIND 4.9.5 name server to distinguish the "quality" of different data from remote name servers. For example, it prevents hackers from firing DNS response packets at your name server with data about hosts in your zone in them, in the hope that your name server will cache the garbage. Here is the hierarchy of data credibility, ranging from the most credible to the least:

*local*

> Data from zone data files, or retrieved via a zone transfer from an authoritative name server, is considered unassailable: less credible data cannot replace it.

*auth*

> These records are data from authoritative answersthe answer section of a response packet with the authoritative answer bit set. These are less credible than local data, but better than anything else.

*addtnl*

> These records are data from the rest of the response packet—the *authority* and *additional* sections. The *authority* section of the response contains NS records that delegate a domain to an authoritative name server. The *additional* section contains address records that may complete information in other sections (e.g., address records that go with NS records in the authority section).

There is one exception to this rule: when the server is priming its root name server cache, the records that would be at credibility *addtnl* are bumped up to *answer* credibility, to make them harder to change accidentally.

The basic rule of credibility is simple: less credible data cannot replace more credible data.

## Administrator-Configurable Mechanisms

### secure_zone TXT Records

Up until BIND 4.9.3, domain administrators had no way to control who could look up data on their name servers. That makes a certain amount of sense; the original idea behind DNS was to make information easily available all over the Internet.

But the neighborhood is not such a friendly place anymore. In particular, people who run Internet firewall may have a legitimate need to hide certain parts of their name space from most of the world, but to make it available to a limited audience. For example, your bastion host might need to know all your internal hosts' domain names and IP addresses. Outside your firewall, however, you might want folks to see only the domain name of your firewall and your external Web server. But if the name server on the bastion host has complete data about your internal zone, how do you protect it?

The *secure_zone* record lets you define an access list of the IP addresses allowed to query your name server for data in a particular zone. Not only does it limit queries for individual resource records, it limits zone transfers, too.

To use secure zones, you include one or more special TXT (text) records in your zone data. The TXT records are special because they're attached to the pseudo-domain name *secure_zone,* and the record-specific data has a special format, either:

```
address:mask
```

or:

```
address:H
```

In the first form, *address* is the dotted-octet form of the IP network you want to *allow* access to the data in this zone. The mask if the netmask for that address. The second form specifies the address of a particular host you'd like to allow access to your zone data. (The H is equivalent to the mask 255.255.255.255.)

Note that the secure zones records apply only to the zones they're in.

## The xfernets directive

Possibly even more important than controlling who can query your name server is ensuring that only your real secondary master name servers can transfer zones from your name server. Users who can start zone transfers from your server can list all of the hosts in your zone. They might use the list to target hosts with particularly juicy names, or to gauge how many hosts you have, or to infer how many employees you have.

BIND 4.9.5's *xfernets* directive lets administrators apply an access list to zone transfers, a feature very similar to secure zones. However, *xfernets* is a boot file directive, unlike secure zones, which is implemented with the special TXT records described in the previous section.

*xfernets* takes as its arguments the networks or IP addresses you'd like to allow to transfer zones from your name server. Networks are specified by the dotted-octet form of the network number. For example:

```
xfernets 15.0.0.0 128.32.0.0
```

allows only hosts on the Class A network 15 or the Class B network 128.32 to transfer zones from this name server. Unlike secure zones, this restriction applies globally, to any zones the server is authoritative for.

If you want to specify just a part of the network, down to a single IP address, you can add a network mask. The syntax for including a network mask is *network&netmask*. Note that there are no spaces either between the network and the

ampersand or between the ampersand and the netmask.

For a primary master name server accessible from the Internet, you probably want to limit zone transfers to just your secondary master name servers.

## bogusns

In your term as name server administrator, you might find some remote name server that responds with bad information. It might run an older version of BIND, and respond with data that your name server can't decipher, causing your name server to complain about a "format error." Or maybe you know that this name server is controlled by a group of hackers or industrial saboteurs, and you want to prevent your name server from listening to its responses, in case they contain spoofed data. If you run BIND 4.9.5, you can configure your name server not to ask questions of this server. Here is the boot file directive you'd use:

```
bogusns 10.0.0.2
```

Of course, you need to fill in the correct IP address.

If this is the only server for a zone, and you just told your name server to stop talking with that server, don't expect to be able to look up names in that zone. Hopefully, there are other servers for that zone that can provide good, reliable information.

## options no-recursion and options no-fetch-glue

Another way to guard against spoofing is to prevent a hacker's queries from causing your name server to query his name server. If a hacker can send a recursive query to your name server, he can induce it to look up a name in a zone under his control. Your name server may then cache the spurious data the hacker's name server replies with and give it out to other, unsuspecting name servers and resolvers.

If your name server only advertises your zone information to the Internet (i.e., your name server isn't used by any resolvers), you can configure it to not accept recursive queries. Processing a non-recursive query is all done locally, so there's much less danger of infection by a remote name server.

The following boot file directive will configure your name server to respond to recursive queries as though they were nonrecursive:

```
options no-recursion
```

You may also want to add

```
options no-fetch-glue
```

to prevent your name server from querying a remote name server for the address that corresponds to an NS record. Together, these directives will make it difficult for a hacker to inject data into your name server's cache. However, they'll also make your name server useless for serving resolvers. If you choose to make one of your servers nonrecursive, do not list this name server in any host's *resolv.conf* file. You can still use it to answer queries from other servers about your zone data, though (i.e., you can still delegate to it).

# Appendix: BIND Resources

## Getting BIND

If you plan to set up your own domain and run name servers for that domain, you'll need the BIND software first. Even if you're planning on having someone else run your domain, it's helpful to have the software around. For example, you can use your local copy of BIND to test your data files before giving them to your remote domain administrator.

Most commercial UNIX vendors ship BIND with the rest of their standard TCP/IP networking software. And, quite often, the networking software is included with the operating system, so you get BIND free. Even if the networking software is priced separately, you've probably already

bought it, since you probably do enough networking to need DNS.

If you don't have a version of BIND for your flavor of UNIX, though, or if you want the latest, greatest version, you can always get the source code. As luck would have it, it's freely distributed. The most up-to-date BIND source, as of the BIND 4.9.5 release), is available on the Web at the Internet Software Consortium's Web site, *http://www.isc.org/*, or via anonymous ftp from *ftp://ftp.isc.org/isc/bind/src/cur/bind-4/bind-4.9.5-P1.tar.gz*. Compiling it on most common UNIX platforms should be relatively straightforward. Paul Vixiincludes sample definitions in the top-level Makefile for most common versions of UNIX, including HP-UX, Irix, AIX, Solaris, and SunOS. A version of BIND 4.9.5 ported to Windows NT is also available from *ftp.vix.com*, in the directory */pub/bind/release/4.9.5/contrib*.

## Handy Mailing Lists and USENET Newsgroups

Instructions on how to port BIND to every other version of UNIX could consume an entire book, so we'll have to refer you to the following resources for further help:

- The BIND mailing list, at *bind@uunet.uu.net*

- The corresponding USENET newsgroup, at *info.bind*

- The bind-workers mailing list, at *bind-workers@vix.com*. This list is used by folks testing the new versions of BIND 4.9.6 and 8.1.1 code.

- Andras Salamon's *DNS Resource Directory* on the World Wide Web for precompiled BIND software. The directory currently has a short list of precompiled binaries at *http://www.dns.net/dnsrd/bind.html*.

- The USENET newsgroup *comp.protocols.dns.bind*, which discusses DNS's BIND implementation

- Paul Albitz and Cricket Liu, *DNS and BIND*, O'Reilly & Associates, 1997. ■

## About the Author

Cricket Liu
5802 Linder Lane
Bethesda, MD  20817
*cricket@acmebw.com*

Cricket Liu is coauthor, along with Paul Albitz, of the O'Reilly & Associates Nutshell Handbook *DNS and BIND*, now in its second edition, and a partner at Acme Byte & Wire, an Internet consulting and training company.

# SECURE CGI/API PROGRAMMING

*Simson Garfinkel with Gene Spafford*

W3J

## Abstract

*Web servers are fine programs, but innovative applications delivered over the World Wide Web require that servers be extended with custom-built programs. Unfortunately, these programs can have flaws that allow attackers to compromise your system.*

*The Common Gateway Interface (CGI) was the first and remains the most popular means of extending Web servers. Practically every innovative use of the World Wide Web, from WWW search engines to Web pages that let you track the status of overnight packages, was originally written using the CGI interface. A new way to extend Web servers is by using proprietary Application Programmer Interfaces (APIs). APIs are faster than CGI programs because they do not require a new process to be started for each Web interaction. Instead, the Web server process itself runs application code within its own address space that is invoked through a documented interface.*

*This article, excerpted from Web Security & Commerce (O'Reilly & Associates, 1997), focuses on programming techniques that you can use to make CGI and API programs more secure.*

## The Danger of Extensibility

Largely as a result of their power, the CGI and API interfaces can completely compromise the security of your Web server and the host on which it is running. That's because *any* program can be run through these interfaces. This can include programs that have security problems, programs that give outsiders access to your computer, and even programs that change or erase critical files from your system.

Two techniques may be used to limit the damage that can be performed by CGI and API programs:

- The programs themselves should be designed and inspected to ensure that they can perform only the desired functions.

- The programs should be run in a restricted environment. If these programs can be subverted by an attacker to do something unexpected, the damage that they can do will be limited.

On operating systems that allow for multiple users running at multiple authorization levels, Web servers are normally run under a restricted account, usually the *nobody* or *httpd* user. Programs that are spawned from the Web server, either through CGI or API interfaces, are then run as the same restricted user.

Unfortunately, other operating systems do not have this same notion of restricted users. On Windows 3.1, Windows 95, and the Macintosh operating systems, there is no easy way to have the operating system restrict the reach of a CGI program.

### Programs That Should Not Be CGIs

Interpreters, shells, scripting engines, and other extensible programs should *never* appear in a *cgi-bin* directory, nor should they be located elsewhere on a computer where they might be invoked by a request to the Web server process. Programs that are installed in this way allow attackers to run any program they wish on your computer.

For example, on Windows-based systems the Perl executable *PERL.EXE* should never appear in the *cgi-bin* directory. Unfortunately, many Windows-based Web servers have been configured this way because it makes it easier to set up Perl scripts.

It is easy to probe a computer to see if it has been improperly configured. To make matters worse, Web search engines can be used to find vulnerable machines automatically.

Another serious source of concern are CGI scripts that are distributed with Web servers and then later found to have security flaws. Because Webmasters rarely delete files from a *cgi-bin* directory, these dangerous CGI scripts may persist for many months or even years—even if new ver-sions of the Web server are installed that do not contain the bug. One example is the *phf* script that was distributed with the NCSA Web server and the many versions of the Apache Web server. An example of an "unintended side effect" (see the next section). The *phf* script can be used to retrieve files from a computer on which it is run-ning.

## CGIs with Unintended Side Effects

To understand the potential problems with CGI programming, consider the script in Example 1.*

**Example 1**

```perl
#!/usr/local/bin/perl
#
# bad_finger
#
sub CGI_GET { return ($ENV{'REQUEST_METHOD'} eq "GET");}
sub CGI_POST{ return ($ENV{'REQUEST_METHOD'} eq "POST");}

sub ReadForm {
  local (*in) = @_ if @_;
  local ($i, $key, $val, $input);

  # Read in text
  $input = $ENV{'QUERY_STRING'} if (&CGI_GET);
  read(STDIN,$input,$ENV{'CONTENT_LENGTH'}) if (&CGI_POST);

  @in = split(/[&;]/,$input);

  foreach $i (0 .. $#in) {
    $in[$i] =~ s/\+/ /g;                  # plus to space
    ($key, $val) = split(/=/,$in[$i],2);# get key and value

    # Convert %XX from hex numbers to alphanumeric
    $key =~ s/%(..)/pack("c",hex($1))/ge;
    $val =~ s/%(..)/pack("c",hex($1))/ge;

    # Add to array
    $in{$key} .= "\0" if (defined($in{$key})); # \0 is the mult. separator
    $in{$key} .= $val;

  }
  return length($in);
}
######################################################################
```

---

* The CGI_GET, CGI_POST, and ReadForm Perl functions are based on Steven E. Brenner's *cgi-lib.pl*. See *http://www.bio.cam.ac.uk/Web/form.html* for more information. The serious Perl programmer may wish instead to use the *CGI.pm* Perl module, which is available from the CPAN archives.

**Example 1**      *(continued)*

```
#
# The real action (and the security problems) follow

print "Content-type: text/html\n\n<html>";

if(&ReadForm(*input)){
    print "<pre>\n";
    print '/usr/bin/finger $input{'command'}';
    print "</pre>\n";
}

print <<XX;
<hr>
<form method="post" action="bad_finger">
Finger command: <input type="text" size="40" name="command"
</form>
XX
```

The first half of Example 1 defines three Perl functions, CGI_GET, CGI_POST, and ReadForm, which will be used throughout this chapter for CGI form handling. There are no problems with these functions—all they do is take input from a CGI GET or POST operation and stuff them into an associative array provided by the programmer.

The second half of Example 1 defines a *finger* gateway. If called by the result of a normal HTTP GET command, it simply generates the HTML for a CGI form:

```
Content-type: text/html

<html><hr>
<form method="post" action="bad_
    finger">
Finger command: <input type="text"
    size="40" name="command"
</form>
```

which produces the expected display in a Web browser, as shown in Figure 1.

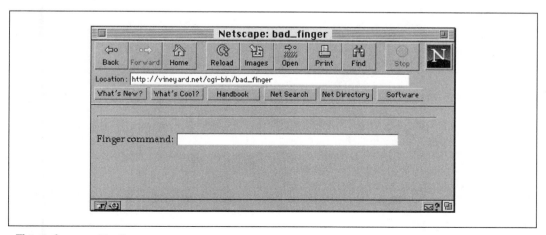

**Figure 1**      The finger gateway

Type a typical user's name into the field, like *spaf@cs.purdue.edu*, hit Return, and you'll get the expected result as shown in Figure 2.

Despite the fact that this script works as expected, it has a serious problem: an attacker can use it to seriously compromise the security of your computer.

You might have some security problems in the CGI scripts on your server that are similar to this one. Security problems in scripts can remain dormant for years before they are exploited. Sometimes obscure security holes may even be inserted by the programmer who first wrote the scripts—a sort of "back door" that allows the programmer to gain access in the future, should the programmer's legitimate means of access be lost.

### The problem with the script

The problem with the script in Example 1 is the single line that executes the *finger* command:

```
print '/usr/bin/finger
    $input{'command'}';
```

This line executes the program */usr/bin/finger* with the input provided and displays the result. The problem with this line is the way in which

the *finger* command is invoked—from Perl's backquote function. The backquote (`'`) function provides its input to the UNIX shell—and the UNIX shell may interpret some of that input in an unwanted manner!

Thus, when we sent the value *spaf@cs.purdue.edu* to this CGI script, it ran the following UNIX command:

```
print '/usr/bin/finger spaf@cs.
    purdue.edu';
```

which evaluated to:

```
/usr/bin/finger spaf@cs.purdue.edu
```

and that then produced the expected result.

The UNIX shell is known and admired for its power and flexibility by programmers and malicious hackers alike. One of these interesting abilities of the UNIX shell is the ability to put multiple commands on a single line. For example, if we wanted to run the *finger* command in the background and, while we are waiting, do an *ls* command on the current directory, we might execute this command:

```
/usr/bin/finger spaf@cs.purdue.edu
    & /bin/ls -l
```

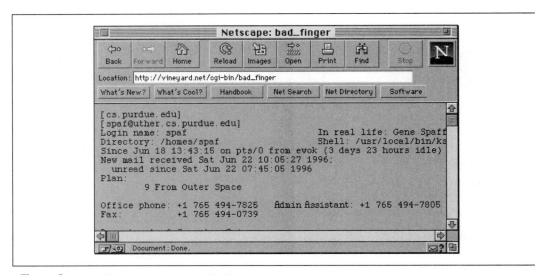

**Figure 2**    The form displayed by the finger script

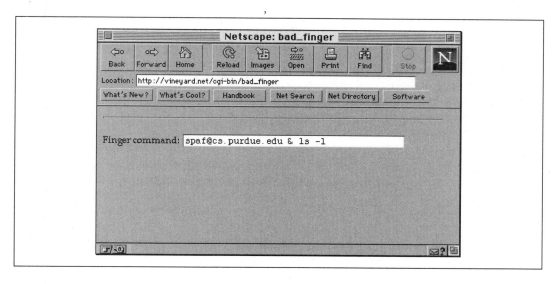

**Figure 3**    Executing the bad_finger script

And indeed, if we type in the name *spaf@cs.pur-due.edu & /bin/ls -l* as our finger request (see Figure 3), the *bad_finger* script will happily execute it, which produces the output you see in Figure 4.

What's the harm in allowing a user to list the files? By looking at the files, an attacker might learn about other confidential information stored on the Web server. Also, the */bin/ls* command is simply one of many commands that the attacker

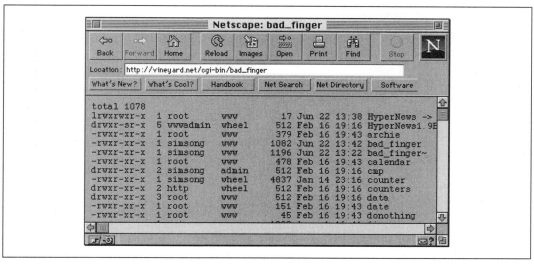

**Figure 4**    Output from the bad_finger script

might run. Just as easily, the attacker could run commands to delete files, to open up connections to other computers on your network, or even to crash your machine.

Although most operating systems are not fundamentally unsecure, few operational computers are administered in such a way that they can withstand an inside attack from a determined attacker. Thus, you want to ensure that attackers never get inside your system. To prevent an attacker from gaining that foothold, you must be sure that your CGI scripts cannot be turned against you.

### Fixing the problem

Fixing the problem with the *bad_finger* script is remarkably easy. All you need to do is not trust the user's input. Instead of merely sending $input{'command'} to a shell, you should filter the input, extracting out legal characters for the command that you wish to execute.

In the case of *finger*, there is a very small set of characters that are valid in email addresses or hostnames. The script below selects those characters with a regular expression pattern match:

```
if(&ReadForm(*input)){
    $input{'command'} =~ m/([\w+@\-
    ]*)/i;# Match alphanumerics, @
    and -
    print "<pre>\n";
    print '/usr/bin/finger $1';
    print "<pre>\n";
}
```

This command works as before, except that it won't pass on characters such as &, ;, or ' to the subshell.

Notice that this example *matches legal characters* rather than *filtering out disallowed ones.* This is an important distinction! Many publications recommend filtering out special characters—and then they don't tell you all of the characters that you need to remove. Indeed, it's sometimes difficult to know, because the list of which characters to remove depends on how you employ the user input as well as which shells and programs are invoked. For example, in some cases you might wish to allow the characters . and /. In other cases you might not, because you might not want to let the user specify the following pathname:

> ../../../../../../etc/passwd

That's why best practice recommends selecting which characters to let through, rather than guessing which characters should be filtered out.[*]

The previous script can be made more secure (and faster) by using Perl's system function to run the *finger* command directly. This entirely avoids calling the shell:

```
if(&ReadForm(*input)){
    $input{'command'} =~ m/([\w+@\-
    ]*)/i;# Match alphanumerics, @
    and -
    print "<pre>\n";
    system '/usr/bin/finger', $1;
    print "<pre>\n";
}
```

The next section gives many "rules of thumb" that will help you to avoid these kinds of problems in your CGI and API programs.

## Rules To Code By

Most security-related bugs in computer programs are simply that: bugs. For whatever reason, these faults keep your program from operating properly.

Over the years, we have developed a list of general principles by which to code. Here, then, is an excerpt from our list, edited for its particular relevance to CGI and API programs:

---

[*] Another reason that you should select which characters are matched, rather than choose which characters to filter out, is that different programs called by your script may treat 8-bit and multibyte characters in different ways. You may not filter out the 8-bit or multibyte versions of a special character, but when they reach the underlying system they may be interpreted as single byte, 7-bit characters—much to your dismay.

1. Carefully design the program before you start.

   Be certain that you understand what you are trying to build. Carefully consider the environment in which it will run, the input and output behavior, files used, arguments recognized, signals caught, and other aspects of behavior. List all of the errors that might occur, and how your program will deal with them. Write a code specification in English (or your native language) before writing the code in the computer language of your choice.

2. Check all values provided by the user.

   An astonishing number of security-related bugs arise because an attacker sends an unexpected value or an unanticipated format to a program or a function within a program. A simple way to avoid these types of problems is by having your CGI programs *always check all of their arguments*. Argument checking will not noticeably slow your CGI scripts, but it will make them less susceptible to hostile users. As an added benefit, argument checking and error reporting will make the process of catching nonsecurity-related bugs easier.

---

## The Seven Design Principles of Computer Security

In 1975, Jerome Saltzer and M.D. Schroeder described seven criteria for building secure computing systems.[1] These criteria are still noteworthy today. They are:

*Least privilege*

Every user and process should have the least set of access rights necessary. Least privilege limits the damage that can be done by malicious attackers and errors alike. Access rights should be explicitly required, rather than given to users by default.

*Economy of mechanism*

The design of the system should be small and simple so that it can be verified and correctly implemented.

*Complete mediation*

Every access should be checked for proper authorization.

*Open design*

Security should not depend upon the ignorance of the attacker. This criterion precludes back doors in the system, which give access to users who know about them.

*Separation of privilege*

Where possible, access to system resources should depend on more than one condition being satisfied.

*Least common mechanism*

Users should be isolated from one another by the system. This limits both covert monitoring and cooperative efforts to override system security mechanisms.

*Psychological acceptability*

The security controls must be easy to use so that they will be used and not bypassed.

---

[1] 14. Saltzer, J.H. and Schroeder, M.D., "The Protection of Information in Computer Systems," *Proceedings of the IEEE*, September 1975. As reported in Denning, Dorothy, *Cryptography and data security,* Addison-Wesley, c1982.

When you are checking arguments in your program, pay extra attention to the following:
- Filter your arguments, selecting the characters that are appropriate for each application.
- Check the length of every argument.
- If you use a selection list, make certain that the value provided by the user was one of the legal values.

3. Check arguments that you pass to operating system functions.

   Even though your program is calling the system function, you should check the arguments to be sure they are what you expect them to be. For example, if you think your program is opening a file in the current directory, you might want to use the index() function in C or Perl to see if the filename contains a slash character (/). If the file contains a slash, and it shouldn't, the program should not open the file.

4. Check all return codes from system calls.

   The POSIX programming specification (which is followed by both C and Perl) requires that every system call provide a return code. Even system calls that you think cannot fail—such as write(), chdir(), or chown()—can fail under exceptional circumstances and return appropriate return codes. When a call fails, check the *errno* variable to determine *why* it failed. Have your program log the unexpected value and then cleanly terminate if the system call fails for any unexpected reason. This approach will be a great help in tracking down both programming bugs and security problems later on.

   If you think that a system call should not fail and it does, do something appropriate. If you can't think of anything appropriate to do, then have your program delete all of its temporary files and exit.

5. Have internal consistency-checking code.

   If you think that a variable inside your program can only have the values 1, 2, or 3, check it to ensure that it does, and generate an error condition if it does not. (You can easily do this using the *assert* macro if you are programming in C.)

6. Include lots of logging.

   You are almost always better off having too much logging rather than too little. Rather than simply writing the results to standard error and relying on your Web server's log file, report your log information to a dedicated log file. It will make it easier for you to find the problems. Alternatively, consider using the *syslog* facility, so that logs can be redirected to users or files, piped to programs, and/or sent to other machines. (Remember to do bounds checking on arguments passed to syslog() to avoid buffer overflows.)

   Here is specific information that you might wish to log:
   - The time that the program was run
   - The process number (PID)
   - Values provided to the program
   - Invalid arguments, or failures in consistency checking
   - The host from which the request came; log both hostname and IP address

7. Make the critical portion of your program as small and as simple as possible.

8. Read through your code.

   Think of how you might attack it yourself. What happens if the program gets unexpected input? What happens if you are able to delay the program between two system calls?

9. Always use full pathnames for any filename argument, for both commands and data files.

10. Rather than depending on the current directory, set it yourself.

11. Test your program thoroughly.

12. Be aware of race conditions. These can be manifest as a deadlock or as failure of two calls to execute in close sequence.

    - *Deadlock conditions.* Remember: more than one copy of your program may be running at the same time. Use file locking for any files that you modify. Provide a way to recover the locks in the event that the program crashes while a lock is held. Avoid deadlocks or "deadly embraces," which can occur when one program attempts to lock file A and then file B, while another program already holds a lock for file B and then attempts to lock file A.

    - *Sequence conditions.* Be aware that your program does not execute atomically. That is, the program can be interrupted between any two operations to let another program run for a while—including one that is trying to abuse yours. Thus, check your code carefully for any pair of operations that might fail if arbitrary code is executed between them.

      In particular, when you are performing a series of operations on a file, such as changing its owner, *stat*ing the file, or changing its mode, first open the file and then use the `fchown()`, `fstat()`, or `fchmod()` system calls. Doing so will prevent the file from being replaced while your program is running (a possible race condition). Also avoid using the `access()` function to determine your ability to access a file: using the `access()` function followed by an `open()` is a race condition, and almost always a bug.

13. Don't have your program dump core except during your testing.

Core files can fill up a filesystem. Core files can contain confidential information. In some cases, an attacker can actually use the fact that a program dumps core to break into a system. Instead of dumping core, have your program log the appropriate problem and exit. Use the `setrlimit()` function to limit the size of the core file to 0.

14. Do not create files in world-writable directories. If your CGI script needs to run as the *nobody* user, then have the directory in which it needs to create files owned by the *nobody* user. (This also applies to the */tmp* directory.)

15. Don't place undue reliance on the source IP address in the packets of connections you receive. Such items may be forged or altered.

16. Include some form of load shedding or load limiting in your server to handle cases of excessive load.

    What happens if someone makes a concerted effort to direct a denial-of-service attack against your server? One technique is to have your Web server stop processing incoming requests if the load goes over some predefined value.

17. Put reasonable time-outs on the real time used by your CGI script while it is running.

    Your CGI script may become blocked for any number of reasons: a read request from a remote server may hang, or the user's Web browser may not accept information that you send to it. An easy technique to solve both of these problems is to put hard limits on the amount of real time that your CGI script can use. Once it uses more than its allotted amount of real time, it should clean up and exit. Most modern systems support some call to set such a limit.

18. Put reasonable limits on the CPU time used by your CGI script while it is running.

A bug in your CGI script may put it in an infinite loop. To protect your users and your server against this possibility, you should place a hard limit on the total amount of CPU time that the CGI script can consume.

19. Do not require the user to send a reusable password in plaintext over the network connection to authenticate himself or herself.

    If you use usernames and passwords, use a cryptographically enabled Web server so that the password is not sent in plaintext. Alternatively, use client-side certificates to provide authentication.

20. Have your code reviewed by another competent programmer (or two, or more).

    After they have reviewed it, "walk through" the code with them and explain what each part does. We have found that such reviews are a surefire way to discover logic errors. Trying to explain why something is done a certain way often results in an exclamation of "Wait a moment . . . why did I do *that?*"

21. "Whenever possible, steal code."

    Don't write your own CGI library when you can use one that's already been debugged. But beware of stealing code that contains Trojan horses.

Remember, many security bugs are actually programming bugs, which is good news for programmers. When you make your program more secure, you'll simultaneously be making it more reliable.

# Specific Rules for Specific Programming Languages

This section gives some rules for specific programming languages.

## Rules for Perl

1. Use Perl's tainting features for all CGI programs. These features are invoked by plac-

ing the -*T* option at the beginning of your Perl script.

Perl's tainting features make it more suited than C to CGI programming. When enabled, tainting marks all variables that are supplied by users as "tainted." Variables whose values are dependent on tainted variables are themselves tainted as well. Tainted values cannot be used to open files or for system calls. Untainted information can only be extracted from a tainted variable by the use of Perl's string match operations.

The tainting feature also requires that you set the PATH environment variable to a known "safe value" before allowing your program to invoke the **system()** call.

2. Remember that Perl ignores tainting for filenames that are opened read-only. Nevertheless, be sure that you untaint all filenames, and not simply filenames that are used for writing.

3. Consider using Perl's emulation mode for handling SUID scripts safely if you are running an older version of UNIX.

4. Always set your program's PATH environment variable, even if you are not running SUID or under UNIX.

5. Be sure that the Perl interpreter and all of its libraries are installed so that they cannot be modified by anyone other than the administrator. Otherwise, a person who can modify your Perl libraries can affect the behavior of any Perl program that calls them.

## Rules for C

It is substantially harder to write secure programs in C than it is in the Perl programming language; Perl has automatic memory management whereas C does not. Furthermore, because of the lack of facilities for dealing with large programs, Perl program sources tend to be smaller and more modular than their C counterparts.

There remains, nevertheless, one very important reason to write CGI programs in C: speed. Each time a CGI program is run, the program must be loaded into memory and executed. If your CGI program is written in Perl, the entire Perl interpreter must be loaded and the Perl program must be compiled before the CGI program can run. Often, the overhead from these two operations dwarfs the time required by the CGI program itself.

The overhead of loading Perl can be eliminated by using the Apache Perl module. Future versions of Microsoft's Internet Information Server are likely to support Perl natively as well. Nevertheless, if you insist on using C, here are some suggestions:

1. Use routines that check buffer boundaries when manipulating strings of arbitrary length.

   In the C programming language particularly, note the following:

| Avoid | Use Instead |
|-------|-------------|
| gets() | fget() |
| strcpy() | strncpy() |
| strcat() | strncat() |

Use the following library calls with great care—they can overflow either a destination buffer or an internal, static buffer on some systems: `sprintf()`, `fscanf()`, `scanf()`, `sscanf()`, `vsprintf()`, `realpath()`, `getopt()`, `getpass()`, `streadd()`, `strecpy()`, and `strtrns()`. Check to make sure that you have the version of the `syslog()` library that checks the length of its arguments.

There may be other routines in libraries on your system of which you should be somewhat cautious. Note carefully if a copy or transformation is performed into a string argument without benefit of a length parameter to delimit it. Also note if the documentation for a function says that the routine returns a pointer to a result in static storage. If an attacker can provide the necessary input to overflow these buffers, you may have a major problem.

2. Make good use of available tools.

   If you have an ANSI C compiler available, use it, and use prototypes for calls.

3. Instruct your compiler to generate as many warnings as possible. If you are using the GNU C compiler, you can do this easily by specifying the -*Wall* option. If your compiler cannot generate warnings, use the lint program to check for common mistakes.

4. If you are expecting to create a new file with the open call, then use the O_EXCL | O_CREAT flags to cause the routine to fail if the file exists.

   If you expect the file to exist, be sure to omit the O_CREAT flag so that the routine will fail if the file is not there.*

5. If you need to create a temporary file, use the tmpfile() or mkstemp() function.

   This step will create a temporary file, open the file, delete the file, and return a file handle. The open file can be passed to a subprocess created with fork() and exec(), but the contents of the file cannot be read by any other program on the system. The space associated with the file will automatically be returned to the operating system when your program exits. If possible, create the temporary file in a closed directory, such as */tmp/ root/*.

### WARNING

The mktemp() library call is not safe to use in a program that is running with extra privilege. The code as provided on most versions of UNIX has a race condition between a file test and a file open. This condition is a well-known problem and is relatively easy to exploit. Avoid the standard mktemp() call. On Solaris, for instance, use tmpfile() instead.

### Rules for the UNIX Shell

Don't write CGI scripts with the UNIX shells (sh, csh, ksh, bash, or tcsh) for anything but the most trivial script. It's too easy to make a mistake, and there are many lurking security problems with these languages.

## Tips on Writing CGI Scripts That Run with Additional Privileges

Many CGI scripts need to run with user permissions different from those of the Web server itself. On a UNIX computer, the easiest way to do this is to make the CGI script SUID or SGID. By doing this, the script runs with the permissions of the owner of the file, rather than the Web server itself. On Mac, DOS, and Windows 95 systems, there is no such choice—scripts run with the same privileges, and can access everything on the system.

Unfortunately, programs that run with additional privileges traditionally have been a source of security problems. The list of suggestions below is based on that list and is specially tailored for the problems faced by the Web developer:

1. Avoid using the superuser (SUID root or SGID wheel) unless it is vital that your program perform actions that can only be performed by the superuser. For example, you will need to use SUID root if you want your CGI program to modify system databases such as */etc/passwd*. But if you merely wish to have the CGI program access a restricted

---

* Note that on some systems, if the pathname in the open call refers to a symbolic link that names a file that does not exist, the call may not behave as you expect. This scenario should be tested on your system so you know what to expect.

database of your own creation, create a special UNIX user for that application and have your scripts SUID to that user.

2. If your program needs to perform some functions as superuser, but generally does not require SUID permissions, consider putting the SUID part in a different program, and constructing a carefully controlled and monitored interface between the two.

3. If you need SUID or SGID permissions, use them for their intended purpose as early in the program as possible and then revoke them by returning the effective and real UIDS and GIDS to those of the process that invoked the program.

4. Avoid writing SUID scripts in shell languages, especially in csh or its derivatives.

5. Consider creating a different username or group for each application to prevent unexpected interactions and amplification of abuse.

6. In general, use the setuid() and setgid() functions to bracket the sections of your code that require superuser privileges. For example:

```
setuid(0);   /* Become superuser to
             /* open the master
             /* file */
fd = open("/etc/masterfile",O_RDONLY);
setuid(-1);  /* Give up superuser
             /* for now */
if(fd<0) error_open(); /* Handle
   errors*/
```

7. Use the full pathnames for all files that you open.

8. For CGI scripts, use the chroot() call for further restricting your CGI script to a particular directory. The chroot() call changes the *root* directory of a process to a specified subdirectory within your filesystem. This change essentially gives the calling process a private world from which it cannot escape.

For example, if you have a program that only needs to listen to the network and write into a log file what is stored in the directory */usr/local/logs*, then you could execute the following system call to restrict the program to that directory:

```
chroot("/usr/local/logs");
```

Only use the chroot() call with CGI programs—never modules that are called by an API. Because of the difficulties with shared libraries on some systems, you may find it easier to use chroot() with Perl than with C.

## Conclusion

Writing secure CGI and API programs is a very difficult task. CGI scripts can potentially compromise the entire security of your Web server. To make things worse, no amount of testing will tell you if your CGI script is error-free.

The solution to this apparent dilemma is to follow strict rules when writing your own CGI or API programs and then to have those scripts carefully evaluated by someone else whom you trust. ∎

## About the Authors

**Simson Garfinkel**
P.O. Box 4188
Vineyard Haven, MA 02568
*simsong@vineyard.net*

Simson Garfinkel is a computer consultant, science writer, and columnist for both *The Boston Globe* and *HotWired*, *Wired Magazine*'s online service. He is the author of *PGP: Pretty Good Privacy* (O'Reilly & Associates, 1994) and the coauthor of *Practical UNIX & Internet Security* (O'Reilly & Associates, 1996). Mr. Garfinkel writes frequently about science and technology, as well as their social impacts. The recently released *Web Security and Commerce* (O'Reilly & Associates, 1997) is his sixth book.

**Euguene H. Spafford**

Purdue University

Department of Computer Science

W. Lafayette, IN  47907-1398

*spaf@cs.purdue.edu*

Eugene H. Spafford is on the faculty of the Department of Computer Sciences at Purdue University. He is the founder and director of the Computer Operations, Audit, and Security Technology (COAST) Laboratory at Purdue. Professor Spafford is an active researcher in the areas of software testing and debugging, applied security, and professional computing issues. He is the coauthor of *Practical UNIX & Internet Security* (O'Reilly & Associates, 1996). He was the consulting editor for *Computer Crime: A Crimefighters Handbook* (O'Reilly & Associates, 1995), and has also coauthored a widely praised book on computer viruses.

# A GUIDE TO SECURE ELECTRONIC BUSINESS USING THE E2S ARCHITECTURE

*Mark Madsen, Andrew Herbert*

## Abstract

*This paper describes the architecture developed for the ESPRIT Project 20.563, "E2S: End-To-End Security on the Internet." E2S is concerned with exploiting the opportunity created by the World Wide Web for supporting global electronic commerce. The project concentrates on the development of the security mechanisms required to support business-to-business transactions, which will define the majority of Internet-based transactions for the foreseeable future.*

## Introduction

The E2S project arose in early 1995 as a result of an expanded range of opportunities in Internet technology, which was driven in turn by the rapid expansion of the Web. The project focused on security mechanisms for protecting information transactions, representing either direct value in the form of money or indirect value in the form of pure but valuable business information, across the Internet. Rather than focusing primarily on electronic payment, the E2S project was chartered to develop security and technological frameworks for supporting real, full scale, business initiatives over the Internet within the time frame set forth (September 1995 through November 1997).

Rather than restricting our work to a purely theoretical investigation of the problems and their possible solutions, we have chosen to develop a set of trial applications, each of which implements an Internet-based solution in real life. These trial systems vary between a sequence of prototypes and a complete final business-quality system, depending on the corporate development philosophy of the user partners that developed the trial system.[*]

The practical work of the project, therefore, has been to work through a classic development sequence involving the analysis of business requirements and risks, the definition of security policies that need to be implemented in order to minimize the impact of those risks, the incorporation of those security policies within an architectural framework that is rich enough to represent each business system as an implementation of the architecture, and finally, the population of the architecture by a set of implementation technologies. Although the development sequence itself is of the classic "waterfall form," its application is unusual in that it is being applied simultaneously to a range of independent business systems.

Though the implementation technologies may differ between business solutions, the architecture should be sufficiently generic to withstand use across a variety of business situations. As a consequence, the electronic business architecture developed for use within E2S is one of the major deliverables of the project, and can be expected to have wide application beyond the confines of the project itself.

---

[*] This varies from throw-away prototyping, through RAD, to semiformal multilevel development within the project. A list of project partners appears at the end of this document.

## Scope and Background

### Structure of This Paper

The next few sections describe the scope of the E2S project, the criteria for building the E2S architechitecture, and the applications of the architecture. Next, we describe the E2S security model and its underpinning requirements and constraints—the security assumptions, relationships, and rules. Then we describe the E2S architecture itself, focusing on the client and server technology. Last, we take a detailed look at the kinds of technologies needed in order to realize functional systems based on the E2S architecture.

This paper sets out the architecture and the common technology framework for the E2S project pilot demonstrators. The architecture identifies, positions, and outlines the function of the main technologies used in the project. Most importantly, perhaps, it determines the trust and security model for the demonstrators.

The E2S architecture was derived from a pragmatic assessment of user partner requirements for technology appropriate to large scale electronic commerce. These requirements determine not only the functionality required by the pilot demonstrators and the constraints on architecture and technology choices dictated by regulatory concerns, but also the availability of standards and market pressures too.* The criteria for building the architecture included the following:

*Universality.* The security provisions should be widely applicable to as many Internet and Intranet electronic commerce scenarios as possible (i.e., the provisions should not be specific to the E2S pilot demonstrators).

*Security.* The architecture should embody the high levels of security required to enable businesses to put trust in electronic processes.

*Reliability.* The architecture should embody the high levels of resilience and recovery necessary to support mission critical functions.

*Portability.* The architecture should accommodate multiple computing platforms.

*Effectiveness.* The architecture should be implementable with minimal changes to existing paradigms and APIs.

*Performance.* The architecture should not make applications slower or more difficult to use.

*Durability.* The architecture should anticipate expected changes in Internet and platform technology.

*End-to-End.* The architecture should provide security for the complete path from a user on the Internet through to the supporting applications and data on the internal networks ("Intranet") of the organization delivering an electronic commerce service to the client.

*Business-to-Business.* In addition to enabling electronic commerce between users and electronic commerce applications, the architecture should allow for business-to-business transactions in which the "user" is a computer application running on behalf of an organization.

## Applications of the E2S Architecture

Within the E2S project, the architecture is being used to develop a common technology framework across four trial demonstrator systems, as described below:

*Secure telecooperation in administration*
    This is being developed at the Technical University of Berlin to allow the university's administrators to send administrative messages securely between destinations on different sites and at different levels of access

---

* Hence the positioning of the architecture as an "implementation architecture" rather than a "reference model."

while maintaining compliance with stringent German data protection laws and keeping the management and use of encryption keys transparent to the end user.

*Customer support for printer servicing and repair*
The Hewlett-Packard Worldwide Customer Service Operation based in Grenoble is developing this trial system in order to move an existing branch of its businesss onto the Web. The principal benefits to HP will be a reduced turnaround time for warranty work and lower costs of authorization and payment.

*Internet investment banking*
The Swiss Bank Corporation is developing this trial system at SBC Warburg in London. It will allow authentication, authorization, and secure access for SBCW client companies to manage their investments remotely at minimal overhead to SBCW, while reducing the system's per-customer deployment costs enough to qualitatively increase the market pool.

*Online third-party merchant services*
Octacon Ltd in Middlesbrough is setting up a Web catalogue marketplace, with itself in the role of the retailer, to a variety of supplier companies whose individual catalogues are securely uploaded to the Octacon server. Octacon therefore gains by taking a share of each transaction, in exchange for which it absorbs the entire risk of exposure to the Internet.

# The E2S Security Model

## Secure Electronic Commerce

This section captures and describes those aspects of security which are crucial to supporting Internet-based electronic commerce.

## Security policy

Security is a balance of risk against cost; it is not practical to defend against every possible threat, particularly when the associated risk (for instance, financial loss or bad publicity) is minimal. Consequently there is unlikely to be a single security design that meets all the needs of all applications. For this reason the E2S implementation architecture consists of a framework containing:

- System components, including trusted components that provide the foundations for security together with (possibly untrusted) components that provide the means of delivering services.

- Rules for combining those components to securely deliver services from end-to-end.

- Guidelines for selecting appropriate components to address specific needs.

The use of the implementation architecture is illustrated in Figure 1. The figure shows how the architecture for an E2S system (e.g., one of the pilot demonstrators) is derived from the E2S implementation architecture.

Figure 1 shows that the *system architecture* specializes the E2S architecture by adding components and functions required to support a business process. The *business process* is constrained by *business policy*—some of which may be required by government or regulation and some of which defines "corporate practice." In addition, the business policy scopes the requirement for security in the system; *security policy* is an outcome of quantifying the acceptable level of risk associated with security threats against the business policy. The security policy defines the level of trust associated with different user roles; the trusted components upon which security is founded; and acceptable technology choices from the E2S implementation architecture. Last, *technology* selected from the E2S implementation architecture provides security functions which

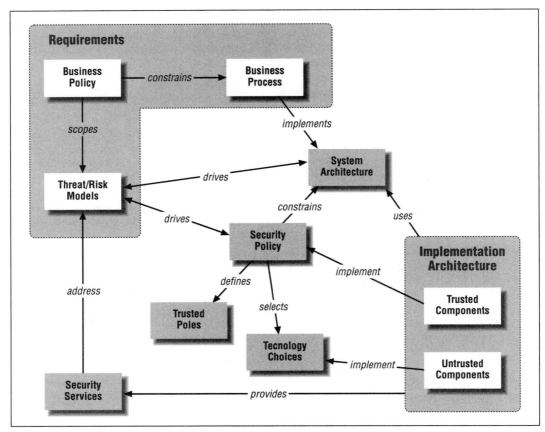

**Figure 1**    The relationships between services, policies implemented by those services, and the implementation architecture

reduce the risks associated with *security threats* to an acceptable level.

### End-to-end security

To argue that a system is secure, the designer must show that business policy, security policy, and security services are consistent. For a large system where many components are involved, this can be a difficult task. The E2S Project has, therefore, focused on end-to-end security, which is easier to analyze. In simple terms, "end-to-end" describes the approach in which security functions are divided between the user and the application to provide a "secure channel" between

them, without requiring any security guarantees from the intervening networks and computers (see Figure 2). This approach is contrasted with conventional "hop-by-hop" security techniques.

An analysis of user requirements shows that the common security requirement of the secure channel is *mutual authentication*—the parties at either end are sure of each other's identity. Other requirements such as confidentiality and transaction integrity are application-specific. Therefore, the scope of the E2S implementation architecture is both a collection of components required to create a mutually authenticated channel end-to-end and a toolkit for building application-specific security protocols.

## Security technology

As a result of a combined analysis of user requirements, available standards, and technology, we have chosen to use smart cards and a public key infrastructure (PKI) as the means to achieve authentication in the E2S project, for the following reasons:

- Public key infrastructures are a widely accepted technology for user authentication. In addition, there is an emerging market of public key infrastructure providers (including Verisign Inc. [1] and Ice-Tel [2]) (available soon).

- Smart cards overcome many of the weaknesses attributed to password schemes and the risks of storing cryptographic keys on insecure computers. They are physical tokens of security that facilitate usability and manageability.

Technology constraints often exist, requiring parts of a system to use conventional security technology—an example is creating trusted network paths to management interfaces. This is permitted by the E2S implementation architecture, but is not included in the security analysis. It is the responsibility of the system designer to show that the introduction of conventional technology has not compromised the integrity of the system.

## Security Analysis

This section presents a security analysis of the trusted components in the E2S implementation architecture.

### Security assumptions

The security of an E2S system depends on the following conditions:

- Public key cryptography, together with encryption, to provide confidentiality

- Controlled access to interfaces based on controlled checking of a user's identity, role, or purpose

- Digital signatures to confirm origin (a digital signature is a bit pattern that can only have been produced by the owner of a private key, and which can be verified only by using the corresponding public key)

- Digital sealing to confirm content (a digital seal is a cryptographic digest of content that can only have been produced by the owner of a private key, and which can be verified by using the corresponding public key)

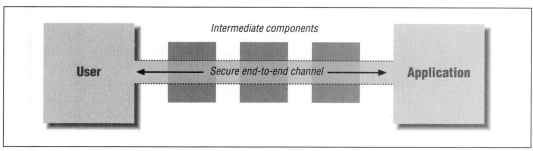

**Figure 2**    End-to-end security built on a channel from intermediate components

- Digital sealing of time stamps, sequences numbers, and so on, to confirm timeliness, prevent replay attack, and tie together transaction steps

- The ability to identify individual people and their roles by name

- The use of smart cards as both a tamper-proof, unforgeable means to store data (in particular, private keys), and a means to apply cryptographic functions over data stored on the smart card as well as input data (such as encryption of messages under a private key)

- Trusted operational support—the assured correct operation of security measures for both operational and backup systems

## Security relationships

The E2S security relationships are illustrated in Figure 3.

The key to the security model are the relationships between the security resources shown in the center of Figure 3 (identity, digital certificate, and so on). These relationships are maintained by a set of security agents (certification authority, rgistration authority, and so on) shown at the bottom of the figure. On the basis of these relation-

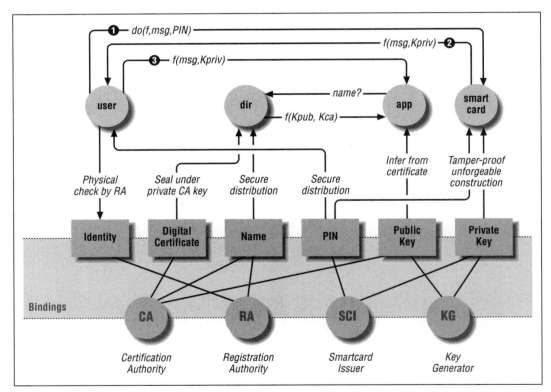

**Figure 3** The E2S security model, showing horizontal (authorization) and vertical (authentication) relationships

ships, the security resources can be distributed between users, smart cards, applications, and directories in such a way that:

- A user can be issued with an individual smart card

- The user can use that smart card as a means of initiating mutual authentication across the Internet with an application

- No other user can achieve authentication, even if that user acquires the smart card

This, in turn, provides the foundation for further interactions to establish access permissions and/ or additional security resources (such as session keys) required for transaction integrity, non-repudiation, and confidentiality.

The basic steps of the authentication process in Figure 3 show the user requesting the smart card to perform a cryptographic function on a message. The smart card returns the result of applying the selected function over a combination of the message and the private key held within the card. This information can be sent across the network and used by the application to authenticate the fact a message was sent by a particular user associated with the private key.

## Security rules

The smart card is not a secret. It is enabled only when inserted in a smart card reader, containing the correct PIN input. The connections between a smart card and the PIN input device, as well as between the application software and the smart card must be secure: this is ensured by using a verified copy of a trusted operating system. The PIN is a secret shared between the user, the smart card, and the smart card issuer; communication between these entities must be secured by either using trusted networks or a safe physical information transfer. The user's public key, in contrast, is not a secret.

The integrity of the binding between a user's public key and the user's name must be trustworthy. To achieve this, the binding must be represented as a digital certificate constructed by a certification authority.[*] The certificate must be made globally available and the private key used by the certification authority to sign and seal the digital certificate must be kept confidential to the certification authority. (This is achieved by creating the certificate offline in a physically secure location). The public key corresponding to the certification authority's private key, on the other hand, is not a secret, and must be available to the application. The public key is trusted and should be globally available. Global availability is achieved by replicating it widely, and by cross-certification with other certification authorities.

By reference to legal documents, physical characteristics, and so forth, the registration authority must use physical means to ensure the validity of the identity associated with the user and bound to the name. Since digital certificates are self-describing, directories of certificates need only be protected against denial of service attacks. The application must include an access control function. In addition, any table of name-to-privilege rules within this function must be stored securely to prevent tampering, and any communication between an application component and the access control function must be secure if they are not in the same physical location.

The registration authority, certification authority, and smart card issuer must cooperate to ensure that, for a given valid smart card, digital certificate, and user triple, the following is true:

- The name in the digital certificate corresponds to the user

- The private key in the smart card corresponds to the public key in the digital certificate

---

[*] For more information on certificate authorities (CAs), see the article "Introducing SSL and Certificates Using SSLeay" in this issue.

- The PIN known to the user is the PIN known to the smart card.

Based on these security assumptions the user can ask the smart card to perform a cryptographic function on some data; as a result, the transformed data will be sent to the application, and the application will verify that the transformed data originated from the user associated with the name. This provides sufficient information to first enable authentication and therefore access control, and to second enable the generation of secure tokens and sequence numbers in business protocols for secure transactions.

Correspondingly, a user's right to access an application can be withdrawn by either of the following processes:

- By changing the application's access control policy, which does not affect the ability of the user to access other applications

- By the certification authority placing the digital certificate in the directory on a certificate revocation list

This effectively "cancels" the user's smart card, provided that applications check the directory as part of the key validation process.

Note that this last action requires the directory to be highly available and efficient.

## Description of the E2S Architecture

As shown in Figure 4, the global areas of technology covered by the E2S implementation architecture are *client technology*, which is concerned with user interaction, *secure connectivity technology*, which is concerned with securing an end-to-

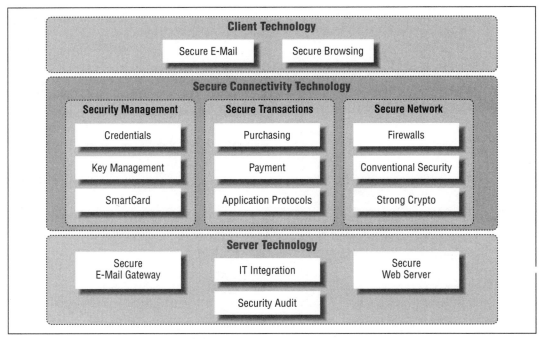

**Figure 4**   The E2S architecture summary diagram showing vertical and horizontal differentiation

end Internet path between users and applications, and *server technology*, which is concerned with supporting Internet applications.

Structurally speaking, each of these technologies is made up of a set of features that an E2S implementation can select from (such as security management). Each individual feature depends upon an underlying set of infrastructures (such as key management), while each infrastructure is made up of a number of architectural components.

The set of features included in the scope of the architecture has been driven both by an analysis of user requirements and a desire to maximize the use of common technology. Thus, the design of the E2S implementation architecture enables the re-use of infrastructure components across a wide set of features and, hence, application scenarios.

The architecture can be used recursively, in the sense that management functions for E2S components can be implemented themselves as end-to-end secure applications; an example is an HTML forms-based interface for updating a registration authority's directory service. In using the architecture recursively, the designer must be sure *not* to create cyclic dependencies.

## Client Technology

Client technology provides the interface between users (i.e., online customers) and the servers that are providing electronic services to those users. In the analysis of user requirements, we have identified the need for two kinds of client features:

*Secure electronic mail.* This is needed for tele-cooperation involving secure exchange of messages, documents, and instructions. This situation primarily occurs in environments where business processes and data protection regulations are formulated in terms of document handling policies. It is also well suited to applications serving users who may not continuously be online—for instance,

out-of-office sales staff with laptop computers.

*Secure web browsing.* This is needed for transactional interactive sessions, to enable activities such as searching, selecting, ordering, and reporting, particularly for applications where rapid access to a wide range of information and a fast response is required. Secure Web browsing requires that the user remain online for the duration of a session—for instance, to purchase a selection of goods. Though most current technology is forms-oriented, the capability to download more intelligent interfaces using scripts and applets will be more common in the future.

Both kinds of client technology require user authentication based on smart cards.

## Secure Connectivity

A prerequisite of end-to-end security is connectivity technology to secure interaction between clients and servers. Analysis of the end-to-end security aspects of E2S user requirements shows the need for three features to secure connectivity:

- *Secure network infrastructure technology* for securing individual components, network links, and/or subnetworks where an end-to-end solution is insufficient, unavailable, or inappropriate.

- *Secure transaction infrastructure,* based on protocols, for ensuring secure electronic business transactions using the following unforgeable signing techniques to confirm origin; unforgeable sealing to confirm content; sealed timestamps or sequence numbers to check timeliness and prevent replay; link transaction steps and encryption to provide confidentiality.

- *Security management infrastructure* components for making, distributing, verifying and revoking cryptographic keys and for issuing smart cards.

These three features are described in the sections that follow.

## Secure network infrastructure

Three types of components are associated with secure network infrastructure:

- *Firewalls* [3], for controlling entry and exit between security domains, and to provide a location for security management and auditing

- *Conventional security technology* (such as trusted operating systems, secure link-level/ transport-level protocols, and password-based authentication), for interoperability with other security architectures

- *Strong cryptography*, where its use is permitted as a means to increase the resistance of security protocols to attack

## Secure transaction infrastructure

An analysis of E2S user requirements shows the need for three features in secure end-to-end transactions:

- An application protocol toolkit to enable construction of protocols (such as GMD's BaKo [4]) to represent end-to-end procedures and maintain appropriate levels of privacy, obligation, and non-repudiation between interacting parties

- An electronic payment infrastructure enabling electronic payments linked via bank card to those organizations deploying the Secure Electronic Transactions (SET [5]) standard* †

- A purchasing infrastructure (including a network of supporting banks) for electronic business-to-business corporate purchasing

such as office supplies, based on corporate bank cards.

## Security management

To support the E2S security model, three features of security management are required:

- A credentials management infrastructure for maintaining relationships between security information belonging to different security domains—for example, a secure electronic transactions domain and a corporate IT domain

- A key management infrastructure for making, distributing, checking, and revoking cryptographic keys used for authentication and access control

- A smart card infrastructure for issuing and verifying smart cards

## *Server Technology*

Our analysis of E2S user requirements demonstrates that two different features are needed to deliver secure services to users: one is based on electronic mail and the other is based on secure user sessions. Alongside the user-facing functionality is a need to integrate electronic commerce technology with "back office" applications. In order to meet a requirement for continued assurance of system security there is additionally a need to monitor and audit server technology. The E2S server technology is made up of the following components:

- A secure email gateway infrastructure to act as the focus for applications based on secure email. The server provides secure mail boxes and functions such as redistribution of mail directed to an organizational unit.

---

* We selected a bank card–based payment system for the E2S project because it is international in scope and has a well understood financial risk model, as compared to other forms of electronic payment. In addition, pilot SET infrastructures are being created in the time scale of the E2S project.
† SET is described in the article "Cryptography and the Web," by Simson Garfinkel and Gene Spafford, in this issue.

- A secure Web server infrastructure to act as the focus for user sessions initiated by client browsers.

- IT integration infrastructure enabling back office applications to be exported via mail gateways and Web servers. It is concerned with the connectivity between the Internet (where clients access services) and internal Intranets (where services are deployed). IT integration includes the capability to download "applets" from the server to the client, to enable customization of the client interface.

- Security audit tools are used to monitor and ensure the integrity of a system implemented using the E2S common technology framework.

# E2S Technology Details

The E2S client technology enables a user to interact with an application securely across the Internet. The components of the client technology include secure electronic mail and secure browsing.

*Secure electronic mail.* This is essential in environments where document handling policies are created for business processes and data protection regulations. It is also well suited to applications serving users who may not be continuously online—for instance, out-of-office sales staff with laptop computers.

Secure electronic mail enables telecooperation based on the secure exchange of messages, documents, and instructions for publication of authentic information; confirmed delivery of information; and secure access to sensitive information.

*Secure browsing.* Users need secure interactive sessions for interactive online applications of electronic commerce. The general WWW view is one where the browser is the user's primary focus of interaction with a service. In E2S, this is extended—the browser is the

agent that needs to be authenticated by a given service, with authorization being handled by the server itself.

In this section, we consider the technological detail of implementing several subsystems that support these two applications. The foundation is the management of secured user identities: the actual key management, smart card, and credential infrastructures. Then we graduate to mission-specific concerns: designing secure business transaction protocols and operational security planning. Finally, we outline some considerations for integrating legacy IT tools into the E2S secure business architecture.

## Security Management

The security of the overall system is enforced through careful management of the cryptographic keys used in secure communications and business protocols. This means enforcing the security of user identities within the key management, smart card, and credential management infrastructures. Figure 5 summarizes the major components of the first two processes. The arrows in the figure denote the principal service requests that occur between the components.

## Key Management

Secure communication based on public key cryptography relies on securing the association between cryptographic keys and their owners as explained above. Creating and tracking that binding is the role of the key management infrastructure, which has several functions implemented amongst different components.

To begin with, as in PGP, either the end-user or an agent of the central key management infrastructure must generate a new public/private key pair. In the former case, users must have their own means to securely store the key; in the latter, the agent has to return the key securely to the owner (e.g., embedded in a smart card). The next step, certification, associates that key with a meaningful name through a digital certificate.

That name, in turn, needs to be registered to a person through online directory services. To prepare the new key for meaningful use in applications the agent can assign attributes such as roles (e.g., "head of department"), capabilities (e.g., "access to sales statistics"), and access privileges or encryption restrictions (e.g., "for bank use only").

Once the key is in circulation, the key management infrastructure is also responsible for verifying that a purported key can be trusted for the purpose to which it is applied (for example, "Giles S. Murchiston, acting in the role of repairs budget holder, purchasing printer spares").

These processes are carried out through coordination of several distinct components of the key management infrastructure. A Certification Authority is responsible for issuing and revoking digital certificates and certificate revocation lists; it also operates a Certificate Repository for storage and retrieval of certificates. These are used by the Client Services module to provide access to the

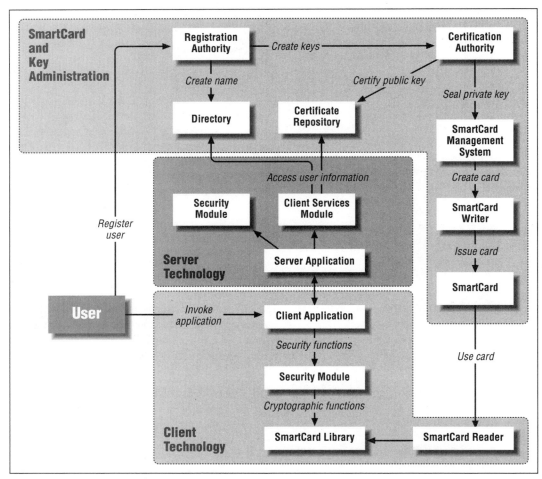

**Figure 5**   The E2S model of the management of keys and smart cards

directory and certificate repository for secure mail gateways, Web servers, and IT inte gration components. A separate Security module handles key storage in a computer and performing cryptographic functions, based on the SecuDE toolkit [6]. Finally, there is an interface to the infrastructure for policy management and audit, called Key Administration.

## Smart Cards

Once an identity has been created, the E2S Secure Business Architecture recommends securing it within a smart card. The smart card management system provides the link between the smart card infrastructure and the key management infrastructure. The smart card management system is responsible for issuing smart cards to users involved in the following activities:

- Receiving a set of private keys from a public key infrastructure manager

- Creating a smart card encapsulating the keys and assigning a PIN

- Delivering the smart card and knowledge of the PIN securely to the smart card user (e.g., by postal mailing in separate packages)

## Credentials Management

Identity is not the end-all of security management. The purpose of credentials management is to maintain relationships between sets of digital certificates. For example, some business processes require both proof of identity and proof of ability to pay. Both of these can be represented as certificates, one issued by the key management infrastructure and the other by a payment infrastructure. Credentials management takes such certificates, verifies them individually, and then delivers an access control decision (perhaps in the form of another certificate, such as a capability) based on the results of the verification and an access control policy.

## Secure Business Transactions

Designing secure business transactions within the E2S architecture means building upon protocols that use cryptographic techniques to ensure that electronic business processes can be trusted. For example, by using cryptographic signing, we can both confirm the origin and content of messages and use cryptographic sealing to protect their confidentiality. E2S's secure transactions component builds up from application protocols to general electronic payment transactions, ultimately leading to corporate purchasing infrastructures, as we'll see in the sections that follow.

## Application Protocols

Application protocols are the electronic analogues of the business contracts we enter into every day, such as updating records, ordering goods or buying services. Business transactions must therefore provide *confidentiality*, so that transactions are only visible to the participants involved; *integrity*, so the transaction follows a correct procedure; *authentication*, so the participants in a transaction are convinced of each other's right to undertake the roles they fulfil in the transaction; and *non-repudiation*, which verifies to each participant at the end of a transaction that the transaction took place.

Because E2S business protocols will be based on exchanges of messages in PEM format, the protocols can use either email or the Web as their transport. Protocols from the SecuDE [6] toolkit will be used for signing, verifying, sealing, and unsealing those messages.

## Secure Payment Infrastructure

Providing means for electronic payment is fundamental to electronic commerce. Given the objectives and timescales of the E2S project, we needed to select a payment system that fulfills the following criteria:

- It is convenient for users

- It spans national boundaries

- It has an accepted status in the financial community

- It is available for use immediately

These criteria led to the choice of electronic bankcards—in particular, the Secure Electronic Transactions (SET) standard [5] and its implementation by VISA International. SET is an open, vendor neutral, non-proprietary, license-free specification for securing online transactions. In order to realize the benefits from this specification, E2S must develop financial relationships with banks who act as issuing banks for SET users and acquiring banks for SET merchants.

## Operational Security

Operational security ensures that electronic commerce and the support infrastructure is safe from network threats such as snooping, replay, and other malicious or erroneous events. Secure networking by itself does not guarantee security; it is also necessary to trust people who perform critical roles in the architecture and to ensure physical protection of critical components. To this end, the E2S architecture builds its defense through the use of firewalls, conventional security technology, and strong cryptography.

### Firewalls

Firewalls are used to selectively isolate computers from the Internet. A firewall creates a security domain encompassing all the computers connected to it. This barrier is erected using successively more complex approaches like filters, gateways, and application-specific proxies. Filters block and/or audit transmission of certain kinds of messages (specified by type, source, destination, or any combination). Gateways forward acceptable messages unmodified from one side of the firewall to the other. Application-specific proxies are programmed to understand those

messages, in order to perform special access controls, monitoring, and auditing.

### Conventional Security Tools

Trusted system components can use conventional security technology, provided that the keys used by the components are physically part of the component (that is, they are a tamper-proof part of its electronics, or an enabling smart card and computer in a physically protected location). Because the E2S architecture promotes end-to-end security, there are limited needs for conventional security technology—concerns such as authentication, confidentiality, integrity and non-repudiation are addressed by the application-oriented, secure, end-to-end transactions part of the architecture, such as smart card-based user authentication and business protocols.

However, in practical systems, there is often a need to interoperate with legacy security infrastructures, or to conform to conventional security standards for access to secured data and system management functions. E2S pilot demonstrators have identified three such areas.

First, there is a need for alternative means of authentication when smart card technology is not available, as shown below:

- To access private keys in security enhanced mailers

- To gain access to server technology local administration functions

- To authenticate a computer as operating on behalf of a user or an organization

Second, there is a need to support existing formats, such as PEM and PGP for encryption of mail and form contents in application protocol.

Third is the need for securing transport protocols such as login and SSL between Web clients and servers, for network access to system management and auditing functions.

## Strong Cryptography

In the end, secure protocols depend upon the strength of the cryptographic algorithms they use and on the length of their keys. Deployment of cryptography is constrained by export regulations, import regulations and government policy.[*] Consequently, the E2S architecture has made only general recommendations to cope with this environment.

To start with, the strongest permissible cryptography should always be used. This implies that security protocol implementations should be parameterized by algorithm and key length so that alternatives can be substituted. Furthermore, those alternatives should not be built into applications as specific algorithms and key lengths (except in the form of constraints on minimum size). Of course, obeying these political constraints requires our system components to associate location information so algorithms and key length can be chosen correctly.

## Legacy System Integration Issues

IT integration technology enables back-office applications to be exported via Web servers to users. These systems provide custom services within E2S, but must be extended carefully to control access to their secure data. Those controls must not only ensure that confidential data will not leak onto the Internet; it must also protect such mission-critical applications from Internet attacks.

At the same time, IT services must be deliverable as custom, branded experiences. This includes control of presentation to the user and the division of processing between browser, IT integration component, and back-office application. The result is user confidence in the system by virtue of trust in the "brand image."

The IT integration technology shown in Figure 6 supports these both together and separately.

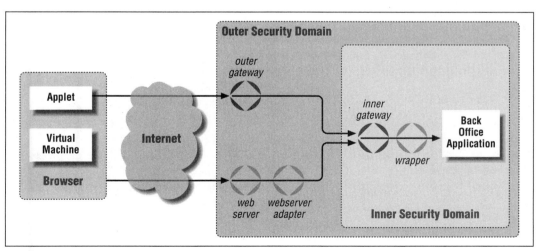

**Figure 6**    The E2S technology framework for information systems integration

---

[*] See the articles "Government Promotion of Key Recovery Encryption: How Current Government Initiatives Will Impact Internet Security," by Clint Smith, and "The Risks of Key Recovery, Key Escrow, and Trusted Third-Party Encryption," also in this issue.

## Summary

The E2S Project is developing an Internet and WWW-based infrastructure for business-to-business electronic commerce that will exploit existing security technology together with appropriate new technologies, such as SET, purchasing protocols, and smart card management systems. The architecture described in this paper is based on the requirements of a deliberately diverse set of applications, and will form the basis for the implementation of those application systems participating in live commercial trials during the coming year. ∎

### References

1. Verisign Inc. *http://www.verisign.com/*.

2. The ICE-TEL Project. *http://www.darmstadt.gmd. de/ice-tel/*.

3. Cheswick, W.R., and Bellovin, S.M., *Firewalls and Internet Security: Repelling the Wily Hacker*, Addison Wesley, 1994.

4. "BaKo: A Protocol for Reliable Exchange of Secured Order Forms." *http://www.darmstadt. gmd.de/TKT/security/Publications/bako/*

5. "SET: Secure Electronic Transactions." *http://www. visa.com/cgi-bin/vee/sf/set/intro.html?2+0*.

6. The SecuDE Toolkit. *http://saturn.darmstadt.gmd. de/secude/secude.html*.

## Acknowledgments

The authors are grateful to their colleagues and partners in the E2S Project and at APM Ltd for their support and comments upon the material discussed in this paper.

The E2S Project is a consortium funded by the European Commission as part of the ESPRIT Programme. The project partners are APM, Gemplus, GMD, Hewlett Packard (European Research Laboratories; Enterprise Networking and Security Division; World-Wide Customer Service Operation) Octacon, TUB, SBC-Warburg, Smart Card Forum and Visa.

## About the Authors

**Mark Madsen**
APM Ltd
Poseidon House
Castle Park
Cambridge CB3 0RD, UK
*Mark.Madsen@ansa.co.uk*

Mark Madsen is the Project Director of E2S. He has held research positions at the Universities of Cape Town, Sussex, Lancaster, Portsmouth and Leicester. Since 1980 he has been involved in projects as diverse as housing demand prediction, physical system simulations, biomedical treatment analyses and evaluations, distributed real time multimedia systems, and distributed information systems design. Since joining APM in 1995, he has contributed to the ANSAweb architecture developed at APM, and to a variety of Internet research programmes.

**Andrew Herbert**
APM Ltd
Poseidon House
Castle Park
Cambridge CB3 0RD, UK
*Andrew.Herbert@ansa.co.uk*

Andrew Herbert is the Technical Director of the E2S Project and of APM Ltd. He has held positions at the University of Cambridge, and has contributed to international standards in distributed object systems, interoperability, and telecommunications. He is a member of the IRTF and a contributor to the OMG.

# The Electronic Medical Record
## Promises and Threats

*Lincoln D. Stein*

## Abstract

*Starting with three fictitious scenarios that illustrate the promises and risks of the electronic medical record (EMR), this article describes the pros and cons of EMRs, the role that the Web will soon play in this arena, and the technological, social, and political challenges to controlling how one's personal medical information should be used.*

## Scenario 1: The Good

The middle-aged male patient is admitted to the emergency room of a Phoenix hospital at 10:32 AM, unconscious and unresponsive, after passersby saw him collapse on the street. Respirations are light and rapid, the pulse thready, and his blood pressure low.

In cases like this one, where someone experiences a sudden loss of consciousness, the range of possible diagnoses is vast. Among the possibilities are heart disease, drug overdose, infection, stroke, and various metabolic diseases. The treatment for each disease is vastly different. Some conditions, like an intracranial bleed, must receive appropriate treatment immediately. Others, like an epileptic seizure, will resolve by themselves if left untreated. Often the key to making the right diagnosis in a timely fashion is the patient's medical history, but an unconscious patient is in no position to answer questions.

In this case, the patient's wallet reveal only his name and an address in Boston; there are no medications to hint at the existence of a medical condition, and no contact information for family members, doctor, or medical facility. He appears to be on a business trip and is not known to anyone in Phoenix.

The traditional medical response to this situation would be to try a little bit of everything: a dose of an opiate-inhibitor to treat potential heroin overdose, an intravenous line of 50% glucose to cover insulin shock in a diabetic, a broad-spectrum antibiotic to treat possible shock from an overwhelming bacterial infection, and an EKG and blood samples to rule out a heart attack. However, the emergency room has just installed a state-of-the-art Internet-based medical record system. While the intern on duty is evaluating the patient in the traditional way, the resident strolls up to one of the ER computers, fires up Internet Explorer 7.0, and connects to the central search service, "MedCrawler." She enters the appropriate authorization codes, types in the patient's name and address, and within a few seconds is browsing the patient's full medical record. There at the top of the patient's "problem list" is the answer: a severe bee-sting allergy. The patient has somehow contrived to get himself stung by a bee. His sudden physical collapse is the result of anaphylactic shock. She and the intern immediately begin the standard treatment for allergic anaphylaxis with *epinephrine* and antihistamines. Half an hour later the patient is up, alert, and very, very grateful.

## Scenario 2: The Bad

A professor at a top-tier school for international affairs is nominated for Secretary of State after the former Secretary was forced to resign for employing an illegal alien as a nanny. The nominee's record is faultless: she is the author of over 200 papers in the field of international relations, and has extensive practical experience in the Pacific rim as a former chief negotiator for the semiconductor industry. Her nomination is widely hailed by the press as a breakthrough, a case in which the nominee's manifest qualifications clearly supersede questions of partisanship politics.

This idyllic situation does not last long. A member of the opposition party, a declared enemy of the reigning administration, quietly hires a hacker to break into the nominee's medical records. Within a day, and without leaving the comfort of his vacation home in the south of France, the hacker has bypassed the security measures on the nominee's records by exploiting an implementation hole in the authentication stack. He downloads the nominee's records, burns them into a CD-ROM, and sends the CD-ROM off by FedEx.

Over the next few days, tantalizing tidbits of information about the nominee are leaked to the press. It's found out, for example, that years ago she had an abortion. This angers abortion-rights opponents. She was briefly treated for depression, raising doubts about her mental stability. A recent uterine biopsy shows hyperplasia, a precancerous condition, but one that raises doubts about her health. Then the stunner. The National Enquirer headlines screams from the grocery store racks: "State Department Pick Cheats on Hubby." Sure enough, a portion of the nominee's psychiatric records has just been leaked. In them, she talks with her therapist frankly about an extramarital affair. Washington's pro-family forces rally against the nomination, forcing the nominee to beat a humiliating withdrawal.

### Scenario 3: The Ugly

A West Coast psychotherapist is finishing up work at the end of a long day when she gets a call from a clerk in the "quality assurance" division of one of the health plans the psychotherapist has recently joined forces with. The clerk is processing some of the electronic paperwork generated by one of the psychotherapist's patients and just needs a few clarifications in order to put the forms through.

"I see that you've coded this guy's diagnosis as DSM-IIIR 300.02: Generalized Anxiety Disorder,"
says the clerk, referring to one of the diagnostic codes in the Diagnostic and Statistical Manual of Mental Disorers, Third Edition (revised).

"Yes, that's right," answers the psychotherapist.

"The plan won't accept that one. You need a more specific diagnosis" says the clerk. "Well, I was wondering . . . I see here that this guy was sexually abused as a kid, so how about if we change this to a 309.81, Post-traumatic Stress Disorder. We use that one a lot here."

The psychotherapist is taken aback. Apparently the full text of her therapy notes, filed with the patient's electronic medical record, is available to the health plan's clerks, accountants, and insurance adjusters. Who else in the plan has access to this information?

## A Mixed Blessing

These three scenarios, none of which is intended to resemble true people or events, illustrate the promises and risks of the electronic medical record. Scenario 1 illustrates the best use of a distributed, Internet-accessible medical record. In this scenario the availability of the electronic medical record went a long way to alleviating the frequent traveler's worst nightmare: getting sick in a strange city far away from one's doctor and friends. Scenario 2 illustrates the worst use: the full, unauthorized disclosure of someone's most intensely personal affairs to the general public. Though dramatic, in some ways this scenario is not so troublesome as the last one, Scenario 3, which portrays medical information percolating gradually through a large and ill-defined group of doctors, therapists, bureaucrats, and other members of the health care community.

The electronic medical record (EMR) is an inevitability. Already every major hospital in this country has some form of EMR, whether a simple system for storing and retrieving laboratory test results, or a comprehensive system for recording the full text of the patient's medical history, medications, progress notes, and test results. As managed care becomes increasingly pervasive and the health care system coalesces into a set of large regional "alliances," the EMR will become essential for coordinating a patient's care among a network of affiliated hospitals, clinics, HMO's, and medical offices.

## A Brief History of the Medical Record

Traditionally, all medical records are maintained on paper in large manila binders called "charts." Typically, a patient has several charts, each maintained at a different location. His primary doctor or health clinic maintains one file, each of the patient's specialists (opthamologist, allergist, orthopedist) has theirs, and any hospital that the patient has ever visited has a chart of its own. When a patient is admitted to the hospital, whether on a scheduled visit or an unscheduled trip to the emergency room, a chart request is sent to the medical records department via courier or pneumatic tube. Minutes to hours later, the patient's chart would arrive.

During the patient's stay, the chart is his constant companion. Every interview, test, order, or medication that the patient receives is entered into the chart, dated, and signed by the responsible physician, nurse, or therapist. As a patient is moved about the hospital, from ward to X-ray to operating room, the chart accompanies him, often dangling from a specially-designed bracket on the gurney. When the patient leaves the hospital, a "discharge note" is entered into the chart. The chart is then returned to medical records for filing.

The paper system has never been much good. Charts are misfiled, pages fall out, notes are entered in the wrong order, and a poorly-placed cup of coffee (or urine specimen) can wipe out a patient's entire medical history. Another chronic problem of the paper record is the well-known illegibility of doctors' handwriting, which can obscure important medical information. Inevitably, mistakes occur during transcription which are propagated throughout the written record. Sometimes consequences of such mistakes are disastrous: a diabetic patient has the wrong leg amputated; a misunderstanding of the pathology report causes the surgeon to remove a benign portion of colon rather than the portion containing the cancer; a patient is nearly given a lethal dose of the anti-cancer drug chlorambucil rather than the antibiotic chloramphenicol.

Over the past twenty years, medical institutions have increasingly turned to computerization for help managing patient information. Inevitably, the first department to be computerized is Accounts Receivable. After that, the next departments to get computer systems are Radiology, whose task involves keeping track of ten thousand or more X-ray, CT, and ultrasound studies per year, and the Clinical Laboratory, which processes hundreds of blood and fluid specimens each day.

When I was in medical school in the mid 80s, the hospitals I worked in had an amusingly inefficient system for incorporating the computerized data from the laboratory systems into the paper chart. One of the medical student's chief duties was to run down to the clinical laboratory at regular intervals, use the computer system to look up patients' test results, run back to the ward, and transcribe the results into the paper record. Really advanced hospitals had dumb terminals at the end of each patient ward. Medical students could log into the lab system and retrieve the results without traveling any great distance. Unfortunately, the terminals were often down and we ended up making the trip anyway.

By and large these early medical information systems weren't integrated. To get a radiology report you had to find a terminal connected to the radiology system. To get the report on a biopsy you had to log into the pathology system. One emergency room that I worked with had two terminals sitting side by side. One was used to retrieve blood gas chemistry results (the concentration of oxygen and carbon dioxide in patients' blood). The other was used to retrieve all other blood analyses!

During the late 80s health care institutions made a concerted effort to weld the individual laboratory computers into integrated "clinical information systems." From a single terminal or PC located in the office or hospital ward, health care workers could retrieve all the patients' test results, including blood chemistry, microbiology, radiology, and biopsy reports. By employing transcription services, hospitals and clinics also began to incorporate important parts of the clinical narrative as well. Surgical operative notes and discharge notes started appearing in the clinical information system, as well as capsule summaries of patient's medical problems ("problem lists") and lists of their current medications.

When managed care changed the face of medicine in the 90s, the face of the medical record changed as well. The spread of multi-institution "partnerships," "plans," and "alliances" across the countryside made it impractical to shuttle paper charts around. Doctors now had many more patients to see, and less time to do it in. Interviews and physical exams had to be efficient, expedient, and to the point. Leafing through a new patient's chart and trying to figure out the person's current medical issues just wouldn't cut it in this new world. Further, in order to keep costs under control, the medical plans needed to closely monitor doctors to ensure that every patient was receiving only the diagnostic tests and therapeutic interventions appropriate for his medical condition.

The computerization of the medical record has accelerated rapidly in recent years. In many centers, essential medical history such as clinic visits, hospital admission notes, problem lists, allergies, discharge orders, diagnostic tests, labor and delivery records, medications, and even dietary notes are kept in electronic form. When a doctor goes to see a patient, all the most important information is now instantly available on the computer or terminal in neatly organized, legible, and searchable form. A few health care providers have even taken the next step—abolishing the written record entirely for a system in which doctors and nurses enter notes into the computer directly and sign them with a digital signature. The notes are crunched into a record-oriented format and stored into a large database.

It's important to emphasize, however, that the traditional written chart is far from dead. Most health care systems still use some combination of electronic medical records and paper charts. It may be a decade or more before the written record is gone for good.

# What's the Electronic Medical Record Good For?

In addition to fixing some of the obvious shortcomings of the traditional paper chart, the electronic medical record offers features that written records simply can't match.

## Consistency

The electronic medical record enforces consistency. Every laboratory result, every radiology report, every progress note follows a standard format. When formats are standardized, incomplete or anomalous information stands out. Health care providers can spend less time figuring out what the report says and more time thinking about its meaning.

## Flexibility

The written medical record is strictly a linear affair. Clinic visit notes, lab results, and progress reports are entered in strict chronological order, like the log book of a seagoing vessel. But medicine is anything but linear. Patients often have multiple, unrelated medical conditions. By forcing everything into a linear narrative the traditional paper chart mixes everything up. The story of the patient's fight with heart disease is interrupted by notes from the podiatrist, the dietician, and the dentist.

In reality, the medical record is more like a hypertext document (Figure 1); only in electronic form can it be expressed with the clarity and flexibility that it requires. If a clinician is interested in following the patient's heart disease, she can rearrange the information so that all the cardiologist's notes are together. She can move all the patient's electrocardiograms together to see how they've changed over the past year. She can even extract a single laboratory value, such as the patient's blood potassium level, and have the computer chart it over time.

## Problem Oriented Approach

At a time when the electronic medical record was just a distant dream, progressive medical and nursing schools were preaching a type of record keeping called the "problem oriented medical record." In this approach, the patient's medical condition is divided into a list of discrete prob-

lems, listed in order from most severe to least. For example, a typical problem list might look like this:

- Coronary artery disease
- Diabetes
- Lower back pain
- Bee-sting allergy
- History of depression
- Lactose intolerance

In this scheme, each entry in the medical record is explicitly organized around the problem list, indicating which problem(s) the note addresses, and summarizing the medical plan in regard to the others. As problems are resolved they're

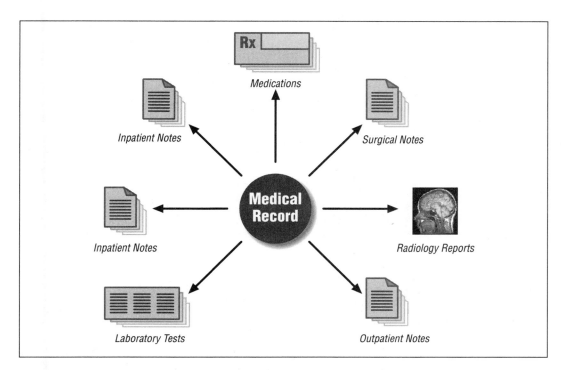

**Figure 1**    The medical record consists of many interrelated parts, just some of which are shown here. Paper records force the parts to follow an artificial chronological order, but the electronic medical record allows their true hyperlinked relationships to be represented.

removed from the list. As new problems appear they're added.

Because of the flexibility of the electronic medical record, the problem oriented approach really comes into its own. Health care providers can instantly focus in on the problem they're interested in. Quality assurance personnel can quickly determine whether each problem is receiving the attention that the standard of care requires.

## Machine-Assisted Decision Making

With the medical record organized in a standard way, the computer can begin to help in a limited way with the medical decision making process itself. The most important aspect of this is the ability of the computer to catch and flag human errors. For example, there are over 3,000 medications in common usage. Most patients take several drugs simultaneously, and quite a few drugs have known adverse interactions with others. It's impossible for the average physician to keep track of all the drug interactions; many are rare, and some have come to light only recently. Here's where the computer system can help. It knows all the patient's meds and has an up-to-date database of adverse interactions. When the doctor prescribes a new medication, the computer scans its database for interactions with any of the patient's existing pharmaceuticals. If an interaction is found, the computer flags the problem and notifies the doctor, emphasizing its point with a capsule review and bibliographic references. The computer can catch misplaced decimal points and other errors that could result in a patient receiving a drug overdose.

Similarly, the computer system can be on the lookout for life-threatening results in the patient's laboratory test data. If routine blood chemistries detect a dangerously low potassium level, the system can raise an alert immediately rather than waiting for someone to notice the problem. Things can also be wired so that the computer will notice problems that arise from interactions *between* different parts of the medical record. For example, some medications are dangerous when

used on patients with certain underlying medical conditions. The antibiotic *gentamicin*, for instance, should not be used in a patient with kidney disease, as it can damage the kidneys even further. If the computer sees "kidney disease" listed on the patient's problem list, or detects anomalous laboratory values that are indicative of kidney disease, it will complain and ask for confirmation if a physician tries to prescribe the antibiotic.

## Quality Assurance

"Quality assurance" is managed care's euphemism for cost control. Quality assurance means that patients shouldn't receive expensive tests and medical procedures that they don't need. Since unnecessary tests and procedures don't improve the patient's life (and sometimes make it much worse) quality assurance is good for everyone. The electronic medical record makes quality assurance practical. The computer system audits the patient's problem list, diagnoses, laboratory tests, medications, and procedure notes. If it sees a test, medication, or procedure that doesn't seem to be justified by the patient's medical condition, it can request further information from the physician or alert someone in the quality assurance department to investigate. The system can also detect physicians who order an unusually high number of lab tests or whose patients have an abnormally high rate of hospitalization.

This may sound big-brotherish, but it's far better than the way quality assurance is now done in institutions that rely on paper records. Here, armies of clerks prowl the wards, reading through patients' charts in minute detail, searching for anomalies.

There's also a more positive side to quality assurance. The computer can help ensure that the medical system applies a uniform and consistently high standard of care. For example, the standard of care at one institution might be that women with an abnormal pap smear are scheduled for a repeat pap smear after six months. If it is still abnormal they are scheduled for a cervical biopsy to investigate the possibility of a cancerous or precancerous condition. The electronic medical record allows the computer system to detect when a woman's pap smear results are abnormal and to set the wheels in motion. It notifies the clinician of the abnormal result and generates the standard letter to the patient. It schedules the repeat appointment, and makes sure that the pap smear actually happens. If the pap is again abnormal, the computer system makes sure that the biopsy is scheduled and performed.

## Online Health Care

Health care is not, and never has been, delivered at a single geographic site. Patients go to one office to see their gynecologists, to another for dental work. If they get sick enough to require hospitalization they'll likely end up in a hospital affiliated with their health plan. Increasingly, many routine lab tests and radiological procedures are now performed and interpreted by outside commercial enterprises rather than by labs located within the hospital walls. By taking advantage of the network infrastructure, electronic medical records allow patient information to be shared among these sites efficiently and rapidly.

An integrated medical record has other potential benefits. With paper records, the patient's medical history is never complete. Little bits and pieces of it are stashed away in file cabinets of all the hospitals and clinics the patient has ever visited. The electronic medical record offers the possibility of a centralized database that can hold the patient's entire medical history, from childhood pediatric visits to geriatric records.

Electronic medical records give health care providers remote access to the chart. Doctors can check up on their patients from home, ask for the advice of outside consultants in distant parts of the country, or follow their patients when they've been transferred to remote locations. This is a major boon to primary care doctors, who have long suffered the experience of being "cut out of the loop" when their patients were admitted to hospitals. Now personal physicians can actively participate in their patients' hospital management, reviewing the daily notes and treatment plan, and adding suggestions of their own to the chart. When radiologists are presented with particularly difficult cases, they can call in specialists for advice, transmitting the relevant X-rays and CT scan images across the Internet (there's even a name for this, *teleradiology*).

Travelers need not fear that they will take sick in a distant locale and be treated by doctors who don't understand their medical needs. With their medical record accessible online, the local doctors can come up to speed rapidly.

# How Does the Web Fit In?

In the preceding discussion I have deliberately soft-pedaled one of the biggest problems of the evolving electronic medical records system: There is no standard for the EMR. Each hospital, HMO, health plan, and clinic has built its own system, sometimes from commercial systems, and sometimes from scratch. As the health care sector contracts, institutions have been seized by merger mania. As they merge, they discover the disconcerting fact that their EMR systems are incompatible. This makes it difficult to effectively share patient information within an institution, let alone distribute it remotely. At first glance, fixing this problem appears to involve massive database conversion, reengineering of existing systems, and the installation of custom software and hardware throughout the consolidated institution.

The Web offers a way out of this mess. With simple standards-based communications protocols (TCP/IP and HTTP), well-understood data conversion techniques (CGI scripts at the server side, Java and ActiveX at the client side), and a widely available, easy-to-use client (the browser), the World Wide Web is the natural platform for the electronic medical record of the future. It provides nonproprietary data encryption and authentication techniques (SSL),* allowing confidential information to remain that way, and a rich array of multimedia formats allowing X-ray images, microscopic images, and even digitized heart sounds to be distributed.

If you do a Lycos or AltaVista search for "electronic medical record," you'll find a dozen or so Web-based EMR systems that are in various phases of research, development, and deployment. One of the nicest online demos is the EMRS project, jointly developed by Laboratory of Computer Science at Massachusetts Institute of Technology and Boston's Beth Israel, Children's,

and Massachusetts General hospitals. It implements CGI gateways to the medical records databases maintained by these three hospitals, translating URL requests into database accesses on the fly, and converting the results into HTML pages, graphs, and other Web documents. You can try it out for yourself on a fictionalized database from this URL:

```
http://www.emrs.org/
```

Figure 2 gives you an idea of what the EMRS system looks like. Each patient's complete demo graphic data is online, as well as the record

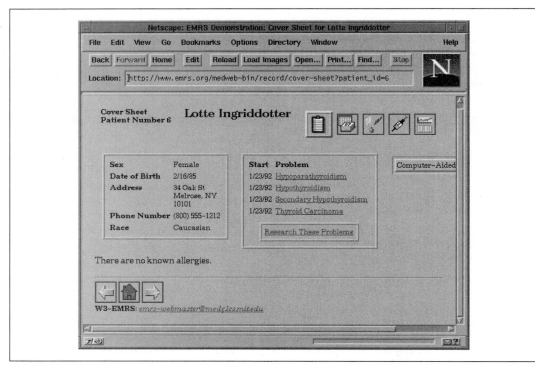

**Figure 2**    An experimental EMR produced by MIT's Laboratory of Computer Science in conjunction with a number of medical hospitals converts the information in the clinical information system mainframe into a set of HTML pages. Hyperlinks lead to the patient's notes, demographic information, medications, and lab results.

---

* For more information on SSL, see the article entitled "Introducing SSL and Certificates Using SSLeay" by Frederick Hirsch, in this issue.

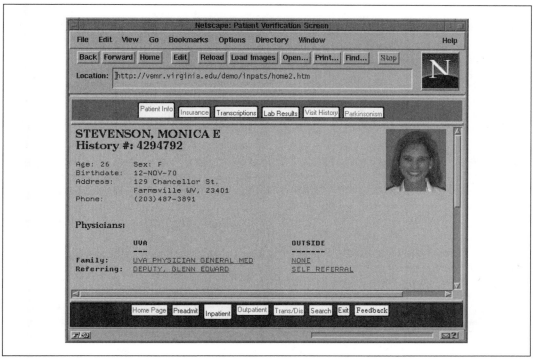

**Figure 3**    A Web-based EMR system in use at the University of Virginia Health Sciences Center department of Neurosurgery incorporates images as well as text. The tabs at the top and bottom of the main frame include components of the problem list (in this example "Parkinsonism") as well as links to other parts of the medical record.

of all visits, procedures, lab tests, and medications. The data can be viewed chronologically, or organized functionally according to the patient's current problem list. Hyperlinks connect relevant parts of the record: you can jump from a progress report on the patient's thyroid disease to the series of lab values showing how the patient's thyroid function has changed over time.

Progress and visit notes are not available at this time because all three of the hospitals that participate in this project still keep these notes in written charts. However the full text of discharge summaries and letters to the patient's personal physician are available.

Another example of a Web-based medical record system is available at:

```
http://vemr.virginia.edu/demo/
      homepg.htm
```

This system, run by the Neurosurgical department at the University of Virginia Health Sciences Center, is a fictionalized demo of an actual system this institution uses to manage patients. Figure 3 shows a page from this system. An interesting feature of its user interface is that it lists items from the patient's problem list in small tabs on a frame at the top of the window. When you click on the tab, all entries relating to the problem are displayed. Hyperlinks take you back and forth between different parts of the record, allowing you to view the patient's history in chronologic order, or to focus in on the aspect of the history that you're most interested in.

# The Dark Side of the EMR

As the scenarios at the beginning of this article suggested, the electronic medical record has its problems too. The main issues are reliability, accountability, and patient privacy.

## Reliability

Despite their many shortcomings, paper charts are still very reliable. They will withstand power outages, electrical storms, air conditioning failures, electromagnetic pulses, and, yes, even the Millenium Bomb. They are also completely impervious to programming errors—public enemy number one of the software world. When I visited a devastated hospital in Uganda soon after their civil war, I found that nearly everything was broken: there was no electricity, no running water, no autoclaves, no medication, no clean syringes. However, the paper-based medical records system, miraculously, was still running smoothly despite the chaos.

An electronic medical record system needs to be at least as reliable as a paper system. The system cannot crash, it cannot hang, it cannot behave capriciously without having potentially life-threatening consequences. This has obvious implications for Internet-based EMR systems. There is no room for network blackouts or slowdowns.

## Accountability

When a physician signs a progress note, a medical order, or a prescription, her signature is a legal statement of responsibility. On the basis of this signature, the pharmacy will fill the prescription, the therapist will begin a round of radiation therapy, or the patient will be led off to surgery. In a world where the only record kept of life and death decisions is in a malleable, easily-forgible medium, it's critical to have a reliable substitute for the signature. Some institutions have addressed this issue by claiming that the secret login key assigned to their employees constitutes a legally binding signature. When a health care worker enters an order, note or diagnostic report, she "signs" it by entering her secret key.

This is an inadequate solution. A typical case is exemplified by one of the hospitals that I have worked at. Although this hospital hasn't abandoned the paper chart yet, it's fairly advanced along that path. Diagnostic reports, medical orders for tests, and inpatient prescriptions are all handled via the clinical information system. To access the system, you must type in your secret key (key only—a user name isn't required), consisting of five uppercase alphanumeric characters. For example, one of my previous passwords was HQ7BB. The user doesn't choose these keys; the system generates them automatically and changes them every six months.

What's wrong with this system? For one thing, by assigning random keys to the users, the system effectively forces users to write their passwords down. My wallet contains various slips of paper containing my current password and several of my previous ones. Written passwords are easily lost, stolen, or read over someone's shoulder. They're also vulnerable to sharing among friends and associates.

For another thing, this password system is prone to guessing. You'd think that the password space for this key system would be 36 (26 letters plus ten numerals) raised to the fifth power, or somewhat more than sixty million possible passwords. However, inspection of a handful of valid passwords suggests that the random number generator always generates a key that contains exactly four alphabetic characters and one numeral. The password space is really more like this:

```
26^4 + 10^4 = 1.04E6
```

or somewhat more than a million possible keys. This might still seem like a lot, but consider that the hospital—plus its various affiliates and outpatient clinics—employ somewhere between 5,000 and 10,000 employees, a substantial proportion of whom have access to the computer system. This means that if you were to guess at keys randomly, you need only try a hundred or so guesses before you hit someone's key. In fact, the odds may be better than this. Nearly everyone who has used this system has had the experience of "breaking in" to someone else's account just by accidentally mistyping their key!

With a system like this in place, how can a patient hold a doctor legally responsible for any order placed in the medical record system? The doctor can simply protest that he lost his key or that someone must have guessed it. How can we guard the system against malicious individuals who plant embarassing or even health-threatening information in the system using a valid, but stolen key? Conversely, how can we be sure that the health care institution itself doesn't tamper with the medical record in order to delete information that might be legally damaging to it?

EMR systems need to use a secure, verifiable, and untamperable form of digital signature, coupled with a message integrity check to ensure that the record itself isn't tampered with. The software industry already has more than enough technical solutions for this particular problem, but makers of electronic medical record systems have been slow to adapt them. At some point, however, I'm confident that some combination of smart card, public key cryptography, secure hash algorithm, and/or digitally signed certificate will ensure that we can trust the elecronic medical record to tell the truth.[*]

## Patient Privacy

This is the most troubling issue for the electronic medical record. Our medical records hold some of our most intimate and private information. Medical records can reveal a history of drug abuse, a venereal disease, or a life-threatening illness. Psychiatric notes reveal inner fantasies, sexual peccadiloes, crimes, or the crimes and abuses of family members. The information from genetic tests can reveal not only that a patient is suscepti-

ble for some disease, but that her children and other family members are susceptible as well. If medical records are disclosed, you can lose your insurance, your job, or even your marriage. Is the price we pay for making our medical records easily accessible to health care providers the complete loss of our privacy?

These concerns, which have been simmering for years, were brought forcefully into the public eye about a year ago, in a well-publicized case in Florida. A worker in a Florida state agency that conducts "anonymous and confidential" testing for the AIDS virus decided that it was his duty to protect the public from infection. He downloaded the list of HIV positive patients to a floppy disk and distributed it to his friends, encouraging them to use the list to avoid picking up the wrong date. Without even the Internet to help out, thousands of people had their medical confidentiality violated in one blow.

If medical records are distributed via the World Wide Web, how are we to ensure that only authorized medical practitioners have access to them? I submit that the Web itself won't present the major problem. The cryptographic protocols, digital signatures, and certificate infrastructure that is being built to protect financial transactions will be more than adequate to protect medical data while it flows across the Internet. To the extent that computer systems can be protected with a combination of firewalls, strong authentication, and hardened operating systems, the databases that store medical records will be made safe from crackers, vandals, and idle thrill seekers.

The problem is to define "authorized medical practitioner." Health care institutions have become vast, and every employee in those institutions is potentially an authorized practitioner. In addition to the doctor and nursing staff, there are medical students, nursing students, physical therapists,

---

[*] These techniques are described in Simson Garfinkel and Gene Spafford's article, "Cryptography and the Web." For more detail on digital signatures, see the DSig 1.0 Signature Label specification in the "W3C Reports" section of this issue.

occupational therapists, dieticians, social workers, radiation therapists, nuclear medicine techs, EKG techs, and a host of other medical and paramedical positions. On top of the caregivers is the bureaucracy entrusted with quality assurance, billing, and insurance coding. The insurance companies themselves feel they have a legitimate right to review the medical record, or at least to know what diagnoses and diagnostic tests are in it. Some people are nosy, some gossip. Others can be bought. When thousands of people have access to the juicy information contained within medical records from the comfort and safety of their own homes, you can be sure that some accesses will not be legitimate. In my own experience I have encountered several cases in which hospital employees have used the clinical information system inappropriately to look up data on recently admitted celebrities, friends, relatives, relatives of friends, and friends of relatives.

Obviously not everyone should have the right to peruse all parts of the medical record. Dieticians should only have the right to see those parts of the record that are relevant to the patient's diet. Physical therapists shouldn't be browsing the psychiatric notes. A doctor shouldn't have access to the records of a patient she hasn't any responsibility for. You would think that you could segment the medical record on a "need to know" basis, the way the military does with classified information. However, this has turned out to be surprisingly difficult to do. In order to do his work properly, the dietician needs to know the patient's allergies, medications, and any relevant medical conditions, such as heart disease, diabetes or renal failure. In a hospital environment doctors frequently cover for one another, and in an emergency no one should be denied the need to access the patient's record just because the system doesn't recognize one's need to know. A large number of medical ethicists, committees, and congressional panels have wrestled with this

problem, and as yet no one has arrived at a satisfactory solution.

Recently, a panel appointed by the U.S. National Research Council met to discuss the privacy threats posed by distributing medical records on the Internet. They concluded that the Internet isn't the problem: the same technical solutions used to protect corporate and financial data can be used to protect patient privacy against interception by people outside the health care system. The real threat, they concluded, is the widespread and unregulated sharing of medical information among the many public and private arms of the medical system, including insurance companies, health care administrators, and government agencies.*

In the absence of a clear solution to this problem, some health care providers have reined back their plans to convert to a completely digital medical record. Recently, the Plymouth Health Plan of Massachusetts, on the eve of unveiling a new electronic medical record system that would completely replace their paper system, had second thoughts. Putting the new system on hold, they held an intensive series of meetings with patient groups, ethicists, and physicians. Eventually, they arrived at a compromise solution. Certain parts of the medical record that everyone felt was important for providing quality care—current medications, allergies, and problem lists—would be incorporated into the electronic system. Sensitive parts, such as psychiatric notes, would be kept in written form only and maintained in the traditional way.

The privacy risks posed by the electronic medical record are not primarily technological ones, but social and political ones. What we need most is well-considered legislation that lays down guidelines on how medical information should be used, who should have access to it, and what parts should be made available. Only when these issues are resolved to everyone's satisfaction can

---

* For details on the report, see *http://www2.nas.edu/cstbweb/*.

the electronic medical record assume its rightful place on the Web. ∎

## About the Author

**Lincoln Stein**
CuraGen Corporation
555 Long Wharf Drive
New Haven, CT 06511
*lstein@genome.wi.mit.edu*

Lincoln Stein is a part-time pathologist, part-time Director of Information Systems at CuraGen Corporation, and a full-time Perl hacker.

# Legislating Market Winners
## Digital Signature Laws and the Electronic Commerce Marketplace

*C. Bradford Biddle*

## Abstract

*This paper argues that certain enacted digital signature laws are premised upon false assumptions, and inappropriately enshrine a business model which would not evolve naturally in the marketplace. In attempting to solve an unsolvable liability allocation problem, such legislation harms consumers and the future evolution of electronic commerce. The article points out that alternative business models can solve the liability allocation problem. Despite obvious flaws, legislation of this type continues to be proposed, partly because the infrastructure created by these laws coincides with the needs of key escrow proponents. Ultimately the article argues that digital signature laws, which impose a particular view of electronic commerce, should be abandoned in favor of laws that remove specific, well-defined barriers to electronic commerce and that allow the electronic commerce marketplace to evolve unfettered.*

The argument goes something like this: Internet commerce is hampered by the authentication problem. There is no reliable way to ensure that the sender of an electronic transmission is in fact who they purport to be. Though digital signatures, supported by a "public key infrastructure" (PKI) of certification authorities (CAs) and certificate databases can solve this authentication problem, CAs will not emerge under the current legal regime because they face uncertain and potentially immense liability exposure. Additionally, the legal status of digitally signed documents is unclear. Therefore, legislation is needed to define and limit CA liability and to establish the legality of digitally signed documents.[*]

This argument has captured an influential segment of the legal community, and has led to the enactment of "digital signature legislation" (described later in the article) in several U.S. states and foreign nations. Unfortunately, the argument is built on fundamentally flawed assumptions, and the legislation enacted based upon it is correspondingly flawed. Much (but not all) of the digital signature legislation enacted to date presumes a vision of electronic commerce that simply is not tenable, and which would not "naturally" evolve in the marketplace. This legislation poses the risk of profoundly distorting an infant market and locking in business models which are harmful to consumers and to the future development of electronic commerce.

The type of public key infrastructure (PKI) envisioned by many of the existing digital signature laws is not viable. The problem is liability. Digital signature legislation drafters have assumed that the potential liability exposure faced by CAs is somehow a flaw of the existing legal regime. This is an erroneous assumption: the liability exposure faced by CAs under the "open PKI" model envisioned by legislation drafters is a product of a business model that cannot internalize the costs associated with its implementation. Moreover, in attempting to limit the liability exposure of CAs, current digital signature laws shift an immense liability burden onto consumers who use the infrastructure envisioned by these laws. Putting

---

[*] For more information on certificate authorities, see the article entitled "Introducing SSL and Certificates Using SSLeay," by Frederick Hirsch. Digital signatures and public key infrastructure are described in the article "Cryptography and the Web," by Simson Garfinkel and Gene Spafford. In addition, the digital signature specification, "DSig 1.0 Signature Labels," can be found in the "W3C Reports" section of this issue.

this type of liability burden on consumers violates long-held tenets of public policy, and is a result which consumers would reject in any truly "bargained for" transaction.

Digital signatures will undoubtedly play a significant role in electronic commerce. However, rather than being implemented in the "open PKI" model envisioned by various digital signature laws, digital signatures are more likely to be utilized under a "closed PKI" system. Under a closed PKI system, the liability problems associated with digital signatures become much more manageable. This article describes the differences between open and closed PKI, and suggests that, in the absence of legislative displacement, certain marketplace trends indicate that closed PKI is indeed the likely market winner.

The open PKI model can and should compete against closed PKI and other authentication technologies, and should not be accorded special legal status via legislation. Such legislation is unnecessary: the "contractual privity problem" which is used to justify open PKI legislation is a red herring. Commercial CAs utilizing the open PKI model can compete in the marketplace without special PKI legislation. These CAs are unlikely to succeed, not because of flaws with the legal system, but because the open PKI model is not a winning business model.

Despite raising the very peculiar specter of regulating an essentially nonexistent industry (CAs), and despite increased recognition of the problems associated with the very specific vision of electronic commerce embodied in these digital signature laws, laws based on the open PKI model continue to be proposed and implemented. This article suggests that one of several factors behind the continued momentum of this legislation, particularly at the federal and international levels, is its synergy with cryptographic "key escrow" proposals. While digital signature legislation ostensibly addresses the use of cryptography only for the purposes of authentication, and not for confidentiality, the infrastructure created by these laws is ideal for implementing a key escrow scheme.

Ultimately this article argues that digital signature laws which impose a particular view of electronic commerce should be abandoned. Laws which remove specific, well-defined barriers to electronic commerce—such as unnecessary "writing" or handwritten signature requirements—and which allow the electronic commerce marketplace to evolve unfettered should be encouraged.

## Background: Digital Signatures and Public Key Cryptography

Digital signatures are a particular application of public key cryptography. No attempt will be made here to explain the rather complex underlying technology in any detail; readers who are unfamiliar with basic cryptographic terminology and techniques should consult some of the many excellent sources available which can provide the relevant technical background. The importance of understanding the technology cannot be overstated: at least some of the flaws in cryptography-related legislation can be attributed to inadequate technical knowledge on the part of policymakers. At the risk of oversimplifying to the point of inaccuracy, creating a digital signature involves encrypting a numerical representation of an electronic message with a private encryption key, which the owner keeps secret; verifying a digital signature involves decrypting the encrypted data using a related public encryption key, which can be made widely available.

Lawyers have largely focused on what digital signatures can accomplish, if implemented in a particular ideal setting. If Alice signs an electronic document with a digital signature and sends it over the Internet to Bob, ideally Bob can be assured of the following:

- First, that the message really came from Alice. Digital signatures can provide assurance that a message has in fact come from its purported sender, a quality called "data origin authentication."

- Second, that the message he received is the exact message that Alice sent. A digital signature enables a recipient of a message to verify that a message has not been intentionally or accidentally altered during transmission, a quality known as "message integrity."

- Third, that Alice cannot later deny that she sent the message. No one else could have sent the message but Alice, and Bob can prove it unequivocally. This quality that digital signatures provide is known as *nonrepudiation*.

Two difficult problems must be overcome in order to actually fulfill the promise of digital signatures: identification and the security of private key.

## Identification

What if Alice never sent the message to Bob at all? Instead, a forger may have generated a cryptographic key pair, and entered the public key in a public key database under the name "Alice." "Alice" and Bob may have entered into some business arrangement whereby Bob performed some service for "Alice," and "Alice" promised to pay Bob. When Bob attempts to enforce his electronic contract, however, he will find that he has been the victim of fraud. Digital certificates, issued by "trusted third parties" called certification authorities, are one attempt to solve this problem of identification.

Certificates are digitally-signed electronic documents issued by CAs that attest to the connection of a public encryption key to an individual (or other entity). Consider this scenario: Alice generates her public and private key pair. She then presents her public key to a CA, along with some form of identification. The CA checks the identification and takes any other steps necessary to assure itself that Alice is indeed who she claims to be. The CA then gives Alice a certificate attesting to the connection between Alice and her public key.

The CA must also somehow provide assurance that it is bound to its public key, which is used to verify Alice's certificate. Thus, the CA could have its own certificate, signed with the digital signature of a "higher level" certification authority. This higher level certification authority might be (as under some of the enacted digital signature laws) a government agency.

When Bob received a message from Alice signed with Alice's digital signature, he could obtain Alice's certificate either directly from Alice or from an online database. If the signature on the message could be verified using the public key listed in the certificate, and the CA's signature verified as well, Bob would know that a CA had authenticated Alice's identity, and that he was not dealing with someone else posing as Alice.

## Security of Private Keys

The second vexing problem presented by public key cryptography is the security of private keys. If a forger somehow discovers Alice's private key, that forger can digitally sign Alice's name on documents. If a criminal discovered a certification authority's private key, that criminal would have the means to commit widespread fraud. As a practical matter, in any large-scale system utilizing public key cryptography, some private keys will become compromised and the certificate containing the corresponding public key will need to be revoked. Certificate revocation lists (CRLs) are designed to prevent people from relying on a compromised or otherwise revoked public key/private key pair.

A CRL is a list of public keys that have been revoked prior to their expiration date. If the private key is compromised, or the key pair is no longer in use for some other reason, the public key would be placed on a CRL. Thus, before Bob relied on the message that he received from Alice, he would check to make sure that Alice's certificate was not on a CRL.

# Digital Signature Legislation

A segment of the legal community, noting authentication problems associated with the Internet, became increasingly enamored with the possibilities of digital signatures. Beginning in 1992, efforts began in earnest to develop legal rules to support the type of public key infrastructure described above. Many of these efforts took place within the framework of the Information Security Committee of the American Bar Association's Section of Science and Technology (the "ABA Committee").

A primary assumption of this group of lawyers was that the specter of large, uncertain liability exposure would prevent the emergence of commercial CAs. The liability problem has several aspects. First, if a criminal defrauded a CA and induced the CA to issue a false certificate, the criminal could impose losses on a large number of third parties who would rely on the erroneous certificate. The CA could take every reasonable step—or even extremely costly, exceptional steps—to confirm identity, but still issue an erroneous certificate. If every party who relied on the certificate had a claim against the CA for any consequent losses, the CA's potential liability could be staggering. CAs would be forced to go to extraordinary lengths to confirm identity in every situation in order to avoid potential liability exposure, even when parties to a given transaction may have been satisfied with a less rigorously-procured (and thus less expensive) certificate.

Additionally, CAs face potential liability for claims by parties who rely on a certificate after the private key associated with the public key listed in the certificate is stolen by a criminal, who then creates forged digitally-signed documents. This type of harm would be difficult for CAs to prevent: they have little or no control over the care a "subscriber" takes in protecting their private key from misappropriation. If CAs bear this risk, it will be reflected in the price of certificates, which might then be uneconomically high.

CAs face catastrophic liability exposure if their private key is compromised. If a criminal obtained a CA's private key, they could commit widespread fraud. Additionally, once the compromise was discovered, all certificates issued by that CA would have to be revoked and new certificates issued, imposing costs on all of the subscribers of that CA. If CAs face liability for these potentially immense losses, entrepreneurs might choose not to enter the CA business at all.

The liability problem was perceived to be particularly intractable because of a "contractual privity problem." CAs could presumably enter into contracts with their subscribers, and allocate risk between the CA and subscriber via contract mechanisms: for instance, the CA could offer certain limited warranties to the subscriber, and limit potential liability to an agreed-upon amount. However, the lawyers looking at this issue believed that CAs would typically not be able to establish a contractual relationship with the parties who would rely on certificates, in order to allocate risk by contract. Therefore, these lawyers concluded, legislation was needed that set out the duties of all parties in this public key infrastructure, and that allocated liability appropriately.

The ABA Committee planned to release a "U.S. Model Digital Signature Act" in June of 1995. Increasingly, however, some members of the committee grew dissatisfied with the planned legislative approach; ultimately, for a variety of reasons, the plan to release model legislation was dropped. In October 1995, the ABA Committee did release its "Digital Signature Guidelines," which it described as:

> . . . general, abstract statements of principle, intended to serve as long-term, unifying foundations for digital signature law across varying legal settings.

The Guidelines set out duties for CAs, subscribers, and relying parties, consistent with the vision for a PKI described above. The ABA Guidelines avoid taking positions on certain detailed issues that legislation in this area would address, however.

In collaboration with the ABA Committee, the state of Utah began developing digital signature legislation, and the Utah Digital Signature Act was enacted (with considerable fanfare) in March of 1995. One of the reporters in the ABA effort was the primary drafter of the Utah Digital Signature Act. Under the Utah Act, a government agency assumes the obligations of being a "top level" CA and, as such, is charged with policymaking, facilitating implementation of digital signature technology, and providing regulatory oversight of private sector CAs through a comprehensive licensing scheme. Licensing under the Utah Act is voluntary; however, licensed CAs are offered certain legal benefits (primarily limited liability). The Utah Act imposes detailed duties on CAs, subscribers, and relying parties that are consistent with the ABA Guidelines. In addition, it allocates liability among these parties and accords special legal status to digitally signed documents created using the services of a licensed CA.

A number of states turned to the Utah Act as model digital signature legislation, a process encouraged by the drafters of the Utah law. In several public communications, a prominent ABA Committee member (who was also involved in the drafting of the Utah Act) indicated that the Utah Digital Signature Act was substantively identical to the unreleased ABA Model Digital Signature Act. In the wake of the enactment of the Utah Act, digital signature legislation based on the Utah law was proposed in nearly a dozen states. By mid-1997 Washington and Minnesota had enacted laws that closely tracked Utah's, and similar bills remain pending in many states. The Utah Act proved influential even when not explicitly followed: for instance, California considered and then rejected the Utah model, enacting a non-technology-specific bill designed to address transactions with government entities. Early drafts of the regulations designed to implement the California law closely followed the Utah model, however.

The "Utah/ABA Guidelines" model has also proven influential at the international level. Malaysia recently enacted legislation based upon the Utah Act; similar legislation is under consideration in Australia, Canada, Germany, Singapore, and at the European Union. The United Nations Committee on International Trade Law (UNCITRAL) is also studying Utah-style model legislation.

Recent legislation proposed at the federal level in the United States and in the United Kingdom adopts the Utah/ABA Guidelines model with an added twist: key escrow. Under these proposed laws, CAs (or TTPs—trusted third parties—as they are called under the U.K. bill) not only serve to bind subscribers to their public encryption keys used for authentication purposes, but also serve as key escrow agents, verifying the escrowing of keys used for confidentiality purposes.

Not all legislative bodies have jumped on the Utah/ABA Guidelines bandwagon. Several U.S. states enacted legislation that addressed "electronic signatures" and other non-public key methods of authenticating electronic transmissions. The most thoughtful legislative effort to date has occurred in Massachusetts, where concerns over the market-distorting effects of Utah-style legislation led to a proposed minimalist bill, aimed simply at removing existing legal barriers to electronic commerce. Similarly, the influential National Conference of Commissioners on Uniform State Laws (NCCUSL) is considering a uniform law on electronic contracting and has not been receptive to arguments in favor of a Utah-style law.

## Open PKI: The Liability "Trilemma"'

The Utah Act and its progeny, and the ABA Guidelines, are premised on an "open system" or "open loop" model of a PKI. The open PKI model envisions that subscribers will obtain a single certificate from an independent third-party CA, which certifies that subscriber's identity. Certificate holders will then use that certificate to facilitate transactions with potentially numerous merchants and/or other individuals.

As discussed above, the open PKI scenario implicates considerable liability risk. Proponents of the open model, enamored with what digital signatures can potentially accomplish, have attributed this risk to flaws in the existing legal regime that must be addressed legislatively. This conclusion is wrong. The liability exposure faced by CAs under the open PKI model is the product of a business model that cannot internalize the costs of the inevitable fraud that will result under any public key-based system. The resulting liability problem is unlikely to be solved at all in the open PKI model, and certainly cannot be solved with any one-size-fits-all legislative solution.

Here's one aspect of the problem: if criminals can obtain something valuable by expropriating an individual's private key, they will. Commentary accompanying existing digital signature laws frequently mentions the concept of storing private keys on tamper-proof smart cards. While such cards would undoubtedly promote the security of private keys, this is simply wishful thinking at this point: smart cards are not commercially deployed in any meaningful way. There is currently no practical way to truly secure private keys, and this problem is going to get worse before it gets better.

Private keys will be expropriated, and third parties will rely on ostensibly valid but fraudulent documents and suffer losses. The aggregate losses could be quite sizable, judging from analogous contexts: Mastercard and Visa lose over $1 billion per year to fraud; phone companies claim to lose $3 billion a year to fraud; in the city of Los Angeles alone fraudulent real estate document filing is said to have cost $131 million in a twenty-seven month period. Who will bear these losses? The relying party? The individual whose key was used to sign the document? The CA who performed the initial binding?

Under the Utah Act, the individual whose key was used to sign the document bears unlimited liability if they failed to exercise "reasonable care" to protect their private key. The Act also imposes difficult evidentiary burdens on the individual. So, if a subscriber (let's call her "Grandmom," just to put things in perspective) doesn't exercise due care, and her key is stolen resulting in losses totaling $25,000 prior to revocation of her key, that subscriber bears the loss—i.e., Grandmom loses her house. Or, if Grandmom *does* exercise due care and her key is still misappropriated, she must present a court with "clear and convincing" evidence (the standard under the Utah Act) to overcome the presumption that a document signed with her digital signature was in fact signed by her. In either case, the result doesn't comport with well-established consumer protection laws (compared with the legislatively imposed $50 consumer liability limit for credit card losses, or the fact that one cannot be bound by a fraudulent handwritten signature). Moreover, no rational consumer would agree to accept this level of risk in a marketplace transaction. The benefits of having a certificate simply do not outweigh the very real possibility of facing extraordinarily large unreimbursed losses.

Yet if the subscriber doesn't bear full liability under this scenario, where else would the loss fall? On the CA? They couldn't prevent the harm, and couldn't realistically insure against such indeterminate losses via pricing mechanisms. CAs presumably wouldn't know whether a particular certificate was going to be used in a purchase of a piece of clip art or in a real estate closing. Thus, the CA couldn't charge a price that would be commensurate with the CA's corresponding risk of loss if the CA were to bear liability for fraud involving the certificate.

Could the loss fall on the relying party? The goals of a PKI would be undermined, and an opportunity for fraudulent collusion would be presented, if the relying party bears the risk.

While the issues are perhaps less stark, this "liability trilemma" plays out similarly for each liability scenario present under open PKI. If CA liability is limited for erroneous certificates issued through no "fault" of the CA, who bears the risk of loss when fraud does occur? The relying party? The individual whose name is on the certificate, despite the fact that they may have no connection to the situation at all? What if CA liability is limited in the event of a compromised CA private key? Will the loss fall on any relying parties who are consequently defrauded? On subscribers who must revoke and replace certificates?

The fundamental assertion of this article is that there is no satisfactory solution to this problem under an open PKI model. Certainly there is no one-size-fits-all solution that can be imposed via legislation. As further described later in the paper, it is conceivable that market mechanisms may be able to solve this "liability trilemma" via contracts, and the "contractual privity problem" is no barrier to this result. However, this result is nonetheless unlikely: the open PKI model is an inherently flawed business model.

## The "Contractual Privity" Red Herring

The "contractual privity problem" as a justification for open PKI-oriented legislation is a red herring. At least one commercial CA, VeriSign, has emerged unsupported by legislation, and is largely pursuing the open PKI model. This CA is betting a substantial investment that they can form "webwrap" contracts with relying parties when the relying parties verify certificates. That is, when relying parties connect to the VeriSign web site to determine whether a particular certificate has been revoked (placed on VeriSign's CRL), they are presented with a "click through" or "webwrap" agreement. This agreement defines the limited warranties VeriSign offers on certificates and strictly limits VeriSign's potential liability. VeriSign enters into a similar agreement with subscribers when the subscriber first obtains a certificate.

Webwrap agreements are not without their problems. The question of whether they are enforceable at all is not definitively settled, and there can be other potential problems depending on specific circumstances. However, this issue is not unique to the CA industry. Most online businesses are forced to rely on webwrap agreements. Several recent court decisions have strongly suggested that they will be enforceable; a legislation-drafting effort underway is close to settling the question. Webwrap agreements present a mechanism by which CAs can attempt to allocate risk contractually.[*]

Accordingly, the open PKI model can compete in the marketplace in the absence of any special legislation. Independent commercial CAs can form enforceable contracts with both subscribers and relying parties, via webwrap agreements, and thus allocate risk contractually. Various CAs utilizing this model would presumably compete on warranty, indemnification, liability limitation, and other contractual terms. This is not a winning business model, however.

Even utilizing the flexibility and dynamism of the market, CAs practicing the open PKI model will not be able to solve the "liability trilemma." In the long run, CAs will not be able to simultaneously offer certificates at low prices along with contract terms acceptable to both subscribers and relying parties. The open PKI model simply poses too much inherent risk of loss that must be borne by one of these three parties.

## The Closed PKI Model

To assert that open PKI is not viable is not to say that public key cryptography won't play an important role in electronic commerce. The closed PKI model offers some significant benefits, and will likely compete—and win—for a variety of applications in the marketplace.

---

[*] One potential hitch is if a court honors a relying party's claim against a CA in a circumstance where the relying party failed to check a CRL, and thus enters into a contract with the CA. This result seems unlikely, however, in light of the "unreasonableness" of not checking a CRL; if this result were to consistently occur it could be dealt with in focused legislation.

A closed PKI has been defined as a system "wherein a contract or a series of contracts identifies and defines the rights and responsibilities of all parties to a particular transaction." This definition came about in response to the assumption that the "contractual privity problem" prevented contract formation with relying parties in an open system. As discussed above, this is an erroneous assumption: CAs can form contracts with relying parties in an open system. Thus, a better definition of a closed system is one where public key mechanisms are used within a specific, bounded context.

Risk management is the critical area of difference between closed and open PKI. Within a bounded context, the liability allocation problems that are intractable under the open model become manageable, primarily because potential liability exposure is quantifiable and limited in scope.

For example, the proprietor of an online "mall" might issue certificates to potential customers and to merchants. The proprietor, acting as a CA, has the opportunity to enter into contractual relationships with both consumers and merchants who will rely on the certificates, and thus can allocate risk contractually. Moreover, the risk to be allocated is relatively small. Unlike under the open model, the CA knows exactly what the issued certificates will be used for. The CA can accurately predict and manage potential losses, and either absorb this cost via pricing mechanisms or assign it to either subscribers or merchants by contract.

Similarly, a merchant might issue certificates directly to its customers. The owner of an online magazine, for example, might mail diskettes containing certificates directly to subscribers of the paper version of the same magazine. Such certificates could be installed the subscriber's Web browser and used to access the online magazine, and perhaps to order related merchandise. The magazine vendor would be well positioned to determine whether such certificates would be sufficiently trustworthy for the purposes for which they were being used. Again, such a scenario does not implicate the difficult risk allocation questions associated with the open model.

Another example might be a business-to-business trading network. Businesses may have processes and equipment in place, enabling them to carefully manage private encryption keys. They may thus be quite willing to agree to contract terms much more "onerous" than the terms imposed by the Utah Act, for example. A business might agree to be strictly liable for all documents signed with its private key, under the appropriate circumstances. A closed PKI system preserves this type of flexibility.

Stephen Kent gave a fascinating talk last year entitled "Let Ten Thousand CAs Bloom." His central theme deserves repeating: let anyone who wants to be a CA be a CA, certifying their own customers, employees, members, and so on. Individuals don't need one overarching identity certificate, to be used in every conceivable circumstance. People can have many certificates, inconspicuously installed in a Web browser, each of which is used in a specific, narrow context. Within the confines of such a bounded context the risk allocation questions that are insurmountable under an open PKI model become much, much easier. Moreover, unlike the rigid, hierarchical structure of an open PKI, such a scenario embraces the chaotic, fast-paced environment of the Internet.

Market trends appear to support the conclusion that the closed model will be the winner in the marketplace. Recall the flurry of announcements concerning commercial CA services which took place in early 1996: VeriSign was spun off from RSA. GTE CyberTrust announced its imminent competing "CyberSign" service. Nortel began issuing demonstration sever certificates, and was rumored to be on the verge of launching full-blown CA activities. MCI, AT&T, and IBM all hinted at planned CA services.

Look at the state of the commercial CA marketplace now. CyberTrust finally started issuing certificates in early 1997—but only for SET,* which presumably will leverage the risk allocation mechanisms already present in the bank card industry. The CyberSign service, based on the open PKI model, has evidently been abandoned in favor of CyberTrust's emphasis on their "customer branded service." The rumors of Nortel's (now Entrust) impending entry into the CA business proved false. Entrust's services focus exclusively on back-end support for other companies that want to offer CA services. Likewise, IBM's offerings focus on back end support. All of these developments are consistent with the dominance of the closed PKI model. Industry players are focusing their attention on "letting ten-thousand CAs bloom."

VeriSign is the only North American company that is actively pursuing the classic open PKI model as a business model. Indeed, judging from their press releases, they are doing so with some success—they are planning innovative ways of addressing problematic aspects of their business model, such as via a recently-announced limited insurance plan for subscribers. However, even VeriSign used the high-profile forum provided by the 1997 RSA Data Security Conference to announce its "Private Label Digital ID Services," which are back-end support for companies that want to offer CA services. Thus, even VeriSign is focusing on offering its services to other companies on an outsourcing basis, consistent with the closed PKI model.

## Open PKI Legislation Lives On

Despite increased recognition of the problems associated with the open PKI model, legislation enshrining this model in law and regulation continues to be proposed and enacted. This can partly be attributed to factors that could be labeled "psychological." The rigid, straightforward hierarchies inherent in the open model are likely deeply appealing to the sensibilities of lawyers and legislators as they contemplate the often chaotic and inscrutable Internet. Moreover, enacting legislation—including legislation that is not well understood—satisfies the legislative urge to "do something" in the face of a rapidly changing economic environment.

Additionally, legislators may be under the mistaken impression that special legal rules are needed to accommodate electronic commerce. In fact, however, the law is quite flexible and supportive of new commercial methods. As a general matter, legislation is not needed in order to accommodate public key cryptography or other emerging authentication technologies. The few areas where existing legal rules impede electronic commerce can be addressed with narrow, targeted legislation.

Another factor behind the continued momentum of open PKI digital signature legislation is less benign: the infrastructure created by such legislation is ideally suited for implementation of a key escrow scheme. Indeed, such an idea was initially broached by the Clinton Administration in a report released in May of 1996. This report described a vision for a PKI consistent with the Utah/ABA Guidelines model, and noted:

> . . . To participate in the network a user needs a public key certificate signed by a CA which 'binds' the user's identity to their public key. One condition of obtaining a certificate is that sufficient information (e.g., private keys or other information as appropriate) has been escrowed with a certified escrow authority to allow access to a user's data or communications. (As noted before, this might be the CA or an independent escrow authority). . . .

Draft legislation designed to implement such a plan was released in April. Similar legislation was introduced in the United Kingdom. The profound civil liberties concerns implicated by such legislation, and the negative effects on commerce of the

---

* See "Cryptography and the Web" for more information on SET.

policies underlying key escrow, are well documented.

## Conclusion

The open PKI model envisioned by many existing and proposed digital signature laws is not viable. This legislation presumes a business model that cannot internalize the costs associated with its implementation. In attempting to solve an unsolvable problem, current digital signature laws shift an immense liability burden onto consumers who use the infrastructure envisioned by these laws. Consumers would reject this result in any true marketplace transaction.

Digital signatures will play a significant role in electronic commerce, but under a closed PKI system where the liability problems associated with digital signatures become manageable. The open PKI model can and should compete against closed PKI and other authentication technologies without the benefit of special legislation. It will not, however, be the winning business model.

Digital signature laws which impose a particular view of electronic commerce on the marketplace should be abandoned. The time for legislation and regulation is after identifiable problems exist in a mature industry, not before an industry even exists. The existing legal infrastructure can accommodate new technologies without dramatic new legislation. Premature legislation and regulation risks creating market distortions which can prevent the market from arriving at much better results than can be envisioned by governmental policymakers. Certainly this is true in the case of open PKI: digital signature legislation based on the Utah/ABA Guidelines model imposes a business model that could not survive under the discipline of the marketplace ∎

## About the Author

**C. Bradford Biddle**
4365 Executive Drive, Suite 1100
San Diego, CA 92121
*biddlecb@cooley.com*

Brad Biddle is the author of several articles on the law and policy of public key cryptography, including Misplaced Priorities: The Utah Digital Signature Act and Liability Allocation in a Public Key Infrastructure, 33 San Diego Law Review 1143 (1996). He is Vice Chair of the Electronic Commerce Subcommittee of the American Bar Association's Committee on the Law of Commerce in Cyberspace, and is an associate in the San Diego office of Cooley Godward LLP, where he served on the legal team advising the Internet Law and Policy Forum's Working Group on Certification Authority Practices.

# The Risks of Key Recovery, Key Escrow, and Trusted Third-Party Encryption

Hal Abelson, Ross Anderson, Steven M. Bellovin, Josh Benaloh, Matt Blaze, Whitfield Diffie, John Gilmore, Peter G. Neumann, Ronald L. Rivest, Jeffrey I. Schiller, Bruce Schneier

## Abstract

*A variety of "key recovery," "key escrow," and "trusted third-party" encryption requirements have been suggested in recent years by government agencies seeking to conduct covert surveillance within the changing environments brought about by new technologies. This report examines the fundamental properties of these requirements and attempts to outline the technical risks, costs, and implications of deploying systems that provide government access to encryption keys.*

The deployment of key recovery–based encryption infrastructures to meet law enforcement's stated specifications will result in substantial sacrifices in security and greatly increased costs to the end-user. Building the secure computer-communication infrastructures necessary to provide adequate technological underpinnings demanded by these requirements would be enormously complex and is far beyond the experience and current competency of the field. Even if such infrastructures could be built, the risks and costs of such an operating environment may ultimately prove unacceptable. In addition, these infrastructures would generally require extraordinary levels of human trustworthiness.

These difficulties are a function of the basic government access requirements proposed for key recovery encryption systems.* They exist regardless of the design of the recovery systems—whether the systems use private key cryptography or public key cryptography; whether the databases are split with secret-sharing techniques or maintained in a single hardened secure facility; whether the recovery services provide private keys, session keys, or merely decrypt specific data as needed; and whether there is a single centralized infrastructure, many decentralized infrastructures, or a collection of different approaches.

All key recovery systems require the existence of a highly sensitive and highly available secret key or collection of keys that must be maintained in a secure manner over an extended time period. These systems must make decryption information quickly accessible to law enforcement agencies without notice to the key owners. These basic requirements make the problem of general key recovery difficult and expensive—and potentially too insecure and too costly for many applications and many users.

Attempts to force the widespread adoption of key recovery encryption through export controls, import or domestic use regulations, or international standards should be considered in light of these factors. The public must carefully consider the costs and benefits of embracing government access key recovery before imposing the new security risks and spending the huge investment required (potentially many billions of dollars, in direct and indirect costs) to deploy a global key recovery infrastructure.

---

\* In his article "Government Promotion of Key Encryption: How Current Government Initiatives Will Impact Internet Security," Clint Smith offers his own policy recommendations for governments in the adoption of KRE.

## Group Charter

This report stems from a collaborative effort to study the technical implications of controversial proposals by the United States and other national governments to deploy large scale "key recovery" systems that provide third-party access to decryption keys [13]. Insofar as is possible, we have considered the impact of these policies without regard to individual encryption schemes or particular government proposals. Rather, we have attempted to look broadly at the essential elements of key recovery needed to fulfill the expressed requirements of governments (as distinct from the features that encryption users might desire). This report considers the general impact of meeting the government's *requirements* rather than the merits of any particular key recovery system or proposal that meets them. Our analysis is independent of whether the key recovery infrastructure is centralized or widely distributed.

We have specifically chosen not to endorse, condemn, or draw conclusions about any particular regulatory or legislative proposal or commercial product. Rather, it is our hope that our findings will shed further light on the debate over key recovery and provide a long-needed baseline analysis of the costs of key recovery as policymakers consider embracing one of the most ambitious and far-reaching technical deployments of the information age.

Although there are many aspects to the debate on the proper role of encryption and key recovery in a free society, we have chosen to focus entirely on the technical issues associated with this problem rather than on more general political or social questions. Indeed, many have suggested that the very notion of a pervasive government key recovery infrastructure runs counter to the basic principles of freedom and privacy in a democracy and that alone is reason enough to avoid deploying such systems. This reasoning is independent of whether the key recovery infrastructure is centralized or widely distributed. The technical nature of our analysis should not be interpreted as an endorsement of the social merits of government key recovery; in fact, we encourage vigorous public debate on this question.

## Background

### Encryption and the Global Information Infrastructure

The Global Information Infrastructure promises to revolutionize electronic commerce, reinvigorate government, and provide new and open access to the information society. Yet this promise cannot be achieved without information security and privacy. Without a secure and trusted infrastructure, companies and individuals will become increasingly reluctant to move their private business or personal information online.

The need for information security is widespread and touches all of us, whether users of information technology or not. Sensitive information of all kinds is increasingly finding its way into electronic form. Examples include:

- Private personal and business communications, including telephone conversations, FAX messages, and electronic mail

- Electronic funds, transfers, and other financial transactions

- Sensitive business information and trade secrets

- Data used in the operation of critical infrastructure systems such as air traffic control, the telephone network, or the power grid

- Health records, personnel files, and other personal information

Electronically managed information touches almost every aspect of daily life in modern society. This rising tide of important yet unsecured electronic data leaves our society increasingly vulnerable to curious neighbors, industrial spies, rogue nations, organized crime, and terrorist organizations.

Paradoxically, although the technology for managing and communicating electronic information is improving at a remarkable rate, this progress generally comes at the expense of intrinsic security. In general, as information technology improves and becomes faster, cheaper, and easier to use, it becomes less possible to control (or even identify) where sensitive data flows, where documents originated, or who is at the other end of the telephone. The basic communication infrastructure of our society is becoming less secure, even as we use it for increasingly vital purposes. Cryptographic techniques more and more frequently will become the only viable approach to assuring the privacy and safety of sensitive information as these trends continue.

Encryption is an essential tool in providing security in the information age. Encryption is based on the use of mathematical procedures to scramble data so that it is extremely difficult—if not virtually impossible—for anyone other than authorized recipients to recover the original "plaintext." Properly implemented encryption allows sensitive information to be stored on insecure computers or transmitted across insecure networks. Only parties with the correct decryption "key" (or keys) are able to recover the plaintext information.

Highly secure encryption can be deployed relatively cheaply, and it is widely believed that encryption will be broadly adopted and embedded in most electronic communications products and applications for handling potentially valuable data. [14] Applications of cryptography include protecting files from theft or unauthorized access, securing communications from interception, and enabling secure business transactions. Other cryptographic techniques can be used to guarantee that the contents of a file or message have not been altered (integrity), to establish the identity of a party (authentication), or to make legal commitments (non-repudiation).

In making information secure from unwanted eavesdropping, interception, and theft, strong encryption has an ancillary effect: it becomes more difficult for law enforcement to conduct certain kinds of surreptitious electronic surveillance (particularly wiretapping) against suspected criminals without the knowledge and assistance of the target. This difficulty is at the core of the debate over key recovery.

## "Key Recovery": Requirements and Proposals

The United States and other national governments have sought to prevent widespread use of cryptography unless "key recovery" mechanisms guaranteeing law enforcement access to plaintext are built into these systems. The requirements imposed by such government-driven key recovery systems are different from the features sought by encryption users, and ultimately impose substantial new risks and costs.

Key recovery encryption systems provide some form of access to plaintext outside of the normal channel of encryption and decryption. Key recovery is sometimes also called "key escrow." The term "escrow" became popular in connection with the U.S. government's Clipper Chip initiative, in which a master key to each encryption device was held "in escrow" for release to law enforcement. Today the term "key recovery" is used as generic term for these systems, encompassing the various "key escrow," "trusted third-party," "exceptional access," "data recovery," and "key recovery" encryption systems introduced in recent years. Although there are differences between these systems, the distinctions are not critical for our purposes. In this report, the general term "key recovery" is used in a broad sense, to refer to any system for assuring third-party (government) access to encrypted data.

Key recovery encryption systems work in a variety of ways. Early key escrow proposals relied on the storage of private keys by the U.S. government, and more recently by designated private entities. Other systems have "escrow agents" or "key recovery agents" (KRAs) that maintain the ability to recover the keys for a particular encrypted communication session or stored file; these systems require that such "session keys" be encrypted with a key known by a recovery agent and included with the data. Some systems split the ability to recover keys among several agents.

Many interested parties have sought to draw sharp distinctions among the various key recovery proposals. It is certainly true that several new key recovery systems have emerged that can be distinguished from the original Clipper proposal by their methods of storing and recovering keys. However, our discussion takes a higher level view of the basic requirements of the problem rather than the details of any particular scheme; it does not require a distinction between key escrow, trusted third-party, and key recovery. All these systems share the essential elements that concern us for the purposes of this study:

- A mechanism, external to the primary means of encryption and decryption, by which a third party can obtain covert access to the plaintext of encrypted data.

- The existence of a highly sensitive secret key (or collection of keys) that must be secured for an extended period of time.

Taken together, these elements encompass a system of "ubiquitous key recovery" designed to meet law enforcement specifications. While some specific details may change, the basic requirements most likely will not: they are the essential requirements for any system that meets the stated objective of guaranteeing law enforcement agencies timely access, without user notice, to the plaintext of encrypted communications traffic.

## Key Recoverability: Government versus End-User Requirements

Key recovery systems have gained currency due to the desire of government intelligence and law enforcement agencies to guarantee that they have access to encrypted information without the knowledge or consent of encryption users. A properly designed cryptosystem makes it essen-

tially impossible to recover encrypted data without knowledge of the correct key. In some cases this creates a potential problem for the users of encryption themselves; the cost of keeping unauthorized parties out is that if keys are lost or unavailable at the time they are needed, the owners of the encrypted data will be unable to make use of their own information. It has been suggested, therefore, that industry needs and wants key recovery, and that the kind of key recovery infrastructure promoted by the government would serve the commercial world's needs for assuring availability of its own encrypted data. Several recent government proposals (along with commercial products and services designed to meet the government's requirements) have been promoted as serving the dual role of assuring government access as well as "owner" access to encrypted data. However, the requirements of a government and the requirements of the commercial world and individual users are very different in this regard, so different that, in fact, there is little overlap between systems that address these two problems.

The ultimate goal of government-driven key recovery encryption, as stated in the U.S. Department of Commerce's recent encryption regulations,

> envisions a worldwide key management infrastructure with the use of key escrow and key recovery encryption items. [15]

The requirements put forward to meet law enforcement demands for such global key recovery systems include:

- Third-party/government access without notice to or consent of the user. Even so-called "self-escrow" systems, where companies might hold their own keys, are required to provide sufficient insulation between the recovery agents and the key owners to avoid revealing when decryption information has been released.

- Ubiquitous international adoption of key recovery. Key recovery helps law enforcement only if it is so widespread that it is used for the bulk of encrypted stored information and communications, whether or not there is end-user demand for a recovery feature.

- High-availability, around-the-clock access to plaintext under a variety of operational conditions. Law enforcement seeks the ability to obtain decryption keys quickly—within two hours under current U.S. and other proposed regulations. [16] Few commercial encryption users need the ability to recover lost keys around the clock, or on such short notice.

- Access to encrypted communications traffic as well as to encrypted stored data. To the extent that there is commercial demand for key recovery, it is limited to stored data rather than communications traffic.

In fact, the requirements of government key recovery are almost completely incompatible with those of commercial encryption users. The differences are especially acute in four areas: the kinds of data for which recovery is required; the kinds of keys for which recovery is required; the manner in which recoverable keys are managed; and the relationship between key certification and key recovery. Government key recovery does not serve private and business users especially well; similarly, the key management and key recoverability systems naturally arising in the commercial world do not adapt well to serve a government.

## Communication Traffic versus Stored Data

While key "recoverability" is a potentially important added value feature in certain stored data systems, in other applications of cryptography there is little or no user demand for this feature. In particular, there is hardly ever a reason for an encryption user to want to recover the key used to protect a communication session such as a telephone call, FAX transmission, or Internet link.

If such a key is lost, corrupted, or otherwise becomes unavailable, the problem can be detected immediately and a new key negotiated. There is also no reason to trust another party with such a key. Key recoverability, to the extent it has a private sector application at all, is useful only for the keys used to protect irreproducible stored data. There is basically no business model for other uses, as discussed below.

In stored data applications, key recovery is only one of a number of options for assuring the continued availability of business-critical information. These options include sharing the knowledge of keys among several individuals (possibly using secret-sharing techniques), obtaining keys from a local key registry that maintains backup copies, careful backup management of the plaintext of stored encrypted data, or, of course, some kind of key recovery mechanism. The best option among these choices depends on the particular application and user.

Encrypted electronic mail is an interesting special case, in that it has the characteristics of both communication and storage. Whether key recovery is useful to the user of a secure email system depends on design of the particular system.

The government, on the other hand, proposes a key recovery infrastructure that applies to virtually *all* cryptographic keys, including (especially) those used to protect communications sessions.

## Authentication versus Confidentiality Keys

Although cryptography has traditionally been associated with confidentiality, other cryptographic mechanisms, such as authentication codes and digital signatures, can ensure that messages have not been tampered with or forged. Some systems provide properties analogous to those of handwritten signatures, including "non-repudiation"—the recipient can prove to a third party that a message was signed by a particular individual.

Much of the promise of electronic commerce depends on the ability to use cryptographic techniques to make binding commitments. Yet some key recovery schemes are designed to archive authentication and signature keys along with confidentiality keys. Such schemes destroy the absolute non-repudiation property that makes binding commitments possible. Furthermore, there are simply no legitimate uses for authentication or signature key recovery. The private sector requires distinct keys for all signers, even when two or more individuals are authorized to send a given message; without that, the ability to audit transactions is destroyed. Government surveillance does not require the recovery of signature keys, either.

However, it is difficult to exclude authentication and signature keys from a key recovery infrastructure of the kind proposed by the government, because some keys are used for both signature and encryption. [17] Nor is it sufficient to exclude from the recovery system keys used only to protect financial transactions, since many electronic commerce schemes use keys that are general in scope. The same key might be used, for example, to encrypt personal electronic mail as well as to electronically sign contracts or authorize funds transfers.

It has been claimed that non-availability of a signature key can be a serious problem for the owner, who will then no longer be able to sign messages. But common practice allows for the revocation of lost keys, and the issuance of new keys with the same rights and privileges as the old ones. Recovering lost signature and authentication keys is simply never required.

## Infrastructure: Local versus Third-Party Control

For a key recovery scheme to be of value to the encryption user, it must allow tight control over depositing, recovering, and maintaining keys, tied to the user's own practices and requirements. Generally, only a small number of individuals will need the ability to recover any individual key, often working in the same location and person-

ally known to one another. When a key does need to be recovered, it will frequently be a local matter, similar to the replacement of a misplaced office key or restoring a computer file with a backup copy. The hours at which the key recovery might take place, the identification of the individuals authorized for a particular key, the policy for when keys should be recovered, and other basic operational procedures will vary widely from user to user, even within a single business. Particularly important is the control over when and how "recoverable" keys are destroyed when they are no longer needed, especially for keys associated with sensitive personal and business records.

Similarly, there is usually no business need for secrecy in the recovery of keys or for the ability to obtain keys without the initial cooperation of the user. When key recovery is used in a business environment, it would generally be one component of the overall data management policy of that business. Users would normally be trusted to participate in assuring recoverability of their own keys, assisted by local management practices and supervision. When a key must be recovered, it will usually be because the users themselves realize that they do not have a copy of the correct key or because the keyholder is no longer available. Even the frequently-cited hypothetical example of the disgruntled employee who refuses to decrypt important files is probably most reliably and economically dealt with through business data management practices (such as management supervision and backup of business-critical plaintext) that do not require any centralized, standard key recovery mechanism. Even in this (rather unusual) case, there is no need to hide from the user the fact that a key has been recovered.

The U.S. government, on the other hand, proposes key recovery schemes that by their nature do not allow local control. The government's requirement for the ability to covertly recover keys on short notice and without notice to the key owner must almost by definition be implemented by a third party whose procedures are entirely divorced from those of the users. Even when the government permits an organization to manage its own keys, the key recovery agent will have to be fairly centralized and remote from the actual users. This requirement eliminates the first line of defense against misuse of key recovery: the vigilance of the most concerned party—the key owner.

## Infrastructure: Key Certification and Distribution versus Key Recovery

As electronic commerce and encryption use becomes more widespread, some form of Certification Authorities (CAs) will be needed in some applications to help identify encryption users. A CA is a trusted party that vouches for the identity (or some other attribute) of an encryption user. It is widely believed that development and use of certification authorities will be essential for secure and trusted electronic exchanges—and, consequently, will become a prerequisite to participation in electronic commerce and online communications. [18]

Although superficially similar, in that they are both concerned with key management, the nature of key recovery is completely different from that of key certification. The most important function of a Certification Authority is to certify the public keys used in digital signatures; key recovery, on the other hand, is concerned with keys used for confidentiality. More importantly, the operation of a Certification Authority does not require handling sensitive user data; a CA generally handles only users' public keys and never learns the associated secret keys. If a CA's secret key is compromised or revealed, the only direct damage is that the certificates from it can be forged. On the other hand, if a key recovery agent's secrets are compromised, the damage can be far greater and more direct: every user of that recovery agent might have its own secrets compromised.

Certification can (and currently does) exist without any form of key recovery. Conversely, a key recovery infrastructure can exist completely independently of any key certification infrastructure.

Several recent government proposals have attempted to associate key recovery with key certification. This proposed linkage between CAs and key recovery makes no sense technically. On the contrary, such linkages have serious liabilities. It is not even clear whether such a system would work. To the extent it might require depositing keys used for signature and identification, such systems create additional security risks; there is no justification (even given government law enforcement requirements) for third-party access to signature keys that, if compromised, could be used to impersonate people, or to forge their digital signatures. In fact, attempts at achieving key recovery through a certification infrastructure would likely be ineffective at meeting the goals of law enforcement. Many (indeed, most) encryption keys are not certified directly, and therefore would be beyond the reach of a certification-based recovery system.

# Risks and Costs of Key Recovery

Key recovery systems are inherently less secure, more costly, and more difficult to use than similar systems without a recovery feature. Key recovery degrades many of the protections available from encryption, such as absolute control by the user over the means to decrypt data. Furthermore, a global key recovery infrastructure can be expected to be extraordinarily complex and costly.

The impact of key recovery can be considered in at least three dimensions:

*Risk*

> The failure of key recovery mechanisms can jeopardize the proper operation, underlying confidentiality, and ultimate security of encryption systems; threats include improper disclosures of keys, theft of valuable key

information, or failure to be able to meet law enforcement demands.

### Complexity

Although it may be possible to make key recovery reasonably transparent to the end users of encryption, a fully functional key recovery infrastructure is an extraordinarily complex system, with numerous new entities, keys, operational requirements, and interactions. In many cases, the key recovery aspects of a system are far more complex and difficult to implement than the basic encryption functions themselves.

### Economic Cost

No one has yet described, much less demonstrated, a viable economic model to account for the true costs of key recovery. However, it is still possible to make sound qualitative judgments about the basic system elements, shared by all key recovery schemes, that will have the most dramatic impact on the cost of designing, implementing, deploying, and operating such systems.

## New Vulnerabilities and Risks

Any key recovery infrastructure, by its very nature, introduces a new and vulnerable path to the unauthorized recovery of data where one did not otherwise exist. This introduces at least two harmful effects:

- It removes the inherent guarantees of security available through non-recoverable systems, which do not have an alternate path to sensitive plaintext that is beyond the users' control.

- It creates new concentrations of decryption information that are high-value targets for criminals or other attackers.

These risks arise with cryptography used in communication and storage, but perhaps even more intensely with cryptography used in authentication. (They are compounded even further if any keys are used for more than one of these purposes.)

### New paths to plaintext

Regardless of the implementation, if key recovery systems must provide timely law enforcement access to a whole key or to plaintext, they present a new and fast path to the recovery of data that never existed before.

The key recovery access path is completely out of the control of the user. In fact, this path to exceptional access is specifically designed to be concealed from the encryption user, removing one of the fundamental safeguards against the mistaken or fraudulent release of keys.

In contrast, non-recoverable systems can usually be designed securely without any alternative paths. Alternative paths to access are neither required for ordinary operation nor desirable in many applications for many users.

### Insider abuse

Like any other security system with a human element, key recovery systems are particularly vulnerable to compromise by authorized individuals who abuse or misuse their positions. Users of a key recovery system must trust that the individuals designing, implementing, and running the key recovery operation are indeed trustworthy. An individual, or set of individuals, motivated by ideology, greed, or the threat of blackmail, may abuse the authority given to them. Abuse may compromise the secrets of individuals, particular corporations, or even of entire nations. There have been many examples in recent times of individuals in sensitive positions violating the trust placed in them. There is no reason to believe that key recovery systems can be managed with a higher degree of success.

The risk of "insider abuse" becomes even more evident when attempts are made to design key recovery schemes that are international in scope. Such abuse can even become institutionalized within a rogue company or government. National law-enforcement agencies, for example, might abuse their key recovery authority to the advantage of their own country's corporations.

## New targets for attack

The nature of key recovery creates new high-value targets for attack of encryption systems. Key recovery agents will maintain databases that hold, in centralized collections, the keys to the information and communications their customers most value. In many key recovery systems, the theft of a single private key (or small set of keys) held by a recovery agent could unlock much or all of the data of a company or individual. Theft of a recovery agent's own private keys might provide access to an even broader array of communications, or might make it possible to easily spoof header information designed to ensure compliance with encryption export controls. The key recovery infrastructure will tend to create extremely valuable targets, more likely to be worth the cost and risk of attack.

The identity of these new rich targets will be highlighted by the key recovery systems themselves. Every encrypted communication or stored file will be required to include information about the location of its key retrieval information. This "pointer" is a road map showing law enforcement how to recover the plaintext, but it may also show unauthorized attackers where to focus their efforts. Moreover, even those systems (such as split key systems) that can decrease these risks, do so with a marked increase in cost. For example, splitting a key in half at least doubles the recovery agent costs. [19] Such systems require multiple agents, costly additional coordination mechanisms, and faster response times necessary to assemble split keys and still provide fast access to plaintext. Regardless of how many times a key is split, law enforcement's demand for timely access will still require the development of fast systems for the recovery of key parts. Both the systems for key part assembly, and the ultimate whole key assembled for law enforcement, will present new points of vulnerability.

## Forward secrecy

Key recovery is especially problematic in communications systems, such as encrypted cellular telephone calls, because it destroys the property of *forward secrecy*. A system with forward secrecy is one in which compromising the keys for decrypting one communication does not reduce the security of other communications. For example, in an encrypted telephone call, the keys for encrypting a call can be established as the call is set up. If these keys are destroyed when the call is over, the participants can be assured that no one can later decrypt that conversation—even if the keys to some subsequent conversation are compromised. The result is that once the call is over, the information required to decrypt it ceases to exist; not even the parties to the call store the keys. Typically, keys are created and destroyed on a per-call basis, or even many times per call. This makes it possible to limit the costs and risks of secure processing and storage to the period of the call itself.

Forward secrecy is desirable and important for two reasons. First, it simplifies the design and analysis of secure systems, making it much easier to ensure that a design or implementation is in fact secure. Second, and more importantly, forward secrecy greatly increases the security and decreases the cost of a system, since keys need to be maintained and protected only while communication is actually in progress.

Key recovery destroys the forward secrecy property, since the ability to recover traffic continues to exist long after the original communication has occurred. It requires that the relevant keys be stored instead of destroyed, so that later government requests for the plaintext can succeed. If the keys are stored, they can be compromised; if they are destroyed, the threat of compromise ceases at that moment.

## New Complexities

Experience has shown that secure cryptographic systems are deceptively hard to design and build properly. The design and implementation of even the simplest encryption algorithms, protocols, and implementations is a complex and delicate process. Very small changes frequently introduce fatal security flaws. Non-key recovery systems have rather simple requirements and yet exploitable flaws are still often discovered in fielded systems.

Our experiences designing, analyzing, and implementing encryption systems convince us that adding key recovery makes it much more difficult to assure that such systems work as intended. It is possible, even likely, that lurking in any key recovery system are one or more design, implementation, or operational weaknesses that allow recovery of data by unauthorized parties. The commercial and academic world simply does not have the tools to properly analyze or design the complex systems that arise from key recovery.

This is not an abstract concern. Most of the key recovery or key escrow proposals made to date, including those designed by the National Security Agency, have had weaknesses discovered after their initial implementation. For example, since the system's introduction in 1993, several failures have been discovered in the U.S. Escrowed Encryption Standard, the system on which the Clipper Chip is based. These problems are not a result of incompetence on the part of the system's designers. Indeed, the U.S. National Security Agency may be the most advanced cryptographic enterprise in the world, and it is entrusted with developing the cryptographic systems that safeguard the government's most important military and state secrets. The reason the Escrowed Encryption Standard had flaws is that good security is an extremely difficult technical problem to start with, and key recovery adds enormous complications with requirements unlike anything previously encountered.

## Scale

Key recovery as envisioned by law enforcement will require the deployment of secure infrastructures involving thousands of companies, recovery agents, regulatory bodies, and law enforcement agencies worldwide interacting and cooperating on an unprecedented scale.

Once widely available, encryption will likely be used for the bulk of network communications and storage of sensitive files. By the year 2000—still early in the adoption of information technologies—fielding the ubiquitous key recovery system envisioned by law enforcement could encompass:

- Thousands of products. There are over 800 encryption products worldwide today, and this number is likely to grow dramatically.

- Thousands of agents all over the world. Proposed systems contemplate many key recovery agents within this country alone; other countries will want agents located within their borders. Large companies will want to serve as their own key recovery agents. Each of these agents will need to obtain U.S. certification and possibly certification by other countries as well.

- Tens of thousands of law enforcement agencies. There are over 17,000 local, state, and federal law enforcement agencies in the United States alone that might seek key information for authorized wiretaps or seized data. [20] National and local agencies around the world will also want access to keys.

- Millions of users. Several million Web users today use encrypted communications whenever their Web browser encounters a secure page (such as many of those used for credit card transactions). There will be an estimated 100 million Internet users by the year 2000, most of whom will be likely to regularly encrypt communications as part of the next version of the standard Internet protocols. Millions of other corporate and home computer users will also regularly encrypt stored information or intranetwork communications.

- Tens of millions (or more) of public-private key pairs. Most users will have several public key pairs for various purposes. Some applications create key pairs "on-the-fly" every time they are used.

- Hundreds of billions of recoverable session keys. Every encrypted telephone call, every stored encrypted file, every email message, and every secure Web session will create a session key to be accessed. (Various key recovery scheme may avoid the need for the recovery center to process these session keys individually, but such "granularity shifts" introduce additional risk factors—see the section entitled "Key Recovery and Scope" below.)

Ultimately, these numbers will grow further as improved information age technologies push more people and more data online.

The overall infrastructure needed to deploy and manage this system will be vast. Government agencies will need to certify products. Other agencies, both within the U.S. and in other countries, will need to oversee the operation and security of the highly sensitive recovery agents—as well as ensure that law enforcement agencies get the timely and confidential access they desire. Any breakdown in security among these complex interactions will result in compromised keys and a greater potential for abuse or incorrect disclosures.

There are reasons to believe secure key recovery systems are not readily scalable. Order-of-magnitude increases in the numbers of requesting law enforcement agencies, product developers, regulatory oversight agencies, and encryption end users all make the tasks of various actors in the key recovery system not only bigger, but much more complex. In addition, there are significant added transaction costs involved with coordination of international key recovery regimes involving many entities.

The fields of cryptography, operating systems, networking, and system administration have no substantive experience in deploying and operating secure systems of this scope and complexity. We simply do not know how to build a collective secure key management infrastructure of this magnitude, let alone operate one, whether the key recovery infrastructure is centralized or widely distributed.

## Operational Complexity

The scale on which a government access key recovery infrastructure must operate exacerbates many of the security problems with key recovery. The stated requirements of law enforcement demand the construction of highly complex key recovery systems. Demands on the speed and process for recovering keys will greatly increase the complexity of tasks facing those trusted with key recovery information. Demands for ubiquitous worldwide adoption of key recovery will greatly increase the complexity and number of entities involved. Each of these will in turn have a significant impact on both the security and cost of the key recovery system.

Consider the tasks that a typical key recovery center will perform to meet one law enforcement request for a session key for one communication or stored file:

- Reliably identify and authenticate requesting law enforcement agents (there are over 17,000 U.S. domestic law enforcement organizations)

- Reliably authenticate court order or other documentation

- Reliably authenticate target user and data

- Check authorized validity time period

- Recover session key, plaintext data, or other decryption information

- Put recovered data in required format

- Securely transfer recovered data, but only to authorized parties

- Reliably maintain an audit trail

Each of these tasks must be performed securely in a very short period of time in order to meet government requirements. For example, the most recent U.S. Commerce Department regulations governing recovery agents require two hour turn-around of government requests, around the clock. The tasks must be performed by agents all over the world serving millions of clients and responding to requests from both those clients and numerous law enforcement agencies.

There are few, if any, secure systems that operate effectively and economically on such a scale and under such tightly constrained conditions—even if these requirements are relaxed considerably (e.g., one day response time instead of two hours). The urgent rush imposed by very short retrieval times, and the complexity of the tasks involved, are anathema to the careful scrutiny that should be included in such a system. If there is uncertainty at any step of the access process, there may be insufficient time to verify the authenticity or accuracy of a retrieval request.

It is inevitable that a global key recovery infra-structure will be more vulnerable to fraudulent key requests, will make mistakes in giving out the wrong key, and will otherwise compromise security from time to time. While proper staffing, tech-nical controls, and sound design can mitigate these risks to some extent (and at considerable cost), the operational vulnerabilities associated with key recovery cannot be eliminated entirely.

### Authorization for key recovery

One of the requirements for a key recovery oper-ation is that it must authenticate the individual requesting an archived key. Doing so reliably is very difficult.

"Human" forms of identification—passports, birth certificates, and the like—are often easily coun-terfeited. Indeed, news reports describe "identity theft" as a serious and growing problem. Elec-tronic identification must be cryptographic, in which case a key recovery system could be used to attack itself. That is, someone who steals—or recovers—a signature key for a law enforcement officer or a corporate officer could use this key to forge legitimate requests for many other keys. For that matter, if a sensitive confidentiality key were stolen or obtained from the repository, it might be possible to use it to eavesdrop on other key recovery conversations.

In contrast, a business's local, day-to-day key recovery process could rely on personal identifi-cation. A system administrator or supervisor would *know* who had rights to which keys. Even more questionable requests, such as those over the phone, could be handled appropriately; the supervisor could weigh such factors as the sensi-tivity of the information requested, the urgency of the request as known *a priori*, and even the use of informal authentication techniques, such as references to shared experiences. But none of these methods scale well to serve requests from outside the local environment, leaving them unsuitable for use by larger operations or when requests come from persons or organizations not personally known to the keyholders.

## New Costs

Key recovery, especially on the scale required for government access, will be very expensive. New costs are introduced across a wide range of enti-ties and throughout the lifetime of every system that uses recoverable keys.

The requirements set out by law enforcement impose new system costs for designing, deploy-ing, and operating the ubiquitous key recovery system. These costs include:

*Operational costs for key recovery agents*
> The cost of maintaining and controlling sen-sitive, valuable key information securely over long periods of time; of responding to both law enforcement requests and legiti-mate commercial requests for data; and of communicating with users and vendors.

*Product design and engineering costs*

New expenses entailed in the design of secure products that conform to the stringent key recovery requirements.

*Government oversight costs*

Substantial new budgetary requirements for government, law enforcement, or private certification bodies, to test and approve key recovery products, certify and audit approved recovery agents, and support law enforcement requests for and use of recovered key information.

*User costs*

Includes both the expense of choosing, using, and managing key recovery systems and the losses from lessened security and mistaken or fraudulent disclosures of sensitive data.

## Operational costs

The most immediately evident problem with key recovery may be the expense of securely operating the infrastructure required to support it. In general, cryptography is an intrinsically inexpensive technology; there is little need for externally-operated "infrastructure" (outside of key certification in some applications) to establish communication or store data securely. Key recovery, on the other hand, requires a complex and poorly understood—and hence expensive and insecure—infrastructure.

The operational complexity described in the previous section introduces substantial ongoing costs at each key recovery center. These costs are likely to be very high, especially compared with the ordinary operational expenses that might be expected in commercial key recovery systems. Government key recovery requires, for example, intensive staffing (7x24 hours), highly trained and highly trusted personnel, and high-assurance hardware and software systems in order to meet the government's requirements in a secure manner. Theses costs are borne by all encryption applications, even those where key recovery is not beneficial to the user or even to law enforcement.

It remains unclear whether the high risk, high liability business of operating a key recovery center, with limited consumer demand to date, will even be economically viable.

## Product design costs

Key recovery also increases the difficulty and expense of designing user level encryption software and hardware. These costs vary depending on the particular application and the precise nature of the recovery system, but could be substantial in some cases. Integrating key recovery, especially in a secure manner, can also substantially delay the release of software. Given the highly competitive nature and short product lifecycles of today's hardware and software markets, such delays could discourage vendors from incorporating it at all, or worse, encourage sloppy, poorly validated designs. Compatibility with older products presents special challenges and further increases these costs.

## End-user costs

Without government-driven key recovery, encryption systems can easily be fielded in a way that is largely transparent to their users. Highly secure communication and storage need require nothing further than the purchase of a reputable commercial product with strong encryption features tested in the marketplace. The use of that encryption need require nothing more than the setting of an option, the click of an icon, or the insertion of a hardware card. We are fully confident that, in an unregulated marketplace, many applications will ship with such high quality user-transparent encryption built in. This is already happening at negligible cost to the user.

In contrast, the use of a secure key recovery system requires at least some additional user effort, diligence, or expense. In addition to the purchase of an encryption product, one or more key recovery agent(s) must be chosen. The user must enter into an important (although possibly implicit) contractual relationship with that agent, a relationship that will govern the potential disclosure of the most sensitive key information—now and for years to come. In many cases, there will need to be some communication of key information between user and the recovery agent. (Although some products will come with a built-in key, prudent users may want to change their keys on a regular basis. Also, software, especially mass-market "shrink-wrapped" software, cannot usually be economically distributed with unique keys installed in each individual copy.)

The burdens on key recovery users continue long after data have been encrypted. Key recovery agents will maintain the ability to decrypt information for years. During that time, an agent might relax its security policies, go bankrupt, or even be bought out by a competitor—but will retain, and in fact must retain, the ability to decrypt. Diligent and concerned encryption users will need to be aware of the fate of their key recovery agents for years after their initial encryption use.

These burdens will apply to all users of encryption. Each use of encryption may entail the entry into a contractual relationship with a third-party key recovery agent. Under any rational business model, each such instance will entail some additional cost.

## Tradeoffs

Some aspects of key recovery can be easily shifted along a spectrum from higher cost to higher risk. While it may be possible to field a particular key escrow system in a relatively secure way, this often results in tremendous costs to the user. While relatively simple and inexpensive key escrow systems exist, they often jeopardize security. For example, a poorly run key recovery agent, employing less skilled, low paid personnel, with a low level of physical security, and without liability insurance, could be expected to be less expensive to operate than a well run center.

Interestingly, security and cost can also be traded off with respect to the design itself. That is, the simplest designs—those that are easiest to understand and easiest to verify—also tend to require the most stringent assumptions about their environment and operation or have the worst failure characteristics. For example, imagine a design in which session keys are sent to the recovery center by encrypting them with the center's globally known public key. Such a system might be relatively simple to design and implement, and one might even be able to prove that it is secure when operated correctly and under certain assumptions. However, this is among the worst possible designs from a robustness point of view: it has a single point of failure (the key of the recovery agent) with which all keys are encrypted. If this key is compromised (or a corrupt version distributed), all the recoverable keys in the system could be compromised. (We note that several commercial systems are based on almost exactly this design.)

### Key recovery granularity and scope

One of the most important factors influencing the cost and security of key recovery is the granularity and scope of the keys managed by the key recovery system. In particular, it is important to understand two issues:

- *Granularity:* the kinds of keys (user, device, session, etc.) that are recoverable

- *Scope:* the consequences of compromising a recovery agent's key

Granularity is important because it defines how narrowly specified the data to be recovered from an agent can be and how often interactions (by the user and by law enforcement) with the recovery agent must take place. Various systems have been proposed in which the recovery agent produces "master" keys that can decrypt all traffic to or from individual users or hardware devices. In other systems, only the keys for particular sessions are recovered. Coarse granularity (e.g., the master key of the targeted user) allows only limited control over what can be recovered (e.g., all data from a particular individual) but requires few interactions between law enforcement and the recovery center. Finer granularity (e.g., individual session keys), on the other hand, allows greater control (e.g., the key for a particular file or session, or only sessions that occurred within a particular time frame), but requires more frequent interaction with the recovery center (and increased design complexity).

Also important is the scope of the recovery agent's own secret. Most key recovery systems require the user software or hardware to send keys to the recovery agent by encrypting them with the recovery agent's public key. If a recovery agent has only a single such key, that key becomes an extraordinarily valuable, global, single point of failure. Worse, because the recovery agent must use the secret component of this key in order to decrypt the keys sent to it (or at least any time a key is recovered), its exposure to compromise or misuse is also increased. To address this vulnerability, a recovery agent may have many such keys, perhaps one or more for each user. However, negotiating and distributing these keys to the users introduces still other complexities and vulnerabilities.

## Conclusions

Key recovery systems are inherently less secure, more costly, and more difficult to use than similar systems without a recovery feature. The massive deployment of key recovery-based infrastructures to meet law enforcement's specifications will require significant sacrifices in security and convenience and substantially increased costs to all users of encryption. Furthermore, building the secure infrastructure of the breathtaking scale and complexity that would be required for such a scheme is beyond the experience and current competency of the field, and may well introduce ultimately unacceptable risks and costs.

Attempts to force the widespread adoption of key recovery through export controls, import or

domestic use regulations, or international standards should be considered in light of these factors. We urge public debate to carefully weigh the costs and benefits of government access key recovery before these systems are deployed. ∎

## References

1. MIT Laboratory for Computer Science/Hewlett-Packard, *hal@mit.edu*

2. University of Cambridge, *ross.anderson@cl.cam.ac.uk*

3. AT&T Laboratories—Research, *smb@research.att.com*

4. Microsoft Research, *benaloh@microsoft.com*

5. AT&T Laboratories—Research, *mab@research.att.com*

6. Sun Microsystems, *diffie@eng.sun.com*

7. *gnu@toad.com*

8. SRI International, *neumann@sri.com*

9. MIT Laboratory for Computer Science, *rivest@lcs.mit.edu*

10. MIT Information Systems, *jis@mit.edu*

11. Counterpane Systems, *schneier@counterpane.com*

12. World Wide Web: *http://www.crypto.com/key_study*
    PostScript format: *ftp://research.att.com/dist/mab/key_study.ps*
    ASCII text format: *ftp://research.att.com/dist/mab/key_study.txt*

13. This report grew out of a group meeting at Sun Microsystems in Menlo Park, CA in late January 1997, including many of the authors and also attended by Ken Bass, Alan Davidson, Michael Froomkin, Shabbir Safdar, David Sobel, and Daniel Weitzner. The authors thank these other participants for their contributions, as well as the Center for Democracy and Technology for coordinating this effort and assisting in the production of this final report.

14. The National Research Council's comprehensive 1996 report on cryptography includes a detailed examination of the rising importance of encryption. National Research Council, *Cryptography's Role in Securing the Information Society* (1996).

15. Dept. of Commerce, "Interim Rule on Encryption Items," *Federal Register,* Vol. 61, p. 68572 (Dec. 30, 1996).

16. For example, the recent British "Trusted Third-Party" system proposes similar law enforcement demands, requiring *one hour* turnaround time for

TTP recovery agents. See U.K. Department of Trade and Industry, "LICENSING OF TRUSTED THIRD-PARTIES FOR THE PROVISION OF ENCRYPTION SERVICES," (March 1997) (Public Consultation Paper).

17. In fact, it is technically straightforward for two parties to use their authentication keys to negotiate encryption keys for secure communication. Any system that distributes trusted authentication keys would *ipso facto* serve as an infrastructure for private communication that is beyond the reach of government surveillance.

18. There is a great deal of debate about the appropriate role of government in regulating CAs. CAs may ultimately be large, centralized, or even government-certified entities, or smaller, locally-trusted entities. At this early stage in their deployment, no consensus has emerged on what government role is appropriate. For an excellent overview of the debate over CA regulation, see Michael Froomkin, "The Essential Role of Trusted Third-Parties in Electronic Commerce," *75 Oregon L. Rev. 49* (1996).

19. Storage of a smaller key part is not necessarily cheaper than storage of the whole key, and the preferred key-splitting methods generally produce key parts each of which is as large as the whole key.

20. U.S. Department of Justice, Bureau of Justice Statistics, *Sourcebook of Criminal Justice Statistics 1995* (1996), p. 39.

## About the Authors

**Harold (Hal) Abelson** is a Professor in the EECS department at MIT and a Fellow of the IEEE. He is co-author of the textbook *Structure and Interpretation of Computer Programs* and the 1995 winner of the IEEE Computer Society's Education Award. Abelson is currently on leave from MIT at Hewlett-Packard Corporation, where he serves as scientific advisor to HP's Internet Technology Group. He can be reached at *hal@mit.edu*.

**Ross Anderson** teaches and directs research in computer security, cryptology and software engineering at Cambridge University in England. He is an expert on engineering secure systems, how they fail, and how they can be made more robust. He has done extensive work on commercial cryptographic systems, and recently discov-

ered flaws in a British government key escrow protocol. He can be reached at *ross.anderson@cl.cam.ac.uk*.

**Steven M. Bellovin** is a researcher on cryptography, networks and security at AT&T Laboratories. He is co-author of the book *Firewalls and Internet Security: Repelling the Wily Hacker*. In 1995 he was a co-recipient of the Usenix Lifetime Achievement Award for his part in creating Netnews. He is a member of the Internet Architecture Board. He can be reached at *smb@research.att.com*.

**Josh Benaloh** is a Cryptographer at Microsoft Research and has been an active researcher in cryptography for over a decade with substantial contributions in the areas of secret-ballot elections and secret sharing methods and applications. Before joining Microsoft, he was a Postdoctoral Fellow at the University of Toronto and an Assistant Professor at Clarkson University. He can be reached at *benaloh@microsoft.com*.

**Matt Blaze** is a Principal Research Scientist at AT&T Laboratories in the area of computer security and cryptology. In 1994 he discovered several weaknesses in the U.S. government's "Clipper" key escrow system. His research areas include cryptology, trust management, and secure hardware. In 1996 he received the EFF's Pioneer Award for his contributions to computer and network security. He can be reached at *mab@research.att.com*.

**Whitfield Diffie** is a Distinguished Engineer at Sun Microsystems specializing in security. In 1976 Diffie and Martin Hellman created public key cryptography, which solved the problem of sending coded information between individuals with no prior relationship and is the basis for widespread encryption in the digital information age. He can be reached at *diffie@eng.sun.com*.

**John Gilmore** is an entrepreneur and civil libertarian. He was an early employee of Sun Microsystems, and co-founded Cygnus Solutions, the Electronic Frontier Foundation, the Cypherpunks, and the Internet's *alt* newsgroups. He has twenty-five years of experience in the computer industry, including programming, hardware and software design, and management. He can be reached at *gnu@toad.com.*

**Peter G. Neumann** is a Principal Scientist in the Computer Science Lab at SRI. He is Moderator of the Risks Forum (comp.risks), author of *Computer-Related Risks* (Addison-Wesley), and co-author of the National Research Council study report, *Cryptography's Role in Securing the Information Society* (National Academy Press). He is a Fellow of the AAAS, ACM and IEEE. He can be reached at *neumann@sri.com.*

**Ronald L. Rivest** is the Webster Professor of Electrical Engineering and Computer Science in MIT's EECS Department. He is also an Associate Director of MIT's Laboratory for Computer Science. He is perhaps best known as a co-inventor of the RSA public-key cryptosystem and a founder of RSA Data Security, Inc. He can be reached at *rivest@lcs.mit.edu.*

**Jeffrey I. Schiller** is the Network Manager at MIT and has managed the MIT campus computer network since its inception in 1984. Schiller is the author of the Kerberos Authentication System, serves as the Internet Engineering Steering Group's Area Director for Security, and is responsible for overseeing security-related Working Groups of the Internet Engineering Task Force (IETF). He can be reached at *jis@mit.edu.*

**Bruce Schneier** is president of Counterpane Systems, a Minneapolis-based consulting firm specializing in cryptography and computer security. He is the author of *Applied Cryptography* and inventor of the Blowfish encryption algorithm. He can be reached at *schneier@counterpane. com.*

# GOVERNMENT PROMOTION OF KEY RECOVERY ENCRYPTION

## HOW CURRENT GOVERNMENT INITIATIVES WILL IMPACT INTERNET SECURITY

*Clint N. Smith*

## Abstract

*This article discusses the market for Key Recovery Encryption (KRE): encryption technology designed to to allow third-party access to encrypted data. We explore how, to what extent, and where the governments and private sectors converge on this issue, and we conclude with policy recommendations for governments in the adaptation of KRE.*

## Introduction

Governments are faced with a pressing policy problem. Encryption is essential to providing security for the ever-growing amount of information in electronic form. But encryption also threatens to increase the expense of, and in some cases preclude, a government's ability to read intercepted or seized information relating to criminal activity or national security concerns.

From the perspective of an increasing number of governments, the most attractive solution is the widespread use of Key Recovery Encryption (KRE). KRE is encryption designed to allow third-party access to encrypted data. Non-Key Recovery Encryption (NKRE), in contrast, is designed so that the user alone controls access to encrypted data. KRE requires the use of Key Recovery Agents (KRA)—trusted parties responsible for safeguarding encryption keys and releasing the keys under established parameters, such as following a court order or at an employer's request.

Government proponents of KRE postulate that KRE meets private sector as well as government needs. In this article, we take a look at both of these groups and the extent to which their inter-

ests converge, and we conclude that they do come together in the following areas:[*]

- System security
- KRA responsiveness
- Secrecy of key requests
- Low cost service

On the other hand, there is little or no convergence with respect to real-time communications, such as encrypted data transferred between a Web browser and server. In this area, which will be the most contentious KRE policy issue to resolve, the government supports the use of KRE while the private sector does not.

We conclude with a series of policy recommendations for governments, which can be summarized as follows. Because of the intersection between government and private sector interests, governments can rely on market forces to produce a system that largely responds to their needs. It would be self-defeating for governments to mandate KRE requirements that do not meet user needs—as over-regulation runs the risk of increasing the cost of KRE to a point where few users will adopt it.

---

[*] This is contrary to a report, also published in this issue, recently released by a group of expert cryptographers. See "The Risks of Key Recovery, Key Escrow, and Third-Party Encryption" [1].

## Overview of the Commercial Market for Encryption

Encryption is the process of protecting confidential information by applying mathematical formulae, thus rendering it unreadable. It has historically been the domain of governments, which have relied on encryption to maintain the confidentiality of their secrets.

Widespread use of encryption in the private sector began in the 1970s, when the international financial services industry began to automate, and recognized the need to secure its payment and clearing systems. In the 1980s other parts of the private sector began to follow the financial services industry's lead, as more information was communicated across global networks and stored in electronic form. Today encryption is considered an essential element of the infrastructure for electronic commerce and information exchange.

Private sector interests in encryption policy are represented by two groups: encryption users and encryption vendors:

*Encryption users* need encryption to secure valued information from commercial as well as state-sponsored surveillance. Demand for encryption has grown dramatically, and is expected to increase in proportion to the growth in the aggregate value of the information stored and transmitted in electronic form.

*Encryption vendors* seek profit from the sale of encryption products and services to users. Just five years ago this group represented only a small core of companies, dependent on government contracts or sector-specific security applications. Today it includes a wide array of the world's most sophisticated technology companies, which have targeted the lucrative global market for security products created by expanding user demand.

KRE vendors are a subset of the vendor group described above. These companies are either vendors of KRE products or service providers (KRAs) who perform key management and recovery services. Though KRE vendors anticipate the demand for KRE products and services, it is currently unclear whether this demand will be driven by government regulation or user needs.

One thing is clear, however: both encryption users and vendors are concerned about government encryption policy. On one hand, users do not want government to restrict their use of encryption. The NKRE encryption generally available without government restriction provides only modest security from concerted attack, and cannot survive state-sponsored attacks. On the other hand, vendors do not want government to restrict their ability to sell encryption. Controls that are not enforced by countries where competitors reside can result in lost sales; controls that are inconsistent from country to country can require investment in more than one version of an encryption product. In addition, both vendors and users incur significant costs in complying with complex governmental licensing or authorization requirements. Despite these costs and concerns, as discussed in the next section, governments maintain a strong interest in restricting what encryption is used and sold, both within and beyond their borders.

## Government Interest in the Regulation of Encryption

Most governments do not control encryption. Of these, a small minority, most notably in Scandinavia, do not control encryption because they view it as an important tool for protecting personal privacy and enabling electronic commerce. For the vast majority of governments in the developing world, there is no need to regulate encryption because domestic use has not yet become widespread.

However, an increasing number of governments have decided to regulate encryption, typically by means of import controls, export controls, and use controls. This government regulation of encryption is driven by two distinct interests:

- A national security interest in collecting all information that implicates the general safety of the country and its citizens

- A law enforcement interest in collecting evidence of specific criminal activity

The military concerns itself with the former, the police with the latter. The prospect of widely available strong encryption threatens both interests, but in different ways.

## National Security Surveillance

The effectiveness of the national security intelligence gathering function depends on the collection of vast amounts of information—typically real-time communications—which are intercepted, sorted, and analyzed. For the most part, national security intelligence gathering depends on the interception and analysis of communications between ordinary people. For example, intelligence agencies would benefit from intercepting a telephone call in which a landlord tells his mother that a tenant, who unbeknownst to them is a terrorist, will be taking a two week vacation. The value of this information is in the way it fits together with other information. A government agency can analyze data to create an accurate, near-real-time picture of unfolding world events. Because of the cost and scale of this kind of undertaking, this type of surveillance is primarily the domain of rich countries such as the United States.

Various governments in the developed world have the legal authority and technical means to conduct this type of surveillance, both within and outside their national borders. Intelligence agencies for these governments might favor encryption import or use controls to facilitate domestic surveillance, and export controls to avoid undermining the effectiveness of their foreign surveillance.

In the U.S., this national security surveillance can be conducted only in accordance with the Constitution and the Foreign Intelligence Surveillance Act. As such (with a few exceptions) national security surveillance must only be conducted if at least one of the parties to the communication is outside the U.S. This explains the long-standing imposition of encryption export controls—limiting the availability of strong encryption outside the U.S. has facilitated the interception and analysis of foreign communications that implicate national security.

## Law Enforcement Surveillance

Law enforcement surveillance involves the collection of specific information related to a certain criminal suspect or activity—for instance, a suspect's real-time communications or stored electronic records.

In contrast to the foreign focus of intelligence gathering, law enforcement surveillance is conducted almost exclusively within a nation's borders. (Law enforcement surveillance outside a nation's borders is generally conducted in collaboration with the law enforcement authorities of the nation in which the surveillance is conducted.) Therefore, law enforcement regulation of encryption focuses on domestic use and import controls: export controls are only of limited value when the surveillance targets are local, not foreign. Nonetheless, law enforcement agencies in the U.S. have used export controls—the existing encryption regulatory vehicle—to promote the domestic use of KRE. This may be because, thus far, they have lacked support for a broader domestic initiative. But other governments, such as the U.K. and France, have proposed regulations that are directly applicable to domestic users.

Law enforcement agencies generally lack the technical means and financial resources for extensive decryption; they consistently receive less funding than foreign intelligence functions. In the U.S., for example, the FBI, state, and local law enforcement agencies budget is dwarfed in comparison to that of the National Security Agency. In addition, while law enforcement surveillance functions are spread out over various federal, state, and local jurisdictions, the national security functions tend to be centralized, well-funded foreign intelligence arms of the military. As a result, proliferation of strong NKRE may pose a greater threat to law enforcement surveillance than to national security surveillance: while national security interests arguably have the capability to deal with widespread use of encryption, law enforcement interests almost certainly do not.

If government encryption policies reflect a balance between these national security and law enforcement interests, recent government policy initiatives indicate that this balance is changing. The pending government KRE initiatives reflect a significant policy shift away from an era of export controls driven by national security interests and toward a future of domestic use controls driven by law enforcement interests.

## Current Key Recovery Initiatives

In this section, we discuss the recently completed OECD Guidelines, as well as government key recovery initiatives at the national and international level. This is not intended to be a comprehensive analysis of pending KRE proposals, but rather a high level explanation of the government and private sector interests at stake. These initiatives all reflect different permutations of the policy shift toward domestic regulation of encryption for law enforcement reasons.

### OECD Guidelines

In March, 1997, the Organization for Economic Cooperation and Development (OECD) adopted Guidelines for Cryptography Policy [2]. These Guidelines were the result of an often contentious process initiated by the U.S. government, which attracted active participation from private sector and privacy advocates.

The text of the Guidelines suggest that no side "won." Because the mandatory key recovery concept was rejected, the Guidelines were not a complete victory for the staunchest government proponents of KRE (such as France). In spite of this, government proponents of KRE did not go away empty-handed: Principle 6, "Lawful Access," established that national encryption policies could permit government access to the plaintext of encrypted information.

As far as private sector input, the Guidelines also contain principles that reflect the interests of vendors and users. The most significant is Principle 5, which suggests that national encryption policies respect the individual's fundamental right to privacy. Principle 2, "User Choice," states that users have the right to choose any encryption method. (The significance of this principle, however, is undercut by the principle being "subject to applicable laws.")

How will OECD member states resolve the conflicts among the Guidelines' eight principles? The Guidelines suggest that the principles are

> . . . interdependent and should be implemented as a whole so as to balance the various interests at stake. No principle should be implemented in isolation of the rest.

But as a matter of international law, the Guidelines are nonbinding on OECD member states. Add to this the ambiguity created by the conflicting principles and it becomes clear that OECD governments remain free to pursue whatever encryption policy they choose.

What, then, was the significance of the OECD process? In the long term, the Guidelines will be seen as a victory for key recovery proponents: for the first time, major governments sent high level representatives to coordinate encryption policy. One practical result has been the establishment of a network of government officials who know the issues and have the authority to speak on encryption policy for an entire government: if nothing else, the OECD process will result in better coordinated national policies. In the end, the Guidelines will result in increased government support for regulation of encryption and/or promotion of KRE.

## U.S. Key Recovery Policy

The foundation of current U.S. encryption policy was set with the much publicized 1992 "Clipper chip" initiative. Clipper chips have a master key, fragments of which are stored with two government agencies. Coordinated action by both government agencies is required to decrypt data encrypted by a Clipper device. Government promotion of the Clipper chip provoked outcry from civil liberties groups such as the Electronic Frontier Foundation, on the grounds that governments would retain back-door access to private communications encrypted with a Clipper device. Despite government assurances that keys would be released only under authority of law, the initiative was perceived by the public as a government assault on personal privacy. Large inventories of the Clipper chip remain to be sold.

Through the course of extensive consultations within the private sector, the Clinton Administration refined its position after the Clipper firestorm. The resulting policy retained Clipper's government access component, but ceded the role of encryption keyholder to a Key Recovery Agent (KRA) chosen by the user. In December 1996, President Clinton issued an executive order allowing the following:

- To export KRE, irrespective of encryption key length or algorithm

- To export 56-bit NKRE as long as the exporter committed to design, build, or market KRE by 1999

The executive order also shifted export control jurisdiction over unclassified encryption from the State Department, which regulates munitions exports, to the Commerce Department, which in turn regulates exports of dual use technology.

The Commerce Department issued regulations on December 23, 1996 for implementing the executive order [3]. These regulations, though ostensibly for export control purposes, are largely directed at establishing a domestic key recovery infrastructure that meets government key recovery needs. To export a KRE product, that product must meet functional key recovery requirements set out in Schedule 4 to the regulations. Keys for exported KRE products, or other information needed to decrypt information encrypted by an exported product, must be maintained by an approved KRA, who must comply with the following requirements set out in Schedule 5:

- Remaining financially solvent

- Responding quickly to government key requests

- Maintaining the secrecy of government key requests

- Maintaining an audit trail of key requests and disclosures

- Implementing policies and procedures that minimize unauthorized key disclosure

The clear intent of the Commerce Department regulations is to drive vendors to create a single KRE system that can be exported as well as used within the U.S.

This "export" policy has been coupled with a modest domestic encryption initiative. The National Institute for Standards and Technology (NIST) will establish a federal standard for KRE, explore the technical feasibility of various KRE systems and promote their interoperability, and oversee KRE pilot projects for civilian government agencies. The Justice Department even went so far as to float for comment draft legislation establishing a domestic KRE infrastructure—though this was quickly withdrawn after it received a negative reaction from privacy advocates.

The U.S. government's export control incentives for developers of KRE systems, and the interest of the U.S. and other governments in mandating or promoting domestic use of KRE, prompted the formation of the Key Recovery Alliance: an industry group investigating KRE opportunities [4]. The Key Recovery Alliance includes more than sixty technology companies, including IBM, Sun

Microsystems, and others who were once vocal critics of KRE. This private sector activity is exactly what the U.S. government wanted: major U.S. technology companies, dedicated to developing and selling KRE products and services.

The most recent U.S. policy announcement is quite significant in that it reflects a departure from promotion of KRE. In a May 9, 1997 speech to the American Bankers Association, Undersecretary of Commerce for Export Administration William Reinsch announced that his department will permit the export of the strongest available NKRE encryption products, as long as they are specifically designed to support a financial institution's transactions. The Commerce Department will allow the sale of direct home banking software of any encryption key length, offered by banks to their customers worldwide. The applications that will be covered include the following:

- International funds transfers

- The Secure Electronic Transaction (SET) standard promoted by Mastercard and Visa for Internet credit card transactions

- Home-banking software

Though this announcement received scant attention, it reveals a significant policy shift: the U.S. government has acknowledged that KRE is not appropriate for certain applications; in this case, home banking and Internet credit card transactions. While this announcement could be dismissed as one more stage in the financial sector's long history of preferential treatment with respect to U.S. export controls, it is essential not to overlook the reasoning behind this policy change: the U.S. government has acknowledged that it does not make sense to escrow encryption keys used only for real-time communications between a client and server, when both client and server would maintain the communication's content in plaintext. Extensions of this reasoning to other applications would result in further liberalization of the current U.S. KRE policy.

The evolving U.S. encryption policy reflects a progressive liberalization of U.S. export controls and an increasing intent to promote domestic use of KRE. Though Vice President Gore has committed not to impose domestic controls on encryption, a mandatory KRE system remains a possibility. A precedent for this was the enactment in 1995 of the Communications Assistance to Law Enforcement Act. CALEA requires that all telecommunications equipment deployed in the public switched telephone network must accommodate government surveillance. CALEA, which passed the Senate by a vote of 98–0, reflects a clear Congressional decision that new technologies should not undermine law enforcement's ability to collect electronic evidence of criminal activity. The same factors that contributed to passage of CALEA could result in a swift and dramatic change in U.S. encryption policy.

## United Kingdom

In a March 1997 public consultation paper entitled "Licensing of Trusted Third Parties for the Provision of Encryption Services," [5] the U.K. government proposed a mandatory licensing regime for Trusted Third Parties (TTPs) that offered encryption key management services. The licensing requirement would only apply to service providers, and would not apply to, or restrict the use of, standalone hardware or software products. Nor would the policy apply to financial transfers, intracompany key management, and certain other encryption services. It is undecided whether encryption services offered to U.K.-based users from abroad will also come under the scope of the U.K. licensing regime.

The proposed access requirements closely follow those adopted by the U.S. government:

- KRAs must be solvent and maintain adequate capital reserves and insurance

- KRAs must have strong security and secure channels for the delivery of keys upon government requests

- KRAs must keep audit trails of key requests and releases

- KRAs must be responsive, with a one hour response time for government key requests

- KRAs must keep the existence of a request secret from the surveillance target

On the grounds of promoting consumer confidence, the U.K. proposal would impose substantial liability on TTPs. TTPs will be strictly liable to customers for compromise or disclosure of private keys, which could reduce the incentive for users to exercise caution in protecting their keys. TTPs could also face criminal liability for the negligent compromise or disclosure of private keys.

The U.K. paper indicates a willingness to adopt mandatory licensing—something that has been resisted so far by the U.S.—but imposes this license requirement only on services, not products. Other key elements of the U.K. paper include:

- An intent to bundle KRE with other commercially promising technology, such as digital signatures

- The importance for other governments to adopt similar licensing regimes—mutual recognition agreements, whereby national licensing authorities would cross-certify each other's TTPs

## France

Last year France adopted a law establishing a legal framework for mandatory KRE, but has yet to issue the regulations necessary to implement the law. The French KRE law, published July 27, 1996 in the *Journal Officiel,* established a mandatory licensing regime for all TTPs, the exclusive providers of encryption services. The law requires TTPs to disclose encryption keys to the French government under certain conditions. Users who escrow their keys with a government-approved TTP will be able to use encryption without further restriction. All other users must obtain an encryption use permit from the SCSSI, the office currently responsible for encryption approvals. If past SCSSI policies are followed, no permits will be issued for encryption with a key length longer than 40 bits.

France exemplifies a country that is willing to mandate KRE for both services and products, as well as prohibiting use of NKRE (notwithstanding the costs this could impose on users). This is certainly the most effective way for governments to protect their ability to conduct electronic surveillance. However, whether other countries will follow France's direct but potentially costly approach will remain to be seen.

## Germany

The German encryption policy debate reflects a battle between the same interests that are driving the encryption policy debate in the U.S. and U.K: private sector interest in the privacy and security of electronic information versus law enforcement and national security interests in obtaining unencryted electronic information.

Recent government pronouncements indicate that Germany's debate is far from settled. The Federal Parliament, in a June 20, 1996 resolution advocating the personal privacy benefits of encryption, found that the constitutional right to confidential communication was extended to include a right to choose appropriate encryption technology for personal communications.

Then in an April 1997 speech, Federal Interior Minister Kanther advocated domestic controls on encryption, to prohibit the use of encryption technologies, except those technologies whose manufacturers had agreed to provide keys to law enforcement upon lawful request. Kanther emphasized:

> Without any regulation [of encryption], the powers of the criminal justice and security authorities to listen in on telephone or data traffic . . . would be practically worthless.

In contrast to Minister Kanther's law enforcement position is the federal Minister of Economic Affairs position. In March 1997, Minister Rexrodt stated that he opposed restrictions on the sale or use of encryption on the basis that encryption was an essential commercial technology. This position was applauded by private sector users and vendors.

An interagency Task Force on Encryption Policy, established in October 1996 with a mandate to develop consensus policy, has yet to find common ground. The German policy debate is a bellwether for other industrialized countries, especially in Europe: how the powerful German high technology companies and privacy advocates fare against the conservative police and military government agencies is likely to be examined by those policymakers in other developing countries, many of whom will likely become involved in a similar policy debate.

### Belgium

A law enacted by the Belgian Parliament in December 1995, which became effective in January 1995, might provide the Belgian government broad latitude to regulate domestic use of encryption. The law prohibits the government-owned telecommunications company "Belgacom" from deploying equipment that renders government surveillance ineffective. The Belgian Institute for Posts and Telecommunications also maintains the right to approve any telecommunications equipment—including encryption devices—used in the country. An aggressive interpretation of these laws could provide the Belgian government the authority to mandate the use of KRE and prohibit the use of NKRE.

Thus far, though the Belgian government has not acted to control domestic use of encryption, the potentially broad laws indicate that other governments seeking to implement KRE initiatives have many ways to do so. For instance, they can rely on existing laws, such as telecommunications homologation requirements and existing electronic surveillance laws, which are equivalent in effect to CALEA in the U.S.

## Government Interests Compared to User Interests

In this section, we analyze the extent to which encryption user interests converge with government interests in KRE. The analysis considers the following government interests, which have been reflected in the U.S., U.K., and French KRE initiatives:

- Scope of key recovery functionality
- System security
- Responsiveness of key recovery agents
- Secrecy of key release
- Perpetual key storage
- Cost of key release

As mentioned in the Introduction, our conclusions differ from a recent report released by a group of leading cryptographers [1]. The general differences include the following; the sections that follow explore the specifics.

- While the Experts focused on the needs of the individual and small enterprise user, our analysis shows that multiuser entities—such as large multinational corporations—will drive demand for KRE.

- By looking to the most common basis for user key recovery requests, such as when the user is cooperative and nearby, the Experts underestimated user demand for KRE. We have identified less common but extremely important circumstances in which key recovery may be necessary; as such, the inability to decrypt data in these circumstances will generate private sector demand for KRE.

- The Experts largely ignored the extent to which government action may drive down the cost of KRE. We suggest several means to achieve this, and suggest that the driving force will be governments promoting the use of KRE.

- In concluding that the creation and operation of a KRE infrastructure is "beyond the experience and current competency of the field," the Experts apparently see no prospect for success in the effort recently undertaken by the more than 60 corporate members of the Key Recovery Alliance, including IBM, Sun Microsystems, and other sophisticated technology companies. We believe that though the effort appears daunting, the KRA may be up to the task.

## Scope of Key Recovery Functionality

What applications do governments want KRE deployed in? All applications. Governments want key recovery functionality both for stored information, such as encrypted files stored on a lawfully seized hard drive, and for real-time communications, such as encrypted cellular telephone conversations, email, and secure internet sessions.

While the government would like to see KRE used for all applications, users want KRE for only certain applications. For example, some users may require key recovery for stored data, but few will require KRE for communications. Generally, encryption keys for communications are neither worth the cost of recovering, nor necessary to recover, because cleartext of the encrypted information will otherwise be available.

Consider telephone conversations. If a user believes a conversation is worth recording, the user will record it. The fact is that despite the low cost, few telephone conversations are recorded. If a conversation is not worth recording, the user will not want the ability to recover the encryption keys for that conversation.

Consider a Web site transaction for which a session key is generated between the merchant's server and the purchaser's Web browser. This encryption is necessary only for transmission of the order and payment information across the public Internet. The encrypted order and payment information will likely reside in unencrypted form behind a firewall on the merchant's network, and perhaps even on the purchaser's desktop computer. Consider also an email, encrypted when transmitted between the server at company headquarters and a server in the company's foreign office. In this example, it is again likely that the email will exist in plaintext on the desktop or internal network of both the sender and the recipient.

With stored records, unlike communications, users may have a legitimate need for key recovery functionality. In addition, the value of stored records is generally longer-lasting, in contrast to the value of real-time communications, which tends to diminish as soon as the information is received. Unlike many encrypted communications, stored records may not exist in unencrypted form. Thus, user demand for KRE is likely to be focused on the stored files; only in rare applications will it extend to communications.

This discussion suggests that without government regulation, KRE will be used primarily for stored communications. Will this limited private sector use of KRE satisfy government surveillance interests? That remains the most important KRE policy question to resolve.

## System Security

Governments have a keen interest in making the security of the KRE systems available to the public—if KRE does not offer an acceptable level of security, it will not be widely deployed. The U.S. government's proposed requirements for licensing KRAs include maintaining high availability systems, encryption of whatever (key or plaintext) is delivered in response to a government request, skilled and trusted personnel, audit trails, and other security-related "best practices," policies, and procedures.

Users have a more direct interest in the security of KRE systems to which their keys are entrusted.

It is hard to imagine that a KRE user who would not want a KRA using high availability systems, employed trusted and skilled personnel, and other best practices, policies, and procedures, as long as it did not result in prices that exceeded the value perceived by the user.

Among the security risks inherent in KRE, the Expert's Report identifies the following:

- The existence of a new path to plaintext, which is outside the user's control.

- In some KRE systems, the existence of a high value target, such as a master key or a customer key database; if disclosed, this would compromise large amounts of information.

There is no doubt that these are real risks—the more important question is how users will balance these against the risk of permanently losing access to information encrypted with NKRE.

Vendors can be expected to develop secure KRE systems in response to user demand. In order to attract customers and limit liability, vendors will invest in the development of the most secure systems users are willing to pay for. Though no KRE system will offer perfect security, vendors will certainly have adequate incentive to design and operate KRE systems that meet user security demands. To suggest that this is impossible either overstates user security requirements or understates a vendor's ability to design acceptably secure systems.

## Responsiveness of Key Recovery Agents

The government is interested in the responsiveness of KRA. Governments also expect KRA to remain solvent. Keys must be available twenty-fours hours a day, seven days a week, 365 days a year. Governments want Key Recovery Agents to make the key available immediately. For example, the U.S. will require key recovery completion in two hours; the United Kingdom in one hour.

Users share this interest in KRA responsiveness. The Experts' Report suggests that

few commercial encryption users need the ability to recover keys around the clock or on such short notice.

Although it may not be the norm for a user to require keys at midnight or with two hours notice, it is easy to consider examples of time-sensitive information for which emergency key recovery might be necessary: an encrypted patent application that must be filed to preserve the rights to an invention; an encrypted lawsuit for which the statute of limitations will run; and, as discussed in the "Secrecy of Key Release" section, sensitive internal investigations. Most commercial users foresee at least an occasional need for recovering a key on short notice, especially given the potential damage that could occur in an emergency. As a result, users do well as the government will prefer a KRA with the capability to respond to these emergency requests.

We expect that vendors will meet this demand for responsiveness. KRAs will operate much like existing network management or data centers, which are staffed around the clock with skilled employees. Response times might easily be accommodated if the key request and release processes were largely automated. A key factor for vendors meeting this demand is the ability to put a price on responsiveness: vendors might charge more for an expedited one-hour key release, for instance, than a standard twenty-four hour release, and more for an after-hours key request than a business hours request.

## Secrecy of Key Release

Maintaining the confidentiality of key requests—and the release of keys or plaintext by KRAs—is in the government's interest. Once a suspect knows that they are the target of surveillance, the surveillance becomes ineffective.

There are times that users will also have an interest in maintaining the confidentiality of key requests. The Experts claim, "there is usually no need for secrecy in the recovery of keys." This statement, however, ignores the occasional need for multiuser organizations to conduct confidential internal investigations, particularly targeted at employees suspected of wrongful conduct. For example, if your company's Chief Technology Officer learned that one of his senior engineers were sending encrypted file attachments to recipients at your company's greatest competitor's domain, the CTO might want to investigate the contents of the files before taking action. While users don't always require secrecy—and indeed may not require secrecy in the majority of cases—secrecy is needed in some of the most important key recovery scenarios. For this reason, some users will demand a KRE system that is designed so a key request is kept secret from the individual user of the key.

Vendors, again, will comply with this requirement. As is currently the case with court wiretap orders (which require the carrier not to inform the target of the proposed surveillance) the KRA will be required by law to maintain the secrecy of government key requests in many cases. Given potential user interest in this area, we can expect vendors to agree by contract to maintain the secrecy of customer key requests as needed.

## Perpetual Key Storage

If law enforcement seizes a hard drive containing evidence, which was encrypted five years earlier, the government will still want access to the key to decrypt that information. As a result, the U.S. government regulations imply a duty to maintain encryption keys in perpetuity.

Few users, on the other hand, will want encryption keys stored in perpetuity. Though many electronic records are stored for defined periods of time—for example, five years for tax records—it is likely that users will want to have keys destroyed after the underlying encrypted information becomes publicly known or loses its value.

The significance of how these interests diverge will depend on the KRA business model that unfolds. If the KRA industry charges periodic key storage fees, users may want to have keys destroyed to avoid unnecessary fees. If storage fees are not charged (perhaps because KRAs obtain revenue from other sources) a user will not object to a KRA maintaining a key in perpetuity—the user will retain the option of deleting the encrypted file, thus rendering the key valueless.

## Cost of Key Recovery

In order to induce its wide use, governments want key recovery to be inexpensive. Keeping the costs down is also important because governments likely will be required to pay prevailing commercial rates for KRA services—both when government agencies store their keys with a KRA and when a KRA releases a key to the government pursuant to a lawful request. Under analogous laws, such as the U.S. federal wiretap statute, government must pay reasonable costs to a telecommunication carrier's placing a wiretap. Extending this principle to KRE, governments may be required to pay a reasonable fee for each key they request from a KRA.

Obviously, that users will also want inexpensive key recovery services. The real question is whether KRE vendors and KRAs can provide it. There is no doubt that the development of systems and procedures will prove to be expensive; however, this has not deterred the members of the Key Recovery Alliance from pursuing KRE product development.

Another factor in increased costs will depend on the extent of government regulation and the legal liability of KRAs. Unnecessary regulation will increase the cost of KRAs by imposing a regulatory compliance burden without a corresponding benefit. But as discussed in the "Conclusion," governments are in a position to reduce the costs of key recovery products and services in the following ways:

- By curbing their urge to regulate KRAs

- By shielding KRAs from extensive liability to customers and third parties

- By using government procurement allowing vendors to quickly realize the increasing returns to scale from a larger KRE infrastructure

Users will also be able to reduce the costs of KRE as follows:

- By agreeing to waive certain liability by contract
- By agreeing to pay higher fees for services which involve higher costs, such as expedited key requests

## Conclusion

Driven by a combination of government initiatives and user demand, what will be the outcome of the contentious debate over KRE? KRE systems will be available in the future. User demand will be determined by a vendor's ability to meet user needs at an acceptable cost—this process is already underway. The following policy suggestions suggest how governments can encourage, but not distort, the growth of user demand for KRE:

### Do not mandate use of KRE

Any government could create instant user demand for KRE if, as France did, the government mandated the use of KRE and prohibited the use of NKRE. But the costs of mandatory KRE, especially when required for all applications, are enormous. If applied to certain applications, like World Wide Web sessions, mandatory KRE would stunt the growth of personal communication and commerce over the Internet.

### Go light on regulation

Every additional regulatory requirement adds to the cost of KRE products and services. As indicated above, government and user interests converge in many areas, such as system security, KRA responsiveness, and the secrecy of key requests. There is no need for governments to require by regulation what customers are likely to demand from ven-

dors. If governments let user demands drive the creation of KRE systems and business models, their interests could be met without imposing regulatory compliance costs on vendors, and thereby raising the costs of KRE.

### Give up promoting KRE for all applications

Governments should not promote KRE for applications for which there is no demonstrable user demand. Prime candidates are the encryption session keys produced by cellular telephones, Internet browsers, and other real-time communications devices. Why should governments give up on these applications? Because in most cases government will have other means to access the desired plaintext. Users will, for their own purposes, keep plaintext of most information the government might later want. For example, if the government could not decrypt a surveillance target's Internet session, the government need only serve a search warrant or subpoena to obtain the plaintext stored by the sender and recipient behind their respective firewalls.

### Regulate to lower the cost of KRA

The most beneficial government regulation would be aimed at limiting the liability of KRAs and thereby reducing the cost of KRE. This could be done by providing KRAs broad immunity from customer and third-party claims relating to KRA services, including a KRA's good faith reliance on a government key request. Governments could also establish per-incident and per-customer caps on KRA liability. This type of regulation would encourage companies to become KRE vendors and KRAs, and reduce the cost of KRE.

### Buy it yourself

If governments believe KRA addresses user needs, then in their capacity as encryption users they should purchase KRE products and services for all appropriate government purposes.

*Invest in alternative means of access*

Encryption is not the first technology that threatens to increase the difficulty and cost of government surveillance. The move from analog to digital technology and the increasing use of compression technologies pose analogous threats. If governments place a high value on the fruits of electronic surveillance, governments must commit a greater budget to developing alternative means to access encrypted data, such as by building better decryption systems and facilities.

*Establish transparent government-to-government agreement*

A recent member survey by the Information Technology Association of America (ITAA) indicated that the greatest perceived challenge to development of a global key management infrastructure is the "difficulty in arriving at international agreements associated with gaining access to encrypted information." [6] Confidential government-to-government agreements will be the subject of private sector distrust. To promote trust in the global KRE system, governments must make the terms of these agreements public so that users and KRAs know the circumstances in which a user's key, or the plaintext derived from that key, may be handed from government to government.

Future developments in encryption policy may depend on the accuracy of the following assessment. KRE seems to benefit law enforcement surveillance rather than the national security surveillance, conducted by intelligence agencies. We can draw two conclusions from this assessment: either national security interests have lost their policy battle with users demanding strong encryption and the law enforcement agencies promoting KRE, or perhaps national security interests, by some legal or technical means—can turn KRE to their benefit. If it is the former, we can expect national security interests to reassert themselves against the spread of stronger, longer key length KRE. If it is the latter, national security interests may sit silently on the sidelines as the KRE market develops. ∎

## Acknowledgments

I would like to thank Stewart Baker and Paul Hurst of Steptoe & Johnson for their insightful comments, and Susan Merk of the MCI Law and Public Policy Department for assistance in preparation of this article. This publication reflects my personal views and does not constitute in any way a statement on MCI's behalf or the position of MCI on the issues addressed herein.

### References

1. *http://www.crypto.com/key_study/report.shtml*

2. *http://www.oecd.org/dsti/iccp/crypto_e.html*

3. *http://www/bxa.doc.gov/ercstart.html*

4. *http://www.ibm.com/security/*

5. *http://dtinfo1.dti.gov.uk/pubs/*

6. *http://www.itaa.org/Softservl.html*

## About the Author

Clint Smith
Associate Technology Counsel
MCI Communications Corporation
1133 19th Street NW
Washington DC 20036
*clint.smith@mci.com*

Clint Smith is an associate technology counsel in the Law and Public Policy Department at MCI Communications Corporation. Clint is responsible for legal issues relating to MCI's Internet, encryption, and electronic commerce services. He is actively involved in the roll-out of MCI encryption products and MCI policy positions on government regulation of encryption.

Prior to joining MCI in 1996 Clint was an associate in the technology and international practice groups at the law firm of Steptoe & Johnson in

Washington D.C. At Steptoe Clint handled corporate and public policy matters for clients developing Internet, encryption, and electronic payment services.

# More Titles from O'Reilly

## World Wide Web Journal

### Fourth International World Wide Web Conference Proceedings

*A publication of O'Reilly & Associates and the World Wide Web Consortium (W3C) Winter 1995/96 748 pages, ISBN 1-56592-169-0*

The *World Wide Web Journal*, published quarterly, provides timely, in-depth coverage of the W3C's technological developments, such as protocols for security, replication and caching, HTML and SGML, and content labeling. This issue contains 57 refereed technical papers presented at the Fourth International World Wide Web Conference, held December 1995 in Boston, Massachusetts. It also includes the two best papers from regional conferences.

### Key Specifications of the World Wide Web

*A publication of O'Reilly & Associates and the World Wide Web Consortium (W3C) Spring 1996 356 pages, ISBN 1-56592-190-9*

The key specifications that describe the architecture of the World Wide Web and how it works are maintained online at the World Wide Web Consortium. This issue of the *World Wide Web Journal* collects these key papers in a single volume as an important reference for the Webmaster, application programmer, or technical manager with definitive specifications for the core technologies in the Web.

### The Web After Five Years

*A publication of O'Reilly & Associates and the World Wide Web Consortium (W3C) Summer 1996, 226 pp, ISBN 1-56592-210-7*

This issue is a reflection on the web after five years. In an interview with Tim Berners-Lee, the inventor of the Web and Director of the W3C, we learn that the Web was built to be an interactive, inter-creative, two-way medium from the beginning. These issues are addressed in selections from the MIT/W3C Workshop on Web Demographics and Internet Survey Methodology, along with commerce-related papers selected from the Fifth International World Wide Web Conference, which took place from May 6–10 in Paris.

### Building an Industrial Strength Web

*A publication of O'Reilly & Associates and the World Wide Web Consortium (W3C) Fall 1996, 244 pp, ISBN 1-56592-211-5*

Issue 4 focuses on the infrastructure needed to create and maintain an "Industrial Strength Web," from network protocols to application design. Included are the first standard versions of core Web protocols: HTTP/1.1, Digest Authentication, State Management (Cookies), and PICS. This issue also provides guides to the specs, highlighting new features, papers explaining modifications to 1.1 (sticky and compressed headers), extensibility, support for collaborative authoring, and using distributed objects.

### Advancing HTML: Style and Substance

*A publication of O'Reilly & Associates and the World Wide Web Consortium (W3C) Winter 1996/97 254 pages, ISBN 1-56592-264-6*

This issue is a guide to the specifications and tools that buttress the user interface to the World Wide Web. It includes the latest HTML 3.2 and CSS1 specs, papers on gif animation, JavaScript, Web accessibility, usability engineering, multimedia design, and a report on Amaya.

### Scripting Languages: Automating the Web

*A publication of O'Reilly & Associates and the World Wide Web Consortium (W3C) By Lincoln Stein, Clint Wong, Ron Petrusha, Shishir Gundavaram, etc. Spring 1997, 244 pages, 1-56592-265-4*

In spite of all the power built into popular web utilities, the informality, ease, and rapid development cycle of scripting languages make them well suited to the constant change common to most web sites. *Scripting Languages: Automating the Web* guides users and developers in choosing and deploying scripting solutions.

In addition, this issue examines the web-wide impact of Perl as the scripting language of choice for webmasters everywhere, with an in-depth article featuring Perl developers Larry Wall and Tom Christiansen.

# Developing Web Content

## Building Your Own WebSite

By Susan B. Peck & Stephen Arrants
1st Edition July 1996
514 pages, ISBN 1-56592-232-8

This is a hands-on reference for Windows® 95 and Windows NT™ desktop users who want to host their own site on the Web or on a corporate intranet. You'll also learn how to connect your web to information in other Windows applications, such as word processing documents and databases. Packed with examples and tutorials on every aspect of Web management. Includes the highly acclaimed WebSite™ 1.1 on CD-ROM.

## Web Client Programming with Perl

By Clinton Wong
1st Edition March 1997
250 pages, ISBN 1-56592-214-X

*Web Client Programming with Perl* teaches you how to extend scripting skills to the Web. This book teaches you the basics of how browsers communicate with servers and how to write your own customized Web clients to automate common tasks. It is intended for those who are motivated to develop software that offers a more flexible and dynamic response than a standard Web browser.

## JavaScript: The Definitive Guide, Regular Edition

By David Flanagan
2nd Edition January 1997
672 pages, ISBN 1-56592-234-4

In this second edition, the author of the best-selling, *Java in a Nutshell* describes the server-side JavaScript application, LiveWire, developed by Netscape and Sun Microsystems.

The book describes the version of JavaScript shipped with Navigator 2.0, 2.0.1, and 2.0.2, and also the much-changed version of JavaScript shipped with Navigator 3.0. LiveConnect, used for communication between JavaScript and Java applets, and addresses commonly encountered bugs on JavaScript objects.

## HTML: The Definitive Guide, Second Edition

By Chuck Musciano & Bill Kennedy
2nd Edition April 1997
520 pages, ISBN 1-56592-235-2

The second edition covers the most up-to-date version of the HTML standard (the proposed HTML version 3.2), Netscape 4.0 and Internet Explorer 3.0, plus all the common extensions, especially Netscape extensions. The authors address all the current version's elements, explaining how they work and interact with each other. Includes a style guide that helps you to use HTML to accomplish a variety of tasks, from simple online documentation to complex marketing and sales presentations.

## Designing for the Web: Getting Started in a New Medium

By Jennifer Niederst with Edie Freedman
1st Edition April 1996
180 pages, ISBN 1-56592-165-8

*Designing for the Web* gives you the basics you need to hit the ground running. Although geared toward designers, it covers information and techniques useful to anyone who wants to put graphics online. It explains how to work with HTML documents from a designer's point of view, outlines special problems with presenting information online, and walks through incorporating images into Web pages, with emphasis on resolution and improving efficiency.

## WebMaster in a Nutshell

By Stephen Spainhour & Valerie Quercia
1st Edition October 1996
378 pages, ISBN 1-56592-229-8

Web content providers and administrators have many sources of information, both in print and online. *WebMaster in a Nutshell* pulls it all together into one slim volume — for easy desktop access. This quick-reference covers HTML, CGI, Perl, HTTP, server configuration, and tools for Web administration.

# Perl

## Programming Perl, Second Edition

*By Larry Wall, Tom Christiansen,*
*& Randal L. Schwartz*
*2nd Edition September 1996*
*676 pages, ISBN 1-56592-149-6*

*Programming Perl, Second Edition*, is coauthored by Larry Wall, the creator of Perl. Perl is a language for easily manipulating text, files, and processes. It provides a more concise and readable way to do many jobs that were formerly accomplished (with difficulty) by programming with C or one of the shells. This heavily revised second edition contains a full explanation of Perl version 5.003.

## Learning Perl, Second Edition

*By Randal L. Schwartz*
*Foreword by Larry Wall*
*2nd Edition July 1997*
*400 pages, ISBN 1-56592-284-0*

This second edition of *Learning Perl*, with a foreword by Perl author Larry Wall, fully covers Perl, Version 5. In this new edition, program examples and exercise answers have been radically updated to reflect typical usage under Perl 5, and numerous details have been added or modified. In addition, you'll find new sections introducing Perl references and CGI programming.

*Learning Perl, Second Edition* is ideal for system administrators, programmers, and anyone else wanting a down-to-earth introduction to this useful language. Written by a Perl trainer, its aim is to make a competent, hands-on Perl programmer out of the reader as quickly as possible. The book takes a tutorial approach and includes hundreds of short code examples, along with some lengthy ones. The relatively inexperienced programmer will find *Learning Perl* easily accessible. For a comprehensive and detailed guide to advanced programming with Perl, read O'Reilly's companion book, *Programming Perl, Second Edition*.

## CGI Programming on the World Wide Web

*By Shishir Gundavaram*
*1st Edition March 1996*
*450 pages, ISBN 1-56592-168-2*

This book offers a comprehensive explanation of CGI and related techniques for people who hold on to the dream of providing their own information servers on the Web. It starts at the beginning, explaining the value of CGI and how it works, then moves swiftly into the subtle details of programming.

## Perl 5 Desktop Reference

*By Johan Vromans*
*1st Edition February 1996*
*44 pages, ISBN 1-56592-187-9*

This is the standard quick-reference guide for the Perl programming language. It provides a complete overview of the language, from variables to input and output, from flow control to regular expressions, from functions to document formats—all packed into a convenient, carry-around booklet. Updated to cover Perl version 5.003.

## Mastering Regular Expressions

*By Jeffrey E. F. Friedl*
*1st Edition January 1997*
*368 pages, ISBN 1-56592-257-3*

Regular expressions, a powerful tool for manipulating text and data, are found in scripting languages, editors, programming environments, and specialized tools. In this book, author Jeffrey Friedl leads you through the steps of crafting a regular expression that gets the job done. He examines a variety of tools and uses them in an extensive array of examples, dedicating an entire chapter to Perl.

# How to stay in touch with O'Reilly

## 1. Visit Our Award-Winning Web Site

### http://www.ora.com/

★ "Top 100 Sites on the Web" —*PC Magazine*
★ "Top 5% Web sites" —*Point Communications*
★ "3-Star site" —*The McKinley Group*

Our web site contains a library of comprehensiveproduct information (including book excerpts and tables of contents), downloadable software, background articles, interviews with technology leaders, links to relevant sites, book cover art, and more. File us in your Bookmarks or Hotlist!

## 2. Join Our Email Mailing Lists

### New Product Releases

To receive automatic email with brief descriptions of all new O'Reilly products as they are released, send email to:
**listproc@online.ora.com**
Put the following information in the first line of your message (*not* in the Subject field):
**subscribe ora-news "Your Name" of "Your Organization"** (for example: subscribe ora-news Kris Webber of Fine Enterprises)

### O'Reilly Events

If you'd also like us to send information about trade show events, special promotions, and other O'Reilly events, send email to: **listproc@online.ora.com**
Put the following information in the first line of your message (*not* in the Subject field):
**subscribe ora-events "Your Name" of "Your Organization"**

## 3. Get Examples from Our Books via FTP

There are two ways to access an archive of example files from our books:

### Regular FTP

- ftp to:
  **ftp.ora.com**
  (login: anonymous
  password: your email address)
- Point your web browser to:
  **ftp://ftp.ora.com/**

### FTPMAIL

- Send an email message to:
  **ftpmail@online.ora.com**
  (Write "help" in the message body)

## 4. Visit Our Gopher Site

- Connect your gopher to:
  **gopher.ora.com**

- Point your web browser to:
  **gopher://gopher.ora.com/**

- Telnet to:
  **gopher.ora.com**
  **login: gopher**

## 5. Contact Us via Email

**order@ora.com**
To place a book or software order online. Good for North American and international customers.

**subscriptions@ora.com**
To place an order for any of our newsletters or periodicals.

**books@ora.com**
General questions about any of our books.

**software@ora.com**
For general questions and product information about our software. Check out O'Reilly Software Online at **http://software.ora.com/** for software and technical support information. Registered O'Reilly software users send your questions to: **website-support@ora.com**

**cs@ora.com**
For answers to problems regarding your order or our products.

**booktech@ora.com**
For book content technical questions or corrections.

**proposals@ora.com**
To submit new book or software proposals to our editors and product managers.

**international@ora.com**
For information about our international distributors or translation queries. For a list of our distributors outside of North America check out:
**http://www.ora.com/www/order/country.html**

O'Reilly & Associates, Inc.
101 Morris Street, Sebastopol, CA 95472 USA
TEL    707-829-0515 or 800-998-9938
        (6am to 5pm PST)
FAX    707-829-0104

# Titles from O'Reilly

*Please note that upcoming titles are displayed in italic.*

## WEBPROGRAMMING

Apache: The Definitive Guide
Building Your Own Web
  Conferences
Building Your Own Website
CGI Programming for the World
  Wide Web
Designing for the Web
HTML: The Definitive Guide,
  2nd Ed.
JavaScript: The Definitive Guide,
  2nd Ed.
Learning Perl
Programming Perl, 2nd Ed.
Mastering Regular Expressions
WebMaster in a Nutshell
Web Security & Commerce
Web Client Programming with
  Perl
World Wide Web Journal

## USING THE INTERNET

Smileys
The Future Does Not Compute
The Whole Internet User's Guide
  & Catalog
The Whole Internet for Win 95
Using Email Effectively
Bandits on the Information
  Superhighway

## JAVA SERIES

Exploring Java
Java AWT Reference
Java Fundamental Classes
  Reference
Java in a Nutshell
*Java Language Reference, 2nd*
  *Edition*
Java Network Programming
Java Threads
Java Virtual Machine

## SOFTWARE

WebSite™ 1.1
WebSite Professional™
Building Your Own Web
  Conferences
WebBoard™
PolyForm™
*Statisphere™*

## SONGLINE GUIDES

NetActivism       NetResearch
Net Law           NetSuccess
NetLearning       NetTravel
Net Lessons

## SYSTEM ADMINISTRATION

Building Internet Firewalls
Computer Crime: A
  Crimefighter's Handbook
Computer Security Basics
DNS and BIND, 2nd Ed.
Essential System Administration,
  2nd Ed.
Getting Connected: The Internet
  at 56K and Up
Linux Network Administrator's
  Guide
Managing Internet Information
  Services
Managing NFS and NIS
Networking Personal Computers
  with TCP/IP
Practical UNIX & Internet
  Security, 2nd Ed.
PGP: Pretty Good Privacy
sendmail, 2nd Ed.
sendmail Desktop Reference
System Performance Tuning
TCP/IP Network Administration
termcap & terminfo
Using & Managing UUCP
Volume 8: X Window System
  Administrator's Guide
*Web Security & Commerce*

## UNIX

Exploring Expect
*Learning VBScript*
Learning GNU Emacs, 2nd Ed.
Learning the bash Shell
Learning the Korn Shell
Learning the UNIX Operating
  System
Learning the vi Editor
Linux in a Nutshell
Making TeX Work
Linux Multimedia Guide
Running Linux, 2nd Ed.
SCO UNIX in a Nutshell
sed & awk, 2nd Edition
*Tcl/Tk Tools*
UNIX in a Nutshell: System V
  Edition
UNIX Power Tools
Using csh & tsch
When You Can't Find Your UNIX
  System Administrator
*Writing GNU Emacs Extensions*

## WEB REVIEW STUDIO SERIES

Gif Animation Studio
Shockwave Studio

## WINDOWS

Dictionary of PC Hardware and
  Data Communications Terms
Inside the Windows 95 Registry
Inside the Windows 95 File
  System
Windows Annoyances
*Windows NT File System*
  *Internals*
*Windows NT in a Nutshell*

## PROGRAMMING

Advanced Oracle PL/SQL
  Programming
Applying RCS and SCCS
C++: The Core Language
Checking C Programs with lint
DCE Security Programming
Distributing Applications Across
  DCE & Windows NT
Encyclopedia of Graphics File
  Formats, 2nd Ed.
Guide to Writing DCE
  Applications
lex & yacc
Managing Projects with make
Mastering Oracle Power Objects
Oracle Design: The Definitive
  Guide
Oracle Performance Tuning, 2nd
  Ed.
Oracle PL/SQL Programming
Porting UNIX Software
POSIX Programmer's Guide
POSIX.4: Programming for the
  Real World
Power Programming with RPC
Practical C Programming
Practical C++ Programming
Programming Python
Programming with curses
Programming with GNU Software
Pthreads Programming
Software Portability with imake,
  2nd Ed.
Understanding DCE
Understanding Japanese
  Information Processing
UNIX Systems Programming for
  SVR4

## BERKELEY 4.4 SOFTWARE DISTRIBUTION

4.4BSD System Manager's
  Manual
4.4BSD User's Reference Manual
4.4BSD User's Supplementary
  Documents
4.4BSD Programmer's Reference
  Manual
4.4BSD Programmer's
  Supplementary Documents
X Programming
Vol. 0: X Protocol Reference
  Manual
Vol. 1: Xlib Programming Manual
Vol. 2: Xlib Reference Manual
Vol. 3M: X Window System User's
  Guide, Motif Edition
Vol. 4M: X Toolkit Intrinsics
  Programming Manual, Motif
  Edition
Vol. 5: X Toolkit Intrinsics
  Reference Manual
Vol. 6A: Motif Programming
  Manual
Vol. 6B: Motif Reference Manual
Vol. 6C: Motif Tools
Vol. 8 : X Window System
  Administrator's Guide
Programmer's Supplement for
  Release 6
X User Tools
The X Window System in a
  Nutshell

## CAREER & BUSINESS

Building a Successful Software
  Business
The Computer User's Survival
  Guide
Love Your Job!
Electronic Publishing on CD-
  ROM

## TRAVEL

Travelers' Tales: Brazil
Travelers' Tales: Food
Travelers' Tales: France
Travelers' Tales: Gutsy Women
Travelers' Tales: India
Travelers' Tales: Mexico
Travelers' Tales: Paris
Travelers' Tales: San Francisco
Travelers' Tales: Spain
Travelers' Tales: Thailand
Travelers' Tales: A Woman's
  World

# International Distributors

## UK, Europe, Middle East and Northern Africa (except France, Germany, Switzerland, & Austria)

**INQUIRIES**
International Thomson Publishing Europe
Berkshire House
168-173 High Holborn
London WC1V 7AA, United Kingdom
Telephone: 44-171-497-1422
Fax: 44-171-497-1426
Email: itpint@itps.co.uk

**ORDERS**
International Thomson Publishing Services, Ltd.
Cheriton House, North Way
Andover, Hampshire SP10 5BE, United Kingdom
Telephone: 44-264-342-832
  (UK orders)
Telephone: 44-264-342-806
  (outside UK)
Fax: 44-264-364418 (UK orders)
Fax: 44-264-342761 (outside UK)
UK & Eire orders: itpuk@itps.co.uk
International orders: itpint@itps.co.uk

## France

Editions Eyrolles
61 bd Saint-Germain
75240 Paris Cedex 05
France
Fax: 33-01-44-41-11-44

**FRENCH LANGUAGE BOOKS**
All countries except Canada
Phone: 33-01-44-41-46-16
Email: geodif@eyrolles.com

**ENGLISH LANGUAGE BOOKS**
Phone: 33-01-44-41-11-87
Email: distribution@eyrolles.com

## Australia

WoodsLane Pty. Ltd.
7/5 Vuko Place, Warriewood NSW 2102
P.O. Box 935, Mona Vale NSW 2103
Australia
Telephone: 61-2-9970-5111
Fax: 61-2-9970-5002
Email: info@woodslane.com.au

## Germany, Switzerland, and Austria

**INQUIRIES**
O'Reilly Verlag
Balthasarstr. 81
D-50670 Köln
Germany
Telephone: 49-221-97-31-60-0
Fax: 49-221-97-31-60-8
Email: anfragen@oreilly.de

**ORDERS**
International Thomson Publishing
Königswinterer Straße 418
53227 Bonn, Germany
Telephone: 49-228-97024 0
Fax: 49-228-441342
Email: order@oreilly.de

## Asia (except Japan & India)

**INQUIRIES**
International Thomson Publishing Asia
60 Albert Street #15-01
Albert Complex
Singapore 189969
Telephone: 65-336-6411
Fax: 65-336-7411

**ORDERS**
Telephone: 65-336-6411
Fax: 65-334-1617
thomson@signet.com.sg

## New Zealand

WoodsLane New Zealand Ltd.
21 Cooks Street (P.O. Box 575)
Wanganui, New Zealand
Telephone: 64-6-347-6543
Fax: 64-6-345-4840
Email: info@woodslane.com.au

## Japan

O'Reilly Japan, Inc.
Kiyoshige Building 2F
12-Banchi, Sanei-cho
Shinjuku-ku
Tokyo 160 Japan
Telephone: 81-3-3356-5227
Fax: 81-3-3356-5261
Email: kenji@ora.com

## India

Computer Bookshop (India) PVT. LTD.
190 Dr. D.N. Road, Fort
Bombay 400 001
India
Telephone: 91-22-207-0989
Fax: 91-22-262-3551
Email: cbsbom@giasbm01.vsnl.net.in

## The Americas

O'Reilly & Associates, Inc.
101 Morris Street
Sebastopol, CA 95472 U.S.A.
Telephone: 707-829-0515
Telephone: 800-998-9938 (U.S. & Canada)
Fax: 707-829-0104
Email: order@ora.com

## Southern Africa

International Thomson Publishing Southern Africa
Building 18, Constantia Park
138 Sixteenth Road
P.O. Box 2459
Halfway House, 1685 South Africa
Telephone: 27-11-805-4819
Fax: 27-11-805-3648

# O'REILLY™

TO ORDER: **800-998-9938** • **order@ora.com** • **http://www.ora.com/**
OUR PRODUCTS ARE AVAILABLE AT A BOOKSTORE OR SOFTWARE STORE NEAR YOU.
FOR INFORMATION: **800-998-9938** • **707-829-0515** • **info@ora.com**

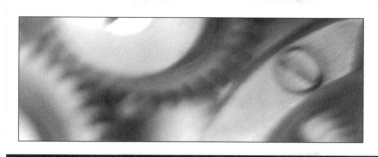

**POST CARD**

The *World Wide Web Journal*, published quarterly by O'Reilly & Associates, Inc, records the work of the World Wide Web Consortium (W3C), and publishes timely, state-of-the-art articles from the wider Web community.

*Visit us online at:*
**http://www.w3j.com/**

The *World Wide Web Journal*, published quarterly by O'Reilly & Associates, Inc, records the work of the World Wide Web Consortium (W3C), and publishes timely, state-of-the-art articles from the wider Web community.

*Visit us online at:*
**http://www.w3j.com/**

PLACE
STAMP
HERE

O'Reilly & Associates, Inc., 101 Morris Street, Sebastopol, CA 95472-9902

NO POSTAGE
NECESSARY IF
MAILED IN THE
UNITED STATES

# BUSINESS REPLY MAIL

FIRST CLASS MAIL   PERMIT NO. 80   SEBASTOPOL, CA

*Postage will be paid by addressee*

**O'Reilly & Associates, Inc.**
101 Morris Street
Sebastopol, CA 95472-9902
Attn: Subscriptions